EUROPEAN ELECTIONS & DOMESTIC POLITICS

CONTEMPORARY EUROPEAN POLITICS AND SOCIETY

Anthony M. Messina, Series Editor

EUROPEAN ELECTIONS & DOMESTIC POLITICS

Lessons from the Past and Scenarios for the Future

edited by

WOUTER VAN DER **BRUG**
and **CEES** VAN DER **EIJK**

University of Notre Dame Press
Notre Dame, Indiana

Copyright © 2007 by University of Notre Dame
Notre Dame, Indiana 46556
www.undpress.nd.edu
All Rights Reserved

Designed by Wendy McMillen
Set in 10.4 / 13 Stone Print by BookComp, Inc.
Printed on 60# Williamsburg White Recycled paper by Sheridan Books, Inc.

Library of Congress Cataloging-in-Publication Data

Eurpean elections & domestic politics : lessons from the past and scenarios for the future / edited by Wouter van der Brug and Cees van der Eijk.
    p. cm. — (Contemporary European politics and society)
  Includes bibliographical references and index.
  ISBN-13: 978-0-268-04369-8 (pbk. : alk. paper)
  ISBN-10: 0-268-04369-8 (pbk. : alk. paper)
    1. European Parliament—Elections, 2004. 2. Elections—Europe.
3. European Union. 4. European Union countries—Politics and government.
I. Brug, Wouter van der. II. Eijk, C. van der. III. Title: European elections and domestic politics.
  JN45.E973 2007
  324.94—dc22   2007020095

♻ *This book printed on recycled paper.*

Contents

Preface vii

Contributors xi

Introduction: Electoral politics in the European Union
and the 2004 enlargement 1
Cees van der Eijk and Wouter van der Brug

1 Effects of space and time on turnout in European Parliament elections 13
  Mark N. Franklin

2 European elections as counterfactual national elections 32
  Marcel van Egmond

3 European Parliament elections and losses by governing parties 51
  Michael Marsh

4 Comparing the views of parties and voters in the 1999 election to 73
  the European Parliament
  Andreas M. Wüst and Hermann Schmitt

5 Locating support for European integration 94
  Angelika Scheuer and Wouter van der Brug

6 The media and European Parliament elections: Second-rate
  coverage of a second-order event? 116
  Claes H. de Vreese, Edmund Lauf, and Jochen Peter

7	Media effects on attitudes toward European integration *Jochen Peter*	131
8	Non-voting in European Parliament elections and support for European integration *Hermann Schmitt and Cees van der Eijk*	145
9	EU support and party choice *Wouter van der Brug, Cees van der Eijk, and Mark N. Franklin*	168
10	The sleeping giant: Potential for political mobilization of disaffection with European integration *Cees van der Eijk and Mark N. Franklin*	189
11	Prospects for electoral change *Martin Kroh, Wouter van der Brug, and Cees van der Eijk*	209
12	European elections, domestic politics, and European integration *Wouter van der Brug and Cees van der Eijk, with Hermann Schmitt, Michael Marsh, Mark Franklin, Jacques Thomassen, Holli Semetko, and Stefano Bartolini*	226
	Postscript: The research agenda beyond the 2004 European elections *Cees van der Eijk and Wouter van der Brug*	262
	Appendix A: The voter study *Cees van der Eijk and Wouter van der Brug*	273
	Appendix B: The media study *Edmund Lauf and Jochen Peter*	277
	Appendix C: Euromanifesto content *Andreas M. Wüst*	283
	Appendix D: Election results, quasi-switching and turnout effects *Marcel van Egmond*	286
	References	295
	Author Index	313
	Subject Index	317

Preface

Elections to the European Parliament are different from elections to national legislative or executive offices. They are often referred to as second-order *national* elections, and this book elaborates why this is the case and discusses some of its consequences. One of the characteristics of these elections is that, although they are ostensibly about the composition of the European Parliament, other—domestic—factors are paramount in the motivations of the most important actors in the electoral process: voters, political parties, and mass media. This generates a number of questions about the ways in which European elections and domestic politics influence each other. These are the questions addressed by this book.

Since 1979 European elections are held every five years in all member states of the European Union, they have been studied systematically by scholars interested in the process of European integration, and by political scientists and communication scientists who took advantage of the comparative laboratory that these elections provide. This book is the product of a group of such scholars, who since 1988 organized themselves in the European Elections Studies Group. Since 1989 this group conducted extensive studies of the European Parliament elections. These resulted in a great number of publications, including two major and integrative 'flagship' publications. This volume builds upon these and constitutes the third of this series.

The first of the two previous volumes is *Choosing Europe?* edited by van der Eijk and Franklin (1996). Using data from the European Election Studies 1989 and 1994 it investigated the electoral behavior of the citizens of the EU member states. It concluded that voters are sensitive to their (national) political contexts, yet also that, in spite of these different contexts, "the populations of the member-states of the European Union constitute a single electorate, and cannot meaningfully be considered as distinct electorates" (p. 404). The second volume in this series is *Political representation and legitimacy in the European Union,* edited by Schmitt and Thomassen (1999). On the basis of the European Election Study 1994 it focused on the quality of representative democracy in the European Union and concluded that, contrary to many pundits, the preconditions for legitimate and effective political representation are clearly present, although the realization of adequate representative democracy still leaves much to be desired. The current volume builds upon these two previous books. It is mainly based on data relating to the European elections of 1999 and compares these, where possible, to similar data from earlier elections to the European Parliament. Moreover, it not only looks into citizens (random samples of whom were interviewed), but also into the other major actors involved in representative democracy: political parties (which are investigated by way of the manifestos that they wrote for the European elections) and mass media (which are studied by way of a systematic content analysis of television news in the various countries of the EU).

Although the empirical material on which this book is based covers the period through 1999, its significance is not limited to that period. This is particularly so because it is *not* primarily a book about the European elections of 1999, but rather an in-depth investigation of more general phenomena, the relevance of which far surpasses this specific election. This book is about the interplay between European elections and domestic politics, about the interactions between voters, political parties, and media, and about the commonalities (or lack thereof) of each of these actors across the member states of the European Union. For reasons that will be elaborated in this book, we have good reasons to believe that it is unlikely that the structural characteristics of these phenomena will change fundamentally in the foreseeable future. In fact, we expect most of these to remain relevant for many years to come. Therefore, the relevance of this volume extends well beyond the period during which most of its empirical material was collected—just as still is the case for the two previous volumes referred to above.

The focus of this third volume is on the ways in which European elections are connected to the national contexts of the member states, their domestic political arenas, and the political processes that unfold there. This connection is a two-way street. The domestic context shapes and influences much of the behavior of citizens, political parties, and mass media in European elections. It does so, however, against the backdrop of profound commonalities that re-affirm the conclusions from the earlier volumes, namely that a single European electorate exists and that the conditions are fulfilled for effective representative democracy at the level of the European Union. At the same time, however, European elections leave their own imprint on domestic politics, and particularly on the strengths of political parties. Indirectly, therefore, European elections also affect member states' policies in the intergovernmental side of European Union politics. This two-way interaction between domestic politics and European Parliament elections unfolds in a climate of increasing contestation over the forms and directions of European integration, particularly when we compare 1999 (and the years since then) to 1994 and earlier. As a consequence, it cannot be taken for granted that the long-standing under-politicization of European integration—documented in the earlier volumes—can be sustained indefinitely. If the integration issue becomes more politicized, this may take quite different forms, owing to the fact that this process will be mainly driven by opportunities provided within the domestic political arenas of the member states. The national specificity of these opportunities is more likely to undermine than to strengthen the preconditions of legitimate and effective representation in the Union, just as it is more likely to fragment rather than strengthen the single European electorate that we show to exist through 1999. The conditions under which these different outcomes may materialize are discussed in the final chapters of this book, taking into account the information that has been provided by the earlier chapters.

When looking at the authorship of these chapters, it is obvious that many people were involved in the making of this book. Not visible, however, are the contributions of countless other individuals and organizations. This research would not have been possible without the financial and material support from a number of institutions and organizations, which are listed in detail in the appendices of this book. We are also indebted to all who have been involved in the collection of empirical information and to everyone who has commented at conferences and expert meetings on preliminary presentations of findings. We would like to thank Wenonah Barton for her invaluable assistance during the final editing stage of this project. Finally, we would like to express our gratitude to the tens of thousands European citizens who, since 1989, have taken part in our surveys, thereby providing the basis of much of our knowledge.

Wouter van der Brug	Cees van der Eijk
Amsterdam	Nottingham and Amsterdam

Contributors

STEFANO BARTOLINI is currently Director of the Robert Schuman Centre for Advanced Studies at the European University Institute, Florence. Previously he was a professor at the Universities of Bologna, Florence, Trieste, Geneva, and at the European University Institute. In 1990 he was awarded the Stein Rokkan UNESCO Prize and in 2001 the Gregory Luebbert APSA Prize. His most recent publications include *The Electoral Mobilisation of the European Left 1880–1980* (Cambridge, 2000), *Maggioritario finalmente? La transizione elettorale 1994–2001*, edited with R. D'Alimonte (Bologna, 2002), and *Restructuring Europe: Centre Formation, System Building and Political Structuring between the Nation State and the EU* (Oxford, 2005).

CLAES H. DE VREESE is Professor and Chair of Political Communication and Scientific Director of The Amsterdam School of Communications Research (ASCoR) in the Department of Communication Science at the University of Amsterdam. He is also Adjunct Professor of Political Science and Journalism at the University of Southern Denmark. His work has appeared in international peer-reviewed journals, including *Communication Research, Journalism Studies, Political Communication, International Journal of Public Opinion Research, Scandinavian Political Studies, European Journal of Communication, West European Politics, EU Politics, Journalism & Mass Communication Quarterly, Mass Communication & Society*, and *European Journal of Political Research*.

MARK FRANKLIN is the Stein Rokkan Professor of Comparative Politics at the European University Institute, Florence. He has published eleven books, including *The Economy and the Vote* (Cambridge University Press, 2007), *Voter Turnout and the Dynamics of Electoral Competition in Established Democracies since 1945*

(Cambridge University Press, 2004), and *Choosing Europe?* with Cees van der Eijk et al. (University of Michigan Press, 1996). He founded the Public Opinion and Participation Section of the European Union Studies Association, has been a director of the European Election Studies project since 1987, has served on the editorial boards of six journals, and is a past Fulbright Scholar and Guggenheim Fellow.

MARTIN KROH is researcher at the German Institute for Economic Research, Berlin. He received his doctorate from the University of Amsterdam. His teaching and research interests include comparative political behavior and statistical methodology. His most current research focuses on the longitudinal study of public opinion and political participation.

EDMUND LAUF is senior researcher for the Dutch Media Authority. He received his doctorate from the University of Muenster, Germany. His research interests include media audience research, content analysis, news media markets, media concentration, and diversity.

MICHAEL MARSH is an associate professor of political science at Trinity College Dublin and Head of the School of Social Sciences and Philosophy. He has been a member of the planning team for European Parliament Election Studies since 1990, was a principal investigator for the first Irish election study (2002), and is a member of the editorial advisory board of *European Union Politics, Electoral Studies* and the *Journal of Elections, Public Opinion and Parties*. He recently co-authored with Michael Gallagher *Days of Blue Loyalty* (2002), a study of the Fine Gael party, and co-edited two books on the 2002 general election: *The Sunday Tribune Guide to Irish Politics* (2002) and *How Ireland Voted 2002* (2003).

JOCHEN PETER received his doctorate in 2003 from the University of Amsterdam and is an assistant professor at the Amsterdam School of Communications Research at the University of Amsterdam. He studied communication science at the University of Mainz, Germany, and at the University of Leicester, England. His research interests focus on political communication and the social consequences of the internet.

ANGELIKA SCHEUER graduated in sociology from University of Mannheim and holds a doctorate from the University of Amsterdam. Her dissertation *How Europeans See Europe—Structure and Dynamics of European Legitimacy Beliefs* is published by Amsterdam University Press. She is currently researcher at the Social Indicators Department of the Centre for Survey Research and Methodology (ZUMA) in Mannheim. Her research interests include attitudes towards the European Union, comparative research, and quantitative methods.

HERMANN SCHMITT is a research fellow of the MZES at the University of Mannheim and a Privatdozent for Political Science at the Free University of Berlin. He was a visiting professor at the University of Michigan (1996-97), Science Po Paris (2001-02), the Australian National University (2003), and the IAS in Vienna (2005). He received his doctorate from the University of Duisburg and his habilitation from the Free University of Berlin. He has participated in various comparative projects, such as the series of European Election Studies (since 1979). He is the author and editor of numerous books and articles on electoral behavior, political parties, and political representation in the EU.

HOLLI A. SEMETKO is the Director of the Halle Institute for Global Learning, vice provost for international affairs, and Professor of Political Science at Emory University since 2003. From 1995 to 2003 she was professor and chair of Audience and Public Opinion Research and chair of the Department of Communication Science at the University of Amsterdam. Her most recent book is *Political Campaigning in Referendums: Framing the Referendum Issue* (London: Routledge, 2004). She also co-edited *The Media, Journalism, and Democracy* (2000), and co-authored *On Message: Communicating the Campaign* (Sage, 1999), *Germany's "Unity Election": Voters and the Media* (1994), and *The Formation of Campaign Agendas* (1991).

JACQUES THOMASSEN is Professor of Political Science at the University of Twente in the Netherlands. He is a member of the Royal Netherlands Academy of Arts and Science. Among his more recent books are *Political Representation and Legitimacy in the European Union*, ed. with Hermann Schmitt (1999), *The European Parliament: Moving toward Democracy in the EU*, ed. with Bernard Steunenberg (2002), and *The European Voter* (2005).

WOUTER VAN DER BRUG (1963) is Professor of Politics at the Department of Political Science at the University of Amsterdam. He received prizes for the best master's thesis (in 1993) and best doctoral thesis (in 1998) in political science in the Netherlands. His work has been published in various international peer-reviewed journals, such as *Comparative Political Studies, British Journal of Political*

Science, European Journal of Political Research, Electoral Studies, Political Behavior, Party Politics, Journal of Theoretical Politics, West European Politics, and *Acta Politica.* He recently co-authored *The Economy and the Vote* (Cambridge University Press, 2007).

CEES VAN DER EIJK is Professor of Social Science Research Methods at the University of Nottingham, England. He is one of the principal investigators of the European Election Studies since 1989, and also of the Dutch Parliamentary Election Studies 1981, 1982, and 1986. He is the author or co-author of fourteen books, including *The Economy and the Vote* (2007), *Citizen Participation in European Politics* (2000), *Choosing Europe?* (1996), and *Electoral Change in the Netherlands* (1983). He is a past Fulbright and NIAS fellow, and a former president of the Dutch Political Science Association.

MARCEL VAN EGMOND received his doctoral degree from the University of Amsterdam. His research focus is on comparative political behavior, especially media and context effects, and his research has been published in the *European Journal of Political Research* and *Electoral Studies.* Since August 2004 he is a Postdoctoral Research Fellow at the University of Queensland Social Research Centre, on the ARC-funded project *Neoliberalism, Inequality and Politics: Public Policy and the Transformation of Australian Society* at the University of Queensland, in Brisbane, Australia.

ANDREAS M. WÜST (1969) is Research Fellow of the Volkswagen Foundation at the Mannheim Center for European Social Research (MZES) at Mannheim University. He studied at the University of Heidelberg, where he received a master's degree in political science in 1996 and a doctorate in 2002. His research interests are voting behavior, political parties, migration, and survey methodology. Main publications are *Wie wählen Neubürger?* on voting behavior of naturalized citizens in Germany (Opladen, 2002) and an edited volume, *Politbarometer,* on Germany's regular opinion poll (Opladen, 2003).

Introduction

Electoral politics in the European Union and the 2004 enlargement

CEES VAN DER EIJK
AND WOUTER VAN DER BRUG

The 2004 enlargement of the European Union is larger and more ambitious than each of the previous ones. Of the ten new member states, only one (Malta) is a relatively well-established and problem-free democracy, but it is by far the smallest of the new members. Of the rest, Cyprus still struggles with its history of civil war and division between Greek-Cypriot and Turkish-Cypriot territories. The remaining eight (Czech Republic, Estonia, Hungary, Latvia, Lithuania, Poland, Slovakia, Slovenia) were communist states that passed through difficult political and economic transitions in the period after 1989, the consequences of which have not yet always fully materialized. The process leading to the formal admission in May 2004 began long before that moment, but the process of actually integrating the enlarged Union—a process that involves the old and the new member states alike—will still require many years thereafter.

When considering the problems that the EU and its members will undoubtedly have to face in this process, one could conceivable take solace from the successful track record of the Union in integrating new members that (at their time) also had only recently experienced transitions to democratic politics (Greece, Spain, and Portugal). Yet the 2004 enlargement poses more formidable challenges than did earlier enlargements. One reason for this is that the EU is not the same as the former European Community (EC). The EC was primarily an *economic* union between sovereign national states. Over the past two decades these national states have transferred much of their sovereignty to the EU, which consequently has increasingly become a *political* union. The treaties of Maastricht, Amsterdam, and Nice in particular increased the breadth of the integration process far beyond that in the 1980s, when Greece, Spain, and Portugal were inducted as new members. Moreover, the number of new members is of a different magnitude than ever before and exceeds that of the three previous enlargements combined. Another important difference is that the new Union of twenty-five member states harbors an even larger variety of historical, political, cultural, and economic differences than the old one. It reaches across the former Iron Curtain into countries that have been separated from the rest of Europe for half a century. It brings together parts of Europe that have traditionally been regarded as 'of a different nature' by such renowned historians and social scientists as Eric Hobsbawm and Stein Rokkan.

The enlargement greatly increased the economic inequalities within the Union at a moment when many economies of the old member states were not doing well at all. When Spain, Portugal, Greece, and Ireland joined the EC, the EC invested heavily in their economies, which subsequently experienced impressive growth. However, in 2004 the old member states are very reluctant to have the EU invest on a similar scale in the new member states, and most of them drew up new regulations to prevent citizens from the new countries freely migrating and finding employment in their own economies.

The challenges for the new Union are daunting. It requires new or renewed institutions and procedures to accommodate the interactions between the member states and the Union as a whole. These are still in the making and will be utterly untested at the time they become operative. It will take at least a number of years to assess to what extent proposals generated by the European Convention can be put into practice and will become successes or failures. Likewise, it will take time to evaluate the wisdom, or lack thereof, of the terms of accession of the new member states negotiated in Copenhagen in December 2002.

The Union, its citizens and elections

The 2004 enlargement affects the older member states as well as the new ones. Even before May 2004 the relations between the older member states had changed, to some extent in anticipation of the consequences of the enlargement to come. The addition of new members will decrease the older ones' share of power in the Union's decision-making processes. The older members may expect a deterioration of the balance of their financial contributions to and transfers from the Union. Their industries and workforce will be subjected to new competition, and so on. All the older member states attempted to avert or at least minimize such anticipated effects, which made their mutual relations more contentious than they used to be. The relations between the older member states themselves have also changed because of the restrictions on their budgetary policies that were imposed by the Stability and Growth Pact. This pact was negotiated to ensure that the euro countries would not loosen their financial discipline after introducing the euro. Differences between the older member states in their willingness to adhere to these obligations—particularly after the economic recession of 2001—also contributed to less congenial relations between them.

These conflicts and problems will unavoidably, and probably more so than in the past, provide opportunities in each of the member states for political contestation over the EU and its policies, over the desirable extent and forms of integration, and so on. Such contestation is largely produced by political entrepreneurs (from existing political parties as well as 'newcomers') in their quest for political profit via the electoral process. Not only do the elections to the European Parliament offer opportunities (and risks) for parties and politicians who politicize European integration and the EU, but domestic elections in the member states do so as well. And the outcomes of both kinds of elections affect in turn the future course of European integration. The relationship between the Union and its citizens will thus be of increasing importance in the first years after 2004, and particularly to the extent that this relation becomes expressed in national and European elections. Obviously, the relationships between the Union and its citizens are inextricably interwoven with those that connect citizens to the political processes in their own country. Both of these relationships will be under substantial pressure until the most important wrinkles of the enlargement process have been ironed out and new institutions and procedures have proved their worth. Even in the unlikely event that the enlargement process does not generate new problems, the extension of the Union itself, and the concomitant reduction of each individual member state's influence on Union policy, can easily increase citizens' apprehensions about a Union that can simply be portrayed as an uncontrolled and uncontrollable Behemoth. How the relationships between the Union, European politicians, domestic politics, and citizens will express themselves in voting behavior and election results can, of course, only be experienced in the years to come. But the basis from which it is to develop can largely be assessed today.

This book focuses on the interplay between European elections, national politics, and the ongoing process of European integration. Below we will set out how national politics affects European elections and vice versa. The book covers the period before the latest enlargement of 2004. Its aim is *not* to provide a timely description of the most recent developments in electoral, domestic, and European politics. It stands in a longer tradition of comparative research on European elections, which resulted in numerous publications, of which two volumes should be mentioned in particular. The first one is *Choosing Europe?* a volume edited by van der Eijk and Franklin (1996) based on data collected for the European elections of 1989 and 1994, and the second one is *Political representation and legitimacy in the European Union*, edited by Schmitt and Thomassen (1999) and based on the European elections of 1994. The current volume covers the period through the European elections of 1999. It aims to do two things. First, it assesses whether and how the character of European elections and of the political representation of citizens' views regarding European integration have changed over the period through 1999. We investigate the electoral expression of the relationships between citizens, their governments, and their domestic political parties and the EU on the eve of the 2004 enlargement. Second, this book provides a basis for evidence-based conjectures (scenarios) about the complex interactions in the years after 2004 between elites and citizens in the interrelated spheres of domestic and European politics. As such, this book aims not only to set a research agenda for studies about the 2004 elections, but also for those covering the period thereafter.

European elections and national politics

In many ways the European Union will, after enlargement as much as before, constitute a level of institutions and policy making that is far removed from its citizens. The existing national identities, the large number of different languages, and the ingrained tendency of citizens, media, parties, and interest groups to look primarily at their own domestic polities hamper the emergence of a Union-wide sphere of political discourse and debate. Moreover, the Union is shielded from popular influence in a myriad of ways. A number of factors contribute to a separation between the Union and its citizens: the absence of trans-European parties and citizens' groups to organize and voice popular concerns at the Union level, the fragmentation of decision making into separate councils that obstructs the emergence of such parties and groups, the reliance on the institutions of the member states to execute Union policies, and the fragmentation of the electoral process by electing the European Parliament via a set of concurrent country-specific elections. Research on voting behavior in European elections has repeatedly shown that national concerns motivate party choice in European elections, the reason why Reif and Schmitt (1980) have labeled them second-order *national* elections. One of the themes running through this book is how European elections are affected by national politics.

The second main topic of this book is how national politics and elections are affected by European politics and elections. From this perspective it is important to realize that the shielding of the Union from its population operates in one direction only. Europe's population is not insulated from the consequences of Union policies. On the contrary, the transfer of policy-making powers from the member states to the Union in the last two decades has increased the likelihood of ordinary citizens being confronted with policy consequences that are to be attributed to the EU rather than to their domestic governments. Notable in this respect is the lack of policy prerogatives of the governments of the member states to deal with disasters in the chain of food production. BSE, foot-and-mouth disease, dioxin contamination of poultry, and aviary diseases all served to highlight the dramatic loss of independent policy-making capacity of national governments. But also in the field of (de)regulation of, e.g., energy suppliers, postal services, and telecom, it has become quite visible to large segments of the public that Brussels has become very important. Increasingly, important domestic political actors such as political parties, labor unions, and mass-based interest groups lament that their traditional access to the centers of domestic political power is no longer sufficient to effectively influence policy. Of course, Europe brings not only policies that are seen as problematic by some, it also brings bonuses, in the form of subsidies, removal of previously existing obstacles, and, in general, demonstrably positive economic effects. But here, too, the insulation of the Union from its citizens has its effects by preventing the Union being credited when credit is due.

This transfer of power from the level of national states to the European level has so far been a largely elite-driven process that has not been politicized in most countries until the early 1990s (e.g., van der Eijk and Franklin 1991; see also chapter 10 of this volume). However, there are signs that the process of European integration is becoming increasingly contested (cf. Marks and Steenbergen 2004) and intertwined with (electoral) politics in the member states. This can be seen in referenda about the treaties of Amsterdam and Nice, the outcomes of which were heavily determined by voters' orientations toward domestic politics (Franklin,

Marsh, and McLaren 1994; Franklin, van der Eijk, and Oppenhuis 1995), and in the success of some anti-EU parties in the European elections of 2004. Paradoxically, however, European elections are not the most appropriate forum for popular influence on European integration. Since national states decide about additional transfers of power to the EU, parties in the national parliaments are to be held accountable for furthering integration (Thomassen and Schmitt 1999a). So, there are good reasons to expect that the debate about European integration will not only become more politicized, but that issues related to it will also become more important in national elections.

The relationship between European citizens and their rulers will, in the years after 2004, remain a complex one. The degree of democratic control that electorates can exert over EU policies is extremely limited. Irrespective of its—increasing—legislative importance, the European Parliament is elected in a way that cannot be construed to yield a policy mandate. Moreover, its composition has no clear ramifications for the composition (and hence the political orientation) of the Council or even of the Commission—although this may change somewhat with respect to the latter if some of the proposals generated by the constitutional Convention were to come into effect. Within their own countries, representative democratic procedures give citizens influence over the distribution of legislative power and, to the extent that political parties and their leaders support different policy packages, also indirectly over the policy direction of their national governments. Yet, the independent policy-making capacity of their national governments is increasingly limited as a consequence of transfers of sovereignty to the EU level. This situation has generated a strategic environment for domestic political elites that can be quite detrimental to European integration. Governmental actors may use the EU as an opportunity for claiming credit and for externalizing blame. Mainstream opposition actors may seek short-term (electoral) gain by refraining from supporting their government's position in EU decision making, even when they would not have taken a different position had they themselves been in power. By doing so, they open up new opportunities to political challengers—political newcomers and non-mainstream opposition actors.

RESEARCH STRATEGY

In order to investigate the relationship between citizens, domestic politics, and the European Union, we focus on electoral politics. With this choice we certainly do not imply that all politics can be reduced to elections. The study of elections is, however, of particular relevance in highlighting the complex interactions and relations between citizens and elites in a multi-level political structure. Electoral politics is highly visible and it is direct in its political consequences, whereas other processes by which groups of citizens affect politics are usually less visible and their implications often take effect only after a longer period of time. Moreover, the way in which elections to the European Parliament are conducted guarantees that the major actors in electoral politics, voters and parties, are virtually the same in European and in national elections. Therefore, European elections have a considerable domestic political significance. National elections also affect European Union politics, but only indirectly so: to the extent that national elections determine the composition of the governments of the member states, they also affect the composition of the European Council and the Councils of Ministers. From previous studies we know that the electoral context is a fruitful one to study how domestic and European politics are interrelated. Finally, more than in the context of opinion studies, the electoral context requires voters to decide how important all different kinds of considerations are when confronted with a situation in which only a single choice can be made.

To sketch possible scenarios for future electoral developments, we have to rely on knowledge about the present, or the not too distant past. When our expectations about the plausibility of the occurrence of different scenarios are based upon the most recent data, we have the most confidence in the reliability of these expectations. In view of this, one possible research strategy would be to focus on the most recent national election studies from individual countries. This strategy has several drawbacks, however. In the first place, such studies contain little information about European elections and about voters' attitudes toward European integration. Moreover, national elections studies are not available for all of the EU member states, and even when they exist, they are conducted at different moments, i.e., in different transnational economic and political circumstances. Finally, differences in the contents and wording of their questionnaires severely limit the potential of national elections studies for cross-national comparative research.

Our strategy is therefore to focus on the European elections of 1999, for which extensive empirical data are available. In almost all chapters of this book, data from the European Elections Study (EES) 1999 are employed—details of this study are provided in appendix A. The EES 1999 consisted of independent cross-sectional surveys fielded in each member state of the EU immediately after the European Parliamentary elections, which ended on 13 June 1999.

The EES survey data are very suitable for cross-national comparative research because the same questions were asked at the same time in each country and in relation to a common event—the European Parliament elections. The fact that the study was designed as a study of European elections ensures that appropriate questions were asked about respondents' attitudes to European integration and the EU. Moreover, it provides information about voters' relations to domestic as well as to EU politics. An additional advantage of the EES 1999 is that this study is in many important respects comparable to European Elections Studies of 1994 and 1989. This allows us to compare the findings of 1999 to those reported in previous works (van der Eijk and Franklin 1996; Schmitt and Thomassen 1999).

A final advantage of the use of the EES 1999 is that the surveys in the fifteen member states were interlinked with two additional data sources. The first of these is a content analysis of the media in the period of the election campaign for the 1999 EP elections. This media study was conducted in fourteen member states of the old EU (all countries except Luxembourg). The second study that can be linked to the voter surveys of the EES is a content analysis of the election manifestos of all parties that obtained seats in the European Parliament in 1999. These two data sources provide invaluable information about the campaign messages that citizens received from media and parties, which in turn can be linked to citizens' attitudes to parties and European institutions.

Some of the contributions to this volume can be seen as 'normal science', by which we mean that the analyses are intended to update findings of previous studies with new data. The results help us not only to confirm the validity of earlier findings, but also to assess to what extent the world has changed. In this respect the book is a logical 'supplementary volume' to the two large-scale and comparative studies on previous European parliamentary elections that were mentioned earlier, *Choosing Europe?* (1996) and *Political representation and legitimacy in the European Union* (1999). The empirical and theoretical knowledge from these and other previous studies enables us to focus on changes over time, which would not have been possible had this volume been the first of such studies. In addition to updating existing knowledge, some contributions incorporate information from previous European elections in the analyses, thus explicitly modeling change. Another novel aspect of this book is that we can link data from media and from party manifestos to survey material (for details see appendices B and C). This provides a broader perspective on the complex interactions between media, parties, and citizens than was available in previous work. Of course, the EES 1999 comprises no data relating to the ten new member states of the 2004 EU enlargement. For these countries we do not have the same kind of information as for the older member states. This will, of course, change once new data becomes available for analysis. New data was collected during the 2004 European elections, but it will still take a number of years before extensive results thereof can be presented.

One of the aims of this book is to provide a basis for understanding the mutual relationship between electoral politics and European integration by way of assessing plausible scenarios for elections—European and domestic elections—after the 2004 enlargement. These cannot be generated by mere extrapolation of current developments as that would not yield valid insights. Whatever trend-like developments may exist, they cannot be reliably estimated on the basis of only five or six time-points (there have been only five European elections through 1999, only six when 2004 could be included). Moreover, in most respects it is impossible to assume *ceteris paribus* to hold. Since 1979 many of the institutional arrangements defining the EC/EU have changed, and they are likely to continue to change. Voters', politicians', and journalists' experiences, perceptions. and expectations concerning the EU, its institutions, and European elections evolve likewise—thus violating the plausibility of *ceteris paribus* conditions on which over-time comparisons depend.

Our approach to discussing possible scenarios is a different one, therefore. We will use the analyses presented in the first eleven chapters of this book to construct models that allow us to assess how election outcomes would be affected by various kinds of political changes. As we argued above, and as we will elaborate in chapter 12, we expect two important developments to take place in the years to come. The first is that issues with respect to European integration will become more important for voters' choices: increasing electoral salience of European integration. The second development that we expect to materialize in the next few years is a change in parties' stands with respect to European integration. For reasons to be discussed in more detail in chapter 12 we expect more parties to advocate Euro-skeptic positions and a greater degree of polarization of these positions. From the results presented in the different chapters of this book we will estimate the electoral consequences of such scenarios.

RESEARCH QUESTIONS AND PLAN OF THE BOOK

The book begins with a focus on (aggregate) election results. Parties, journalists, and voters alike tend to view European elections as second-order national elections (Reif and Schmitt 1980). One of consequences is that fewer people vote in European elections than in national (first-order) ones. Turnout in European elections declined in 1999 for the fourth time in a row, which is seen by many as threatening the legitimacy of the democratic process. In chapter 1 Mark Franklin analyzes aggregate turnout levels in all EU member states in all European elections since 1979 and explores various structural causes for turnout decline that would not raise such questions about democratic legitimacy. Another consequence of European elections being second-order elections is that party choice may be different from that in a national parliamentary election. Chapter 2 by Marcel van Egmond first assesses the extent to which such differences occur and then continues to assess whether this implies a structural advantage for particular kinds of parties. Chapter 3 by Michael Marsh also focuses on differences in patterns of electoral behavior in European and national elections, which lead to different aggregate outcomes. By comparing the results of European elections with those from the most recent preceding national elections he tests various explanations that have been proposed in the literature to explain these differences.

The second part of this book explores the locations of support for and opposition against European integration. Until the second half of the 1990s, the European project has been mainly elite driven in most European countries. In the 1990s referenda about issues involving the EU were held on several occasions. These referenda increased the political importance of citizens' opinions about integration, particularly after some referenda failed to provide the necessary consent for governments' proposals. They also raised the importance of parties' public stances with respect to European integration. In chapter 4, Andreas Wüst and Hermann Schmitt analyze the positions that parties occupy in this respect by means of the coded content of party manifestos drafted for European elections. They study to what extent parties present a European perspective in their programs for European elections. In addition they map positions of parties on European issues. Finally, they assess how voters' perceptions of parties relate to the contents of these manifestos. Chapter 5 by Angelika Scheuer and Wouter van der Brug focuses on the same type of questions, but now from the perspective of citizens rather than that of parties. They investigate the social and political location of support for and opposition against the EU in the different member states. The chapter identifies where in society and where in the political spectrum the groups are located that strongly oppose or support the EU and European integration.

The third part of the book focuses on the election campaign. Much of what citizens know about politics in general, about the EU, the elections to the European Parliament, and the campaigns for those elections has been acquired from the mass media. Chapter 6 by Claes de Vreese, Edmund Lauf, and Jochen Peter identifies the main differences among the countries in the tone and visibility of the campaigns for the European elections in the media. They also describe to what extent the media present the campaign from a European or from a domestic political perspective. Large differences were observed between the different countries, which are partly determined by the absence or presence of a viable anti-EU party. Chapter 7 by Jochen Peter focuses on the effects of campaign contexts on voters' attitudes toward European integration. He demonstrates that the existence of a viable anti-EU party is an important moderator for the effect of media content. These findings are highly relevant for our discussion of possible future scenarios and the likelihood of increasing or decreasing popular support for the EU.

The fourth part of this book focuses on individual-level voting behavior in European elections. This part consists of two chapters that address the two types of choices voters are confronted with: first, whether or not to vote, and only if so, second, which party to vote for. Chapter 8 by Hermann Schmitt and Cees van der Eijk focuses on the factors that influence whether or not citizens make use of their voting rights. The main question addressed is whether non-voting in European elections is fuelled by opposition to the EU and by (dis)satisfaction with the domestic government. Chapter 9 by Wouter van der Brug, Cees van der Eijk, and Mark Franklin focuses on party choice and attitudes toward European integration. The key question they address is to what extent party choice is motivated by support for or opposition against European integration or EU policies, and to what extent it is motivated by other considerations deriving from the domestic political environment.

In the fifth part we shift our focus to the electoral opportunity structure in which parties and voters find themselves. The electoral opportunity structure of parties depends upon the positions of voters and on the positions of competing parties on important policy dimensions. Positions that are densely populated with voters but not represented by any parties provide opportunities for existing parties to move to those positions, or for new parties to form and position themselves there. The electoral opportunity structure of voters is determined by the choices that parties offer between different sets of policies. Chapter 10 by Cees van der Eijk and Mark Franklin explores parties and voters on two dimensions: left-right and pro- or anti-European integration. After mapping this two-dimensional space, they identify the positions where many voters are located, but which are not represented by parties. Chapter 11 by Martin Kroh, Wouter van der Brug, and Cees van der Eijk focuses on patterns of electoral competition. It charts the groups in the electorates of the member states that have a high propensity of switching between parties, assesses their size, and evaluates the implications for short-term shifts in vote shares that parties may acquire and the conditions under which this may happen.

Chapter 12 is the product of a working conference in which a number of scholars joined forces to reflect on parties' and citizens' responses to further European integration. We discuss how future European elections are likely to be affected by domestic political circumstances and how attitudes toward the EU will affect the outcomes of future elections. We argue that the issue of European integration is likely to become more politicized and to become more important for party choice, and we model the consequences thereof in the form of three scenarios. The first scenario is one in which voters' orientations toward European integration become more important determinants of their votes, but where their own positions and those of parties are unchanged. In a second scenario, positions of parties become more Euro-skeptic, and in the third scenario positions of both parties and voters are changed in such a way that distances between voters and parties on a European integration dimension are given equal play to affect voters' choices as the left-right dimension, which has until now been the most important domestic political orientation in all of the member states. Obviously, these scenarios are ideal-types, and it is unlikely that future developments will play out exactly in these stylized forms. But we do think that these scenarios contain some of the most important elements of how the relations between voters, member states, and the EU will develop in future years.

CHAPTER ONE

Effects of space and time on turnout in European Parliament elections

MARK N. FRANKLIN

The idea that turnout responds to levels of public esteem for democratic institutions is deep seated and recurrent. Though it has been argued (Franklin 1999, 2004; Franklin, van der Eijk, and Oppenhuis 1996) that turnout reflects nothing of the sort—certainly not unless one first controls for other factors more immediately responsible for turnout levels—this argument has evidently not been widely heard. The significant drop in turnout registered at the fifth elections to the European Parliament conducted in all the member countries of the European Union in June 1999 provided an opportunity for commentators and politicians to point to those elections as demonstrating a supposedly low and declining level of support for European institutions (never mind that previous research had found little evidence that turnout in such elections was driven by attitudes to Europe—see chapter 8 of this volume).[1] Much was made of the fact, evident in table 1.1, that these elections represented the fourth successive occasion upon which turnout at European elections had fallen, and that the rate of decline (whether we look at the weighted or unweighted averages)[2] appeared to be accelerating.

One point neglected by virtually everyone is that the European Union of 1999 is not the same place as the European Economic Community of 1979. In 1979, nine countries participated in the first elections to the European Parliament, ten if we include Greece, where the first EP elections were held

Table 1.1 Turnout at elections for the European Parliament, 1979–1999

Country	1979	1981	1984	1987	1989	1994	1995	1999	Average
Austria							67.7	49.4	58.6
Belgium+	90.4		92.2		90.7	90.7		91.0	91.0
Britain	32.2		32.6		36.2	36.1		24.0	32.2
Denmark	47.8		52.4		46.2	52.9		50.5	50.0
Finland							60.3	31.4	45.9
France	60.7		56.7		48.7	52.7		46.8	53.1
Germany	65.7		56.8		62.3	60.0		45.2	58.0
Greece+		78.6	77.2		79.9	71.2		75.3	76.4
Ireland	63.6		47.6		68.3	44.0		50.2	54.7
Italy+	84.9		83.4		81.5	74.8		70.8	79.1
Luxembourg+	88.9		88.8		87.4	88.5		87.3	88.2
Netherlands	57.8		50.6		47.2	35.6		30.0	44.2
Portugal				72.4	51.2	35.5		40.0	49.8
Spain				68.9	54.6	59.1		63.0	61.4
Sweden							41.6	38.8	40.2
EU Average	65.8	78.6	63.8	70.7	62.9	58.4	56.5	52.9	60.5
EU Average*	(67.1)		(65.0)		63.6	(58.0)		52.8	
Weighted by voting age population*	(62.8)		(60.3)		58.8	(54.3)		47.6	
N	9 (10)	1	10 (12)	2	[12]	12 (15)	3	15	64

*Includes the first election of new members in the columns for preceding EU-wide elections.
+Compulsory voting country (in Italy only until 1993, see text).
Source: Compiled from official sources.

in 1981. In 1999, fifteen countries participated. The progressive enlargement of the (soon to be) European Union brought about two changes that need to be taken into account in any assessment of turnout decline. In the first place, the proportion of countries that employed compulsory voting declined as a consequence of additions to the EC/EU. This will have reduced average turnout at these elections. In the second place, most countries participating for the first time in European Parliament elections see higher turnout than in subsequent EP elections, perhaps because of the greater media coverage given to initial events of this type (see below). The relative number of such countries necessarily declined over time. A third development, also quite mechanical in its operations, will have further accentuated the decline. This has to do with the point within their national election cycle that each country has reached at the time of a European Parliament election. When such elections fall early in a national election cycle (soon after national elections have been held) turnout is almost invariably lower than when EP elections are held late in a national election cycle, shortly before or coinciding with national elections. By chance, the time since the last national elections had in 1999 increased, on average over all countries, by about 5.3 months; reducing the turnout we would expect to find by some 1.6 percent (Franklin, van der Eijk, and Oppenhuis 1996, 318).

These three structural factors need to be taken into account in any assessment of turnout change. The purpose of this chapter is to see how far the decline in turnout observed in European Parliament elections over the course of the first five elections to that body can be ascribed to mechanisms associated with the structural factors of first-time voting, compulsory voting, and time until the next national election (which we will refer to as 'electoral salience' for reasons explained below). First we will elaborate the reasons for the three effects. Then we will use data from the EP elections of 1979 to 1999 to estimate the effects of the three variables of interest. The resulting coefficients are used to model the turnout that would have been observed in the absence of the three mechanisms (i.e., with a constant number of compulsory voting countries, constant time to the next national election, and no first-time turnout boost). Additionally, we will see whether turnout in particular countries deviates significantly from expectations derived from our model.

THEORY

The theory underpinning the effects of compulsory voting is well understood. Countries that impose a sanction on those who do not vote (even if the sanction is small and not always applied) do see higher and less variable turnout than other countries. What is unusual in the case of elections to the European Parliament is the magnitude of the effect. Compulsory voting in national elections only adds about 9 percent to turnout (Powell 1986; Jackman 1987; Jackman and Miller 1995; Blais and Dobrzynska 1998; Gray and Caul 2000; Franklin 2002b). In elections to the European Parliament the effect of compulsory voting is magnified more than threefold (Franklin, van der Eijk, and Oppenhuis 1996) because turnout in these elections is so very low in the absence of a compulsion to vote (the average turnout among non-compulsory voting countries in table 1.1 is 49.8 percent). Table 1.1 also shows that, in 1979, three of the nine countries voting in that first election to the European Parliament employed compulsory voting. In 1981, newly admitted Greece conducted its first EP election also under conditions of compulsory voting. Between 1981 and 1999 five more countries joined the EC/EU, but none of them were compulsory voting countries.

Most tables of turnout at EP elections do not show the separate elections of newly admitted members, but average the turnout at those elections with turnout at the previous EP election (as is done in the second EU Average row of table 1.1). So the tables we normally look at (containing only columns for years ending in 9 or 4 in table 1.1) have a first column in which close to half the participating countries used compulsory voting and subsequent columns in which progressively smaller proportions of citizens voted under these conditions.

Turning to the boost that turnout appears to get in most countries voting at their first European Parliament election, this has often been noted by commentators, but it has never really been explained. First election has been found important for explaining turnout not only in European Parliament elections but also in national elections. High electoral turnout in the first elections conducted in Eastern Europe following the fall of communism and in South Africa following the end of minority white rule there were widely noted in the press. Franklin (2002b) notes the same thing, and also the fact that turnout is higher after a temporary suspension of democratic elections (for example during World War II). Commentators have generally assumed that the first-time boost for European Parliament elections (evident for all countries other than compulsory voting countries in table 1.1 except for Britain and Denmark) is due to the excitement surrounding a novel experience (Reif 1984; van der Eijk, Franklin, and Marsh 1996).[3] This excitement manifests itself in the sort of media attention that journalists would normally give to a national election. Blumler (1983) and Blumler and Fox (1982) describe in detail the amount and type of attention given to the European Parliament elections of 1979. They point out that much of it had to do with explaining to readers the role of the European Parliament and how the elections would change its complexion (up until then the EP had consisted of appointed members drawn from national parliaments). No similar systematic studies have been conducted of subsequent EP elections, but such reports as have appeared (e.g., in the country chapters of van der Eijk and Franklin 1996) make it clear that coverage of more recent elections was much less. This makes sense because the type of information contained in much of the 1979 election coverage was not the sort of information that would be news in later elections. Reading between the lines we can surmise that journalists learned from their first experience that European elections provide very little material for them to use in filling the pages of their newspapers or the minutes of their news programs. So in subsequent elections they would know better than to give the process much attention.

But the journalists of each new member country in turn apparently needed to learn the same lesson. We judge this from the fact that the first-time boost has on three occasions been followed by a drop-off at subsequent EP elections: in 1984 when ten countries were voting for the second time, in 1989 when two countries were voting for the second time, and in 1999 when three countries were voting for the second time. This pattern would by itself have produced the appearance of declining turnout over the EU as a whole, even without the waning effect of compulsory voting.

Electoral salience is the last of the structural variables we will deal with in this chapter. As argued at length elsewhere (Franklin 1999, 2002b, 2004; Franklin, van der Eijk, and Oppenhuis 1996; Franklin and Hirczy 1998), turnout responds to the importance of the election in the minds of voters. In really important elections almost everyone votes. Elections for less important offices, or when the result is a foregone conclusion, or when it is unlikely to have policy consequences, see lower turnout. Elections to the European Parliament have about as little salience in their own right as it is possible to imagine. The institution is poorly understood and generally (though wrongly) considered to be of little consequence (van der Eijk and Franklin 1996; Blondel, Sinnott, and Svensen 1998; Franklin 2005). More importantly, elections to the European Parliament do not set in train a process of government formation, so they have no immediate policy implications. Most importantly of all, the campaigns that lead up to European elections do little to mobilize voters on issues of importance to the governance of Europe (Blumler 1983; van der Eijk and Franklin 1996; van der Eijk, Franklin, and Marsh 1996—and see chapter 6 in this volume). On the other hand, European elections do 'borrow' some importance as means for commenting on national politics in the member countries. Results are often interpreted as barometers for how well parties would perform in 'real' (i.e., national) elections (Anderson and Ward 1996; Franklin, van der Eijk, and Oppenhuis 1996; Franklin 2005). In this way they can sometimes act as 'primary elections' that help parties choose policies and even leaders whom they think might have the best chance of making gains (or avoiding losses) in a national election.

The extent to which European Parliament elections serve this purpose depends almost entirely on timing. European elections occur every five years, but in most member countries they do not always occur at the same point in the national election cycle. In most European countries, the timing of national elections is not fixed. Only the maximum length of time between elections is prescribed by law. Moreover, the maximum term of a national parliament is generally four years rather than five, and national elections can be (and often are) called long before this. Because national elections generally occur more frequently than European Parliament elections (the exception is Luxembourg which has always held European Parliament elections on the same day as national elections), the position of EP elections in the national election cycle is variable between countries and over time. EP elections that occur soon after national elections have no role as barometers. A better indicator of the standing of national parties already exists in the outcome of the recent national election. Moreover, no one is much interested in a barometer of public opinion when the next election will not occur for several years. However, as the next national election approaches, interest in the standing of the parties increases. And the passage of time also renders the previous national election outcome less and less useful as an indicator of the next election's probable outcome. So, European elections that occur in the shadow of forthcoming national elections can arouse considerable interest in the media and among politicians. Voters become aware of the possible importance of the election outcome in domestic political terms and are more likely to vote as a consequence. Indeed, extensive research has shown that time until the next national election serves as an excellent surrogate measure of the importance of the EP election (Franklin 2002b, 2005; van der Eijk and Franklin 1996).[4] Turnout (when corrected for other influences) does vary in step with variations in electoral salience, even in compulsory voting countries (though in such countries the variation is more muted than elsewhere—see table 1.1).

This third variable goes some way toward explaining one of the two exceptions to the general rule that countries see lower turnout at their second EP election, except when compulsory voting keeps turnout high. The two exceptions are Britain and Denmark. The British exception can be at least partially explained by the fact that the second election in that country occurred a full year later in the electoral cycle than their first EP election. For that reason we would have expected turnout to be more than 3 percent higher. Because actual turnout hardly changed, we do in fact see the operation of the 'first-election boost' in that country. Denmark is more difficult to explain. This is the one country to have seen a clear rise in turnout between its first and second election to the European Parliament. The first election also happened only four months before a national election, so we would have expected turnout to be even higher at that election. The first-election boost should have joined with electoral salience to produce particularly high turnout at that first EP election. The fact that it did not must surely be bound up with specifics of Danish politics, which are beyond the remit of this chapter. Denmark has always been idiosyncratic in its behavior at European Parliament elections, often for good reason (see note 12).

Modeling Turnout at European Parliament Elections

Apart from the three variables of major concern to us in this chapter, turnout at EP elections has been found in past research to respond to a number of additional factors which would have to be taken into account in any properly specified model of EP turnout. In this research we are mainly concerned to see whether the effects we have drawn attention to can, alone, account for observed turnout decline. It is indeed possible that some other factors have played a role in turnout variations at EP elections, which would reduce the strength of effects ascribed in this chapter to structural factors. Our intent is to show, however, that the observed decline in turnout does not itself *require* that additional factors be identified.[5]

The dataset used in all analyses reported in this chapter is a country-level dataset derived from official turnout statistics, along with other variables to be described below. This dataset has sixty-four cases: ten for 1979 (including Greece which in reality conducted its first EP election in 1981), twelve for 1984 and 1989 (including Spain and Portugal in the 1984 time-point even though their first EP elections were in reality conducted in 1987) and fifteen in 1994 and 1999 (including Austria, Finland, and Sweden in the 1994 time-point even though their first EP elections were held in 1995). In format this is a pooled cross-section study design and so we will analyze it using panel-corrected standard errors (Beck and Katz 1995) and test for time serial correlation in the data. However, because our data have many fewer time-points than is generally thought necessary for the use of this procedure (Stata 1999), we also employ a random effects model (Stata 1999) as a check on the findings.

A potential problem arises because of the nature of the dependent variable. Though turnout is measured as a percentage of registered voters (see below), and is thus interval-level, it is subject to ceiling effects. For this reason it has the same limitations in regression analysis as do binary variables, and Ordinary Least Squares may yield the same sort of biased coefficients as with a dummy dependent variable. To see whether this was occurring in practice, we subjected our dependent variable to a logistic transformation and used OLS regression with the resulting transformed variable.[6] This analysis explained less variance than the corresponding analysis with an untransformed dependent variable, indicating that a linear dependent variable better represents the data (additionally, none of the predicted values of this variable actually exceed 100 or are less than 0). With the methodology out of the way, we can turn to the coding of specific variables.

Turnout

As already mentioned, turnout is measured in terms of valid votes as a percentage of the registered electorate. The sources for the different elections are official returns from the various countries. Useful compendia are to be found in Mackie (1991, 1996) and Mackie and Craig (1980, 1985) and these formed the basis for our turnout data. However, because turnout figures are often corrected following their initial release (sometimes dramatically) and we have tried to use these corrected figures whenever we could find them, our numbers (shown in table 1.1) do not exactly duplicate those found in Mackie or any other sources (these sources themselves show differences in specific turnout figures).

The independent variables

We code compulsory voting as a dummy variable that takes the value 1 for Belgium, Greece, Italy, and Luxembourg. Otherwise it takes the value 0. In Italy, non-voting has never been a crime punishable by law. However, even where non-voting is considered a crime it is seldom punished, and in Italy non-voters used to have this fact recorded on their identity cards, with the possibility of real or imagined repercussions. Italy has traditionally been treated as a compulsory voting country for this reason, but the practice of recording the voting record of citizens ended in 1993 and officially Italy is no longer a compulsory voting country. However, it is not clear to what extent Italian voters have adapted to the change. Turnout in Italy at European Parliament elections was lower in 1994 (by 7 points) and in 1999 (by 11 points) than in previous EP elections, but this decline is small compared to the 30 points that generally separates countries with compulsory voting from those without in EP elections. Moreover, about half of the drop in turnout that actually occurred in 1994 would have been expected on account of the fact that the election was held a year earlier in the national election cycle than had been the case in 1989 (see above). So it seems that Italian turnout is actually falling rather gradually as Italian voters come to terms with their new freedom not to vote, at a rate of about 4 percent per European election. At that rate it will take nine elections or forty-five years for Italian voters to completely forget the behavior associated with compulsory voting—a reduction of 0.125 in the value of the compulsory voting variable per election, which is how the process has been modeled in this research.[7]

In our data, first election is coded 1 in 1979 for the six countries without compulsory voting whose citizens voted in that election and 0 otherwise. For Portugal and Spain the variable is coded 1 for the election of 1984 (which in these countries was not in fact conducted until 1987) and 0 in subsequent elections. For Austria, Finland, and Sweden it is coded 1 in 1994 (though the actual election occurred in 1995) and 0 in 1999. Countries (Austria, Finland, Portugal, Spain, and Sweden) that did not participate in the first EP elections are not included in the dataset for elections prior to the one in which they first took part.

Finally, time until the next expected national election is measured in years and parts of years (to three significant digits with a maximum of 5.00 and a mean of 2.02). The variable is coded with reference to recent history, using the average time between elections over the past three elections as a basis for the expected date of the next national election unless that election occurred in conjunction with the European Parliament election, in which case time to the next election is coded 0.[8] Time to the next election is also coded 0 for compulsory voting countries, where we expect turnout to be sustained by the compulsion to vote even in elections that lack salience. A measure of electoral salience is derived from this by subtracting it from 5, thus producing a variable that increases as the election becomes more important to voters, commentators, and politicians. It runs from 0 to 5 with a mean of 3.01.

Findings

Table 1.2 displays the effects of the three independent variables in three models explaining turnout variations. Models A and C employ GLS regression with panel-corrected standard errors, even though this procedure is not recommended for models in which the number of time-points is less than the number of groups (Stata 1999). Model C, in addition to correcting the standard errors for panel effects, also assumes an AR1 autoregressive process.[9] Model B serves as a check on the findings, by assuming random effects over space and time using OLS regression.

Though all three models yield very similar values for the coefficients of importance to us in this research (unstandardized regression coefficients), model A

Table 1.2 Results of regression analyses (Standard Errors in parentheses)

Variable	Model A (Panel corrected)	Model B (Random effects)	Model C (Panel corrected AR1)
Constant	31.73 (3.51)***	33.78 (3.58)***	34.26 (4.00)***
Compulsory voting	25.16 (2.15)***	27.65 (4.60)***	28.04 (2.63)***
For non-compulsory voting countries:			
Electoral Salience	5.54 (0.96)***	4.69 (1.07)***	4.46 (0.99)***
First election	10.51 (2.17)***	10.76 (2.13)***	10.34 (2.48)***
Adjusted R^2	0.822	0.819	0.819
N	64	64	64

* Significant at 0.05 level; ** Significant at 0.01 level; *** Significant at 0.001 level.

comes closest to fitting the variations in turnout actually found in the data (as shown by its slightly higher variance explained) so in what follows we will employ coefficients from that model. In the next section we will see to what extent we can explain the decline in European Parliament electoral turnout on the basis of these effects.

Modeling the Effects of Changing Composition

We saw in table 1.1 that average unweighted turnout in European Parliament elections has declined by 14.3 percent. To what extent can we explain this decline by taking account of the changing composition of the EC/EU? As pointed out in the introduction, accessions of new members have had two effects: (a) reducing the proportion of Europeans who vote under conditions of compulsory voting, and (b) multiplying the instances when turnout did not benefit from a first-time boost.

By 1999 all member countries (except compulsory voting countries) had experienced the drop-off in turnout characterizing their second and subsequent trips to the polls. The total effect of this variable will thus be the effect of first election in model A (table 1.2) multiplied by the proportion of non-compulsory voting countries (11.25/15).[10] Multiplying this proportion by 10.51 (the appropriate coefficient in table 1.2's model A) yields 7.9 percent. The consequence of the de-

Table 1.3 Mean expected turnout when composition and timing effects are removed

Year	N	actual turnout	corrected turnout
1979	10	67.1	56.1
1984	12	64.9	60.3
1989	12	63.6	59.8
1994	15	57.9	56.5
1999	15	52.8	54.4

clining proportion of EC/EU countries going to the polls under conditions of compulsory voting is calculated in a similar fashion. The coefficient of 25.16 in model A has to be multiplied by the proportion by which compulsory voting countries have been reduced: 0.4 to 0.25 which is 0.15. This proportion of 25.16 is 3.8. So we can expect turnout to have been reduced by close to 4 percent on account of the declining proportion of countries with compulsory voting. Added to the 7.9 percent due to subsequent election drop-off, this gives us a total of 11.7 percent—rather less than the 14.3 percent decline that actually occurred.

But this is not all. The remaining variable in table 1.2 also has the opportunity to contribute to an explanation of turnout decline. Electoral salience is not the same on average at the time of each European election. Over the whole period from 1979 to 1999, average time to the next election increased by 0.44 years which, when multiplied by the appropriate coefficient in model A (5.54), yields an expected decline in turnout of 2.4 percent among non-compulsory voting countries, or 1.8 when averaged over all countries. Taken with the 11.7 percent decline due to the other two variables, the total comes to within 0.8 of matching the drop in turnout that actually occurred.[11]

A more elaborate procedure that amounts to nearly the same thing is to estimate the average turnout that would have occurred in each European Parliament election had the proportion of countries with compulsory voting remained constant, had there been no first-election boost, and had the average salience of the election remained the same as in 1979 (2.79 among non-compulsory voting countries). To do this, we apply the following equation:

$$\text{Corrected} = \text{Turnout} - (25.16 \times \text{COMPULS}) - (10.51 \times \text{FIRST}) - (5.54 \times (\text{SALIENCE} - 3.01)) + 6.29$$

Apart from average electoral salience, most of the coefficients come straight from model A of table 1.1. The constant term at the end of the equation is the increase in turnout we get from having 3.75 out of fifteen countries with compulsory voting at the end of our period, rather than none (6.29 = (3.75/15) × 25.16). This equation yields the values for corrected turnout shown in table 1.3. There we find that corrected turnout is lower by only 1.7 percent in 1999 compared with its value in 1979. More interestingly, the intervening years did see considerable turnout variations. Turnout in 1979 would have been quite low without the first-election boost that year, but would have risen by over 4 percent in 1984. Thereafter there would have been a slight decline. Notably, however, most of this decline occurred in a single step between 1989 and 1994, when turnout fell by 3.3 percent. Between 1984 and 1989 corrected turnout fell by only 0.5 percent while between 1994 and 1999 the drop in corrected turnout was only 2.1 percent. It is natural to suppose that the 1994 decline was due to the accession of Austria, Finland, and Sweden whose first elections to the European Parliament, though they occurred the following year, are counted in our data as having occurred in 1994. However, this is the reverse of the case. Without these countries, the drop between 1989 and 1994 would have been 3.8 percent and the drop in turnout after 1994 would have been reduced to 1.3 percent.

Outliers

The analysis reported in model A of table 1.1 produces two outlying countries, Britain and Sweden. These are the only countries whose elections see turnout that is lower on average than expected (by a highly significant 16 percent in the case of Britain, and by 10.5 percent in the case of Sweden). There is not much that can be said about Sweden as that country had in 1999 participated in only two European elections, but in Britain, not only in 1999 but (to a lesser extent) in every European election, voter turnout was significantly less than would have been expected on the basis of that country's lack of compulsory voting and the timing of the EP election in its national electoral cycle. It would be easy to blame this on Euro-skepticism, except that the other main Euro-skeptic country, Denmark, does not deviate significantly from the turnout expected on the basis of its political characteristics.[12] Some of the size of the British outlier is due to the particularly low turnout registered in Britain in 1999, but even when that outlier is taken into account by means of a specific dummy variable, the overall British residual retains its significance and only drops two points to 14 percent.

The additional drop in 1999 is surely due to the unfamiliarity of a new electoral system and the lack of evident connection between votes under List PR and votes under a first-past-the-post system that would still prevail at the next (national) general election. It accounts for fully 1 percent of the EU-wide decline in turnout after 1994. By introducing so radically different an electoral system for EP elections, the British have effectively removed any easy means for translating the outcome into domestic political terms. So European elections in Britain can no longer readily serve as barometers for the standing of parties in the national political arena. Even though commentators and politicians largely ignored this fact, if British voters responded to it this would not be the first time that voters have shown themselves to be smarter than their representatives. (Until 1999 the British residual had been steadily declining and was less than 10 percent in 1989 and 1994.)

But this leaves us little closer to understanding the large difference between turnout in Britain and turnout elsewhere. When proportionality of the electoral system was included in the prediction equation (in earlier studies of EP election turnout), Britain was less of an outlier, because low turnout in Britain was picked up by this variable (Franklin, van der Eijk, and Oppenhuis 1995, 1996). Substantively, the low British turnout was blamed on the wasted vote syndrome that was thought to apply to systems that were not highly proportional. The British no longer use that electoral system in European elections,[13] but it is unlikely that British voters have immediately adapted to the change. Indeed, we argued above that the change was very likely responsible for lower turnout rather than higher. If we assume that British voters still retain the attitudes inculcated by poor proportionality of their historic electoral system, this could go some way toward explaining the British case.

Discussion

If this chapter has any important message it is that composition effects should be taken seriously when considering change in political variables. Electorates do not consist of the same individuals from election to election, and the European Union does not consist of the same countries from election to election. Admittedly the major composition effect we discovered in this analysis was an odd one, having to do with the removal of a one-time increase in the turnout of most countries at their first EC/EU election, but even the more straightforward effect of the reducing proportion of compulsory voting countries will have accounted for close to a 4 percent drop in turnout over twenty years.

The findings have implications for turnout in elections to the European Parliament from 2004 onward. Since none of the new member countries employ compulsory voting, the long-term impact of new members should be to reduce turnout somewhat, as the overall effects of compulsory voting in the increasingly small proportion of compulsory voting countries are further diluted. Counteracting this long-term trend, we might nevertheless have expected a short-term boost to average turnout in 2004 as each new country contributed its own 'first-election boost' comparable to the one that other new members had previously enjoyed. This does not in fact appear to have occurred. Indeed, citizens in several of the new member states voted at especially low levels in the EP elections of 2004 (Franklin 2005), perhaps because these elections closely followed referenda in the new countries that might have somehow interfered with this 'first-election boost'.

With or without the accession of new countries, turnout can be expected to rise somewhat when average time to the next national election goes down. This average cannot continue to rise indefinitely, and at some point it must drop as the happenstances of electoral timing bring a random shift, on average, in that direction. This did happen in 2004 among established member countries, which saw on average virtually no change in turnout since 1999 (Franklin 2005).

A possible concern about our findings comes from the fact that turnout has been observed to decline in national elections in Europe, raising a question as to why corrected turnout is not declining in European Parliament elections as well. Other research (Franklin 2004) shows that in most EU countries (all except the Netherlands) decline in national election turnout since 1979 has been slight and can be explained on the basis of changes in institutional arrangements and party competitiveness that would not necessarily impact turnout in European elections.[14] We have admittedly made no attempt to apportion responsibility for turnout decline between the variables investigated in this study and other potential effects on turnout, so there is still the possibility that other influences may have played a part, attenuating the effects we measure in this chapter. To the extent that there are in fact other reasons for turnout decline, those reasons might have caused declining turnout at EP elections even in the absence of the structural factors we identify in this study. It is, however, notoriously difficult to correctly apportion effects that are shared between different variables, and even if we had identified additional effects, those effects might have been accidental rather than causal. With the small number of time-points at our disposal for studying European Parliament elections it is unlikely that we would be able to arrive at definitive conclusions about this. More worrying is the fact that a residual decline in turnout at EP elections, beyond what could be explained by any and all measured influences, would have been consistent with other aspects of the evolution of EP elections (see below).

One surprise in our findings was the size of the effects that can arise (for countries without compulsory voting) due to changes in average time to the next

Table 1.4 Effects on turnout of changes in mean time to next national election for non-compulsory voting countries

				Effect on turnout	
Year	N*	Mean	Difference from previous election	Non-compulsory voting countries	All countries**
1979	6	1.36	—	—	
1984	8	1.39	+0.03	−0.17	−0.12
1989	8	1.20	−0.19	1.05	0.77
1994	11.12	1.68	+0.48	−2.66	−1.98
1999	11.25	1.80	+0.12	−0.66	−0.50

* Italy counts as 0.88 of a compulsory voting country in 1994; 0.75 in 1999 (see note 7).
** Note that, after the next enlargement of the EU, effects for all countries will be much closer to the effects for non-compulsory voting countries.

election. Table 1.4 shows these mean figures for each of the election years, together with the effect on turnout of the difference between each mean figure and the mean for the previous year. The biggest difference between two successive years occurred between 1989 and 1994, when turnout could have been expected to drop almost 2 percent simply because of the fact that, on average, the 1994 European Parliament elections occurred six months earlier in the national election cycles of member countries than had been the case at the previous EP election.

The variables of greatest moment in this chapter are easily derived from the public record that exists at the time of each European Parliament election. The number of compulsory voting countries is certainly known.[15] The number of new members, and whether they are conducting their first or subsequent election to the European Parliament, is also known. The average time until the next national election is harder to compute for most countries, since the position of European Parliament elections within each nation's electoral cycle is not well known. Yet the approximate position in the electoral cycle of each country is easily derived from the date of the previous national election together with the legal maximum length of parliaments in each country (four or five years). This measure can be refined by looking at the empirical record of recent parliaments in each country to find the average length of time between elections there, but this makes little difference in practice to the estimates of turnout that can be derived from the resulting figures. When considering turnout at future EP elections it will be easy enough to correct reported figures by performing the rudimentary calculation

FIGURE 1.1   Uncorrected and corrected turnout at EP elections, 1979–1999

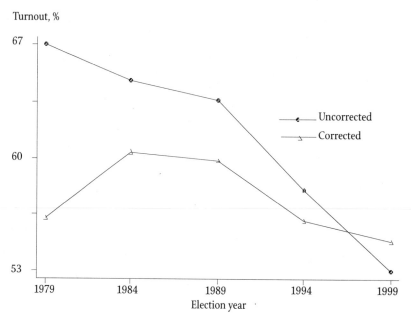

upon which table 1.3 was based before speculating about the implications of turnout at such elections.

What implications can we draw from the pattern of corrected turnout shown in table 1.3? The picture given is one of stability (especially when we consider that 1.2 percent of the fall in turnout since 1979 can probably be attributed to generational replacement in the Netherlands—see note 14). This is demonstrated graphically in figure 1.1, which plots corrected and uncorrected turnout at EP elections since 1979. Nevertheless, turnout at EP elections (even if fairly stable) is very low in most countries, almost certainly reflecting a general perception that these elections are of little importance. Citizens would not be wrong in such a perception. The political complexion of the European Parliament has historically had no effect on the political complexion of the Commission and has not even the possibility of affecting the complexion of the European Council. Yet it is this latter body that is increasingly perceived as the source of most of the important decisions regarding Europe. So, low turnout at European Parliament elections comes as no surprise. The surprise is that, once corrected for compositional differences and matters of timing, the decline of turnout in elections to this body has apparently ended even though awareness of its powerlessness (being largely a matter of familiarity with the facts) could have been expected to have become more widespread than ever. In respect to such matters as being willing to vote for different parties in EU elections than they would have voted for in national elections (Franklin 2005), citizens of the EU do appear to be adapting to the realities of European Parliament elections. Why not with regard to the pointlessness of turning out to vote? This is the real puzzle we are left with after explaining away the apparent decline of turnout in EP elections since 1979.

NOTES

This is a revised version of an article published in *European Union Politics* (Franklin 2001). I am grateful to be able to reuse my work published in that venue. I am also grateful to three anonymous reviewers for suggestions that greatly improved that manuscript. That article in turn was based on a paper presented at the Annual Meeting of the American Political Science Association, Washington, D.C., September 2000. I am grateful to panel participants, to Vanessa Baird, and to Michael Marsh for helpful comments.

1. See Schmitt and Mannheimer (1991) and van der Eijk and Franklin (1996). Blondel, Sinnott, and Svensson (1997, 1998) did find some impact of attitudes to Europe, but it is not clear that all confounding influences were controlled in their analysis. Attitudes to European Parliamentary institutions are part of a syndrome of attitudes toward democratic institutions in general. Those who think little of such institutions are less likely to vote in any elections, not just elections to the European Parliament (van der Eijk and Oppenhuis 1990; van der Eijk and Schmitt 1991). If the only indicator of this syndrome included in an analysis is one that measures attitudes to European institutions, then it is attitudes to Europe that appear to play a role.

2. Strictly speaking, weighting turnout by population gives the best view of turnout level and turnout change over the EU as a whole because it is expressed in terms of the average voter. However, most analyses of turnout decline treat each country equally in the calculation of average turnout, so that the figures normally seen correspond to the unweighted row of table 1.1. In this chapter, the analysis is conducted at the country level and it would have added a layer of complexity to weight the countries, so our findings are also expressed in terms of unweighted turnout. The measures are in any case not that different. Weighted turnout is lower than unweighted turnout, but it only declines by 0.9 percent more (15.2% instead of 14.3%).

3. A first-time boost is not expected in countries where a compulsion to vote keeps turnout high even in elections that generate little interest. The Danish and British exceptions will be addressed below.

4. Not only does time until the next election serve as a strong predictor of turnout, but it also relates to the choices made at an EP election. On the basis of time until the next national election we have been able to characterize the choices made by voters as being

made 'with the heart', 'with the head', or 'with the boot'—the latter being our label for protest voting. In important elections, people vote 'with the head'. Models were tried that replaced electoral salience with time since the previous election and the presence of concurrent national elections (two possible components of an alternative measure of electoral salience) but neither separately nor together did these variables perform as well as the measure we employ here.

5. In an earlier version of this chapter three additional variables (Sunday voting, proportionality of the electoral system, and links to social groups) were in fact included as controls, but were not found to be significant in explaining turnout change (see Franklin 2000).

6. The transformation is achieved by taking LOG ((turnout / MAX(turnout) / (1 − turnout / MAX(turnout)))).

7. The rate of decline is close to what we would find if only new voters were responding to the fact that compulsory voting is no longer in effect, and this is probably what is happening (see Franklin 2004 for an extended analysis of the generational basis of turnout change). The dummy variable for compulsory voting is thus adjusted in the case of Italy so that in 1994 it takes on the value 0.875 and in 1999 the value 0.75. Models (not shown) were run that kept the value of compulsory voting unchanged but included an additional variable taking on values of 1 and 2 respectively for the 1994 and 1999 Italian cases, and 0 otherwise. These models gave very similar results to those presented in table 1.2 but make the computation of estimated effects later in the chapter more complicated.

8. This coding is a departure from the way in which the variable was coded in past work, where the actual date of the next election was employed. The reasoning in past work was that this date provided us with an indicator of the salience of the election. However, it has been pointed out (private communication with Wouter van der Brug) that, at the time of a European election, the time of the next national election is generally unknown. All that people certainly know is when the next national election is expected to occur. A measure of electoral salience based on this expectation performs significantly better than a measure based on the actual dates of national elections.

9. A model was also evaluated that allowed for panel-specific autoregressive processes, but this explained even less variance and in any case is hard to justify when there is no theoretical reason for expecting the over-time dependencies to be different in each panel (see Beck and Katz 1996, for a discussion of the difference between the two procedures). The fact that we get a better fit to the data when we do not assume any time-serial dependencies accords with the findings of the random effects model (model B) in which the Breusch and Pagan Lagrangian multiplier test found the effects to be random. Note that the STATA Prais-Winsten regression procedure with panel-corrected standard errors calculates much inflated values of R^2 when corrections are made for time-serial dependencies. Variance explained in these analyses was thus computed by correlating the predicted values of the dependent variable with the dependent variable itself, squaring the result and then adjusting for the number of independent variables.

10. Taking account of the fact that Italy had by 1999 taken two steps toward becoming a non-compulsory voting country—see note 7.

11. The total decline in (unweighted) turnout between 1979 and 1999 was 14.3 percent, 0.8 more than what we get from adding the three components calculated above. See note 2 for a discussion of why we use unweighted turnout in this chapter.

12. This could be because in Denmark, alone among countries participating in elections to the European Parliament, EP elections do have an importance in their own right. Two parties vie for votes in these elections that have platforms specifically geared to European Union affairs. See Worre (1996) and Franklin, van der Eijk, and Marsh (1996) for a discussion of this point.

13. With the change in electoral system that took effect in 1999 for EP elections, new analyses (not shown) indicate that the proportionality of the electoral system is no longer a significant predictor of turnout in EP elections.

14. That study found turnout in the Netherlands to have been declining mainly because of the progressive replacement of electoral cohorts socialized into habits of high turnout before the abolition of compulsory voting in that country in 1970. It seems evident that the same process will have occurred for EP election turnout in that country. Were we to take the Dutch decline as having been partly 'explained' by generational replacement, this would reduce the fall in Dutch turnout between 1979 and 1999 by some 13 percent (half of the 25.1 effect of compulsory voting, since half of the Dutch electorate would have been replaced over the twenty-five–year period since 1979), accounting for much of the otherwise unexplained decline in EU-wide EP turnout that occurred after 1979.

15. Though the declining residual effects of compulsory voting in the Netherlands and Italy might be thought to cause a problem (see notes 7 and 14), this should not be the case as long as commentators are only comparing adjacent elections.

CHAPTER TWO

European elections as counterfactual national elections

MARCEL VAN EGMOND

European Parliament (EP) elections are not national parliamentary (NP) elections, yet it is tempting to speculate about the consequences of EP election outcomes as if they were national parliamentary elections. Indeed, politicians and the media often discuss the outcomes of the European elections in terms that refer to the national, not the European political arena. In doing so, it is commonplace to present the election outcome in terms of the composition of the national parliament had this election been a national one. Such a counterfactual representation, in which European parliamentary elections are presented as national parliamentary elections, will form the central perspective of this chapter.

There are several reasons why a counterfactual representation of EP election outcomes may be of interest to us. If voters act similarly in European and national parliamentary elections, the outcomes of European parliamentary elections may have considerable consequences for the *national* political arena. Parties that fared well in the EP elections—when compared to the preceding NP elections—may see an increase in their national political clout. A coalition partner with a particularly successful EP result may want to cash in on its European success at the national level by demanding a greater say in government—even though their *national* vote share has not changed. The consequences may vary from a change in the direction of a government's policies to a complete collapse of the coalition and fall of the government,[1] all on the basis of European elections that were treated as if they were national elections. However, the counterfactual representation may also show us the flipside of the coin: what if voters do *not* act the same in European and national parliamentary elections? What if they would not decide to back the same party in EP and NP elections, but instead support one party in European and another one in national parliamentary elections? As will be shown below, some voters do actually vote for different parties in the different elections, even in those countries where these two elections are held on the same day. This outcome is not surprising at all. Since national and European elections are different elections for different representative bodies in different political arenas, there is no compelling need for voters to support the same party in both instances. In countries where national and European parliamentary elections are held concurrently, the actual election outcome offers us an opportunity to see to what extent party choice in European and national elections actually differs. In countries where the two elections are not held concurrently, we need to use the counterfactual approach which involves assessing how people would have voted had not European elections but national ones been on the calendar. This chapter explores the differences in election results between the 1999 EP election outcome and a NP election that would have been held on the same day (or that actually was concurrent, as happened in a few countries).

There are several leads available to us if we want to answer the puzzles set out above. Existing research into EP elections has already taught us a few things, including the notion that these elections may be viewed as second-order national elections (Reif and Schmitt 1980), dominated mainly by *national*, not European political issues. Other scholars (van der Eijk and Franklin 1996) have reported on previous European parliamentary elections and explored the possibilities to treat these as counterfactual national parliamentary elections. Both these strands of research will be further discussed below. In some countries, however, we need not make counterfactual comparisons, since EP and NP elections were held concurrently in these countries. In Luxembourg, EP and NP elections have been held concurrently ever since the first European Parliament elections of 1979. In other countries, the concurrence of the two elections is due to happenstance—both electoral cycles ended at the same moment, as was the case in Belgium where the two elections were held concurrently as well. These coinciding elections enable us to compare turnout and voting patterns for both elections directly.[2] The distribution of votes for both elections in Luxembourg and Belgium is presented in table 2.1.[3]

Are European parliamentary elections a good indicator of the outcome of national parliamentary elections? Table 2.1 shows that in Luxembourg and Belgium,

Table 2.1 European (EP) and national (NP) parliamentary election results in Luxembourg and Belgium—distribution of valid votes

Country	Party	EP vote (%)	NP vote (%)	Difference (EP – NP)
Luxembourg	CSV/PCS	31.9	30.2	1.7
	DP/PD	20.8	22.0	–1.2
	LSAP/POSL	23.1	24.2	–1.1
	ADR	8.6	10.5	–1.9
	Déi Greng	10.7	7.5	3.2
	Other	4.8	2.8	2.0
Belgium: Flemish parties	SP	7.7	9.6	–1.9
	VLD	11.9	14.3	–2.4
	Agalev	6.6	7.0	–0.4
	CVP	12.2	14.1	–1.9
	Vlaams Blok	9.0	9.9	–0.9
	VU-ID21	6.6	5.6	–1.0
Belgium: Walloon parties	PS	11.6	10.2	1.4
	PRL-FDF-MCC	12.1	10.1	2.0
	Ecolo	10.2	7.4	2.8
	PSC	2.6	5.9	–3.3
	FN	0.7	1.5	–0.8
	Other	9.0	4.4	4.6

the differences in outcomes between the two elections are small. Nevertheless, in both countries the two elections do not result in identical outcomes, and in some cases the differences are substantial. Some parties—Déi Greng in Luxembourg, the Parti Socialiste and Ecolo in Belgium—did markedly better in the European elections than in the national elections. The reverse is true for ADR in Luxembourg and all of the Flemish parties, who fared better in the national elections than they did in the European elections. Clearly, the outcome of European and national elections are not identical, even if the two elections are held on the same day. In addition, minor aggregate level shifts may conceal substantial variation at the individual level in the form of vote switching or split-ticket voting (see also table 2.4 below). On the other hand, the aggregate level differences are rather small, at least in these two countries, which suggests that one can very well regard the outcome of the EP elections as a proxy for NP elections at the same moment in time—they indeed seem to be second-order *national* elections.

What then if we want to make inferences about the national political situation based on European elections in countries where no concurrent national parliamentary elections were held? In those cases we need to revert to a counterfactual comparison. The European Election Studies of 1999 makes such a comparison possible by asking respondents what party they would have voted for if national parliamentary elections would be held the next day. On the basis of these answers, we can get an insight into what the distribution of votes would be at the national level. Since the respondents were also asked what their voting behavior was in the EP elections, we can compare the differences and similarities in voting behavior and aggregate outcomes for the two arenas. To what degree do European Parliament elections differ from national elections in the different countries? Is there any systematic pattern in the differences that occur that is comparable across countries, or are these differences purely national affairs?

COMPARING EUROPEAN AND NATIONAL PARLIAMENTARY ELECTIONS

The respondents in all countries of the European Union were asked how they would have voted were national parliamentary elections being held the next day.[4] Respondents were asked to indicate the party they would have voted for, or that they would not participate in the elections. Table 2.2 presents, as an

Table 2.2 Germany, distribution of votes in European parliamentary and (hypothetical) national parliamentary elections, 1999

	EP vote (%)	*Counterfactual NP Vote (%)*	*Difference (EP – NP)*	*Actual 1998 NP Vote (%)*
CDU/CSU	48.7	52.8	−4.1	35.1
SPD	30.6	33.2	−2.6	40.9
Bundis90/Grünen	6.4	5.9	0.5	6.7
FDP	3.0	2.0	1.0	6.2
PDS	5.8	1.0	4.8	5.1
Other	6.4	5.1	1.3	6.0
Pedersen index			6.7	

example, the results for Germany, first for the European Parliament elections, followed by the (hypothetical) national parliamentary elections, and the difference between the two.[5] For illustrative purposes, the actual election results for the preceding 1998 national parliamentary elections have been included.

Table 2.2 shows that parties fare differently in the European Parliament and in (hypothetical) national elections in Germany. This pattern is repeated in the other EU countries, the results of which are presented in appendix D of this volume. As was the case in Luxembourg and Belgium, the German electorate distinguishes between European and national parliamentary elections and adjusts its voting behavior accordingly, even if these are hypothetical elections. The differences must not be exaggerated: on the whole, no electoral landslides occur. A difference of four percentage points between elections, however, as the Christian democratic CDU/CSU would experience, is a substantial difference. For the social democratic SPD, the difference amounts to well over two percentage points. Both parties do worse in the European elections than they would have in national parliamentary elections.

A crucial advantage of the comparison of EP and *counterfactual* NP elections is illustrated if we compare the 1999 EP result with the actual parliamentary elections of 1998 in Germany. A straightforward comparison of the two outcomes suggests that the German electorate had a considerable change of heart in the period of about one year, with the CDU/CSU the clear winner and the SPD in the doldrums. But that would be comparing apples and pears, as one can imagine the SPD response would be: the German electorate may simply prefer the CDU/CSU for the European Parliament, while still supporting the SPD for the national Bundestag. In other words, different political arenas may create different political winners. The counterfactual results disprove this reasoning, however. As the counterfactual 1999 NP vote shows, the CDU/CSU is winning in the EP elections, and it would do so in national elections as well. In 1999 the electoral tide in Germany was indeed shifting away from the SPD. Regardless of the fact that the SPD would improve their vote share in NP elections, the gap between SPD and CDU/CSU would still increase from the actual 18.1 percent in the EP elections to 19.6 percent, had NP elections been held. And more importantly, the CDU/CSU would have gained an absolute majority—a feat not achieved since the mid-1950s.

Using the Pedersen index as a measure of change between the European and the national parliamentary elections, the change for Germany is 6.7 percent.[6] This underlines what was stated before, namely that no political landslides occur between concurrent elections for different parliaments, fought by the same set of parties. Germany is slightly below average in this respect, compared to the rest of the European Union member states, as table 2.3 testifies.

Table 2.3 Pedersen index: Difference between EP and NP party vote share

Country	Difference EP – NP	Country	Difference EP – NP
Austria	9.8	Greece	8.0
Belgium: Flanders	8.9	Ireland	13.3
Belgium: Wallonia	7.1	Italy	9.8
Britain	20.5	Luxembourg	4.6
Denmark	31.6	Netherlands	10.8
Finland	7.3	Portugal	8.8
France	22.7	Spain	4.2
Germany	6.7	Sweden	13.3
EU average			11.7

Table 2.3 shows that the Pedersen index for change between the European and national parliamentary vote shares varies between a low 4.2 percent in Spain to a high of 31.6 percent in Denmark. The average Pedersen index for the whole of the EU is 11.7 percent.[7] Denmark's high score on this measure is explained by the fact that two of its political parties—the Junibevaegelsen and the Folkebevaegelsen—do not compete in national elections, but only in European Parliament elections, and do so very successfully. Supporters of these two parties will have to switch to a different party in national elections, leading to a high Pedersen index.

SOURCES OF VOTE SHARE VARIATION

Two causes can be distinguished for the differences between EP and (counterfactual or concurrent) NP election results presented in the previous section. Voters may either vote for different parties in the two elections, or they may participate unevenly in them.

Quasi-switching

One obvious explanation for differences in party distributions between elections is that voters support different parties in each election. Over time, this change is of course—to a certain degree—common to any party landscape: parties evolve in terms of performance, policies, leaders, and so on, and individual voters may change in their political experiences, outlook, and opinions. Together, they almost unavoidably result in different choices of individuals in different elections, a major source of differences in election results over time. But our focus here is on comparison of simultaneous choices (one of which is of a counterfactual nature). Apparently, for whatever reasons, some voters prefer one party for the European Parliament and a different one for the national parliament. This is not an uncommon feature in electoral behavior; it is comparable to what is called split-ticket voting in American elections, where voters often support a presidential candidate from one party and a congressional candidate from the other party. In this chapter, this concept of split-ticket voting will be referred to as switching, or rather as *quasi-switching*, since we are referring to hypothetical national elections for all but two countries.[8] Part of the variation in party vote share may be caused by quasi-switching.

Table 2.3 suggests that the impact of quasi-switching is likely to be limited in most countries if we look at electoral outcomes at the aggregate level. Shifting the focus to the level of the individual voter shows that this would actually be a rash conclusion, as table 2.4 demonstrates.

Table 2.4 presents the percentage of EP voters that qualify as quasi-switchers. As the table shows, in most countries this is a substantial number of voters, with the EU average varying between 17.6 and 20.5 percent for different European election years. This means that on average no less than one out of every five voters

Table 2.4 Quasi-switchers as percentage of all EP voters, per country 1989–1999

Country	1989	1994	1999	Country	1989	1994	1999
Austria	—	—	13.4	Greece	8.1	12.4	9.6
Belgium: Flanders	15.6	16.5	10.9	Ireland	28.7	23.8	32.3
Belgium: Wallonia	10.3	20.0	23.3	Italy	19.7	20.7	32.0
Britain	13.0	16.0	22.3	Luxembourg	15.0	14.3	15.5
Denmark	35.4	42.9	39.8	Netherlands	12.4	19.6	13.9
Finland	—	—	17.7	Portugal	9.7	12.7	7.5
France	27.2	40.8	25.4	Spain	22.2	12.5	15.5
Germany	11.8	14.2	16.9	Sweden	—	—	24.2
EU average							
(12 countries)					17.6	20.5	20.4
(15 countries)					—	—	20.0

Note: Data for 1989 and 1994 from van der Eijk, Franklin, and Mackie 1996, table 17.3.
No 1989 and 1994 data available for Austria, Finland, and Sweden.

votes for a different party in the EP elections than they would in a national parliamentary election at the same moment.

Table 2.4 also shows that the percentage of quasi-switchers is not constant; it varies between countries, and within countries over time. Some countries such as Denmark and Ireland show particularly high numbers of quasi-switchers, while others such as Greece and Portugal are consistently low in this respect. France and Spain show considerable variation in the percentage of quasi-switchers over time. This variation within and between countries may have several causes, which makes this variable by itself worthy of further exploration. The degree of quasi-switching may be a characteristic of the political culture of a country: a high degree of party loyalty in a system will depress the number of quasi-switchers, while the opposite creates the potential for high numbers of quasi-switchers. But the variation may also be influenced by characteristics of the party system. In Denmark, two of the most successful parties in the EP elections do not compete in the national parliamentary elections, forcing its following to choose a different party in the NP elections. This will, by definition, create high numbers of quasi-switchers, as mentioned above.

Turnout effects

Currently, one significant feature of European parliamentary elections is their rather poor turnout in most EU countries (see also chapter 1). In the absence of compulsory voting, turnout levels for the 1999 elections were half, or even less than half of the level of turnout common for national parliamentary elections in many EU countries. Table 2.5 presents an overview of the EP participation rate compared to the previous national parliamentary elections in the respective countries.[9] In countries where compulsory voting laws are in effect (Belgium, Greece, Italy, and Luxembourg), turnout is very similar in European and national parliament elections. In countries without compulsory voting, EP turnout is on average 32.3 percent lower.

By itself, turnout variations need not influence the distribution of votes. If supporters of all parties participate in both elections in equal proportions, no variations in vote shares will occur. The point is, of course, that we cannot beforehand rule out that turnout may be selective, and indeed it is often suggested by politicians and commentators alike that supporters of different parties do not participate in equal proportions in both elections. Selective turnout effects may cause variation in the electoral success of parties between the two types of elections and are therefore a second possible source for variation in party vote shares.

Table 2.5 Turnout rates in European and most recent preceding national elections

Country	Turnout EP	Turnout preceding NP	Country	Turnout EP	Turnout preceding NP
Austria	49.4	86.0	Ireland	50.2	66.1
Belgium*∞	91.0	90.6	Italy∞	70.8	82.9
Britain	24.0	71.5	Luxembourg*∞	87.3	86.5
Denmark	50.5	86.0	Netherlands	30.0	73.2
Finland	31.4	65.3	Portugal	40.0	66.3
France	46.8	68.0	Spain	63.0	78.1
Germany	45.2	82.2	Sweden	38.8	81.4
Greece∞	75.3	76.4			
EU average				52.9	77.4
EU Average (non-compulsory voting countries only)				42.7	74.9

* National parliamentary elections concurrent with European parliamentary elections.
∞ Compulsory voting.

Of course, it is impossible to determine from aggregate numbers to what degree differences in parties' vote share in the EP and NP can be attributed to quasi-switching or to turnout effects. The two effects may even work in different directions: a positive quasi-switching effect may be offset, partially or completely, by a negative turnout effect, and vice versa. To determine what effect worked in what direction for a particular party in a given EU country we need more than mere election outcomes.

Fortunately, the European Election Survey data is able to give us an insight into the importance of quasi-switching and turnout effects for the difference between national and European election outcomes. This is because we not only know what party each respondent (would have) voted for in the two elections, but also whether they would (or did) participate in the elections.[10] By comparing the voting behavior of participants of the EP election with those who did not turn out to vote, we can determine which parties lost out because of selective turnout effects and which parts of the electorate switched from one party in the EP elections to another party in the national elections.

Establishing quasi-switching effects and turnout effects

Table 2.6, below, presents a partial repeat of table 2.2, above, showing how the German parties fared in the European Parliament elections and how they

Table 2.6 Germany, quasi-switching and turnout effects, EP 1999 (Positive effects indicate gain in European election, compared to counterfactual national election)

	EP Vote (%)	NP Vote (%)	Difference (EP – NP)	Quasi-switching	Turnout Effect
CDU/CSU	48.7	52.8	–4.1	–5.9	1.8
SPD*	30.6	33.2	–2.6	0.9	–3.5
Bundis90/Grünen*	6.4	5.9	0.5	0.0	0.5
FDP	3.0	2.0	1.0	0.8	0.2
PDS	5.8	1.0	4.8	4.7	0.1
Other	5.4	5.1	0.3	–0.6	0.9
Pedersen index			6.7	6.5	3.5

* Government parties at the time of the EP 1999 elections.

would have done were a national parliamentary election held at the same time. In addition table 2.6 presents the extent to which these differences were brought about by quasi-switching and by selective turnout. To determine which part of the vote share variation for a party can be attributed to quasi-switching or to a turnout effect, we need to know three things: choice of party in the European elections, the choice of party in the (hypothetical) national elections for the whole of the sample, and again the choice of party in the (hypothetical) national elections, but now only for participants in the European elections.[11] The turnout effect is determined as the difference in NP vote share for participants in EP elections, compared to the vote share of that party for all respondents in the sample. In other words, the popularity of the party among those who turned out to vote in EP elections is compared to the popularity of the party among the whole of the electorate. To determine quasi-switching, we compare the vote share of a party in the EP elections to the vote share of that party in the (hypothetical) national elections for participants in the EP elections only. Both of these effects can be positive or negative, and the sum of the two equals the difference in party success in EP and national elections.

Table 2.6 shows that the CDU/CSU combination polled over four percentage points lower in the EP elections than it would have if a national parliamentary election would have been fought. However, this change cannot be attributed solely to voters making different choices in different types of elections, nor can it be attributed solely to the effect of selective turnout. As the negative quasi-switch effect in table 2.6 shows, 5.9 percent of the electorate would have voted for the CDU/CSU if this were a national election, but instead opted for another party in the EP elections. Compensating this, however, is the fact that CDU/CSU voters prove to have a higher tendency to participate in the EP elections than the German electorate in general. As a consequence, there is a positive turnout effect of 1.8 percent pushing up the CDU/CSU vote share in the European elections. The net effect is therefore a vote share that is 4.1 percent lower than it would have been in a national parliamentary election.

In overview, table 2.6 shows us several findings regarding quasi-switching and turnout effects. The first is that most of the differences are small in magnitude. No great shifts occur—neither in total nor in terms of the two components separately. In addition, there is little regularity to be observed in the direction of turnout and quasi-switching effects: both may occur in the same direction or in conflicting directions, and no clear patterns in positive of negative effects can be observed.[12] However, in general, turnout effects tend to be substantially smaller than quasi-switching effects, a pattern that is repeated in all countries of the European Union but one—the Netherlands—as table 2.7 shows.

Table 2.7 shows that there is considerable similarity in size for the quasi-switching effect in the different countries of the European Union, as is the case for

Table 2.7 Pedersen index: Total, quasi-switching and turnout effects, EU countries

	Total Difference	Quasi-switching	Turnout
Austria	9.8	7.6	5.2
Belgium: Flanders	8.9	9.2	0.5
Belgium: Wallonia	7.1	7.7	7.1
Britain	20.5	12.7	11.0
Denmark	31.6	31.4	2.8
Finland	7.3	13.0	7.6
France	22.7	22.6	1.9
Germany	6.7	6.5	3.5
Greece	8.0	8.1	1.0
Ireland	13.3	14.5	4.1
Italy	9.8	11.0	1.7
Luxembourg	4.6	4.6	1.1
Netherlands	10.8	2.7	10.5
Portugal	8.8	6.2	2.6
Spain	4.2	4.0	1.5
Sweden	13.3	12.0	7.7
Average	11.7	10.8	4.3

the turnout effects in the different countries.[13] For quasi-switching, the largest value is found in Denmark. This is not surprising, considering the fact that there are a number of successful anti-EU parties active in Denmark that participate only in EU elections. As mentioned, their success is by definition a manifestation of quasi-switching: in national elections their supporters will have to choose another party. Turnout effects prove smaller than quasi-switching effects in all countries except the Netherlands, where the average turnout effect is nearly four times larger than the quasi-switching effect. No ready explanation that reaches beyond the level of *ad hoc* explanations is available here.[14] Findings for other countries are in line with findings for previous EP elections (cf. van der Eijk, Franklin, and Mackie 1996).

EXPLAINING QUASI-SWITCHING AND TURNOUT EFFECTS

The previous section showed that it is possible to distinguish between two sources of differences between outcomes of European and national parliamentary elections, namely quasi-switching and turnout effects. As table 2.6 and the tables in appendix D show, the magnitude of these two effects varies considerably between parties. In this section, these variations in turnout and quasi-switching effects will be investigated at the party level by means of OLS regression analysis. Our units of analysis will be the political parties participating in the European Parliament elections of 1999. In all, 111 parties are available for analysis. Can the characteristics of these parties explain why some of them encounter a positive, while others a negative turnout or quasi-switching effect? And what determines the size of these effects?

Quasi-switching

It has been argued frequently that European Parliament elections are elections that are *not* about European issues, but instead about national issues. In this respect, the term *second-order* national elections has been coined by Reif and Schmitt (1980). Such elections are dominated by the domestic political system. The elections are thus not fought on the issues that concern the body to be elected—i.e., the European Parliament—but rather on issues that are of importance to the domestic political arena such as, for instance, a vote in favor or against the national government.

If indeed EP elections would be dominated by national policy issues, a party's policy stance on European issues would be of no consequence for its electoral success in European elections. We will therefore analyze whether a party's perceived position regarding European integration is of influence on the degree of quasi-switching for that party. The party stance on EU integration is measured as the interpolated median of a party's stance as perceived by the respondents of the European Election Study 1999. Low values indicate an adverse, while high values indicate a positive stance toward EU integration. Absence of a statistically significant effect for this explanatory factor would indicate that parties' enthusiasm or skepticism regarding European integration is no reason for voters to switch parties between EP and NP elections. A significant effect would put some limitations on the second-order theory. The direction of any significant effect indicates what kind of parties benefit from a quasi-switch effect: negative when Euro-skeptic parties benefit from quasi-switching, positive when pro-integration parties benefit. Previous research (Oppenhuis, van der Eijk, and Franklin 1996) could not establish a statistically significant effect of this variable.

A tendency that could be established in previous research (Oppenhuis, van der Eijk, and Franklin 1996) was the propensity of voters to vote for smaller or politically more extreme parties in European elections. The reasoning for this can again be connected to the second-order theory. If elections appear to be less consequential to voters, they may be more willing to vote for more radical or less influential parties. Such parties may actually better reflect a voters' political preference in the national political arena, but at the same time carry too little political clout or appear too much of a risk to be supported in a first-order election. Second-order elections would then prove an excellent opportunity for these voters to support the party they actually prefer—without any of the possibly nasty consequences. This thesis will be tested through the use of three variables. Two of these variables measure the extremity of a party's stance on the aforementioned EU integration issue and on the left-right dimension by calculating the distance of a party's perceived median position and the midpoint (5.5) of each of the two scales. Positive effects for these variables would suggest that extreme parties are more successful in the EP elections than in a national parliamentary election at the same time. The third variable is the size of a party, measured as its vote share in the preceding national election. Smaller parties are expected to do better in EP elections than in NP elections (i.e., negative relation between size of party and quasi-switching) since they will be less burdened by their limited size in EP elections than in NP elections. The last party characteristic included in the model is a party's perceived left-right position. Although of potential interest, no prior assumptions toward both the existence as well as the direction of any effect of this variable will be specified here.

Any of the effects of party characteristics mentioned in the previous paragraph may be influenced by characteristics of the election or of the political context. Several such contextual characteristics have been suggested in the literature: the state of the economy, the position of the EP election in the domestic electoral cycle, and so on. National parliamentary elections following shortly on the European Parliament elections may turn the latter into a crucial last rehearsal, of particular importance for government contenders. To test for such potential interactions, a variable indicating the position of the EP election in the domestic electoral cycle is included in the model. In the analyses, the electoral cycle is standardized to correct for differences in term length between countries, and runs from 0 to 1, with 0 indicating that the EP elections were held 'the day after' national parliamentary elections and '1' indicating that both elections are held concurrently.[15]

Table 2.8 presents the outcome of a regression analysis on quasi-switching in which the explanatory potential of the factors described above was tested. Only few of the factors yielded statistically significant coefficients, and only these were included in the model presented in table 2.8. Variables not included in the model did not prove influential in explaining quasi-switching.[16]

Table 2.8 presents a model that attempts to explain quasi-switching effects in European Parliament elections. The model is based on a regular OLS regression analysis, with political parties as the units of analysis. Robust standard errors (Huber/White/sandwich estimation, Huber 1967; White 1980) are used because the dependent variable is related for subgroups of the sample: one party's gain in an election means other parties will have to lose.

Table 2.8 Determinants of quasi-switching (OLS regression, robust standard errors, n = 111)

	B	Beta	Sig
Party stance on EU integration (adverse-favorable)	−.836	−.327	.007
Party left-right position	−.323	−.167	.065
Extremity of party left-right position	−.968	−.300	.000
Size of party (votes share in last NP election)	−.240	−.739	.001
Electoral Cycle (0–1)	−3.074	−.231	.049
Electoral Cycle (0–1) * size of party	.256	.550	.027
Constant	10.200		.000
R^2		.34	

The first variable of the model in table 2.8 indicates that, although at times it is argued otherwise, EP elections are, at least to a certain degree, influenced by European issues. The significant and negative estimate of a party's stance on EU integration indicates that this issue is of importance to voters: parties that take a negative stance toward EU integration benefit systematically (albeit slightly) from quasi-switching in the 1999 EP elections. EP elections are thus, at least to some extent, also about European issues, or more precisely about anti-European issues.

The left-right position of parties is included in the model in two ways. The negative estimate for left-right position by itself indicates that left-wing parties fared better in the EP elections of 1999 than right-wing parties did. This estimate is, however, not statistically significant, in contrast to findings of, for instance, Pacek and Radcliff (2003). When controlling for left-right position, the extremity of a party's left-right position *is* of significant influence. Perhaps surprisingly in view of previous findings (cf. Oppenhuis, van der Eijk, and Franklin 1996), and in view of what second-order election theory suggests, extreme parties do *not* systematically benefit from quasi-switching, but do rather worse in these terms, as is indicated by the negative estimate (at least as far as 1999 is concerned).

The most influential factor of the model is size of party, measured here as vote share (0–100%) in the previous national parliamentary election. In the model it is the most influential factor, and, in accordance with expectations, smaller parties perform better than larger parties.

Lastly, two factors concerning the electoral context are examined. Although the EP elections are all held at virtually the same moment—10 or 13 June 1999—this moment can take a different position in the domestic electoral cycle of each country. In some countries, such as Finland, the EP elections followed shortly upon the national parliamentary elections, while in other countries such as Ireland they fell somewhere in the middle of the cycle. In Austria and Portugal the 1999 EP elections fell shortly before the national elections, while, as we have seen, in Belgium and Luxembourg the EP elections actually coincided with national elections. As Oppenhuis, van der Eijk, and Franklin (1996) argued, EP elections held shortly before a national election may take on a role of increased importance, giving voters a last option to air their opinions without too many consequences for government power, while parties may get a last indication about their electoral position. Large parties may thus fare better late in the cycle, compared to how they would have done in EP elections following shortly after a national election.

The influence of the electoral cycle by itself does not allow for substantive interpretation.[17] It is included in the model because its interaction with size of the party is significant. This interaction term indicates whether the effect of party size on quasi-switching varies over the course of the domestic electoral cycle. The positive sign of this effect (see table 2.8) indicates that larger parties are less hurt by quasi-switching in EP elections toward the end of the cycle—in other words, when a European election is held shortly before national elections. This interaction term therefore offsets the negative effect of party size, although it fully compensates for this negative effect only at the very end of the cycle: at 94 percent of the cycle, to be exact.[18] In a standard four-year term, this would mean that the size of a party will have a positive impact only if the EP election is held within three months before the national elections. If the EP elections are held earlier in the cycle, the size of the party has a negative impact.

Turnout effects

Turnout effects are actually selective turnout effects: some parties benefit, while others are hurt by the typically lower turnout rates in European Parliament elections (see also the tables in appendix D of this volume). It may be that certain parties are particularly susceptible to a turnout effect because their electorate proves particularly unwilling to participate in EP elections, or because they manage poorly in mobilizing their potential voters for lack of effort, or sundry other reasons. Conversely, some parties may benefit because their electorate shows a particularly high propensity to participate. Parties that are able to mobilize their support can gain considerably in elections where turnout is relatively low.

Explanations of turnout effects should therefore be cast in terms of characteristics of parties that would be related to the stability and dedication of their support base. A series of similar regression analyses as reported above was conducted with parties' turnout effect as dependent variable. As independent and contextual variables we used the same factors as in the analyses of quasi-switching. None of these showed any statistically significant relationships, however.[19] The implication is that although parties are differentially affected by selective turnout, the factors that determine the direction and the magnitude of these effects are largely idiosyncratic in nature, not captured by general party characteristics (size, government status, ideological position, or extremity).

Conclusion

It was the aim of this chapter to explore the differences between parties' electoral success in European and national parliamentary elections. The outcomes of EP elections were compared to concurrent (actual and counterfactual) NP elections. The results showed that EP and NP elections are different. Parties' vote shares differ in European election from what they are or would have been in national elections at the same moment in time. Moreover, as table 2.5 showed, substantial numbers of voters support different parties for different jobs—national or European. The differences in electoral success in the two kinds of elections are the sum of two different components: the effect of differential turnout on the one hand, and the—on average much larger—effect of quasi-switching on the other. When looking at parties, we found that how they are affected by differential turnout is largely inexplicable by general party characteristics. This contrasts sharply with how they are affected by quasi-switching. As the regression analysis of table 2.8 showed, these differences can to a considerable extent be explained by characteristics of the political parties. The analysis showed that their position pro or contra further integration plays a significant role. Parties touting an anti-integration stance proved to benefit from quasi-switching in the 1999 EP elections, something which could not be established in previous EP elections. In line with expectations, smaller parties also largely benefited from this, although progressively less so toward the end of the national electoral cycle, where the relationship is reversed.

Notes

1. To illustrate various national consequences of the 1989 European elections: the outcome of the European elections played a role in the eventual downfall of British Prime Minister Mrs. Thatcher (Franklin and Curtice 1996, 95); in Spain, electoral success in those same EP elections prompted the ruling PSOE to call early national elections (del Castillo 1996, 266); while the reverse was the case in Italy, where the governing parties decided against calling early national elections following their disappointing showing in the European elections (Mannheimer 1996, 200).

2. One could wonder whether the differences between the results of concurrent elections are caused by differences in eligibility. Although such differences do indeed exist, all available evidence suggests that they concern such small numbers of people that the differences documented in table 2.1 and further down in this chapter cannot be attributed to them.

3. In table 2.1, the outcome for national and European elections is presented for Belgium as a whole. The party systems of Wallonia and Flanders, the two regions that make up the Belgian federal state, differ fundamentally, however. In the remainder of this chapter, Flanders and Wallonia will therefore be analyzed as separate political systems.

4. In Belgium and Luxembourg the actual voting behavior was asked.

5. Note that the sample has been weighted so that the distribution of votes for the European Parliament reflects the distribution of the actual election outcome.

6. The Pedersen index is defined as the sum of the absolute differences in vote share for all parties, divided by two.

7. The analyses presented here exclude Northern Ireland. The party system of Northern Ireland differs to such a degree from the British system that inclusion in that system would not be fruitful, while the small sample size for Northern Ireland precludes inclusion in the analyses as a separate system.

8. Confer for the concept of quasi-switching to van der Eijk and Franklin 1996.

9. For Belgium and Luxembourg, this comparison involves the concurrent national election, not the most recent previous one.

10. Of course, this data is not without its flaws. There is some discussion in the literature as to the validity of questions regarding electoral participation (cf. Katosh and Traugott 1981; see also Visscher 1995; Smeets 1995). Typically, respondents would rather not admit that they did not participate in the election, leading to an inflated rate of participation. In our case, the problem is not so great. The rate of participation in the EP elections in most countries of the EU is so low that most respondents appeared to have no qualms admitting they did not participate.

11. On this matter, see van der Eijk and Franklin 1996, chapter 3.

12. Correlation coefficients per country computed at the party level for the relations between quasi-switching and turnout effects prove significant in only three out of sixteen cases: Italy (-0.55), Finland (-0.91) and Portugal ($+0.96$). The magnitude of the correlation in especially these last two countries suggests that further investigation into this matter (especially over time) is warranted. Such lies outside of the scope of this chapter, however.

13. Separate country tables reporting quasi-switching and turnout effects per party are presented in appendix D of this volume.

14. In the 1994 EP elections in the Netherlands, the turnout effect was larger than the quasi-switching effect too, though to a far lesser degree. In the 1989 elections, however, the turnout effect was slightly smaller than the quasi-switching effect.

15. The specification of the model tests for a linear effect of this variable, although a curvilinear relationship, in which more emphasis is put on the period shortly before or after a national election can be conceived of as well. Additional analyses proved that the two operationalizations produced virtually identically fitting models.

16. The estimated model presented in table 2.8 consists of the variables presented in that table only. A number of variables (measures of the potential and unshared electorate of a party) did show a significant bivariate relationship with quasi-switching. However, none of these produced statistically significant effects in the multivariate regression models.

17. The position of the EP election in the electoral cycle is a system characteristic, and thus applies to all parties in a system equally. As quasi-switching can have a positive effect for some parties and a negative effect for other parties within a political system, a uniform

system characteristic such as the electoral cycle cannot explain quasi-switching. The electoral cycle may be of influence on the *absolute* size of the quasi-switching effect, but that requires a different analytical approach from the one presented here.

18. Direct effect of party size (0.240) divided by interaction between electoral cycle × party size (0.256) = 0.9375. Therefore, if electoral cycle is 0.937 or larger, party size will have a positive influence.

19. Cross-national analyses of turnout effects will suffer from heteroskedasticity problems, as the differences in turnout—and hence possible turnout effects—vary substantially between countries. Various approaches can be taken to amend this problem, including the use of quasi-likelihood estimation (Papke and Wooldridge 1996) or the inclusion of the size of the national drop in turnout as a controlling factor (signed positive or negative, in accordance with the turnout effect. Cf. van der Eijk and van Egmond, forthcoming). Both approaches were applied in separate analyses, without leading to a change in outcomes.

CHAPTER THREE

European Parliament elections and losses by governing parties

MICHAEL MARSH

The fifth set of elections to the European Parliament in 2004 saw twenty-five countries sending representatives to the parliament in Brussels and Strasbourg, more than twice the number who participated in the first elections in 1979. On the face of it this presents anyone wishing to predict what may happen at such elections with a great deal more uncertainty than previously, but this would ignore the fact that we have learned a lot about European Parliament elections in the last twenty-five years. We have observed significant regularities in the behavior of European voters and have developed a theory—second-order election theory—which provides a sensible account of such regularities. On this basis we certainly have a set of expectations about such elections. This is not to say that our expectations are very precise, nor that our theory is without blemish. Uncertainty remains to cloud any predictions, and there remain both features of behavior that are unexplained by theory as well as facts which fit uncomfortably with it. This chapter reviews the performance of the theory of second-order elections to date and also considers the alternative merits of two theories which were developed to explain regularities in the behavior of US voters in the congressional elections that occur in presidential midterm which show significant parallels with those of European Parliament elections.

Elections to parliaments within member states are held according to various timetables. Occasionally national and EP elections coincide (they always do in Luxembourg); more typically they do not, and European elections fall somewhere within the national parliamentary election cycle in each member state. While those elected to the European Parliament sit in European Party Groups, they are in reality elected to represent national parties, and hence it is possible to compare the performance of national parties in European Parliament elections with their performance in the preceding national election. It is also possible to compare turnout. When we do so we observe two pretty general patterns: governments lose votes compared to the preceding national election and turnout falls. In the US there are national elections every two years for Congress and every four years for the president. Congressional elections take place coincidentally with presidential elections, and again in the middle of a president's term of office—a 'midterm' election. And congressional midterm elections differ from the preceding congressional election in two respects: the president's party wins fewer votes, and turnout is lower. This pattern has endured throughout the twentieth century, almost without exception.

The theories that will be discussed here have generally sought to link the regularities in each context, to see the turnout and government or presidential loss as connected rather than separate phenomena. In the European context it is a central aspect of Karlheintz Reif's theory of 'second-order national elections' (Reif and Schmitt 1980; Reif 1985b; Reif 1997). In the US context this is the contribution made by the theory of 'surge and decline' advanced by Angus Campbell (1960, 1966). A further common aspect of both theoretical approaches is that the results of the less important election are seen as interpretable only through an understanding of something exogenous. In the European case this is the national parliamentary election cycle; in the US case this is the presidential election cycle.

In the next section we will review two sets of theory. Special attention will be given to two things: first, what is the source of the explanation and second, what is the mechanism of decision making at the level of the individual that provides the expected change. Having done that we can then move on to consider the manner in which these theories can be applied to European Parliament elections, what they explain, and what sort of expectations they generate about the future.

Second-order theory and some alternatives

Second-order theory

The concept of a second-order national election in fact has its roots in observations of electoral patterns in US midterm elections, as well as German regional elections. It was used by Reif and Schmitt (1980) to account for the results of the first direct European Parliament election. Reif and Schmitt point out that elections differ in terms of how important people think they are and assume that national general elections will be considered more important than European Parliament elections. Rather than distinguish elections as such they refer to different arenas of politics, with elections to bodies in the most important arena of primary importance and elections in other arenas of lesser consequence. Given that national politics remain preeminent, general elections in parliamentary democracies are therefore first-order elections. All others are second-order. Voters can be expected to behave differently in the two types of elections because of their differential importance. For a start, they will be less likely to vote in second-order elections because they and the parties know that such elections are less important. When they do turn out voters will be more mindful of the political situation in the first-order arena than that of the second-order arena. First-order issues, for instance, will dominate second-order ones. In particular, voters may take the opportunity to signal their dissatisfaction with government policy despite the fact that the second-order election has no direct implications for government composition. Additionally, in making their choice voters will be more inclined to follow their 'heart' in second-order elections, whose relative un-importance means there are no consequences for the voter. This explains why their behavior may differ from that in first-order elections, in which voters follow their 'head'.

Although Reif and Schmitt do not develop a theory of the voter, some points are implicit in what they say. Essentially, at the core of second-order theory is a relatively strategic voter and implied in this notion is a voter who has a preference structure across two or more parties with more than one non-zero element. In other words, a voter does not simply support one party and reject the rest.

This strategic aspect can be further developed. Reif and Schmitt suggested that governments would perform particularly poorly when second-order elections occurred at midterm. The rationale for this is that midterm is a normal nadir of government popularity, brought about by a combination of political business cycles and the inevitability of unrealized expectations (see below). However, this is disputed by Oppenhuis, van der Eijk, and Franklin (1996) who reject the inevitability of such popularity cycles and instead focus on the importance of the election as a signaling device. This is also a function of the time since the last general election, and the time expected until the next one. When a second-order election follows close on, or is simultaneous with, a general election, it passes almost unnoticed. Hence turnout will be particularly low. Those who do vote will please themselves, voting with the 'heart'. However, when a second-order election takes place on the eve of a general election, its importance as a sign of what will happen at that general election is considerable. In such circumstances turnout will be higher (relative to other second-order elections) and voters are more likely to signal their discontent with a party or government. The 'referendum' element of second-order elections is thus contextually located, not by levels of government dissatisfaction or economic trends but by the timing of the second-order election in the first-order election cycle.

A second development of second-order theory is the suggestion that the differential importance of elections is better represented by a continuum than by a categorization (van der Eijk, Franklin, and Marsh 1996). Not all second-order elections are equally unimportant but not all first-order elections are equally important either. In fact, where general elections have few implications for the choice of government, because a system of consociational democracy operates for instance, then they may differ little from second-order elections in the same system. Perhaps only in countries where general elections are expected to bring about some alternation of government control does it make sense to see local or European Parliament elections as second-order.

We now turn to some alternative theoretical approaches, developed to account for US midterm election results. We begin with the theory of surge and decline, and then deal more fully with the so-called referendum element of such elections, already alluded to above.

Surge and decline

The original theory of 'surge and decline' was presented by Angus Campbell (1960). We will call this Campbell-1. The theory seeks to explain differences in turnout and support for the president's party between midterm and preceding presidential elections in the US, but Campbell himself saw it as having a more general relevance. In his original formulation of surge and decline theory Campbell suggested that although the theory was specifically intended to illuminate well-established patterns in US political behavior it was likely that:

> the basic concepts . . .—political stimulation, political interest, party identification, core voters and peripheral voters, and high- and low-stimulus elections—are equally applicable to an understanding of political behaviour in other democratic systems. (Campbell 1960, 62)

The explanation for midterm loss and low turnout is that in presidential elections people are more likely to depart from their 'normal' pattern of political behavior.

This is because such elections are (relatively, in the US context) high-stimulus elections. The higher stimulus of a presidential election promotes two types of change. First, it draws those to the polls who do not usually vote, those Campbell calls 'peripheral' voters. Lacking a strong party attachment, peripheral voters are likely to be swayed disproportionately by the circumstances of the moment to vote for the winning party. At the next midterm election, these voters stay at home, thus adversely affecting the president's party. The high stimulus also means that regular or 'core' voters are more likely to be swayed by the advantage circumstances give to the winning party to depart from their normal partisan behavior, only to return to their habitual behavior in the lower stimulus midterm. Again, this is to the disadvantage of the president's party. Presidential elections are thus a departure from an equilibrium that is restored at the subsequent congressional election.

After reviewing some individual-level evidence and arguing that it does not support classic surge and decline theory, James Campbell (1997) provides a revised version of surge and decline in which the mechanism of a higher or lower stimulus remains much the same but the impact of that stimulus on different types of voters changes. We will call this Campbell-2. On the basis that the individual-level evidence does not support the differential turnout of independent voters in the two types of election, James Campbell argues instead that the difference in the result is caused by the return to the midterm electorate of partisans of the losing party in the previous election ('disadvantaged partisans') who were cross-pressured by short-term forces and abstained, and the switching back of weaker partisans who defected due to the same cross-pressures. In his revised version of surge and decline theory it is strong partisans who move from abstention to voting, and weak partisans and independents who switch. The key additional concept used in the revised model is that of cross-pressure. Strong partisans may find themselves cross-pressured in a presidential year, wanting to vote for their normal party but preferring the candidate of the opposition. They resolve the conflict by abstaining. Weaker partisans have no problem with the cross-pressures and simply switch parties. Campbell-2 is thus a revision of Campbell-1.

Referendum theory

A quite different explanation for midterm losses is the referendum theory advanced by Tufte (1975). In sharp contrast to surge and decline, which finds the roots of inter-election decline in the upsurge at the previous election, referendum theory locates it in the record of the administration. However, as in surge and decline theory, the roots remain external to the election itself, since they are located in the record of a president rather than of a congress. Midterm elections are essentially a referendum on the government's performance, in which voters express their approval or disapproval through voting for or against those representing the president's party. The mechanism of change lies in the decision by at least some midterm voters to reward or punish the party of the president. The election provides an occasion at which voters can signal their dissatisfaction. This view is expressed most clearly by Tufte and we will refer to his theory as Tufte-1.

Tufte cites two separate measures of performance: the public's general satisfaction with the president's performance and the trends in economic indicators. His analysis uses these to predict the magnitude of swings against the incumbent party, and he shows these can predicted with a high degree of accuracy. There is nothing in the theory of a referendum itself to explain why swings are almost always adverse, but Tufte suggests that this stems from two further trends. The first is that presidential popularity tends to decline through a term of office; the second is that the performance of the economy tends to be better at the time of presidential elections. Of course, to the extent that neither is the case, the president's party should not suffer at midterm.

Unlike surge and decline, Tufte's referendum theory does not directly link turnout and midterm loss but others have attempted to do so within referendum theory. Kernell (1977) asserts a 'negativity' hypothesis. Like Tufte, Kernell sees the midterm election as strongly influenced by perceptions of the president's record but he offers a more fundamental account of why this is bad news for the president's party. According to Kernell, judgments on presidential performance are always biased in a negative direction because—as a social-psychological rule—negative impressions are always more salient than positive ones. Moreover, voters are more likely to act on negative impressions. Hence, there will be more people dissatisfied with the president than there were two years ago; dissatisfied voters will also be more likely to turn out than satisfied ones, and, having turned out, will be more likely to vote against the president's party.[1]

Having outlined various theories we now turn to examine their relative value in accounting for features of European Parliament elections. The following analysis deals largely with the central point at issue between the competing theories, the explanation of government losses. It deals only indirectly with turnout, in as much as differential turnout is essential to such explanations.

Explaining government vote loss in European Parliament elections

Aggregate data analysis

We will start with the aggregate data on government performance in European Parliament elections. What we want to know is how well the different theories can account for the pattern of government losses in European Parliament elections. A number of concepts used require operationalization.

- *Government loss:* the difference between the percentage vote in the European election and the last national election.
- *Normal vote:* the percentage vote at the national election before last.
- *Election cycle:* the timing of the European election within the term defined by the two adjoining national elections. This variable ranges theoretically between -0.5 and $+0.5$, with 0 as the midpoint. Where the date of a succeeding national election is not known it has been estimated according the normal pattern of a country.
- *Economic record:* the change in GDP, unemployment, and inflation in the calendar year prior to that in which the European Parliament election takes place (which is always in June).
- *Alternation:* the existence of a norm that elections may bring about substantial change in the partisan control of the government. We judge here that this exists in all EU countries other than Belgium, Luxembourg, the Netherlands, and Italy (prior to the system upheaval of the early 1990s).

Specific hypotheses, derived from the discussion above, are as follows:

- H1.1. Timing of election within the national cycle is important for defection rates (second order).
- H1.2. Government losses will be a function of the surge at the previous general election: i.e., the difference between that election and the preceding national election (surge and decline).
- H1.3. Government losses will be a function of the economic performance in the previous year (referendum).

We have estimated a model including cycle and cycle squared, allowing for a greater loss around midterm, as well as surge and economic record. We have

Table 3.1 Importance of national election cycle, previous surge, and economic performance of government vote loss in European Parliament elections: OLS estimates

	European Parliament elections in countries with governmental alternation				All non-concurrent European Parliament elections			
	b	se	b	se	b	se	b	se
Cycle	−4.35	2.43	−6.45*	2.76	−3.40	2.03	−3.82	2.49
Cycle Squared	33.33*	11.43	41.96***	9.68	22.00	11.39	29.4**	9.69
Surge	0.18	0.21			−0.08	0.25		
Record (GDP)	−0.16	0.41			−0.53	0.37		
Constant	−6.16	4.58	−6.16	3.31	−2.13	3.54	−4.36	2.93
Adj R²	.26		.26		.26		.21	
F	23***		69***		29***		7.3**	
	(8.11)		(7.11)		(8.13)		(6.13)	
N	39		41		49		52	
Root MSE	5.77		6.04		5.62		6.07	

*** Significant at .001 level; ** Significant at .01 level; * Significant at .05 level.
Dummies included for the European Parliament (1–5) included with the 1979 as the reference category but results not shown. Country clustered standard errors.

done so, first, for all countries, excluding only those with concurrent national and European Parliament elections, and second, for only those countries that normally experience a pattern of governmental alternation, on the basis that it is perhaps only in such countries that the idea of a second-order election damaging governments makes sense. This analysis essentially replicates and extends a previous analysis that covered only those European Parliament elections between 1979 and 1994 (Marsh 1998). This present analysis includes all European Parliament elections through 1999. We also included dummies for the five directly elected European Parliaments to date to control for time differences.[2]

The results (see table 3.1) confirm previous work in demonstrating the importance of the timing of the election, and supporting the quadratic function of the timing of the degree of government losses (Marsh 1998). Estimates in the simplified form of the model for countries with governmental alternation are very similar to those for the 1979–94 period: −6.5 as against −6.7 (for the election

FIGURE 3.1 Expected government losses in countries with norms of alternation, by point in national election cycle

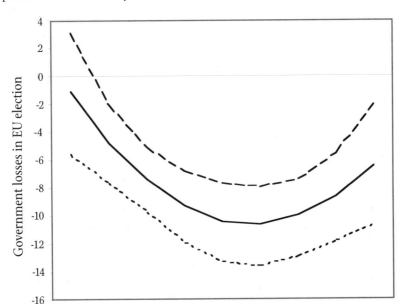

cycle variable) and 40 as against 42 (for the squared cycle variable). Similarly, for all countries estimates are −3.8 as against −7.7 (cycle) and 29 as against 22 (cycle squared). The variables designed to examine surge and decline and referendum theories proved not significant in any specification. Surge has no effect, nor does GDP, nor the alternative economic indicators (not shown). What sort of losses can be expected at what point in the election cycle? Figure 3.1 plots the estimated losses by governments in countries with alternation from the simplified model (column 2) showing the upper and lower bounds of those estimates. While the overall mean loss expected is no more than 7 percent, the higher losses around midterm, around 13 percent, are clear.[3]

At least at the aggregate level these results demonstrate the strength of the second-order theory in predicting government vote loss moderately well and much better in those countries where it would be expected to be more appropriate, i.e., those with a norm of alternation. They also indicate a weakness, in the European context, of basic referendum and of surge and decline theories. Admittedly, the referendum test is a very crude one that could easily be bettered, but it closely parallels Tufte's original analysis. Information on government popularity might be more appropriate, but that is not available for all elections. The surge indicator is also crude. Another operationalization was also tried: averaging across three general elections with the previous general election as the midpoint of the three. This allows for some trend in parties' support over time. However, this also failed to produce significant estimates.

Individual-level analysis

These 'successes' of second-order theory in this context are unsurprising and in line with previous work at this level. Moving to the individual level is more challenging as it brings into question not so much what is happening but who makes it happen. In particular we want to observe the pattern of voter mobility across the two elections (general to EP) and see how well it matches the expectations of the various theories already discussed.

Specific expectations, again derived from the discussion above, are as follows:

- H2.1. Most of the change is away from the government (surge and decline: Campbell-1).
- H2.2. The government will lose more votes to non-voting than opposition parties, and many more voters will switch parties away from them than toward them (surge and decline: Campbell-1).
- H2.3. Independent voters are less likely to turn out at European elections than general elections, relative to partisans (surge and decline: Campbell-1).
- H2.4. Low-interest voters are more likely to switch or abstain from government parties (surge and decline: Campbell-1).
- H2.5. There should be a higher defection of partisans at general elections than European elections (surge and decline: Campbell-1).
- H2.6. Opposition partisans who abstained last time will rejoin the opposition side (surge and decline: Campbell-2).
- H2.7. Weak opposition partisans who voted for the government last time will return to the opposition (surge and decline: Campbell-2).
- H2.8. There should be a shift away from the government by voters dissatisfied with its record (referendum).
- H2.9. Satisfied government supporters abstain more then dissatisfied ones who are more likely to switch (referendum).

- H2.10. The shift away from government is greater when there is another favored party (second order).
- H2.11. Second-order arena concerns are not relevant: i.e., European attitudes do not affect the decision of voters to switch (second order).

Data for this section is from the European Election Study of 1999.[4] Between 500 and 3,000 voters in each country were interviewed by telephone immediately after the 1999 elections (300 were interviewed in Luxembourg but this country has been excluded from what follows as the two elections occurred simultaneously). Country samples have been weighted so that each sums to 500. Operationalizations are as follows.

- *Vote change:* differences between recalled vote at the last national election and reported EP vote.[5]
- *Partisanship:* feeling of being close to a party, measured on a four-point scale: not close, sympathizer, quite close, very close. This is coded from -3 (very close to opposition party to $+3$ (very close to government party) with not close as zero.
- *Government popularity:* approval or disapproval of the government's record to date, running from -1 (disapproval) through 0 (DK) to $+1$ (approval).
- *Multiple party preferences:* these are measured by the 'propensity to vote for party x' questions (PTVs) standard in European Parliament election studies as well as several national election studies (see Tillie 1995; van der Eijk and Franklin 1996). Respondents are asked for each party how likely is it that they would ever vote for this party, with responses on a ten-point scale from 1–10. Three measures are calculated from this. The first is a measure of support for a/the government party and is the highest of the PTV's for the various government parties. The second is an equivalent measure of support for an opposition party. The third is simply the difference between the two, which we call PTV_maxdif. It is scaled from -9 (PTV $=10$ for an opposition party, no more than 1 for any government party) to $+9$ (PTV $=10$ for a government party, no more than 1 for any opposition party).
- *Views on Europe:* an item on attitude to unification which uses a one to ten point scale to indicate whether integration has gone too far or should be pushed further. This is recoded here as a ten-point scale from -4.5 (too far) to $+4.5$ (further). Respondents were also asked to place each party on this scale and we have used the same technique as explained above with respect to differences in party preferences to measure the perceived difference between government and opposition on Europe.

- *Political interest:* a four-point scale self-assessed interest in politics from none (0), a little, somewhat, to very (4). Missing values were coded 0.

We have so far maintained a simple government *vs.* opposition focus in line with the US system which serves as the basis for both surge and decline and referendum theories but this now needs some relaxation. Hence table 3.2 and subsequent analysis indicates voters' movements between the two elections, general and European: whether respondents voted for the same government party, the same opposition party, *or a different government or opposition party,* or did not vote.[6] This addition is required because voters may change their party support without crossing the government or opposition boundary and it is important to find out how far this happens. Table 3.2 provides evidence of various types of change and so gives us a basis for evaluating some of the surge and decline hypotheses H2.1–H2.3 and H2.6. We can see from table 3.2 that the government parties did not on average lose a higher proportion of their original voters than did the opposition parties. Government parties kept only 43 percent of their voters but opposition parties retained only 44 percent. This is not what would have been expected on the basis of surge and decline. It is true that the impact of change is more negative for the government because so much of the change from opposition parties is toward other opposition parties. It thus remains within the fold, whereas for government parties it does not. More voters also cross from government to opposition than move in the other direction, although the numbers moving in either direction are quite small. Erstwhile government (and opposi-

Table 3.2 European Parliament election vote and recalled national election vote

	European Parliament election vote							
	Opposition voter				Government voter			
Recalled national vote	Same Opp party	Opp	Different Opp party	Did not vote	Same Govt party	Govt	Different Govt party	n
Opposition	44		20	32		4		4671
None		14		80		6		1334
Government		13		43	39		5	4419

Note: Original n's shown in table but then weighted to equalize country size for analysis.

tion) supporters are also more likely to abstain than they are to defect. Among clear non-habitual voters (those in the second column) the government also did better last time than the opposition, 43 percent as against 32 percent (a valid comparison as the row totals are nearly equal). All this is in accordance with hypotheses drawn from Campbell-1 (H2.1; H2.2). There is relatively little evidence of significant shifts from abstention to voting as might be expected from Campbell-2 (H2.6) although what shifts there were did benefit the opposition.

Surge and decline theories also direct attention to the party attachments of voters, arguing that tendencies to stay, abstain, or switch vary across different levels of attachment. We thus need to know something of the character of the voters in the different cells. Table 3.3 makes this clearer, breaking down the voter transition matrix in table 3.2 by party attachment, coded here as simply 'Opposition', 'None', and 'Government'.

Campbell-1 (H2.3) would lead us to expect independents who voted for the government in the national election to abstain in the European Parliament election, whereas partisans who crossed over should return. This is what we find. Of independents who voted for the government last time, 51 percent abstained in the European election and more stayed with the government party they supported last time (27%) than switched to the opposition (18%), although 5 percent switched government party which may or may not have been consistent with party attachment. Partisan defection was rare in the general election but of the 'disadvantaged' partisans who defected to the government last time, 47 percent returned, compared to only 11 percent who stayed and 43 percent who abstained. Campbell-2 (H2.6) predicts partisans of the non-government party should move from abstention back to their party. However, there are few enough of them and, while 37 percent returned, 61 percent continued to abstain. Campbell-2 (H2.7) also predicts that independents should switch back from the government but, as we have seen, such a move was less common than abstention.

A further expectation from Campbell-1 (H2.5) is that there should be more defections—that is, those identifying with one party but voting for another—in general elections than in European ones. The numbers are very small here but 7.4 percent (as a percentage of partisans voting) defected[7] in the general election and 5.9 percent in the European election, which is consistent with H2.5.

While this detailed analysis is necessary to test some ideas of surge and decline theory and to give some idea of the numbers involved, a more general and multivariate analysis is preferable to consider the other expectations. Such an analysis also allows us to control for the country factor in our dataset. We are particularly interested in those voters in the first and third rows, those who voted for

Table 3.3 Recalled national vote by party attachment and European Parliament vote

	European Parliament election vote							
	Opposition voter				Government voter			
Recalled national vote Party Attachment	Same Opp party	Opp	Different Opp party	Did not vote	Same Govt party	Govt	Different Govt party	n
Opposition								
Opposition	57		19	22		2		2563
Independent	31		21	42		5		1929
Government	25		12	38		25		179
TOTAL	44		20	32		4		4671
None								
Opposition		37		61		2		182
Independent		11		84		5		1018
Government		2		75		23		134
TOTAL		14		80		6		1334
Government								
Opposition		47		43	11		0	408
Independent		18		51	27		5	1799
Government		5		36	53		6	2212
TOTAL		13		43	39		5	4419

Note: Cell entries are row percentages. Original n's shown in table but then weighted to equalize country size for analysis.

or against the government last time, and in how their behavior in this 1999 election is related to characteristics like partisanship, satisfaction, and their views on Europe.

Taking each row in turn we could simply regress the pattern of 1999 behavior on four characteristics, controlling for country, using standard OLS regression. Apart from concerns about the distribution of the dependent variables, a central problem would be the need to assume that the characteristics that lead to abstention are also those that lead to switching parties. This may be the case, but the assumption seems unwise to make at this point, especially since in many of the

Table 3.4 Characteristics of vote-switchers from government party: Multinomial logit estimates

	Voted government last general election					
	European election voted opposition		European election non-voter		European election different gov. party	
Variables	Odds ratios	SE	Odds ratios	SE	Odds ratios	SE
Approval of government	0.88	0.10	0.84*	0.07	1.21	0.15
Positive attitude to Europe	0.88**	0.04	0.93***	0.02	0.94	0.03
Party differential on Europe	1.02	0.04	1.01	0.02	0.93	0.05
Partisan attachment to a govt party	0.59***	0.05	0.78***	0.03	0.76***	0.04
PTV_maxdif	0.75***	0.02	0.87***	0.02	0.96	0.03
Interest in politics	1.04	0.11	0.60***	0.06	1.00	0.21
McFadden's R^2			0.30			
Log likelihood			−2501			
n			3087			

Note: Reference category is those voting for the same opposition party; country dummies not shown.
*** Significant at .001 level; ** Significant at .01 level; * Significant at .05 level.

expectations above abstainers and switchers are expected to behave differently. For that reason we have chosen to use multinomial logit which allows a categorical variable to be regressed on a number of independent variables.

Table 3.4 contains a set of odds ratios which indicate the odds first of shifting to the opposition, second of abstaining, and third of shifting to another government party rather than staying with the government party (this is the reference option). So a shift of one point in government approval (e.g., from 0 to 1) lowers the odds of an erstwhile government supporter shifting to the opposition to 0.88:1, in other words, by 12 percent. A shift from −1 to +1, the maximum, would drop it to 0.76:1, thus lowering the odds by 24 percent although as the standard error indicates, this is not enough to be significant at the 0.05 level. In

66 *Michael Marsh*

Table 3.5 Characteristics of vote-switchers from non-government party: Multinomial logit estimates

	Voted opposition last general election					
	European election voted government		European election non-voter		European election different opposition party	
Variables	Odds ratios	SE	Odds ratios	SE	Odds ratios	SE
Approval of government	1.19	0.22	0.94	0.06	0.85*	0.07
Positive attitude to Europe	0.95	0.04	0.94	0.04	0.96	0.03
Party differential on Europe	0.93	0.05	1.03	0.03	1.03*	0.01
Partisan attachment to a govt party	1.69***	0.14	1.34***	0.07	1.26***	0.06
PTV_maxdif	1.33***	0.10	1.13***	0.03	1.08*	0.04
Interest in politics	1.27	0.16	0.66***	0.05	1.08	0.06
McFadden's R^2			0.22			
Log likelihood			−2884			
n			3093			

Note: Reference category is those voting for the same opposition party; country dummies not shown.
*** Significant at .001 level; * Significant at .05 level.

table 3.5 the odds ratios apply to the likelihood of switching to the government, or abstaining, or switching to another opposition party relative to staying with the opposition. The odds ratios of 1.19:1 and 0.94:1 indicates a one unit shift in approval increase the odds of someone switching to the government by 19 percent and decreases the odds of abstaining by 6 percent, having voted for the opposition last time. However, neither of these effects is significant.

We can use these two tables as evidence in relation to our expectations outlined earlier, starting again with those from surge and decline theory. Partisanship is linked to abstention or defection patterns. As partisanship inclines toward the government it seems to have more impact on defection from the government to the opposition (0.59) than abstention (0.78), but defection by strong partisans is infrequent.[8]

On interest (H2.4) it is apparent that less interested voters are much more likely to abstain than stay. This holds for both government (0.60:1) and opposition (0.66:1) parties.

Expectations H2.8 and H2.9 from referendum theories offer two different possibilities: that defection or abstention from the government is a function of approval (Tufte), and that abstention is not a function of approval but that defection is negative voting. Results are inconclusive but if anything they point to the weakness of negative voting theory. There is the expected tendency for voters to leave the government when they are dissatisfied but, as we have already illustrated above, this is hardly very strong. There is no sign at all of negative voting, which would require a link between disapproval and switching but not between disapproval and abstention. In fact, only the reverse is true. The only significant link is between (dis)approval and abstention. In general, approval is not linked significantly to changes in the behavior of either erstwhile supporters of government or opposition parties, although dissatisfied opposition supporters are more likely to shift opposition parties than stay with their former party.

Second-order theory rests on the assumption that voters have preferences across a number of parties and that different elections provide different contexts in which they select from their set. The PTV_maxdif variable uses this insight, measuring the differential utility of voting for different parties, in this case government or opposition.[9] A low value for this variable indicates a low government-opposition differential, a high value indicates that one is preferred to the other by a big margin. We would expect (H2.10) that those who shift will have a lower party differential. This is the case. An increase of only one point in the differential (running from -9 to $+9$) reduces the chances of defecting from the government side by over 50 percent. On the opposition side, the differential has a much weaker impact on the odds of moving from opposition to government—about 35 percent—and on moving to abstention, where a one point change alters the odds by about 12 percent. Arguably, abstention is the option of people who have no other party to vote for.[10]

Perhaps the most striking result of all, however, is that with respect to EU orientations, something that we would not expect to be important given second-order theory. Hypothesis H2.10 is certainly not confirmed in this data as negative attitudes to Europe drive voters who voted for the government last time to switch or abstain. A one point increase on the European attitude scale (which runs from -4.5 to $+4.5$) reduces the odds of a voter switching to the opposition by

12 percent and the odds of abstaining by 7 percent. Hence the odds of a voter strongly supportive of more integration changing her vote are almost 100 percent smaller than of a voter who is strongly opposed, and the odds of her abstaining 50 percent less. There is no significant link between a positive attitude to Europe and moves from opposition to government but as it happens government parties were more supported at the last set of general elections by pro-Europe voters than were opposition parties. The mean attitude to Europe on the scale used here was 0.39 to the opposition's 0.20. In the European Parliament elections the difference increased: 0.74 to 0.29—half a point on the scale. Non-voters, too, are much less pro-European in European elections than in general elections, 0.08 as against 0.46.

What is problematic about this significant shift from governments is that it is unrelated to the perceived party differential on Europe. We would have expected the shift to be more pronounced among those who see the opposition as closer to their own position on Europe than is any government party, yet this is not the case. The inclusion into the model of a variable indicating whether a respondent is closer to a government party than any opposition party proved generally insigificant.[11] It appears that voting against the government, or abstaining, is often an anti-European act, which is carried out regardless of whether the government or opposition is closer to the voter on the issue! Whether they like it or not, and whether or not they deserve it, governments appear to stand as a proxy for the EU itself when it comes to European Parliament elections and any widespread anti-EU sentiment imperils support for government candidates in such election.

Discussion

This chapter has sought to examine the expectations we might have about forthcoming elections in the light of available theoretical work both on European Parliament elections and the analogous US midterm elections. We contrasted the US-based theories of Angus Campbell and his successors with Reif and Schmitt's theory of second-order elections on the basis that all seek to explain the comparable patterns of regularity in different political systems. There are differences between the several theories. These lie chiefly in different conceptions of what motivates the average voter, with the second-order theory allowing for more strategic, 'rational' behavior than the US theories, but they also lie in the behavior that each was developed to explain. Surge and decline and referendum theories focus on behavior in a two-party system with a separation of powers and an electorate which is easily categorized as identifying with one party or another. In parliamentary democracies none of these conditions applies. Two-party systems are rare, even if they are liberally defined; there is no separation of powers[12] and party identification, as the concept is understood in the US, is much less easily separated from immediate voting intentions. Nonetheless, the assumption with which this chapter began was that such theories are at least potentially applicable in the different circumstances. Second-order election theory has grown out of this literature but offers explanations for matters outside the normal ambit of US-focused studies, such as the shift of votes from larger to smaller parties, as well as adapting previous insights to understanding electoral change in sub- and supra-national elections.

On the whole we discovered that second-order theory provides us with a better understanding of European Parliament elections than its potential rivals but these do offer some understanding of the mechanics of individual vote change. The expectations derived from surge and decline theory are only in part confirmed by the data. First of all, there is mixed evidence that government losses can be seen as a consequence of voters returning to 'normal' behavior. Aggregate losses are not linked to the size of a surge at the previous election. However, as predicted, it seems that defections by partisans were more apparent in general elections than European elections, a finding which runs counter to some popular wisdom that European elections are contexts in which partisanship counts for little. We also see at the individual level that independent voters are more likely than others to abstain at the lower stimulus election, and that partisanship is linked to shifts in and out of the voting public in some of the expected ways, although it is evident that 'peripheral' voters alone are not responsible for the losses suffered by governments. It must be acknowledged that these findings may be distorted by the fact that we have only recall evidence for the last national election, and must assume no change in partisanship or PTV differentials, perhaps a somewhat heroic assumption. We badly need widespread panel data on these elections, something that is not yet available for more than the odd country. Even so, the distortions in recall might be expected to strengthen links between partisanship and recalled choice rather than weaken them and the evidence here should certainly not be discounted on that point. In general the findings give more value to Campbell's original formulation that his namesake's revised version. While not every expectation is fulfilled, not all can be dismissed.

Referendum theory and its developments generally perform less well. The aggregate data showed no sign that the economy mattered, and the individual-level analysis revealed weak results with respect to government popularity.[13] There was no support for the negative voting hypothesis.

Evidence with respect to second-order theory confirms previous analyses at aggregate level on the importance of timing for the extent of government losses. This result obtains even when the economic record is controlled for. These controls could certainly be specified in a more sophisticated way. However, if the result is accepted it raises the important question as to why voting with the heart rather than the head disadvantages the government. In our analysis this is probably a consequence of the fact that the opposition is more fragmented than the government. Vote switching is thus more likely to hurt the government than the opposition. This does not explain why the degree of loss follows the cyclical pattern that it apparently does.

The individual-level findings provide further support for the idea that voters have a set of party preferences rather than a single loyalty. Voters with another option are more likely to defect than abstain. However, the most striking finding relates to the significance of attitudes to Europe on defection and abstention. A central tenet of all the theories reviewed here is that midterm or second-order elections are not quite what they seem. European Parliament elections are supposed to be primarily decided by national concerns, not by the politics of the 'European' arena. If European Parliament elections are wholly second order then 'Europe' would not matter at all but the evidence here suggests that European orientations do seem to matter to some degree in voters' decisions to stay with or switch from their general election party choices. A puzzle is the absence of evidence that defection is prompted by a perception that the 'other party' is closer to the voter on the European issue. Rather 'Europe' is tied up with the government, and disaffection with Europe means disaffection with the government. More research is needed to ensure this pattern differs from what has been found in previous years and is not just a different result generated by a different methodology, but it does seem to mark a departure from past behavior.

This chapter has largely focused on a review of theories of lower stimulus elections, exploring differences and similarities between them, in order to assess what each can tell us about European Parliament elections. Most of them offer something of value, although some have a wider potential than others. What we can say is that we certainly do not lack useful tools for generating expectations about future elections and for analyzing them in retrospect. We have shown several clear patterns in previous results, many of them quite consistent with theory and thus interpretable in such terms. Yet we have also found the unexpected. The vulnerability of governments is well known, and we have plotted the cycle of that vulnerability in figure 3.1. The source of some of that vulnerability in anti-European sentiment is less well known and anyway this finding remains tenuous at this point. However, as at present support for the European project generally appears to be waning rather than waxing among the European public, the prospects for government parties in these elections are hardly rosy.

NOTES

1. For a concise review of some other variants that we have no space to discuss here see Campbell (1997).

2. In a previous analysis a variable indicating the sequential number of the European Parliament (i.e., 1st, 2nd, 3rd, etc.) was included in the regression analysis. This reflected the tendency of anti-government swings to increase since 1979 (Marsh 1998, 603). With a smaller anti-government swing than in 1994, 1999 proved an exception to this trend, necessitating the use of dummies here instead.

3. These were calculated using the CLARIFY software authored by Tomz, Wittenberg, and King (2000). See also King, Tomz, and Wittenberg (2000).

4. See appendix A of this volume.

5. An alternative operationalization would be to contrast the EP vote with vote in a hypothetical general election at the same time. This was used by Oppenhuis, van der Eijk, and Franklin 1996, 287–305, and also by van Egmond in chapter 2 of this volume. It has the advantage of removing the bias of recall data but the disadvantage of being subject to the same second-order effects of any opinion poll taken between elections. However, Oppenhuis et al.'s findings on the existence of switching and abstention contributing to government party losses are similar to those in the analysis here (below). A more complete comparison of the consequences of the alternative operationalizations will be the subject of further work.

6. In the analysis that follows, all data are weighted to give close approximations to actual results, resulting in an average loss of 6 percent.

7. Defection here is limited to defection across the government or opposition divide.

8. The means of the different groups reinforce this point. Loyal government supporters average 1.5 on the party attachment scale. Abstainers have weaker attachment, averaging 0.9. Switchers to the opposition, however, average -0.3. These results are closer to Campbell-1 than Campbell-2.

9. One objection that might be raised here is that the PTV-based variables and the government satisfaction variable are doing much the same job, and that the importance of the PTV variables in fact supports the referendum case. While there is some truth in this, in fact the variables are not highly correlated. Pearson's r is only 0.37 between the PTV for the most favored government party and government satisfaction. The relative weakness of the government satisfaction variable is certainly not due simply to multicollinearity. Dropping the PTV-based variables does result in significant estimates for the impact of government satisfaction on the behavior of government supporters (defection and abstention) and opposition supporters (defection) but depresses the R^2. Dropping

government satisfaction has little impact on R^2. Hence these results are more supportive of Tufte's referendum thesis but not Kernall's theory of negative voting.

10. If we look at the means for each of the different groups who voted for the government last time, the party differential for those who stayed with the government is 3.2, for those who abstained is 2.0 and for those who switched is -0.9. The equivalent figures for those who voted opposition last time show a similar pattern: stayers -4.1, abstainers -2.9, switchers to government -0.2 and switchers within the opposition -3.2.

11. In case the party attachment and PTV items were acting as intervening variables in the relationship between proximity on Europe and defection from the government these were dropped, but the proximity variable was still insignificant

12. Although of course in the context of a European Parliament election the difference is less important.

13. Mixed results have also been found in the US context; see Niemi and Weisberg 1993, 209.

CHAPTER FOUR

Comparing the views of parties and voters in the 1999 election to the European Parliament

ANDREAS M. WÜST
AND HERMANN SCHMITT

The increasing transfer of policy-making powers from the member states to the European Union during the past decades has generated relatively little political controversy in most of the member states. The exceptions to this general pattern—particularly Denmark and Britain, to some extent also Sweden—indicate that this state of affairs cannot be regarded as a 'natural' development. Both the general trend as well as the exceptions raise important questions with respect to the role of the electoral process in European integration and its democratic character. Addressing these questions requires, at the very least, a focus on political parties, on voters, and on the electoral connection between them. This chapter deals mainly with political parties, which are among the most important actors in the process of politicization of issues. Where do parties position themselves on the issue of European unification, and how are these positions perceived by voters? To what extent do parties in the various member states offer voters a choice between different views on the future of the EU? The question of political representation—how well voters' attitudes toward European unification are represented by parties—will be discussed briefly in this chapter, and will be assessed in more detail in chapter 10.

The analysis of parties' positions in this chapter will be based on data from a systematic analysis of the contents of their manifestos for the European elections (appendix C). The question of how adequately voters perceive parties' positions will be addressed by juxtaposing parties' positions as derived from their manifestos with voters' perceptions as derived from the voter survey of the European Election Study (appendix A).

We use party manifestos as a source of information to gauge parties' positions on various issues. Manifestos are authoritative statements of party policy. In spite of the facts that they are usually drafted by small groups of specialists within a party and that they are issued prior to an election so that they do not address issues that will become salient at later times, it has been established that what parties advocate in parliament and what parties do when in government is indeed to a large extent in line with the contents of their manifestos for national elections (Klingemann, Hofferbert, and Budge 1994).

Thus, election manifestos constitute an important source of information on parties' input into the electoral connection, and it is therefore that they take a prominent place in any 'extended design' of comparative electoral research (Thomassen 2000). Their relevance as sources of information on party positions is not diminished by the fact that they are usually hardly read by voters, although this observation prompts the question of how manifesto content and voter perceptions of party positions are related.[1]

Empirical analyses of party manifestos must be based on a systematic coding of the contents of these documents. This can be done in different ways. Probably the most prominent strategy is to code the issues raised, or referred to, in the manifesto. Statistical analyses can then determine how often (in absolute and relative terms) certain issues are mentioned, and the analyst can use this as a proxy for the party-specific saliency of these issues. This is in a nutshell what the multilateral Manifesto Research Group (MRG) does. The beginning of this research group dates back to the mid-1970s (cf. Robertson 1976). By that time, a coding frame was conceived that later was further developed and utilized to generate empirical information on the content of election programs of parties in twenty-five countries from 1945 onward (Budge et al. 2001). The MRG scheme focuses on the emphasis that parties put on various issues as manifested by the number of arguments devoted to them (see also the next section).[2] All in all, MRG coding provides frequencies for arguments in fifty-six coding categories which are grouped into the following seven policy domains: external relations, freedom and democracy, the political system, the economy, welfare and quality of life, the fabric of society, and social groups.

In this chapter we report first findings of a research project which closely follows the footsteps of the MRG. In this project the experience and the particular approach of the MRG research group has been applied to a different political level: the manifestos that parties issue at the occasion of European Parliament elections. These Euromanifestos, as we call these documents, are usually different from national election manifestos.[3] Most parties in the member countries have produced such Euromanifestos for each EP election in which they participated.[4]

While we aim at applying the well-established MRG coding scheme to the new subject area as closely as possible, this cannot be done without adaptation and change. The reason is that parties give considerably more attention in their Euromanifestos than in their national manifestos to 'Europe', the European Union (formerly the European Community), and its institutions and policies. This emphasis cannot be covered adequately by the MRG schemes as they are and requires a cautious adjustment of the original coding scheme.

CODING THE CONTENTS OF THE EUROMANIFESTOS OF POLITICAL PARTIES

On the data side, the purpose of the Euromanifesto project has been to collect all available manifestos parties have issued for European Parliament elections since 1979. Coded are not entire manifestos, or sections or chapters in it, but individual 'arguments'. An argument is defined as the verbal expression of a political idea or an issue. A sentence coincides with an argument most of the time, as it is the basic or natural unit of meaning. When a sentence comprises more than one argument, it is broken down in as many quasi-sentences as there are arguments, and these quasi-sentences are coded.[5] In the end, our unit of analysis is an argument, which often—but not always—coincides with a natural sentence. These arguments are coded according to a modified and 'mirrored' MRG coding frame. While the modification was necessary to add EU-specific issues (thirteen categories and various sub-categories were added to the MRG scheme), the mirroring was done to identify which level of government is involved when referring to an issue.[6]

In the original MRG coding frame, only two codes are provided for the coding of EC/EU related arguments: EU positive [code 108] and EU negative [code 110]. While these codes might suffice to capture the EU-related arguments of national party manifestos, they are obviously not enough for an adequate coding of the contents of Euromanifestos. We have kept these two 'original' codes that now denote general pro- or anti-EU arguments and arguments regarding a further deepening of the EU, respectively. In addition, however, we have split the domain 'political system' [domain 3] into two sub-domains, 'political system in general' [domain 3.1] and 'political system of the European Union' [domain 3.2] in an effort to cover most of the more constitutional issues of the debate on the future of the EU. Party positions on the most important dimensions of institutional development of the EU political system, on enlargement, and on unspecified protest to the system as such can now be coded in a number of specific categories (as described in table 4.1). Wherever necessary, we have, in addition to the codes of the new domain, added EU-specific sub-codes to existing codes, an example being 'lack of democracy in the EU', which was added to 'democracy in the EU'. Note, however, that all codes of the new domain and all sub-codes can be regrouped into the two original codes 'EU-positive' and 'EU-negative', which allows the EMCS findings to be compared with the contents of national manifestos that have been coded according to the original MRG coding scheme.

Not only have we added new code categories to the MRG coding scheme, table 4.1 indicates another major difference: in our coding we distinguish the level of government to which each argument refers. Is a poor performance of

Table 4.1 Categories of the "new" domain 3.2 of the EMCS

Code	Content of the Argument
2–306	Competences of the European Parliament: Positive
2–307	Competences of the European Parliament: Negative
2–308	Competences of the European Commission: Positive
2–309	Competences of the European Commission: Negative
2–310	Competences of the European Council/Council of Ministers: Positive
2–311	Competences of the European Council/Council of Ministers: Negative
2–312	Competences of the European Court of Justice: Positive
2–313	Competences of the European Court of Justice: Negative
2–314	Competences of other EC/EU institutions: Positive
2–315	Competences of other EC/EU institutions: Negative
2–316	EC/EU enlargement: Positive
2–317	EC/EU enlargement: Negative
2–318	Complexity of the EC/EU political system

the economy due to national or to European factors? Should immigration be regulated by EU or by national political authorities? In a multi-level polity like that of the European Union, issues and policies can originate and be dealt with at different levels, as these examples demonstrate. Any effort to grasp the role and importance that parties assign to the European Union in their Euromanifestos must therefore identify the level of government of the argument involved.[7] This level of government can be identified by two meaning elements and two decision rules (Wüst and Volkens 2003, 7f.).

The two meaning elements are:

- the governmental frame of an argument: codes (1) national government, (2) EC/EU government, and (3) world government or unspecific; and
- the policy scope of an argument: codes (1) the nation or sub-national entities, (2) the EC/EU/Europe, and (3) the world or unspecific.

The two decision rules are:

- if only one meaning element is present, it defines the code;
- if both elements are present but do not suggest the same code, governmental frame beats policy scope.

Generally, almost all arguments can refer to all three levels of government. However, the categories of the new domain 'political system of the EU' can only refer to the European level, as a discussion on institutional aspects of the EU is framed by definition in terms of European government. In addition, there are a few sub-codes that are also limited to either the national (e.g., financing the EU: negative) or the European level of government (EMU/European currency: positive/negative).

Order of presentation

Based on the coding scheme described above, we first present results of a content analysis of the manifestos that political parties have issued ahead of the European Parliament election of 1999.[8] We compare those findings with the results of the Voter Study of the European Election Study 1999. In doing so, we focus on issues. Issues are problems that parties and voters deal with in an election campaign.

Issues differ, among other things, with regard to saliency and framing. Saliency is measured, on the side of the parties, by the frequency with which an issue is mentioned in an election program. How often particular issues are stressed is taken as an indicator of the emphasis parties put on them, which in turn is indicative of the saliency they attribute to particular issues.[9] On the voters' side, the saliency of issues is measured by asking respondents from a representative sample what they see as the most important political problems (agenda question).

With regard to framing, one important dimension is the level of government parties refer to when discussing an issue, and where voters think problems ought to be solved. We will empirically determine in which governmental frame parties put the issues they are talking about in their manifestos, and the level of government that voters envisage for the problems that are salient to them.[10]

We will also study the positions of political actors with regard to the European Union and European integration. On the parties' side, this will be done in two ways. First, for each party the shares of Euro-positive arguments (fourteen code categories) and Euro-negative arguments (fifteen code categories) are calculated and the balance between these two is determined.[11] This difference is a measure of each party's pro- or anti-EU position. Second, we analyze the expert coders' assessment of each party's position on a ten-point pro- or anti-EU scale. It turns out that the two measures correlate very strongly ($r = 0.81$), which suggests that the content analysis produced valid measures of parties' positions toward the EU. With regard to the voters we rely on the European Election Study where representative samples of voters were asked to position themselves and the nationally relevant parties on this same pro- or anti-Europe dimension.[12]

Empirical findings

In presenting our empirical findings, we will first look at the party side and hence the Euromanifestos, then add the pertinent information for the voters from the European Election Study 1999, and finally compare the two with one another.

Governmental frame and pro- or anti-EU positioning of political parties

What governmental frame do political parties use in their Euromanifestos, national or European? Do they primarily stress the EU level of government and address European-wide political issues and problems? Or do they rather have the national polity in mind, perhaps even suggesting re-establishing its independence from and sovereignty vis-à-vis the ever-growing policy scope of the Union? Analyzing the level code assigned to each argument, we find that political parties present their arguments predominantly in a European Union perspective in their 1999 Euromanifestos. With very few exceptions, a majority of arguments of the 1999 manifestos are put in an EU governmental frame (see table 4.2). And these exceptions do not follow a clear pattern.[13] When shifting our focus from parties to member states, there is some evidence that the parties from founding members discuss more arguments within a European frame than parties in countries that have joined later—like Ireland, Denmark, Portugal, Greece, and Austria. However, Finland, Sweden, and Spain do not fit in that pattern.[14]

Table 4.2 may be read as support for what Bosch and Newton (1995) referred to as 'familiarity breeds content', by which they meant that the longer a country belongs to the Union, the more its parties support the Union's basic rules and procedures. We do find support for this thesis, but also remarkable variation between party families in this respect. Taking the adherence to one of the political groups of the European Parliament as a sorting criterion, social-democratic (PES) and green parties (EFGP) put the largest share of arguments in an EU governmental frame (table 4.3). This is particularly pronounced for all social democratic parties with the exception of Greek's PASOK. Of all parties belonging to the green group, only Belgium's Groen is framing its arguments as overwhelmingly national. The parties in the other two big parliamentary groups, the Christian democrats and conservatives (EPP-ED) and the liberals (ELDR), tend to frame their political arguments more frequently in a national perspective. Yet, there are as well notable exceptions. In the EPP-ED group, France's UDF, the Belgian Social Christian Party (PSC), the Christian Democrats of Germany (CDU) and of the Netherlands (CDA) frame more arguments as European. Among the Liberals, it is D66 of the Netherlands and CiU of Spain that present almost all arguments in a European frame. There is one overtly EU-critical group in the fifth directly elected European Parliament, 'Europe of Democracy and Diversity (EDD)' whose member parties to a larger extent view the world through a national lens than all other parliamentary groups. Compared to EDD, 'Europe of Nations (UEN)', a group of patriotic and partly nationalist parties, turns out to be more moderate in its views on Europe as indicated by the balance of its pro- and anti-EU arguments. The top ten parties promoting an explicitly anti-EU program are mostly located at the far right and far left end of the political spectrum.[15] However, the British Conservatives are also among the parties with more anti-EU (23%) than pro-EU arguments (12%).

The governmental frame that parties apply co-varies to some extent with their positions on a pro- or anti-EU dimension. We find a moderate positive correlation

Table 4.2 Governmental frame and the shares of pro-EU and anti-EU arguments in 1999 Euromanifestos and coder evaluation by country

Country*	Governmental frame of arguments			Pro-EU (14 codes) and anti-EU (15) arguments			pro/anti EU (coder evaluations)
	National (%)	European (%)	not specified (%)	pro EU (sum %)	anti EU (sum %)	difference pro-anti EU	scale values (pro-anti, 1–10)
Austria	19.5	72.0	8.5	16.0	12.1	3.9	3.4
Belgium	13.8	76.5	9.7	19.8	5.9	14.0	3.2
Flanders	20.1	66.9	13.0	16.1	6.6	9.5	3.5
Wallonia	3.8	91.7	4.5	25.8	4.7	21.1	2.6
Denmark	12.7	71.0	16.3	21.3	11.5	9.8	5.0
Finland	7.7	81.0	11.3	17.1	2.6	14.5	4.5
France	12.9	80.6	6.5	15.6	10.9	4.7	4.4
Germany	6.7	91.8	1.5	18.3	7.2	11.1	3.5
Greece	72.5	24.1	3.5	7.8	3.8	4.0	3.3
Ireland	32.5	60.0	7.5	12.8	2.7	10.1	3.4
Italy	16.6	74.0	9.4	26.1	3.1	23.0	2.9
Luxembourg	11.7	79.7	8.6	23.1	6.5	16.6	2.5
Netherlands	1.8	89.2	9.1	19.8	4.7	15.1	4.2
Portugal	23.6	74.7	1.7	19.3	6.3	13.1	2.8
Spain	13.2	84.1	2.8	16.4	2.1	14.3	1.7
Sweden	7.2	80.9	12.0	13.5	6.2	7.3	4.5
United Kingdom	18.0	78.7	3.8	13.3	13.4	-0.0	6.2
Britain	17.5	78.7	3.8	13.4	13.3	0.1	6.2
Northern Ireland	32.7	65.5	1.8	10.6	14.4	-3.8	6.0
Summary (15 countries)*	15.8	78.3	6.0	17.5	7.2	10.3	4.8
EC founding countries*	11.0	82.8	6.2	19.9	6.8	13.1	3.6

* Weighted by seats in EP.

Table 4.3 Governmental frame and the shares of pro-EU and anti-EU arguments in 1999 Euromanifestos and coder evaluation by parliamentary groups

Parliamentary groups/parties		National (%)	Governmental frame of arguments		Pro-EU (14 codes) and anti-EU (15) arguments			pro / anti EU (coder evaluation)
			European (%)	not specified (%)	pro EU (sum %)	anti EU (sum %)	difference pro-anti EU	scale values (pro-anti, 1–10)
EP groups*	All parties (118 manifestos)	15.8	78.3	6.0	17.5	7.2	10.3	3.8
Conservatives and Christian democrats	EPP-ED (25 manifestos)	18.9	76.6	4.6	17.6	8.3	9.3	4.0
Social democrats	PES (19 EM)	8.0	87.7	4.3	18.3	1.6	16.7	2.7
Greens	EFA (17 EM)	9.7	80.7	9.6	13.2	5.6	7.6	4.0
Liberals	ELDR (17 EM)	19.9	68.9	11.2	20.3	3.3	17.0	2.9
Socialists	GUE/NGL (15 EM)	15.3	75.8	8.9	9.6	10.5	-0.9	5.7
Nationalists	UEN (5 EM)	17.8	78.2	4.0	17.0	19.0	-2.1	5.5
Euro-skeptics	EDD (5 EM)	27.6	59.7	12.8	5.0	25.3	-20.3	9.1
None	Non-attached (7 EM)	29.8	66.8	3.4	14.0	15.9	-2.0	5.1
Euro-Parties	EPP	0.0	92.7	7.3	14.6	0.0	14.6	4.0
	PES	0.0	98.4	1.6	14.5	2.0	12.5	4.0
	ELDR	0.0	96.1	3.9	17.5	5.3	12.1	3.0
	EFGP	0.0	87.7	12.3	5.6	0.4	6.0	4.0

* Weighted by seats in EP.

FIGURE 4.1 Co-variation of the share of arguments put in an EU governmental frame and the position taking of parties on a pro- or anti-EU scale

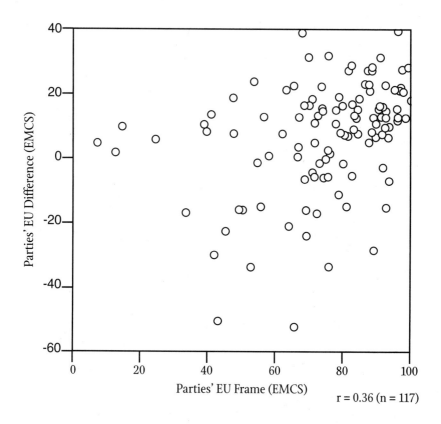

of r = 0.36 between the proportion of EU governmental frames and pro- or anti-EU positions (figure 4.1). Parties with a clear Euro-positive position tend to put more arguments in a European frame than others. Most prominent outliers at the bottom right of the graph are Germany's Republikaner, on the left the main Greek parties (PASOK and New Democracy) and Groen of Belgium. While the Euromanifesto of the former is filled with negative arguments on the EU, the latter do not talk much about the EU, but if they do, they refer to it positively.

Issue emphasis of political parties

Having analyzed the framing of issues and its relationship with the position taking of parties on a pro- or anti-EU dimension, we move on to the specific issues that parties emphasize in their Euromanifestos. What do parties talk about in their EP election programs? This question was central to a computerized content analyses of the programs of the European party federations (Schmitt and Binder 2004). The basic finding of this study was that parties are preoccupied with the polity of the European Union, thus leaving hardly any room for other topics. We find some traces of that as well in our present analysis of expert coders' evaluation of national parties' Euromanifestos. In virtually all these documents, the 'EU in general' and 'EU institutions' play central roles (table 4.4).

When it comes to differences between the parties, the political agendas of the Christian-conservative EPP-ED and of the socialist PES have much in common, even though some of the issues that they put forward reflect the traditional center-right and center-left profiles of these European party families—examples are 'decentralization', 'agriculture and farmers', and 'law and order' (rank 10; 3.3%) for the EPP-ED and 'internationalism', 'non-economic demographic groups' (rank 7; 3.9%), 'social justice' and 'creating jobs' (rank 9; 3.1%) for the PES. The green party group, by contrast, puts the strongest emphasis on 'environmental protection', followed by 'democracy', the post-materialist issue of an 'anti-growth economy' and 'EU institutions'. 'Environment' and 'democracy' as well as the 'welfare state' (rank 7; 4.6%) are very important for the liberal parties as well, but the ELDR member parties give also significant weight to 'decentralization' and the various EU issues. The GUE/NGL parties on the extreme left discuss Marx within a European frame (top five issue) and pay more attention to 'social justice' than the parties of the other parliamentary groups. For the Euro-skeptic parties of EDD, UEN, and the non-attached, the (loss of a) 'national way of life' is a top ten issue in their Euromanifestos. In addition, the various institutional aspects of the EU get more attention by the parties belonging to the UEN and the non-attached than from the parties belonging to the two largest groups.

All in all, it is not trivial to say that Euromanifestos contain a mix of issues. Party-specific issue profiles are clearly visible, most pronounced for the parties belonging to one of the smaller groups, and somewhat less distinct for member parties of the predominant EPP-ED and the PES.

Voters' governmental frame

Let us now move on to the voters. The governmental frame here is the level of government—sub-national, national, or European—that in their view is or should be in charge of particular issues.[16] Findings of the 1994 European Election Study suggest that Europe is considered to be a powerful political actor by many,

Table 4.4 Arguments in 1999 Euromanifestos by parliamentary groups (share of grouped issues in %)

All Euromanifestos		Issue	EPP-ED		PES		Greens		ELDR		GUE/NGL		EDD		UEN		N.A.	
Rank	%		Rank	%	Rank	%	Rank	%	Rank	%	Rank	%	Rank	%	Rank	%	Rank	%
1	8.5	EU in general/deepening of the EU	1	8.2	2	7.1	7	4.5	3	6.6	4	7.4	1	16.1	1	10.5	2	9.5
2	7.1	Political authority	2	8.1	4	5.8	16	2.2	14	2.7	1	8.3	2	13.5	5	4.4	3	8.6
3	5.5	Environmental protection	6	4.0	3	6.3	1	14.0	1	8.6	9	3.6	6	7.3	13	3.2	22	1.5
4	5.1	Democracy	9	3.7	6	4.6	2	8.2	2	8.5	2	7.7	5	8.7	8	3.5	13	2.3
5	4.8	EU institutions	8	3.9	9	3.3	4	5.8	4	5.8	8	3.6	7	5.5	2	9.3	4	8.4
6	4.2	Decentralization	3	5.4	19	1.9	5	5.7	5	4.9	11	2.9	3	10.1	6	4.4	6	4.6
7	4.0	Internationalism	12	3.0	5	5.0	6	5.0	6	4.7	6	5.2	12	2.3	3	7.3	15	2.1
8	3.8	Social justice	21	2.3	1	7.1	11	3.3	17	2.0	3	7.6	32	0.2	27	1.4	27	0.9
9	3.4	Freedom and human rights	5	4.2	11	3.1	8	4.4	9	4.1	15	2.3	15	1.1	20	2.0	23	1.4
10	3.1	Agriculture and farmers	4	4.5	27	1.3	10	3.3	10	3.7	17	2.0	11	3.2	17	2.0	5	6.2
14	2.5	National and European way of life	13	2.9	28	1.3	26	1.1	32	0.7	31	0.8	4	8.7	9	3.5	1	9.5
28	1.2	Single market	29	1.2	33	1.0	32	0.5	25	1.2	32	0.7	28	0.4	4	5.5	28	0.9
37	0.8	Anti-growth economy	46	0.0	34	0.9	3	6.0	38	0.2	27	1.1	33	0.2	38	0.8	40	0.1
40	0.4	Marxist analyses	42	0.2	48	0.0	47	0.5	47	0.0	5	5.3	46	0.0	44	0.0	39	0.2

Note: The top ten issues based on all Euromanifestos plus the top five issues for the parties of each parliamentary group are presented. Percentages refer to all Euromanifesto content.

Table 4.5 Most important problem (MIP) being solved on the European Union level: Perception (in %), preference (in %), and differences by country

Country	Governmental level in charge of most important problem			Governmental level that should deal with most important problem			Difference (preference and perception)
	regional	national	European	regional	national	European	European
Luxembourg	7	47	47	11	50	39	−7
Greece	16	39	44	19	44	37	−8
Austria	18	39	42	20	37	44	1
Spain	25	42	33	43	27	30	−3
Denmark	16	51	33	10	59	31	−2
Belgium	15	53	33	12	58	30	−2
Germany	32	37	31	25	37	38	7
Ireland	17	54	29	31	46	23	−6
Netherlands	12	59	29	16	38	46	18
EU-15	19	54	28	22	44	34	6
Italy	15	61	23	18	47	36	12
UK	24	53	23	30	45	25	2
France	23	55	22	24	40	36	14
Finland	20	61	19	24	63	13	−5
Portugal	4	78	18	29	35	35	18
Sweden	32	51	17	29	51	20	3

Source: European Election Study 1999. Weighted data are reported; a combination of the political weight and the EU population weight has been applied.

and that a good number of EU citizens want the European level of government to become even more powerful (Schmitt and Scheuer 1996; De Winter and Swyngedouw 1999). These earlier findings are nicely confirmed by the 1999 results. As table 4.5 displays, 28 percent of EU citizens think that the problem that is most important to them *is* currently dealt with on the European level (national level: 54%), while 34 percent think their most important problem *should be* dealt with on the European level (national level: 44%). There is considerable cross-national variation both in the perception and in the preference for solving problems on the EU level. In countries in which the EU level of government is perceived to play less of a role, people would rather prefer more problems should be solved there (exception: Finland), while the opposite tendency is found in countries where the EU is perceived to be in charge of many problems (exception: Austria).[17]

On the parties' side, we found a moderate and positive correlation between the relative frequency with which political parties put their arguments in a European governmental frame and their pro- or anti-EU position taking. We can replicate this analysis for the voters by relating both their perception and preference of the governmental level in charge of the most important problem to their attitudes toward European integration. Perceptions of reality, while possibly colored by preferences and deeper rooted values, should not systematically co-vary with pro- or anti-EU positions. This is different with preferences about where a political problem *should* be dealt with. There we expect at least some co-variation between the proportion of problems discussed in a European governmental frame and the general attitude toward European unification. And this is indeed what we basically find. Figure 4.2 shows that the level of government perceived to be in charge is not related to one's attitude about European unification. Preferences are different. Preferences for the EU level of government are modestly, and positively, correlated to general appreciations of the process of European unification. This suggests that preferences for a particular level of government are not

FIGURE 4.2 Preference for EU government being in charge for most important problem by voters' attitudes toward European unification (% share by scale values)

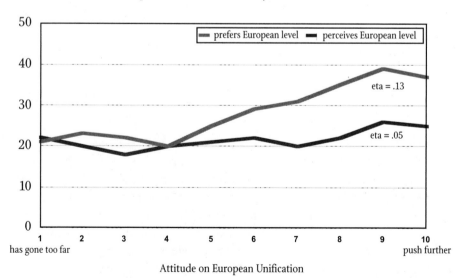

only determined by the 'nature' of the issue at hand. A general approval of the process of European unification seems to strengthen the 'specific support' (Easton 1975) people have in the problem-solving capacity of the EU's political authorities and institutions.

At this point, we can draw a few preliminary conclusions. First, the data suggest that voters attribute fewer issues and policies to the European Union than parties do. This at least is the impression one gets from a comparison of parties' governmental frame as applied in their Euromanifestos with their voters' preferences about where the most important political problem should be dealt with—at the sub-national, the national, or the European level.[18] Our second preliminary conclusion is that voters want to see more problems dealt with by the European Union than what they think is already the case. It is noteworthy that there is some association between voters' EU-competence perceptions and preferences: the more problems and policies they perceive to be already in 'European hands', the less increase do they advocate (cf. the 'thermostat' hypothesis advocated by Franklin and Wlezien 1997).

Issue agendas compared

Looking at the issues that voters want to be solved on the European level, it becomes obvious that, in European Parliament elections, parties and voters have quite distinct agendas (for a detailed analysis, see Schmitt and Binder 2004). For the voters, unemployment (48% of respondents mention it as most important) is by far the most important European issue, followed by issues related to crime and law and order (5%) and health care (3%). Note that the distribution is heavily skewed, with unemployment being by far the single most important issue among voters. All other issues rank far behind.

No single EU issue ranks among the top ten issues of the voter agenda. Even all EU issues combined make up less than 5 percent of all issues mentioned. Yet, at least the key issues that parties emphasize in their Euromanifestos enjoy some prominence in the agendas of their voters. Examples are protection of the environment for green party supporters and creating jobs for the voters of social-democratic parties. However, the voters' agenda also contains a number of issues that are hardly emphasized in the Euromanifestos (see table 4.3) like law and order (4%), migration (4%), or drugs (3%).

To sum up, there is not much congruence in the agendas of voters and parties in European Parliament elections. Parties in their manifestos seem to be preoccupied by the politics of the European Union, while voters when asked what the important problems are come up with much more mundane concerns—unemployment being the most prevalent among them. Having said this, we want to add a warning note based on methodological grounds. Perhaps voter and party agendas as measured in this study cannot really coincide, and we are thus looking for an impossible finding. There are limits to congruence that originate in the very nature of documents and data compared. Consider for a moment a party manifesto that spends about 50 or more percent of its arguments on unemployment: parties might issue such a manifesto as a special policy document, but hardly as a general election platform. Voters, on the other hand, when asked in a standardized interview what the most important problem is in their view, can only come up with one or a few issues. Upon this background, perhaps, the signs of similarity between voters' concerns and parties' agendas that we still found are less meager than it seems at first glance.

Pro- and anti-EU positions compared

Last but not least, we return to the pro- and anti-EU differentials of political parties as they can be derived from their Euromanifestos. There are two purposes for doing this. One is to compare these scores with the perception of voters about where the parties are. The other is to relate party and voter positions to each another. Voters' perceptions of party locations, and voters' self-location, are again drawn from the post-election survey of the European Election Study 1999.

Previous studies have shown that parties' positions toward the EU and European integration play a negligible role both for voters' decisions to participate in elections (e.g., Schmitt and van der Eijk 2003, see also chapter 8 of this volume) and for their party choice (e.g., van der Eijk, Franklin, and van der Brug 1999; Schmitt 2001; see also chapter 9 of this volume). This can be the result of at least two different constellations, one being that voters do not know where the parties are and the other that they do not care. It is obvious that the two possible backgrounds suggest different political consequences. If voters would not know where the parties are, a more effective campaign could help to solve the problem and parties would be well advised to invest in political communication. However, if voters do not care, the only remedy would be to raise the saliency of 'Europe', and parties' strategies should concentrate on developing the institutional and procedural preconditions of more salient European politics.

How accurate is the voter perception of parties' 'true' position on the general pro- or anti-EU dimension? Again, we have previous evidence to start out from. Van der Brug and van der Eijk (1999) estimated party positions by the judgment of party candidates: they were taken to be the experts and their average party placements were considered to be as good an estimate of 'true' party positions as one could get at the time in the absence of a more objective measure. They concluded that the voters have a rather vague perception of party positions on three EU policy dimensions—common currency ($r = 0.63$), borders ($r = 0.69$), and employment program ($r = 0.71$). This was considered a rather poor fit on the background of a much higher correlation between voters' and parties' left-right positions ($r = 0.89$).

What if we do not rely on the expertise of party candidates, but rather determine the parties' pro- or anti-EU positions on the basis of arguments they make in their Euromanifestos? The fact that we then deal with a general dimension rather than with specific policies could lead us to expect a stronger correlation than the ones van der Brug and van der Eijk found for 1994. However, Euromanifestos are indeed hardly read by the public at large, which may lead to an expectation of even weaker correlations with voter perceptions. What we find is surprisingly similar to the earlier results, however. There is a substantial positive correlation between parties' 'true' positions as reflected in their Euromanifestos and voters' perceptions of these party positions, but this correlation is not too strong ($r = 0.67$). Among the main outliers are the Greek ND and the Portuguese PSD as well as PSP: these parties are perceived to be more supportive of European unification than they actually are on the basis of their Euromanifestos. On the other hand, the Welsh Plaid Cymru, the Danish Progress Party (FP), and Junibevaegelsen are perceived to be more EU-skeptical than their Euromanifestos suggest (see figure 4.3), which replicates the results of van der Brug and van der Eijk (1999) for these parties.

Moving on from perceptual accuracy to the congruence of positions of voters and parties, we finally can address the question whether voters' EU orientations are in accord with their parties' positions on this same dimension. The electoral connection between citizens and EU politics can only add to the democratic nature of EU politics if voters choose parties on the basis of issue considerations, or at least, if their own preference and that of the party they support are consonant. In other words, representative democracy requires some basic issue congruence between voters and parties.

In the European Representation Study of 1994 we found a strong positive correlation between mean left-right self-placements of voters and their representatives ($r = 0.86$). The correlation was considerably weaker with regard to the position on a common currency (to $r = 0.52$), and it dropped even further on the question of open borders between EU member countries (to $r = 0.41$; cf. Thomassen and Schmitt 1999b). These earlier findings gave rise to concerns about a possible loss of contact between voters and parties on EU matters. We

FIGURE 4.3 Difference between pro- and anti-EU arguments in Euromanifestos and voters' party perceptions (interpolated medians) toward European integration

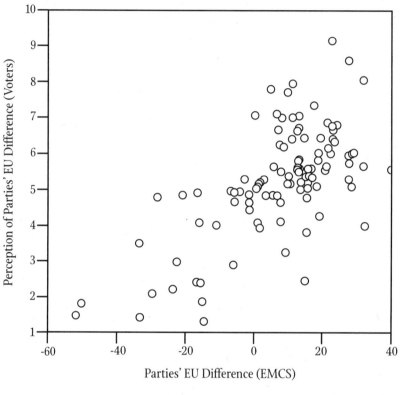

r = 0.67 (n = 105)

must underline these concerns on the basis of our current results. If we correlate party positions toward European unification as measured by the EMCS with their voters' positions—which is only possible for sixty-four voter-party–dyads[19]—we find a correlation of r = 0.46. For a significant number of cases we have to conclude that voters and parties live in different European worlds. And the cases in which voters and parties deviate most can be grouped as follows: parties of the predominantly left center like the Danish or Luxembourgian liberals and some social-democratic parties which are more pro-EU than their voters and quite extreme parties like Austria's FPÖ or the Greek Communists which take far more critical positions on the EU than their voters. Yet, beyond this general picture, we realize that the fit between parties and voters differs between countries, and it seems to be somewhat closer on the British Isles and in Denmark than elsewhere.

This can be read as if congruence between voters and parties is the higher the more controversy and opposition exists in a national public over questions of European policy making. Plausible as that may be, the empirical basis of these observations is very thin and we will not dwell on this for the time being.

CONCLUSION

Our analysis of issues and the governmental frame in which they were put in the 1999 election to the European Parliament has shown that European Union politics play different roles for parties and for voters. While parties in their Euromanifestos discuss issues predominantly in an European Union frame, their voters are still more oriented toward the nation-state. Moreover, voters and parties seem to be concerned about different things. Voters care overall about unemployment first; parties in their Euromanifestos deal with the EU, its institutions, and its future. While these differences may be partly due to the very nature of the different sources analyzed, they are telling nevertheless. It seems that parties and voters talk a great deal past one another, and that the political messages of the parties are only in part received at the voters' side.

Differences are less pronounced if it comes to general pro- or anti-EU positions. Voters do not know well enough where the parties position themselves toward European unification. This confirms earlier findings. However, in contrast to earlier assessments, it seems to us that parties do not 'hide' Europe, do not avoid the politicization of the European issue, as the variation of party positions aptly demonstrates. There is no party conspiracy (Franklin, van der Eijk, and Marsh 1996, 370–388) on the European issue. But nevertheless, the electoral connection was again found to be weak with regard to EU politics. The positions of voters and parties on questions of European Union politics are only weakly related to one another. Based on these findings, parties may be well advised to adjust their European electoral rhetoric to the language of ordinary citizens in order to be better understood. And voters may then want to have a closer look at what happens in Brussels and elsewhere in the EU political arena that is of utmost relevance to their daily lives.

NOTES

This chapter reports on the findings of the Euromanifestos project. This project was funded by a research grant of the German Science Foundation DFG (grant identifier:

SCHM 835/4–1). For more information on the project and its objectives visit http://www.euromanifestos.de.

1. Voters may perceive parties' positions through other sources than election manifestos, and on possibly 'outdated' information. Therefore we expect the match between voter perceptions and partisan offer to be less than perfect.

2. The MRG coding scheme has been criticized for not consistently providing directional information: whether parties are favoring or opposing certain issue positions. However, this coding scheme does apply a distinction between pro- and anti-positions for thirteen of the fifty-six issues covered, the remaining forty-three issues being of a valence-type that does not require this (Volkens 2002).

3. We tend to find a common (national and EP) election manifesto only when EP elections are held concurrently with national first-order elections, as it is regularly the case in Luxembourg.

4. We note however that a growing number of national parties use as their Euromanifesto an adaptation from the manifesto of their European party organization, rather than drafting a new one from scratch.

5. Note that the identification of multiple arguments in sentences is a difficult area even for expert coders, and one source of less than perfect inter-coder reliability.

6. Our notion of 'governmental frame' here refers to the level of government that parties envisage when discussing an issue: do they mention it with reference to the national level of government, to the European level of government, or is no level of government specified?

7. Note that this coding strategy does not distinguish between empirical and normative references to levels of government, i.e., whether a policy or problem *is* or *should be* dealt with at a particular level of government. It is the relative emphasis a party puts on a particular level of government that interests here, either in a descriptive or a prescriptive manner.

8. These include a few parties that had previously been represented in the EP, like Germany's Republikaner. The manifestos of the European party federations are also included in the analysis. Some data for Italy (four out of twenty-two Euromanifestos), for Spain (two regional alliances), and for the Belgian CVP are missing.

9. Note that it is relative frequencies that are indicative of emphasis and saliency. Relative frequencies are calculated as the proportion of arguments referring to a particular issue or problem in all arguments.

10. Note that on the voters' side, the European Elections Study survey includes questions on which governmental level the most important political problem *is* and *should be* dealt with.

11. In each Euromanifesto, the *pro-EU share* is calculated as the sum of emphasis on the following categories: 108s, 2–203, 3021, 306s, 308s, 310s, 312s, 314s, 316s, 4041, 4084, 4086, 2–601, 1–602. The *anti-EU share* is the sum of the following: 110s, 2–204, 3011, 307s, 309s, 311s, 313s, 315s, 317s, 318s, 4011, 4085, 4087, 1–601, 2–602 (for detailed descriptions of each code, see Wüst and Volkens 2003, appendix 1).

12. The respective survey question provides a scale from (1) 'European Unification has already gone too far' to (10) 'European Unification should be pushed further'.

13. The exceptions are PASOK and New Democracy (Greece), Groen and VLD (Belgium), Front National (F), the Christian Democratic CCD (Italy), Fine Gael (Ireland), the UK Independence Party, the Liberal Democrats (Britain), the Scottish National Party, and DUP (Northern Ireland).

14. The party-specific data (framing, pro- and anti-EU positions, coder evaluations) are available on the internet [http://www.mzes.uni-mannheim.de/projekte/manifestos/eestab.pdf].

15. These are Germany's Republikaner (REP), the UK Independence Party (UKIP), Austria's FPÖ, the Danish People's Party (FP) as well as Folksbevægelsen (FB), the French Front National (FN) and Lutte Ouvrière (LO), DUP of Northern Ireland, and the Dutch as well as the Swedish extreme left/communists.

16. Note that in the 1999 Voter Study, the agenda question first asked from respondents what in their view was the most important problem; second, which of the national parties would be best in dealing with it; third, which level of government was actually in charge; and fourth and finally, which level of government should be in charge of it. We are analyzing here parts 1, 3, and 4 of this complex question.

17. A methodological problem could arise from the fact that the likelihood of different issues to be attributed to the European level of government varies. We know, however, from earlier work that national agendas are rather similar (Thomassen and Schmitt 2004) so that we can put those worries to rest.

18. We realize that this is perhaps a bit of a far-fetched conclusion as the instruments from which those findings are drawn differ considerably between the parties' and the voters' level. However, valid conclusions do not need to be based on identical, but functionally equivalent instruments (van Deth 1998). Functional equivalence in this case would require at the very least that in their Euromanifestos parties do address all the issues that are salient to them rather than a just subset of issues that in their view belong in the realm of the European Union. Whether or not this form of equivalence exists can and will be tested elsewhere by comparing the content of Euromanifestos with that of national manifestos.

19. Parties which in the voter study of the European Election Study 1999 are represented by less than twenty-six respondents are not included in these analyses.

CHAPTER FIVE

Locating support for European integration

ANGELIKA SCHEUER
AND **WOUTER VAN DER BRUG**

Until the 1990s the European project has been largely elite driven. As long as the European Union was mainly an economic union, the (potential) issue of whether further European integration was desirable was hardly politicized. To be sure, there were often protests against European policies, but there is little evidence that these protests also reflected sentiments against the process of European integration in general. Moreover, these protests came usually from very specific and small groups in society with special interests, such as farmers, and not from large sections of the general public.

Since the debates aroused by the ratification of the Treaty of Maastricht, the EU has acquired a much more political dimension, and it was issues particularly relating to that political dimension that generated referenda, and thereby supplemented the elite drive character (which is still there) with a set of non-elite checks. A series of referenda about European treaties (of Maastricht, Amsterdam, and Nice) and about the introduction of the Euro helped to politicize the question of further European integration. Because of the increasing importance of the European level of decision making on the policies of the member states, it is hardly surprising that the question of European integration becomes a political issue relevant to many ordinary citizens in European democracies, and not only to those who were until recently most directly affected by EU policies. This shift from narrowly felt to broadly experienced consequences of integration makes it important to study the extent of public support for European integration in the member states. Moreover, from a normative perspective, it is also important to study public support for decisions concerning European integration, the legitimacy of which largely depends on it (e.g., Sinnott 1995a, 1995b; Thomassen and Schmitt 1999b; Semetko, van der Brug, and Valkenburg 2003).

In chapter 9, which analyzes voting behavior, we will assess to what extent attitudes toward European integration affect party choice. In this chapter, we describe and explain these attitudes toward European integration. Thereby, we aim to achieve two things. First, we want to provide insight into country differences in support. Second, we want to assess which social and political groups in society support or reject the European project.

Research on EU support

When studying variations in support for European integration, we first have to conceptualize and measure the dependent variable. Previous studies have shown that attitudes toward Europe are of a multi-dimensional nature (e.g., Semetko, van der Brug, and Valkenburg 2003; Scheuer 2005; Niedermayer and Sinnott 1995; Gabel 1998a). However, some of these dimensions have been found to exist only in some of the countries. Some attitude dimensions were found to be unstable, and many specific attitudes that relate to particular aspects of integration have never been shown to affect party choice or other kinds of political behavior (e.g., Niedermayer and Sinnott 1995; Gabel 1998a). In this chapter, we will concentrate on an affective attitude dimension, of which it has been demonstrated that it can be measured in a comparable way in all countries of the EU. In contrast to evaluative attitudes that focus particularly on policy output, this dimension is rather stable and independent of external short-term political processes (Scheuer 2005). Because of its measurement characteristics, we can compare the distribution of attitudes on this dimension between the member states of the EU. We measure support for European integration on a three-point scale (range 0 to 2); country means on this scale are presented in figure 5.1.

Figure 5.1 demonstrates that the (average) support for European integration varies considerably between the populations of the member states, from a low of 0.51 in Sweden to a high of 1.28 in Luxembourg. The pattern shown in figure 5.1 confirms previous findings (Hewstone 1986; Inglehart and Reif 1991; Eichenberg and Dalton 1993; Gabel 1998a). Citizens of Luxembourg, Greece, Portugal, and the

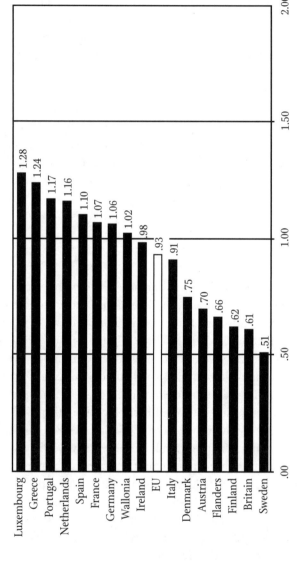

FIGURE 5.1 National levels of support for European integration

Data source: EES 1999.

Netherlands tend to be the strongest supporters of further European integration, whereas people in Sweden, Flanders, and Finland are least supportive. The following general patterns can be detected which were also found in earlier studies (Marsh 1995; Niedermayer 1995). The original six countries that founded the European Coal and Steel Community (Germany, France, Italy, the Netherlands, Belgium, and Luxembourg) all demonstrate high support for European integration (with the exception of the Flemish part of Belgium). The northern and western countries that joined later (Britain, Denmark, Sweden, and Finland) display comparatively low support (with the exception of Ireland). The southern countries that joined during the 1980s all register high support.

Much of the existing research on support for European integration aims not only at describing, but also at explaining differences between countries in EU support, which requires the use of country characteristics that can replace country names as explanatory variables (for an example in this field, see Eichenberg and Dalton 1993). In general two different kinds of explanations can be pursued to account for sources of country differences in support for European integration: contextual differences and differences in the distribution of individual-level determinants of such support for European integration. In what follows, we will first try to explain differences between countries in terms of individual-level determinants of EU support for integration. In a next step, we will assess to what extent country characteristics still add to the explanation while controlling for the effects of individual-level determinants of EU support. Finally, we will add contextual variables to explain the remaining differences.

EXPECTATIONS ABOUT EXPLANATORY FACTORS

Background variables

Two types of individual-level determinants of European attitudes can be thought to be relevant for explaining differences in support for European integration: socio-economic and political characteristics. Of the first category we investigate age, gender, urbanization of residence, religion, social class, and union membership.

It can be demonstrated that age is a determinant of support for European integration in two different ways (Scheuer 2005, 107). Age (or rather, year of birth) reflects first of all generational (or cohort) differences. Younger generations have been socialized in a world in which the already existing EU (or previously the EC or EEC) was an integral part. As a result, we expect them to be more supportive of the European integration than older generations who were socialized in times of war (or their immediate aftermaths) between countries that now share membership in the EU. On the basis of Scheuer's earlier work we also expect life-cycle effects, which express themselves in the age-differences in support for integration. Such differences may be due to different levels of political attentiveness in different stages of people's lives: quite little in their youth, more during their professional time, and again rather little when retired.

Gender is an individual characteristic with important and deep-rooted social consequences. A gender gap in support for European integration is regularly observed in opinion research, with women being less supportive than men (e.g., Rosch Inglehart 1995; Eurobarometer). Since European integration *per se* does not yield any disadvantages to women, there is no good explanation for this. Scheuer (2005, 101) presents causal analyses (path analyses) on the basis of 1994 data. She demonstrates that gender has no direct effect on EU support, but that it does exert an indirect effect via political attentiveness. When this variable is included in an explanatory model, the effect of gender disappears. In other words, apparent gender effects reflect differences in socialization and daily activities that result in women being less attentive to political affairs than men. The same is observed for education. Formal education is commonly found to be a determinant of support for European integration: the better educated are more likely to support integration than those with less formal education. This effect disappears after controlling for levels of political attentiveness (Scheuer 2005, 101). We include gender and education in our analyses here to replicate the analyses from 1994 with 1999 data.

Urban residence is expected to be important because living in capitals and big cities involves being connected to the nodes of worldwide communication networks. Moreover, cities profit more from international trade and exchange. Greater familiarity with other cultures is likely to positively affect support for European integration. Occupation describes an individual's position in the labor market, which shapes people's interests as well as their social environment and is thus likely to affect attitudes toward integration.

Social class and religion are important elements of the social environment into which individuals are socialized and which contribute to the formation of their goals, ambitions, and value orientations, and possibly also to their support for European integration. Although the importance of social class and religion as determinants of political values and behaviors (such as electoral behavior) has decreased substantially in most western democracies since the late 1960s (e.g., Franklin 1985, 1992), both variables are still systematically connected to political attitudes, the reason why they are included in our analyses. Finally, we include union membership as an independent variable. The European Union has promoted free trade and privatization of businesses—policies that were often strongly criticized by trade unions. Union membership is therefore expected to promote (critical) attitudes toward integration.

Political attitudes

In addition to socio-structural determinants of attitudes toward European integration, there are a number of political-attitudinal variables that can be expected to affect support for integration. The first of these is political attentiveness.[1] Citizens who are generally more attentive to politics are better informed and perhaps more familiar with advantages and disadvantages of European integration. This could affect their attitudes toward the EU; earlier studies suggest that this relationship is generally a positive one (Scheuer 2005, 120).

The European project has mainly been promoted by mainstream parties of the center-left and center-right. Opposition to the EU was most often voiced by radical right-leaning parties (with nationalist arguments), as well as by radical left-leaning parties and groups (who argue that the EU promotes free market capitalism). On this basis we may expect that citizens with different ideological positions on the left-right dimension will differ (in a curvilinear fashion) in their support for European integration.

Party identification is possibly important for attitudes toward integration as it is usually linked with trust in important political institutions, including European ones. Identification with a political party is conceptually divided into two components, strength and direction. Strength of party identification alone turned out to affect support for European integration by way of political attentiveness (Scheuer 2005, 103). With respect to direction, we expect that identification with a mainstream political party will have a different effect than identification with a radical right or radical left party because radical parties most often voice opposition to the European project. Therefore, we also tested for interaction effects between party identification and left-right extremity. Since these interaction effects turned out to be not significant, we do not present them in this chapter.

Finally, we include as independent variables three attitudinal variables in our analyses that describe the extent to which citizens are satisfied with the workings of European as well as national political institutions. These variables are: satisfaction with EU democracy, satisfaction with national democracy, and the approval of the record of the national government. We expect that citizens who are more satisfied with the way democracy works, as well as with the performance of the national government, will be more inclined to support European integration than those who are dissatisfied.

System characteristics

We have now described the individual-level determinants of EU support for European integration. What about systemic and contextual factors? We expect, first of all, that duration of membership of the EU matters. Countries became member of the EU at different times. The longer a country is member of the EU, the more its citizens will have grown accustomed to it, and the less resistant to integration they will be. A second contextual variable is the duration of democratic governance. Citizens in countries that have experienced a democracy for only a brief period of time when entering an integrating Europe (like Germany, Italy, Spain, Portugal, and Greece) may be more inclined to regard the EU as an institution that strengthens and safeguards the democratic character in their country, which we expect to increase support for integration. The third and fourth contextual variables relate to the economic benefits or costs associated with membership of the EU. Since British Prime Minister Margaret Thatcher's successful attempt to reduce Britain's payments to the EU in 1984, the issue of which countries are net contributors and which ones are net recipients became increasingly prominent and part of public awareness and discourse. We expect that citizens in net recipients will—again, *ceteris paribus*—be more supportive of integration than those from net contributors.

DATA AND OPERATIONALIZATION

For the analyses in this chapter we used survey data from the European Elections Studies 1999, which are described in detail in appendix A of this book. As in the other chapters, we distinguish sixteen political units, because we differentiate between two Belgian regions, Flanders and Wallonia. The dataset contains two indicators of attitudes toward European integration:

- *Membership:* "Generally speaking, do you think that [your country's] membership of the European Union is a good thing, a bad thing, or neither good nor bad?"
- *Push further:* "Some say European unification should be pushed further. Others say it already has gone too far. What is your opinion? Please indicate

your views using a ten-point scale. On this scale, 1 means unification 'has already gone too far' and 10 means it 'should be pushed further'. What number on this scale best describes your position? You may use any number between 1 and 10 to specify your views."

The first variable (membership) is one of the items that in previous research has been employed in scales measuring support for European integration. The structure of such scales is found to be stable across time and robust across countries (van der Eijk and Oppenhuis 1996; van der Eijk, Franklin, and van der Brug 1999; Scheuer 2005). Other items of this scale that were included in earlier studies were not part of the questionnaire of the EES 1999. The 'push further' item, however, was found to form a strong scale with the 'membership' item, which means that they both can be considered to be strong indicators of a single, unidimensional attitude. As this latter item was a (very strong) component of the support for integration scale documented in earlier studies, the resulting two-item scale that could be constructed from the 1999 data can conceptually and operationally be considered to be comparable with the more extensive scales in the studies reported above. To conclude: our dependent variable—support for European integration—is measured by the score on a two-item additive scale comprising the 'membership' and 'push further' items. The results of the scale analysis are reported in the appendix with this chapter.[2]

The individual-level determinants of EU support were treated as follows. In order to tap the possibly nonlinear effect of age, we created three dummy variables to distinguish four age groups. The youngest group consists of respondents of 18–39 years. This group is busy with education and settling their professional and familial life. The second group consists of those who are 40–54 years old. This group is in full professional life and charged with familial responsibility. The third group (55–69 years old) is completing professional careers and retires. The eldest group (70 years and older) is retired but has, of all four age groups, the most extensive memories of the world before European integration.

For 'urban residence', two dummy variables were constructed to distinguish three groups: rural areas, small towns, and large cities. Social class was measured with a survey question that invites respondents to indicate their own social class. Four groups are distinguished by dummy variables: 1) upper and upper middle class, 2) middle class, 3) lower middle class, and 4) working class.

Measuring religion in a comparative context often turns out to be difficult because denominations vary across countries. In addition, in some countries the variable is almost constant. As a case in point, 94 percent of the Greek respondents declared to be Greek Orthodox. To some extent, differences between religions coincide with the countries of origin, so that effects of religion may turn out to be spurious. In the analyses we will control for this. Four groups are distinguished: Roman Catholic, Protestant, Orthodox, and not religious. In addition, we include information about the importance of religion to citizens' personal lives. The best indicator for this is church attendance (how often does someone attend religious services). In contrast to denomination, this variable presents ample variance within each of the countries.

Levels of education are difficult to compare across countries. In the EES this was done by asking the respondent how old she was when she finished her last full-time education. We consider those who finish their education at a later age as better educated than those who finished earlier. Three levels of education were distinguished by means of dummies: low (finished education at age 15 or younger), medium (finished education at ages 16–20), and high (finished education at age 21 or older). Employment was likewise measured with dummies, distinguishing working, being in school, doing the household, being unemployed, and being retired. Union membership only has two categories (whether any member of the household is a member of a trade union or not). Political attentiveness is an additive scale of four indicators: 1) attention paid to news about politics, 2) attention paid to news about the economy, 3) interest in politics in general, and 4) interest in the European election campaign. These four items form a strong unidimensional scale that is robust across all sixteen countries.

Ideological positions are measured by asking respondents to indicate their position on a ten-point left-right scale, of which only the extremes are labeled (1 is labeled 'left' and 10 is labeled 'right'). In order to capture a potential nonlinear relationship between left-right ideology and EU support, we distinguished four ideological groups by means of dummy variables (1–3 is radical left, 4–5 is moderate left, 6–7 is moderate right, and 8–10 is radical right). Party identification is dichotomously measured with a question that asks respondents whether or not they consider themselves to be close to any particular party.

Satisfaction with EU democracy and satisfaction with national democracy were measured with the following survey questions: "On the whole are you very satisfied, fairly satisfied, not very satisfied, or not at all satisfied with the way democracy works in [name of your country] / the European Union?" The response categories of both questions are recoded into a dichotomy: 'very satisfied' and 'fairly satisfied' (coded 1) and 'not very satisfied' and 'not at all satisfied' (coded 0). Government approval, finally, is measured with the survey question: "Do you approve or disapprove of the government's record to date?" The response categories are 'approve' (coded 1) and 'disapprove' (coded 0).

The first two contextual determinants of EU-support are measured in a very straightforward way. Length of EU membership and length of democratic governance are measured in years (Inglehart 1997, 358). Whether a country is a net payer or net recipient is more difficult to establish because many of the EU subsidies are not structural. Moreover, various subsidies (such as those for scientific research) are given to international consortia, which makes it difficult to trace how much member states benefit from each of these subsidies. It is not very useful therefore to treat the variable (net sum of contributions and subsidies) as an interval variable. Moreover, being a net recipient may not have the opposite effect from being a net contributor. Therefore, we distinguished three groups of countries: those who were at the time of the European elections of 1999 net recipients on a structural basis (Greece, Portugal, Spain, Ireland, and France), those that were net contributors (Germany, the Netherlands, Austria, and Sweden), and the remaining countries that by and large 'broke even'. Two dummy variables were created to distinguish these three groups of countries.

Analyses

Figure 5.1 showed substantial differences in support for integration across the various EU member states. The two possible explanations that we distinguish are differences in distributions of individual-level determinants of support for integration on the one hand and contextual differences on the other. We will first explore the effects of individual-level determinants of support for integration. Table 5.1 describes the contrasts between the categories of our independent variables in terms of their means on the dependent variable support for integration (using the pooled data of all fifteen EU countries).

Table 5.1 shows that, on an EU-wide basis, a clear and linear relationship exists between levels of political attentiveness and EU support. The same is true of the effects of education and social class. The better educated, the more attentive, and those in higher social classes tend to be most supportive of European integration. In line with many previous studies, we also find men to be more supportive of European integration than women. Differences among the age groups are quite marginal, albeit that the oldest generation is somewhat less supportive of the EU than the younger generations. Support for the EU is somewhat higher in the cities, particularly large ones, than in rural areas. Those who attend religious services are more supportive of the EU than others. By and large, Catholics and Orthodox show more support for European integration than Protestants. People who identify with a political party are more supportive than people without party

Table 5.1 Mean support by groups across countries (data of all EU systems pooled)

Educational level			*Union membership*	
Low	0.83		Yes	0.97
Middle	0.89		No	0.85
High	1.03		*Political attentiveness*	
Social class			Lowest level	0.73
Working class	0.80		1	0.90
Lower middle class	0.83		2	0.94
Middle class	0.99		3	1.01
Upper middle class	1.13		Highest level	1.13
Upper class	1.17		*Party identification*	
Gender			Without PI	0.83
Men	1.02		With PI	1.04
Women	0.85		*Satisfaction with national democracy*	
Age			Dissatisfied	0.80
18–39 years	0.95		Satisfied	1.01
40–54 years	0.93		*Satisfaction with EU democracy*	
55–69 years	0.91		Dissatisfied	0.81
70+ years	0.89		Satisfied	1.12
Urbanization			*Approval of government record*	
Rural area	0.89		Disapprove	0.79
Small/middle town	0.93		Approve	1.07
Large town	0.99		*Left-right self-placement*	
Church attendance			Left	0.97
Church attendants	0.98		Center Left	0.94
Non attendants	0.92		Center Right	0.94
Religious denomination			Right	0.99
Roman Catholic	0.99		Don't know	0.77
Protestant	0.75			
Orthodox	1.23			
Not religious	0.89			
Occupational status				
Working	0.95			
In school	1.05			
Household	0.92			
Retired	0.89			
Unemployed	0.76			

identification. Those who are still in school or who are employed are more supportive of the EU than the unemployed, retired, and housewives. As expected, respondents who are more satisfied with the functioning of democracy in their own state and in Europe also tend to be more pro-integration, as are those who evaluate the government record positively.

The only unexpected finding in table 5.1 is that citizens at the radical left as well as citizens at the radical right tend to be marginally more in favor of integration than those who have more centrist ideological leanings. When compared, however, to those who do not (or cannot) place themselves in left-right terms, respondents at all positions of the left-right dimension score high on support for integration. Evidently then, the inability to use the most important political dimension in the political systems of the EU as a framework for describing one's own political views is strongly linked to lack of support for the integration process. Whether this signifies the importance of cognitive factors or of a kind of political alienation cannot be deduced from these findings.

The magnitude of the differences between the means of different groups of people is to some extent indicative of the strength of the relationship between the various factors and support for integration. It does not tell us, however, the strength of the effect of the independent variables on the dependent one. Moreover, we do not know whether such effects are the same in all countries. To answer these questions, we conducted a large series of regression analyses for each of the countries separately as well as for the pooled data set. We tested a number of multivariate models in a block-recursive fashion. The first group of independent variables to be included in the model consists of demographic variables, thereafter other social characteristics are added, and finally we included political-attitudinal variables. There is little to be gained from presenting all the details of all these regressions. We will focus on their explanatory power (adjusted R^2) in table 5.2 and subsequently on the regression effects in table 5.3. The R^2s in table 5.2 do not tell us whether the effects are similar in sign and magnitude across all countries, but we will comment upon this at the end of this section.

In most countries, the explained variance of the model increases gradually with the addition of each block of independent variables. In some cases, there is quite a 'jump' in R^2s when specific variables are added to the model. Examples of this are Italy and Sweden, where political attentiveness has a particularly strong effect on the model's explanatory power. In Italy, Denmark, and Sweden we find similar 'jumps' when left-right positions and party identification are included, and in Flanders and Denmark satisfaction with the EU democracy strongly contributes to R^2. In Flanders, finally, we find that satisfaction with national politics

Table 5.2 Explained variance by individual determinants of EU support (adjusted R^2)

Model	1	2	3	4	5	6	7	8
Austria	.04	.07	.08	.09	.11	.12	.14	.18
Belgium: Flanders	−.01	.03	.08	.10	.10	.10	.18	.26
Belgium: Wallonia	.01	.03	.10	.11	.11	.12	.12	.11
Britain	.01	.02	.05	.08	.10	.11	.12	.13
Denmark	.02	.05	.06	.07	.07	.10	.19	.21
Finland	.02	.05	.04	.06	.07	.06	.10	.12
France	.01	.02	.05	.05	.05	.06	.07	.09
Germany	.03	.05	.06	.11	.13	.14	.15	.17
Greece	.02	.03	.02	.05	.05	.06	.08	.13
Ireland	.01	.02	.03	.03	.03	.02	.06	.06
Italy	.01	.02	.03	.09	.09	.14	.17	.18
Luxembourg	−.00	.03	.05	.07	.07	.08	.08	.10
Netherlands	.02	.04	.06	.06	.06	.06	.08	.09
Portugal	.08	.10	.14	.16	.16	.16	.20	.24
Spain	.07	.08	.08	.13	.13	.15	.19	.19
Sweden	.04	.09	.09	.14	.14	.19	.23	.23
EU-15	*.01*	*.04*	*.05*	*.07*	*.10*	*.11*	*.14*	*.16*

Model 1: demography (gender, age);
Model 2: model 1 plus social conditions (social class, place of residence);
Model 3: model 2 plus social behavior (education, occupation, union membership);
Model 4: model 3 plus political attentiveness;
Model 5: model 4 plus religion (denomination, church attendance);
Model 6: model 5 plus ideological position (left-right and party identification);
Model 7: model 6 plus European political attitudes (satisfaction with EU democracy);
Model 8: model 7 plus national political attitudes (satisfaction with national democracy, government approval).
Note: In Italy the question about the respondent's place of residence is missing.

strengthens the explanation in particular. In most countries, however, all independent variables contribute a little to the explained variance. The most fully specified model (model 8) produces an R^2 of 16 percent in the pooled data (with country-specific values ranging between 9% and 26%), which is not very strong.

Table 5.3 Results of multivariate regression models (EU-wide analyses)

	Model A	Model B	Model C	Model D	Model E
Socio-economic factors					
Residence: Big cities	.029**	.023**	.023**	.025**	.022**
Class: middle	.109***	.075***	.052***	.069***	.053***
Class: upper (middle)	.122***	.085***	.059***	.068***	.060***
Education: high	.062***	.068***	.062***	.061***	.064***
Occupation: working	.041***	.045***	.051***	.036***	.049***
Occupation: in school	.043***	.048***	.049***	.049***	.048***
Union membership	−.084***	−.072***	−.008		
Political factors					
Political attentiveness		.125***	.147***	.137***	.148***
Catholic		.072***	.007		
Protestant		−.058***	.004		
Orthodox		.118***	.014		
Party identification		.088***	.048***	.086***	.048***
Satisfaction EU democracy		.144***	.119***	.119***	.119***
Satisfaction national democracy		.026**	.068***	.040***	.069***
Government approval		.134***	.119***	.133***	.119***
Contextual factors					
Duration of membership				.198***	.163***
Democratic experience				−.038**	−.322***
Net payer				.025**	.002
Net receiver				.188***	.161***
Country dummies					
Austria			−.196***		−.022*
Belgium: Flanders			−.155***		
Belgium: Wallonia			−.055*		.094***
Britain			−.202***		
Denmark			−.189***		
Finland			−.211***		.034**
France			−.071**		−.111***
Germany			−.068**		
Ireland			−.112***		
Italy			−.073**		
Luxembourg			−.026		.274***
The Netherlands			−.042		.105***
Portugal			−.025		−.038**
Spain			−.053*		−.070***
Sweden			−.243***		
R² Adjusted	.038	.146	.211	.173	.211

*** Significant at .001 level; ** Significant at .01 level; * Significant at .05 level.
In Model C the base category for country dummies is Greece.

Given the large number of factors included in model 8 and its weak explanatory power, the general conclusion must be that all kinds of social and political groups differ relatively little in terms of their (average) support for European integration. On average the explained variance in these sixteen systems is over 20 percent, somewhat higher than the 16 percent of explained variance in the pooled data. This suggests that either some of the differences in country averages (see figure 5.1) are not adequately accounted for by model 8 or that the effects of the independent variables are to some (limited) extent country specific. We will explore both possibilities.

Table 5.3 presents the regression coefficients of a number of models that were estimated on the pooled data. Model A is a model with only the socio-structural characteristics that exert significant effects on support for integration. The signs of the effects are in line with our earlier bivariate results (table 5.1). Yet, the very low R^2 of 3.8 percent implies that these social characteristics contribute only marginally to an explanation of individual differences in EU support.

When adding political-attitudinal variables to the model (model B), the R^2 increases to 14.6 percent which shows that these variables exert stronger effects than social characteristics. Most support for integration is found among those who are politically involved, who approve of the record of the government of their countries, and who are satisfied with the way the democracy in the EU works. Religious denominations also affect attitudes toward Europe. Some of these effects do not primarily reflect individual differences but differences in the composition of the populations of the various countries. This is shown by model C, in which we included country dummies in order to tap aggregate level differences among countries that cannot be explained by different distributions of individual-level variables. The addition of these country dummies increases explained variance by 6.5 percent (from 14.6% to 21.1%). This means that differences in distributions of the individual-level determinants of EU support do not explain all of the aggregate country differences that were described in figure 5.1. Had these aggregate differences been brought about by differences in the composition of national populations, none of the country dummies would yield significant coefficients. Differences in the distributions of individual-level variables do explain some of the aggregate differences among countries, however. This is evidenced by the fact that a model with only the fifteen country dummies explains 10.5 percent of the individual-level variance (not presented in table 5.3), whereas the increase in explained variance by the country dummies is only 6.5 percent.

Country dummies are rather uninformative, however. They just indicate that (average) support for integration differs between countries even after controlling for individual-level variables, but why this is so cannot be deduced from them.

The aim of comparative analysis is thus to replace the effects of country dummies (or, in Przeworski and Teune's [1970] terminology: *proper names*) by theoretically meaningful variables at the system level. Earlier in this chapter, we suggested such characteristics. We include these in model D and exclude the country dummies. We find that each of the system characteristics has a significant effect on support for integration. Duration of EU membership and duration of democratic governance have the kind of effects we expected. Support for integration is positively affected by length of EU membership and by the recency of non-democratic experiences (as is reflected in the negatively signed effect of the latter variable).

The third factor, whether a country is a net contributor or recipient, is represented by two dummy variables in model D. As was as expected, there is a positive effect on support for integration by one's country being a net recipient. Somewhat unexpected, however, is that living in a net-contributing country also has a positive effect (both categories have to be contrasted to the base category, which consists of countries that more or less 'break even'). In this case, the causal chain could also point in the opposite direction. Countries in which integration is strongly supported could be somewhat more willing to contribute to the EU. In any case, these findings indicate that—as far as support for integration is concerned—financial balances are not a zero-sum game. There is clear evidence that receiving money from the EU enhances support for integration, without being a net contributor decreasing it.

Model D explains 17.3 percent of the variance in support for integration, which is 3.8 percent less than model C, but 1.7 percent more than model B. This means that only some, but not all of the country differences can be explained by the individual and country-level variables included in the model. Yet, in view of the fact that a model with only the country dummies explained 10.5 percent of the variance, we can conclude that most of the country differences can be accounted for by the variables included in model D. Model E extends model D by—again—including country dummies in a stepwise procedure. We see that the number of significant country dummies is reduced, as could be expected from the inclusion of system-level variables in the model. For some country dummies, the effect has even reversed sign. In principle, one could use the coefficients of the country dummies for generating hypotheses about omitted system-level variables. Inspection of the coefficients did not, however, lead to specific suggestions in this respect. Therefore, we refrain here from drawing substantive conclusions from the effects of these dummies.

A potential complication that we have not yet assessed is that the effects of the individual-level variables may vary between systems, in their magnitude and even in their sign. Modeling such differences would require interaction effects between the country dummies on the one hand and the individual-level variables on the other. To check whether or not we should include such interactions in the model we used the following procedure. First, we estimated model B for the pooled data (i.e., for all systems combined), and we saved the residuals. These residuals represent the part of the variance not explained by this pooled analysis. Then we selected one of the countries and estimated a regression model with the same independent variables and the residuals as the dependent variable. If a significant interaction exists, it will manifest itself in the form of a significant coefficient in this latter regression analysis. This procedure was repeated for each of the sixteen countries in turn.

As model B contains fifteen individual-level variables and as we have sixteen political systems, we test with this procedure for each of 240 different interactions whether or not it is significantly different from zero. Standard significance tests will find a few of them significant, even if the null-hypothesis of no effect is true. To be on the safe side, we should only look for interaction effects that are significant at $p < 0.001$. The main conclusion of this extensive exploration of 240 interaction effects is that only twelve of them were found to be significant.[3] This leads to two complementary conclusions. First, minor variations exist between systems in the relationship between the independent variables and support for European integration. Second, the general pattern of relationships between dependent and individual-level independent variables is remarkably robust, reason for us to accept model E (without interactions) as a satisfactory model.

Conclusions and Implications

In this chapter, we explored the differences in support for European integration among countries and individual citizens. We found that the degree of support differs considerably between the different political systems of the EU. The pattern of differences is in concordance with previous research: support is lowest among the Scandinavian countries, Britain, Austria, and the Flemish part of Belgium, and it is highest in Luxembourg and the Mediterranean member states. As our measure of support is comparable across these systems, these differences are not mere artifacts but empirical findings that stand in need of explanation. Our first line of explanation was by way of individual-level characteristics: to the extent that populations differ in the proportions of the kinds of people that tend to be high (or conversely: low) in support, population averages in support will differ as well. Our second line of explanation focused on country characteristics. Countries may differ in ways that are intelligibly linked to levels of support. Moreover, these same differences may affect the way in which individuals differ in support.

Individual-level differences in support for integration do indeed exist. They help to explain part of the differences between countries' average support rates. This illustrates the relevance of (variations in) the composition of populations in terms of the independent variables we employed. Some groups of citizens turned out to be somewhat more supportive of European integration than others. The most supportive groups are in particular those who are better educated, more politically involved, who have more confidence in the way democracy works (at the national and at the EU level), and who approve of the performance of their national government. This last finding demonstrates the existence of a spill-over between attitudes toward the national and European levels of governance. In general, attitudes toward the domestic and the European political system are not compensating each other: negative attitudes toward domestic politics do *not* result in positive ones toward the European system (or the other way around). Rather, more generalized political attitudes seem to exist that are expressed toward the domestic as well as the European level (cf. van der Eijk and Oppenhuis 1990).[4]

Our analyses showed that only a small part of the individual-level differences in support for European integration are explained by the independent variables used. As these variables cover most of what is suggested as relevant explanatory variables in the literature, the general conclusion is that support for and opposition against integration is not very concentrated in specific groups, but widely dispersed instead. A corollary of this conclusion is that all kinds of groups in a population are bound to be internally divided in this respect. This is also the case for groups that can be distinguished by their ideological (left-right) positions (see also van der Eijk and Franklin 2004), which implies that parties that attempt to politicize the issue of European integration (to promote more integration, or to oppose it) run the risk of losing the support of many of their (potential) supporters.

The extent to which country differences in average support for integration can be explained by the distributions of individual-level independent variables is quite small. We gain some explanatory power by looking at characteristics of political systems rather than of individuals. Support is somewhat higher the longer a country is member of the EU, the shorter its history is of democratic governance, and when it is a net recipient. The implication hereof for the ten new member states of 2004 is that their populations' support for integration—clearly demonstrated in the referenda on admission to the EU—will not be sustained by duration of membership, which will be short for some time to come. This will in all likelihood be compensated, however, by their recent democratic transformations and by any positive balance of financial transfers, were that to materialize.[5] These effects of system characteristics have an across-the-board nature, as hardly any of the interactions between country and individual variables were found to be significant. However, these system characteristics explain only about two-fifths of the variance in average support between the countries, which implies that some major sources of the differences illustrated in figure 5.1 remain unknown.

The political relevance of (differences in) support for integration is particularly to be found in the realm of the legitimacy of the existing Union, and of the changes it will experience in the years to come. In a very specific form, such support may be important in future referenda on (further) integration, or on the outcomes of the constitution-building process.[6] The lack of support for the 'EU constitution' in referenda held in 2005 in the Netherlands and France, two of the founding countries of the EU, is rather surprising, particularly in view of our finding that length of membership has a positive effect on EU support. However, in many cases, votes cast in such referenda reflect only partially the more generic support for the EU. Other considerations, such as lack of support for the government, as well as particular aspects of the topics of the referenda decide whether new steps in the direction of further integration will be publicly supported. This issue will be addressed in more detail in the postscript. Whether or not support for integration is of importance for individual-level behavior, e.g., for party choice in European elections, is not predicated by this, and will be assessed as a separate question in chapter 9 of this book.

Appendix

Two variables in the analyses reported in this chapter are composite scores, which combine information from (answers to) different survey questions. One of these is the dependent variable used in this chapter (support for European integration), the other is one of the most important individual-level independent variables (political attentiveness). To assess the validity of these combinations, Mokken scaling was employed (Mokken 1971). The most important diagnostic to assess whether items form a scale is the H-value (which is a measure of the homogeneity or unidimensionality of the items). Mokken gives the following criteria to interpret these values:

Table 5.A.1 Scaling coefficients (H-values) for the two Mokken scales employed in this study

	EU-support	Political attentiveness
Austria	.61	.46
Belgium: Flanders	.48	.60
Belgium: Wallonia	.45	.55
Britain	.59	.51
Denmark	.62	.51
Finland	.53	.49
France	.48	.50
Germany	.70	.55
Greece	.34	.43
Ireland	.35	.43
Italy	.49	.46
Luxembourg	.79	.52
Netherlands	.78	.51
Portugal	.56	.72
Spain	.47	.68
Sweden	.53	.41

H < 0.30	no scale
0.30 ≤ H < 0.40	weak scale
0.40 ≤ H < 0.50	medium scale
H ≥ 0.50	strong scale

Table 5.A.1 presents the H-values of the Mokken scales for all systems. These results show that the scalability of the items is robust across all EU member states. The strength of both scales is satisfactory in all systems, often even quite strong.

Notes

1. To measure political attentiveness, we combined a number of separate items, after having assessed with Mokken scaling that they clearly surpass requirements for unidimensionality. For details, see table 5.A.1 in the appendix of this chapter.

2. In this study, we employ the same dependent variable in all sixteen different countries. The validity of our analyses depends largely on the question whether the dependent variable has the same meaning in all countries. For practical purposes, it would be easiest to use the original ten-point scale of the unification item as our measure of the dependent variable. Single-item measurement, however, leaves no room for assessing construct validity and comparability, other than by *fiat*. When using multiple items, a more rigorous test can be derived from Mokken scaling (e.g., Mokken 1971; Jacoby 1991). The values for the unidimensionality of the items are all well above minimum requirements in this respect (see table 5.A.1 in the appendix of this chapter). For the purpose of the scaling analyses, the 'membership' item was coded 'Good thing' = 1 and 'Neither good nor bad', 'Bad thing', DK, NA = 0. The 'push further' item was coded 8–10 = 1 and 1–7, DK, NA = 0.

3. When testing 240 interaction effects, standard significance tests will in many cases find a few of them being significant, even when the null-hypothesis of no effect is true. In order not to capitalize on chance, we describe here only the twelve effects that were significant at $p < 0.001$. In Austria significant negative interaction effects were found for 'Roman Catholic' and 'Protestant' and the adjusted R^2 of a model to explain the residuals is 0.04. In Flanders significant interaction effects were found for 'high education' (positive) and 'government approval' (positive), and the adjusted R^2 of a model to explain the residuals is 0.10. In Wallonia significant interaction effects were found for 'union membership' (positive) and 'being still in school' (positive), and the adjusted R^2 of a model to explain the residuals is 0.06. In Britain no significant interaction effects were found, and the adjusted R^2 of a model to explain the residuals is 0.01. In Denmark a positive significant interaction effect was found for 'satisfaction with the EU democracy', and the adjusted R^2 of a model to explain the residuals is 0.04. In Finland no significant interaction effects were found, and the adjusted R^2 of a model to explain the residuals is 0.01. In France no significant interaction effects were found, and the adjusted R^2 of a model to explain the residuals is 0.01. In Germany a significant positive interaction effect was found for 'satisfaction with the national democracy', and the adjusted R^2 of a model to explain the residuals is 0.04. In Greece no significant interaction effects were found, and the adjusted R^2 of a model to explain the residuals is 0.02. In Ireland a significant positive interaction effect was found for 'political attentiveness', and the adjusted R^2 of a model to explain the residuals is 0.06. In Italy no significant interaction effects were found, and the adjusted R^2 of a model to explain the residuals is 0.01. In Luxembourg a significant negative interaction effect was found for 'still studying', and the adjusted R^2 of a model to explain the residuals is 0.03. In the Netherlands no significant interaction effects were found, and the adjusted R^2 of a model to explain the residuals is 0.00. In Portugal significant positive interaction effects were found for 'being employed' and 'still studying' and the adjusted R^2 of a model to explain the residuals is 0.05. In Spain no significant interaction effects were found, and the adjusted R^2 of a model to explain the residuals is 0.02. In Sweden no significant interaction effects were found, and the adjusted R^2 of a model to explain the residuals is 0.05.

4. This interpretation is consistent with findings that citizens sometimes use referenda about (further) European integration as opportunities to cast a vote of non-confidence in the current government (Franklin, Marsh, and McLaren 1994; Franklin, Marsh, and Wlezien 1994; Franklin, van der Eijk, and Marsh 1995).

5. This same logic suggests a somewhat different outcome for Malta, which has a much longer tradition of democratic governance, and which will most likely benefit less from transfer payments than the new member states in Eastern Europe or Cyprus. Support for integration will therefore be more vulnerable to erosion in Malta than in the other new member states.

6. This statement is not in contradiction with the findings of spill-over of support for domestic and European politics as that operates in a superimposed fashion on top of levels of support generated by other factors (e.g., system characteristics).

CHAPTER

The media and European Parliament elections: Second-rate coverage of a second-order event?

CLAES H. DE VREESE, EDMUND LAUF,
AND JOCHEN PETER

European elections are often referred to as second-order national elections. Following the first elections for the European Parliament in 1979, Reif and Schmitt (1980) asserted that European elections are not essentially about 'Euro-politics' but about national, domestic politics. As a result citizens rely mainly on their relationship to the domestic political arena when deciding whether and how to vote. Reif and Schmitt (1980) offer three propositions about second-order elections: first, turnout is likely to be lower; second, national government parties are likely to suffer losses in European Parliament elections; and, third, larger political parties are likely to do less well than smaller parties. The second-order election model has been tested, refined, and largely supported in subsequent European elections (e.g., Oppenhuis, van der Eijk, and Franklin 1996; Marsh 1998).

So far, the second-order election perspective has not been used in the analysis of the media. This is surprising. After all, media play a crucial role in the linkage between citizens and the political realm. Citizens' experiences with politics are largely mediated by the mass media (e.g., Swanson and Mancini 1996; Bennett and Entman 2001). Even more so than for domestic politics is this the case for a distant institution such as the European Parliament, its elections, and the accompanying campaigns (e.g., Blumler 1983).

This chapter analyses news coverage of the campaigns of the European elections of 1999 and tests a number of expectations that can be derived from the second-order election literature and from previous research on contextual differences between second-order elections. Studies of election outcomes and voter behavior demonstrate that a second-order election's location in the domestic electoral cycle affects the extent of government and big party losses (Oppenhuis, van der Eijk, and Franklin 1996; Marsh 1998; also chapters 1, 2, and 3 of this volume). Other studies suggest that the extent of polarization of elite opinions affects the presence or absence of public debates about Europe and its effects on public opinion (Peter 2003).

This chapter addresses three main aspects of news coverage of the elections and their campaigns: *visibility* of the coverage, presentation as a *domestic* or *European* political contest, and *tone* of the coverage. For the first two aspects we analyze the impact of the aforementioned contextual differences.

Expectations

The logic of second-order election theory and findings in previous research give rise to clear expectations about the three aspects of news coverage we want to analyze. As far as *visibility* is concerned, we first of all expect this to be low in the case of European elections in comparison to coverage of first-order domestic elections. In view of the low salience of European elections for voters and parties, we could hardly expect their visibility in the media to be very high.

The most encompassing study of a campaign for the European elections so far dates back to the first European election in 1979 (Blumler 1983). A comparative analysis of television coverage in all member states of the (then) EC showed that 'Europe' did not surface on the media agenda before the actual campaign started. However, as the campaign progressed, the amount of television attention to the European elections increased (Siune 1983). Media coverage and political communication were hardly investigated during later European elections. One of the few available studies concluded that, while the first elections did receive some degree of media coverage because of the novelty of the event, this aspect had already vanished from the second elections (in 1984) onward. As of the second time around, the campaign was 'nothing special' (Leroy and Siune 1994, 52–53).

However, no previous analyses of media investigated whether cross-national variation in the visibility of news coverage of the election campaign can be linked to contextual factors such as polarized elite opinion and the timing of the European elections in the domestic electoral cycle. From what we know about such variations in election results and in the behavior of voters and parties, we expect that the European elections will be more prominent in the news in countries that are close to an upcoming general election because the relevance of these elections in the domestic political arena is then largest (for an extended presentation of this argument, see Oppenhuis, van der Eijk, and Franklin 1996). We also expect more prominent coverage in countries where elite opinion on European integration is polarized as the presence of such differences of opinion increases the news value of the election and the campaign.

With respect to the *presentation* of the elections and the campaign in domestic or European terms, the logic of the second-order model suggests that a domestic frame will be strongly dominant. After the 1979 election for the European Parliament, it was concluded that the news coverage was in most countries predominantly Europe-oriented (Siune 1983, 235–236), although in quite a few countries a strong 'domestic pull' exerted itself on the news. However, as the 'novelty' aspect of European elections has worn off, a stronger emphasis on domestic matters can be expected. Contrary to this expectation one could argue that the increasing amount of autonomy and legislative power that has been transferred since 1979 from the member states to 'Brussels' will lead to a stronger presentation of the European aspects of the elections. A study of the 1989 elections, however, found that most of the coverage of the European elections was domestic in nature with only little reference to the European dimensions of the issues in question (Leroy and Siune 1994).

From the second-order election perspective and previous research about the effects of the domestic electoral cycle, we expect that media coverage of European elections will be more domestic (as opposed to European) in countries that are close to an upcoming general election. Moreover, because elite disagreement over matters concerning European integration exists primarily between domestic political actors, we also expect election coverage to be more domestic in countries where such elite opinions are polarized.

As far as the *tone* of coverage is concerned, the second-order election perspective does not directly yield any expectations. Low visibility and dominance of the domestic political arena may coexist with either a positive or a negative tone of the news. However, the tone of news is one of the most important characteristics of news coverage. Positive or negative coverage of candidates, institutions, and political parties can affect voters' perception of and preference for these (Herr 2002; McCombs, Lopez-Escobar, and Llama 2000; Norris et al. 1999). We expect the news to be, by and large, neutral or slightly negative with respect to the objects covered. This expectation flows from the findings in studies of national news which demonstrate the existence of a so-called 'negativity' bias (e.g., Kepplinger 1998, 2002).

DATA AND OPERATIONALIZATION

In this chapter we focus exclusively on television news. Television has repeatedly been identified as the most important source of information about European issues (Eurobarometer 54, 2001) and television is generally seen as the most influential mass medium (e.g., Chaffee and Kanihan 1997).[1] During the campaign, television news in all countries of the EU was videotaped.[2] We selected for each country two news programs, one each from the public and private channels with the largest audience. A complete listing of the networks and news programs included is given in appendix B of this volume. The data collection covered the two weeks preceding Election Day because the news tends to cluster toward the end of the campaign (Leroy and Siune 1994; Siune 1983).

The contents of the taped news bulletins were coded by native speakers of each of the languages involved. Coders were trained by the research team at the University of Amsterdam, which also supervised the coding process. The coding scheme was extensively pre-tested to fit the news bulletins from different countries. The unit of analysis and of coding was the news story (defined as semantic entity with at least one topic) and all stories in each news bulletin were coded. Ultimately, we coded 369 news bulletins containing a total 5,479 news stories. Stories were coded in terms of length, place in the respective news bulletin (first, second, etc.), topic, and, if it was political in character, the actors involved and their characteristics.[3] Inter-coder reliability tests are reported in the appendix.

We are interested in the effect of two contextual variables—the location of the European elections in the domestic electoral cycle and the nature of elite opinion on issues of European integration—on the visibility of news about the European elections and on the 'Europeanness' of the news coverage. We use the distance to the next national election (expressed in number of months) as our indicator of the location of the European elections in the domestic electoral cycle. For each country we created a dummy variable expressing the presence (1) or absence (0) of polarized elite opinion. The presence or absence of polarized elite opinion about the EU was operationalized in terms of the existence of a sufficiently visible anti-EU party. An anti-EU party was defined as a party that had, in a survey among experts (Ray 1999), received on average a score of 2 or lower (*opposed to*

European integration) on a seven-point scale.[4] Because the influence of a *sufficiently visible* anti-EU party is to be assessed, parties had to have gained at least 5 percent of the votes in the latest general election (assessed with reference to the year 1999).

Kosovo and poisoned chickens: The competitive news environment during the campaign

The visibility of an event or topic in the news depends on what it has to 'compete' with in terms of newsworthiness. Across potential topics, visibility is a fixed-sum characteristic, the sum being determined by the length of the news bulletin. This is no different for European elections than it is for any other topic or event. During national elections, the campaign is often 'upgraded' in the allocation of additional resources, journalists, and time in the news program to cover the elections (e.g., Blumler and Gurevitch 2001). For the 1999 European elections this was not the case. Though several news programs initiated advance planning and increased staff and research budgets, none of the news programs designated a special segment to the European elections (de Vreese 2003b).

There is always a multitude of other events that compete for attention and visibility, but during the weeks preceding the European elections of 1999 the competition was particularly stiff. The Kosovo conflict had entered its hottest phase in the form of military intervention by NATO forces. News of atrocities against civilians, of bombing raids, casualties, and dramatic suffering captured the headlines during the two weeks leading up to the June elections. In addition, a food-safety scandal in Belgium generated considerable unrest in that country and many of its neighbors. Dioxin pollution in chicken food caused a widespread scare about health hazards of poultry and eggs. Earlier food-safety problems and bio-industry epidemics (BSE, foot and mouth disease, etc.) had primed media and public opinion for a strong reaction to a problem that, in retrospect, was of a relatively minor nature.

We coded the topics of new stories by means of a set of eleven categories. One of these was devoted specifically to the European elections, one other to 'other EU-related news' during the campaign. The other categories concerned specific topics such as 'Kosovo' and 'food safety' that played an important role during the campaign while yet other ones were more general such as 'economy'.[5] Using these categories, table 6.1 shows the visibility of each of these topics in the two weeks leading up to the European elections of 1999.[6]

Table 6.1 Visibility of the campaign on television

Country	EP-elections	Other EU-topics	Party and governmental	Economy	Food safety	Law and order	Foreign affairs	Kosovo	Disaster & Human Interest	Sport	Misc.	Total N
Austria	12 (16)	5 (6)	5 (9)	3 (7)	4 (6)	3 (6)	8 (13)	32 (25)	12 (20)	<1 (5)	14 (29)	142
Belgium	2 (16)	1 (5)	15 (122)	3 (35)	48 (435)	4 (45)	<1 (6)	13 (106)	5 (81)	5 (75)	4 (40)	966
Britain	5 (10)	1 (3)	8 (19)	3 (14)	4 (14)	4 (15)	6 (17)	46 (82)	8 (31)	13 (46)	<1 (3)	254
Denmark	13 (24)	<1 (2)	9 (30)	7 (20)	3 (15)	6 (23)	8 (21)	30 (60)	17 (52)	2 (6)	5 (19)	272
Finland	8 (20)	3 (10)	14 (39)	8 (21)	3 (13)	10 (28)	2 (7)	37 (83)	2 (15)	2 (8)	12 (29)	273
France	12 (51)	<1 (3)	5 (42)	3 (31)	13 (71)	5 (61)	1 (12)	43 (227)	4 (45)	6 (49)	8 (55)	647
Germany	<1 (2)	2 (9)	11 (34)	6 (43)	8 (27)	5 (26)	2 (10)	33 (62)	15 (75)	14 (57)	3 (16)	361
Greece	8 (72)	2 (11)	2 (24)	2 (15)	14 (50)	25 (120)	2 (16)	15 (80)	15 (97)	11 (90)	4 (35)	610
Ireland	3 (3)	3 (2)	11 (10)	5 (7)	4 (7)	10 (18)	11 (13)	29 (22)	7 (11)	10 (22)	7 (10)	125
Italy	8 (26)	1 (6)	4 (17)	4 (28)	7 (24)	12 (47)	1 (4)	31 (98)	9 (43)	16 (42)	8 (35)	370
Netherlands	2 (2)	<1 (2)	33 (62)	4 (15)	10 (18)	7 (24)	1 (9)	25 (29)	8 (33)	2 (9)	7 (16)	219
Portugal	27 (34)	2 (5)	16 (59)	4 (27)	6 (22)	3 (26)	2 (23)	18 (42)	8 (52)	9 (51)	5 (30)	371
Spain	3 (13)	<1 (3)	8 (50)	4 (32)	8 (43)	5 (38)	2 (17)	27 (123)	12 (82)	27 (167)	3 (29)	597
Sweden	12 (23)	3 (7)	12 (36)	4 (24)	3 (11)	22 (62)	3 (10)	28 (48)	6 (26)	2 (13)	4 (12)	272
All countries	8 (312)	2 (74)	11 (553)	4 (319)	10 (756)	9 (539)	3 (178)	29 (1087)	9 (663)	9 (640)	6 (358)	(5479)

Note: Entries are percentage of length for a particular topic in all countries (sum of length per topic in all countries [sum of length per topic divided by total length]. In brackets: number of stories.

Table 6.1 shows clearly that the election campaign was heavily dominated by the events in former Yugoslavia. The national news programs in the countries of the European Union devoted, on average, almost one-third of their time to the events in Kosovo. The saliency of the elections was low in comparison with other topics as well as in absolute terms. In total, 312 news stories were devoted to the European elections on the news programs in all the EU countries. The average time spent on the election for all EU member states was 8 percent. Belgium, Britain, Germany, Ireland, the Netherlands, and Spain devoted even less than 5 percent of the news to the elections. Austria, Denmark, Finland, France, Greece, Italy, and Sweden are somewhat above average, spending 8 percent to 13 percent of the news on European elections, while television news in Portugal outdid all other countries with 27 percent of the news dealing with the elections.

Clearly, the European elections were not center stage on the news agenda during the election campaign. This is underscored by a different indicator of visibility that involves the place of items in the ordering of an entire news bulletin. Topics that are considered most important and pertinent by journalists are typically placed at the beginning of a news program rather than at the end. We coded this place and averaged it over bulletins in such a way that a score of 0 for a topic means that this topic was, on average, placed as the middle story in a news program. A score of -10 means that a topic is placed 10 percent after the average story and so forth. Figure 6.1 reports the relative place of the European elections in the news programs across Europe.

News about the European elections was typically placed in the second part of news bulletins, as is indicated by the negative values in figure 6.1. This pattern holds for most countries. Only in Austria, Ireland, and Spain was news about the European elections (on average) placed early in the news programs. The single issue that scored highest in this respect was the Kosovo conflict (not shown in figure 6.1). This news was almost always located in the first part of the news programs, ahead of all other topics.

The conclusion of these two analyses is that the visibility of the European elections in terms of amount of time and placement in the bulletin was typically low in the national television news programs. Although there is little hard comparative information, all country-specific studies we know indicate that the visibility of the European elections is considerably lower than for the visibility of national (first-order) elections.[7]

As discussed above, we expect systematic variation between countries in visibility as a function of the context within which these second-order elections take place: their location in the domestic electoral cycle, and the presence or absence

FIGURE 6.1 Importance of the European elections in the news by story number

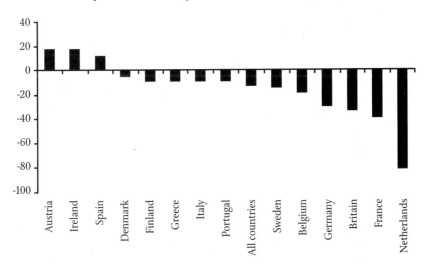

of polarized elite opinion on European integration. To test this we estimated a regression model, the results of which are presented in table 6.2.

We did not find any support for the expectation that the European elections were more visible in the news in countries in which national elections were approaching. Distance to the next general election was not significantly associated

Table 6.2 Visibility of EP elections in television news

	beta	b	S.E.
Constant		2.90	(1.42)
			t = 2.04
Polarized elite opinion (1 = yes)	0.86	7.51	(1.42)
			t = 5.31
Distance to next general election (in months)	0.16	0.05	(0.05)
			t = 0.98
R^2		0.74	
N		13	

Note: Luxembourg is excluded due to missing content data. Portugal is excluded as a single outlier case.

with the amount of news coverage. The presence of polarized elite opinion was, however, a strong positive predictor of the amount of news coverage of the elections. Indeed, political rows over European issues tend to be institutionalized within existing, national party–political structures in the *de facto* absence of a European-level party system (Mair 2000).

A Union without face or voice: A domestic or a European election?

So far, we focused our analysis on the visibility and priority of the news coverage of the European elections. We now turn to the domestic or European nature of the news coverage. To investigate the 'Europeanness' of the event, we use two indicators. First of all, we assessed whether the actors involved in news stories were domestic or European in character. Our second indicator distinguishes whether the location where the news took place and the location ostensibly affected by the news topic were domestic, European, or otherwise.

Our first indicator derives from similar work by McQuail and Bergsma (1983), who also assessed the visibility of *European* level versus *domestic* actors in the news. We identified the nationality of the actor except when she or he was to be considered a *European* actor. We defined as European actors institutions such as the Commission, the Parliament, and the European Central Bank and persons directly affiliated with these institutions, such as MEPs, members of the Commission, etc.[8] This indicator covers almost all news stories about the European elections as no fewer than 295 of the 312 relevant stories portrayed one or several actors that could be coded in this manner.

From table 6.3, we learn that (Europe-wide) no more than 7 percent of the actors in the news were EU-level actors, 9 percent 'other' (typically from NATO), and no less than 83 percent domestic.[9] This emphasizes strongly the second-order national character of news content during the campaign of the European elections. When looking at the results with the news story as a unit of analysis (not shown in table 6.3), we find that more than 80 percent of the relevant news stories did not contain a single European actor. To put it bluntly: since the European elections were overwhelmingly represented by domestic actors from the different countries, the European Union was an entity without a face.

The picture becomes only more dismal when we look at Europe's 'voice'. Arguably a mere count of the presence of actors is only part of the story about the importance of actors in the news. Quoting an actor in a news story gives her or

Table 6.3 Percentage of EU actors, domestic actors, and other actors in EU election stories

Country	EU actors	Domestic actors	Other
Austria (n = 74)	18	61	21
Belgium (n = 45)	4	60	36
Britain (n = 45)	4	96	0
Denmark (n = 109)	16	78	6
Finland (n = 62)	5	65	31
France (n = 200)	7	85	8
Germany (n = 3)	0	67	33
Greece (n = 260)	8	88	4
Ireland (n = 18)	0	100	0
Italy (n = 130)	3	89	8
Netherlands (n = 11)	64	36	0
Portugal (n = 133)	1	97	2
Spain (n = 28)	18	82	0
Sweden (n = 97)	1	77	22
All countries (n = 1,215)	7	83	9
	(n = 86)	(n = 1,006)	(n = 123)

Note: Percentages do not all add up to 100 due to rounding errors. The 86 EU actors were mentioned in 55 news stories, which equals 19% of the total number of EU stories.

him additional presence and weight. We therefore analyzed also the distribution of quotes. In all the stories about the European elections, EU-level actors delivered 4 percent of the quotes whereas domestic actors provided 89 percent. In other words, the European Union had neither a face nor a voice during the campaign for the European elections.

Our second measure of 'Europeanness' of the news involved the locations where the news took place and where the content of the news was said to be felt. A BBC news story, for example, from Frankfurt, Germany, about the impact of the exchange rate of the euro for British exports was coded as Germany (location of the news) and Britain (location affected). A story on the Italian RaiUno about an Italian candidate would be coded as 'Italy' for both measures. These two 'location' measures indicate the degree to which news about the European elections was predominantly domestic or European in nature. On average, more than 85 percent of the news was reported domestically (from the country of the respective news program) and it strongly emphasized domestic implications.[10]

Table 6.4 'Europeanness' of EP elections in television news (percentage EU actors)

	beta	b	S.E.
Constant		25.47	(9.32)
			t = 2.73
Polarized elite opinion (1 = yes)	–.11	–3.62	(9.27)
			t = –.39
Distance to next general election (in months)	–.50	–.58	(.32)
			t = –1.79
R^2		.25	
N		13	

Note: Luxembourg is excluded due to missing content data. Portugal is excluded as a single outlier case.

Having established that the logic of the second-order election model extends to the 'Europeanness' of media coverage, we still have to address the question of the relevance of differences in the context within which these elections take place. Earlier, we elaborated on the expectation that news coverage was likely to be more strongly domestic in a context of upcoming domestic elections and in countries with polarized elite opinions on European integration. To test this expectation, we estimated a regression model, which is presented in table 6.4.

The results show that the data do not support these expectations. Even though there were somewhat fewer European actors—and more domestic actors—in countries with upcoming national elections, this effect is not statistically significant.

Neutral or negative: The tone of the coverage

We finally turn to the *tone* of the news coverage. The second-order election perspective and the nature of elite opinion do not yield any expectations about the tone. Positive or negative coverage of candidates, institutions, and political parties may, however, affect voters' perceptions and preferences. For each of the actors portrayed in the news we analyzed whether she, he, or it was evaluated. Evaluations may either be unfavorable (e.g., negative aspects, emphasis on failure, unresolved problems) or favorable (e.g., positive aspects, emphasis on success, problems solved, successful solutions) or mixed (combining positive and negative aspects). We aggregated all the individual evaluations to arrive at an overall view of the tone of the coverage. This is measured on a scale ranging from −100 to +100. This overall tone is assessed for different kind of actors: EU actors, domestic actors, and other (international) actors. A score of 0 means that the actors received neutral or balanced coverage (on average), a negative score means that the actors received more negative than positive coverage and a positive score indicates the reverse.

Table 6.5 gives an overview of the tone of the news coverage of these different groups of actors. Most actors were treated neutrally and if they were evaluated this was in an unfavorable direction. This dovetails with Siune's (1983) observations about the news coverage of the 1979 European elections and Kepplinger's (1998) work on national elections. However, of the three groups of actors, EU actors were evaluated most unfavorably in the news. Combined with the results from the previous section, we can therefore conclude that EU actors were only marginally present in the news and when they were presented they were evaluated slightly more negatively than other actors.

Table 6.5 Evaluation of actors in EU election stories

Country	EU actors	Domestic actors	Other	Mean all actors
Austria	0	−2	0	−1
Belgium	0	−4	−6	−4
Britain	0	12	—	11
Denmark	−24	−11	0	−12
Finland	0	−8	−5	−6
France	−23	−7	0	−7
Germany	—	0	0	0
Greece	−44	−20	−18	−22
Ireland	—	6	—	6
Italy	0	−9	−18	−9
Netherlands	−14	0	—	−9
Portugal	0	0	0	0
Spain	80	35	—	39
Sweden	0	−7	0	−5
All countries	−15	−7	−5	−8
Cases (n)	86	1006	123	1215

Note: Mean ranging from −100 to +100.

Discussion

At the outset of the chapter, we argued that the news and information environment during an election is of great importance. News media provide information and cues which voters may be exposed to and which may affect their decision to turn out to vote and how to vote and which may shape political evaluations that persist even beyond the elections. Drawing on the model of second-order elections, we hypothesized that news coverage of European elections and their campaigns would be low in visibility and low in 'Europeanness'. These expectations were borne out by our data, even stronger than we anticipated. The visibility of the campaign in the news was extremely low. This can be explained partly by competing events, of which the Kosovo war was the most dramatic. Yet, this is only part of the reason. We suspect that even without this war, the visibility of the election campaign would have been low, and that topics other than the election would have benefited more from the absence of this competing event.[11] Not only did news programs give little attention to the election campaign, to the extent that they did so coverage was overwhelmingly domesticized. A 'European' perspective was largely absent. Actors portrayed or quoted were almost exclusively domestic actors and news content took place at mostly domestic locations.

Our expectations that country-variations in coverage can be attributed to the context within which European elections take place were not supported by our data. Whether these elections fall early or late in the domestic electoral cycle hardly explains whatever differences in coverage we find between countries. This negative finding can to some extent be attributed to restricted variance. In addition, it seems likely that country-specific (and possibly also channel-specific) factors create these differences. One difference between countries is quite clear, however: where there is elite disagreement on matters concerning European integration, the visibility of European elections in the news was much higher.

In terms of tone we found that most actors received either neutral or unfavorable evaluations. Of the three groups of actors, EU actors were evaluated most unfavorably in the news. This pattern, however, was not so pronounced that it allows for generalizations about the evaluation of EU actors in the news. Moreover, other studies of the news coverage of important EU events (such as the introduction of the euro) or EU summits and Council meetings found no difference in the pattern of evaluations when comparing EU actors with domestic political actors (de Vreese 2003a). It would therefore be incorrect to conclude that the media in Europe are 'stigmatizing' EU actors or treating them structurally different from any other type of domestic or international political actor.

In addition to the presence or absence of elite disagreement, what may explain the cross-national variation in the amount of news coverage? The answer is most likely to be found in several factors both within and outside journalism. Research focused on factors within journalism has shown that editorial choices made in the newsroom about the priority and topical focus of the news played a significant role in determining the news in the 1999 election campaign (de Vreese 2003b). For example, editors and journalists in several countries all characterized the campaign for the European elections as being of marginal interest only and they described European issues as complex. But this common appraisal led to entirely different reactions in terms of coverage. Dutch broadcasters, for example, chose to almost entirely neglect the elections, while their Danish colleagues chose to invest in coverage of the elections (de Vreese 2003b; see also table 6.1).

From a democratic perspective, a campaign has the potential to inform and mobilize voters to elect representatives. The media play a crucial role in this process. Did the 1999 campaign for the European elections fulfill this role? In some countries, the picture painted of the news coverage of the European elections is gloomy from the perspective of the campaign providing citizens with information. The European elections were given low priority in the news, they rarely made the opening of the news bulletins, the coverage was domestic in nature with most stories taking place in the home country and addressing issues with implications for the home country. Only few representatives of EU institutions made it into the news and these EU actors were rarely quoted and they were evaluated less favorably than other actors. In other countries, however, there was a considerable amount of coverage of the elections, especially given the somewhat unusual nature of the general news environment which was heavily dominated by the Kosovo conflict.

How alarming are the patterns in terms of media attention? A case can certainly be made that the campaign, as presented by the news media, did not enable the European electorate to make an informed choice. To which extent this is caused by media or by parties and politicians is a matter beyond the scope of this chapter. Finally, the question remains whether the news coverage affected public perceptions of, and support for, European integration. This question will be addressed in the next chapter.

Notes

1. The research reported here also investigated newspaper coverage of the European elections in all member states of the European Union. Limitations of space prevent us from presenting the newspaper analyses here.

2. The analysis of television news excludes Luxembourg due to technical problems related to finding appropriate coding collaborators.

3. A story was categorized as political if it contained at least two references to, quotes from, or depictions of politicians, political groups, political institutions, or political organizations.

4. The results from the 1996 survey are used.

5. The categories were: 'European Parliament elections'; 'Other EU-related topics'; 'Party and governmental issues' (e.g., politics, party conflicts); 'Economy' (e.g., unemployment, government budget, wages and earnings); 'Food Safety' (e.g., dioxin); 'Law and Order' (e.g., crime and trials); 'Foreign affairs' (e.g., relations between states); 'Kosovo' (all about the Balkan conflict); 'Disaster and human interest' (e.g., earthquakes; epidemics, lottery winners); 'Sports', and 'Miscellaneous' (i.e., other topics).

6. Table 6.1 reports relative visibility of the different topics in terms of length of the news stories in seconds. This is a more accurate measure of the visibility of topics than the number of news stories because the total length of the different programs varied and some networks opted for only a few rather lengthy stories whereas others opted for more and shorter stories for given topics such as the European elections.

7. Evidence from national election studies in, for example, Britain, Germany, the Netherlands, and Spain consistently show that national elections are more visible in the news (e.g., Kleinnijenhuis et al. 1998; Schoenbach, de Ridder, and Lauf 2001; Norris et al. 1999; Semetko and Canel 1997; de Vreese 2001).

8. Members of the European Parliament in the period 1994–1999 were coded as EU-level actors while first-time runners for the Parliament were coded as domestic actors as they are essentially not representing an EU institution. The latter category was rarely used.

9. These figures show relatively little variation across countries. However, not too much can be made out of the seemingly aberrant figure for the Netherlands (64% of all actors being European) in view of the extremely small n (11) on which it is based.

10. The major exceptions to this overall pattern are Belgium and Germany, which both displayed a below-average emphasis on domestic impact locations.

11. This expectation is mainly based on circumstantial and non-comparable evidence. An interesting comparison can be made, however, for the Netherlands. During the first Gulf War of 1991 elections for Provincial Councils were conducted in the Netherlands. These elections are clearly of the second-order type, and the councils to be elected are extremely invisible to Dutch voters. The lackluster campaign for these elections had to compete in the news with a war, just as was the case in the 1999 European elections. In spite of that, their visibility in national television news bulletins in the weeks prior to the election was considerable higher than we documented in table 6.1 for the Netherlands. For further details, see van der Eijk and Schild (1992).

CHAPTER SEVEN

Media effects on attitudes toward European integration

JOCHEN PETER

The previous chapter described patterns of media coverage of the 1999 European election campaign. This chapter deals with the effects of this coverage on citizens' opinions about the EU. More specifically, the chapter investigates whether the coverage affects (a) the perceived importance of European integration and (b) citizens' support for European integration. As in chapter 6, the analyses in this chapter focus on *television* news coverage of the European election campaign. One of the main reasons for this focus is that television is known to be the most important source of information about EU affairs for European citizens (Eurobarometer 51, 1999). The coverage of 'the news' in television is particularly relevant in this respect.

A number of scholars have argued that television news coverage of European elections may play an important role in voters' opinion formation during the campaign (e.g., Blumler and Thoveron 1983; Schulz 1983). Nevertheless, research on opinion formation during European election campaigns has largely ignored television news as a potential influence. The few existing studies suggest that exposure to media coverage affects voters' awareness and interest in the campaign (e.g., Cayrol 1983, 1991; Schoenbach 1981, 1983). However, these studies do not explicate how *specific* characteristics of coverage and news content influence citizens' attitudes toward European integration. Moreover, it remains unclear whether the effects of television news coverage on citizens' opinions are the same in all

EU member states or whether they depend on a particular context. As a result, this chapter investigates first whether specific characteristics of television news coverage of the campaign for the European elections shape citizens' attitudes toward European integration. Furthermore, it asks whether potential effects of coverage are conditioned by particular country characteristics.

Effects of the amount of coverage on the perceived importance of European integration

The amount of coverage of the 1999 European elections and the campaigns that preceded them differs considerably between the member countries of the EU (see chapter 6). This raises a simple, yet important question. Does the mere amount of European election coverage influence attitudes toward European integration and, in particular, perceptions of how important further EU integration is? Such effects are often referred to as 'agenda-setting'.[1] Miller and Krosnick (2000) demonstrated that attitudes toward the importance of an issue are important moderators for more complex evaluations and, potentially, for behavior. This suggests that factors that influence such attitudes toward importance of integration may provide new insights into antecedents of, for example, turnout and vote choice.

Research from the agenda-setting tradition (McCombs and Shaw 1972; for reviews, see Dearing and Rogers 1996; Rössler 1997) has repeatedly confirmed that the amount of coverage that media devote to a particular issue can shape the extent to which citizens consider the issue important. But we know little about whether the coverage of European election campaigns increases the perceived importance of European integration. With respect to the first European parliamentary elections in 1979, Schönbach (1981) found that higher exposure to television news was associated with more frequent perceptions of European integration as an important matter. However, the actual amount of media coverage was not assessed. This is important because it is unclear whether agenda-setting effects also occur for issues that are not covered prominently such as European election campaigns (see also chapter 6 on the limited share of the European elections in news coverage).

In addition to this lacuna, we also lack knowledge about the context-dependency of agenda-setting effects. Although such effects have been studied for a variety of issues in a variety of countries (for review, see Dearing and Rogers 1996; Rössler 1997), no study to date has investigated whether their presence (let alone their strength) varies with country characteristics. With respect to European elections it stands to reason that consensus or polarization in elite opinion on European integration could be such a conditioning factor for the emergence of agenda-setting effects. In this chapter, elite opinion refers to the opinions of political parties with respect to European integration. The extent of consensus or polarization of these opinions is a macro-level phenomenon that defines a part of the context in which European elections, and media coverage thereof, take place.

In much research on the EU, elite-driven approaches serve to explain public support for European integration or EU-related opinions (e.g., Eichenberg and Dalton 1993; Inglehart 1970; McLaren 2001; Wessels 1995). The basic idea is that citizens use cues from political parties to form attitudes toward European integration (for empirical evidence, see for example van der Eijk and Franklin 1991; Wessels 1995). Banducci, Karp, and Lauf (2001) applied this notion in the realm of media influence on support for European integration. They found that the nature of elite opinion conditions media influence on support for European integration. Depending on the nature of elite opinion as consensual or polarized, the amount and tone of coverage elicited opposite effects on support for European integration. This finding raises the question whether the conditioning impact of elite opinion also holds for perceived importance of European integration, which is conceptually and attitudinally different from support for European integration (cf. Scheuer 2005).

However, before we can specify expectations, a few conceptual remarks are in order about the two components of the presumed moderator—its elite character and its consensual or polarized nature. Agenda-setting research has only indirectly discussed the role of political elites on the agenda-setting process (Rogers and Dearing 1988).[2] Although scholars have studied how political elites try to influence the media agenda (for review, see Dearing and Rogers 1996), it is still unclear whether and how the interaction between political elites may condition the effect of the amount of media coverage on citizens' perceptions of the importance of an issue. Nevertheless, it seems plausible that the interaction between political elites provides citizens with cues about issue importance.

Polarization of (elite) opinions about an issue has been studied only marginally in agenda-setting research. There is, however, some tentative evidence that the polarization of issues strengthens agenda-setting effects (McCombs and Gilbert 1986). Generally, polarization of opinions about an issue indicates that it is important to the contestants involved and that it needs to be solved. It has been reported that consensus among political elites prevented European integration from becoming an issue of importance in most campaigns for European elections (cf. van der Eijk and Franklin 1996; Duch and Taylor 1997). Elite consensus may project the impression that the issue is not very important for choosing between parties because of the lack of political contestation. Conversely, elite polarization may signal citizens that an issue is sufficiently important for elite actors to invest time and effort in clarifying their stands and attempting to mobilize support.

Based upon these considerations, we expect the following regularities. The nature of elite opinion on European integration will moderate the basic agenda-setting pattern. The manner in which (individual) exposure to EU coverage affects one's perception of European integration as important depends on the nature of elite opinion. When elite opinion is consensual, agenda-setting effects will be weak at best: greater levels of coverage of the election campaign will not increase the perception that European integration is an important political issue. When elite opinion is polarized, however, we expect that greater levels of coverage will increase the perception that European integration is important. Technically speaking, we expect a two-way interaction between the (contextual) nature of elite opinion and the amount of coverage to which individuals are exposed.

Effects of the Tone of Coverage on Support for European Integration

From chapter 6, we know that the tone of coverage of the European election campaign varied between countries. What effects a favorable or unfavorable tone of coverage has on attitudes toward European integration has rarely been studied (exceptions are Banducci, Karp, and Lauf 2001; Norris 2000). This is striking because political commentary frequently suggests that the tone of coverage affects what citizens think about European integration. More specifically, we know hardly anything about whether and how the tone toward EU actors shapes people's attitudes toward further European integration.[3] Research in other contexts has shown, however, that the tone in the coverage of political actors presents a powerful influence on citizens' attitudes toward a variety of political issues (e.g., Cappella and Jamieson 1997; Kepplinger 1998; Valentino, Buhr, and Beckmann 2001; Valentino, Beckmann, and Buhr 2001). Therefore, it seems worthwhile to investigate whether and how the particular tone in news coverage of EU actors influences citizens' attitudes toward European integration.

When dealing with the tone of coverage, media consonance is an important concept in cross-national comparison. Elisabeth Noelle-Neumann (1973, 78–79) defines consonance as "a large extent of similarity in the presentation of certain material in all the media," which, according to her, may increase the effects of mass media on audiences. With respect to the subject matter of this chapter, consonance refers to the similarity of the tone in the coverage of EU actors across the media in a particular country. If all media in a given country evaluate EU actors similarly, the citizens of that country have little chance to be confronted with different evaluations. As a result, they may adjust their own opinions to the prevailing evaluative tone of the coverage.

It goes without saying that no individual is exposed to the entire media coverage in a given country. He or she uses only particular outlets. This means that the consonance of the entire coverage is a contextual factor rather than an individual one. Consonance or dissonance of the entire media coverage (including newspaper coverage) may thus moderate the effects of television news to which individuals are actually exposed. The basic question, then, is whether the coverage that people are exposed to has a stronger influence if the 'surrounding' coverage as a whole (i.e., the coverage of all media in a given country) is consonant. From the literature and our discussion above we expect the following: the tone in television coverage of EU actors influences citizens' support for European integration if the coverage of EU actors as a whole is consonant; it has no or a very weak influence on citizens' opinions if the coverage is dissonant. Technically speaking, this implies an interaction between the (contextual) consonance or dissonance of coverage as a whole and the tone of coverage in the outlet(s) an individual is exposed to.

PROCEDURE AND MEASURES

In the analyses of this chapter, two kinds of empirical information are linked. On the one hand, I use data from a content analysis of television news coverage of the June 1999 European election campaign. The design and procedure of these content data have been discussed in detail in chapter 6 (see appendix B for further details). On the other hand I make use of the voter survey of the European Election Study 1999 (see appendix A for further details).

Dependent, independent, and control variables

To assess how important people feel European integration to be, the following question was used: "Thinking about European integration, is this compared to other important topics in [your country] a topic of great importance, some importance, little importance, or no importance at all?" The variable was inversely coded so that 4 means *great importance*. Citizens' support for European integration was gauged with the question "Some say European integration should be pushed further. Others say that it has already gone too far. What is your opinion?" Response categories ranged from 1 (*unification has already gone too far*) to 10 (*unification should be pushed further*).

The amount of EU television coverage was operationalized as the sum of EU stories during the two weeks prior to the European election, i.e., news stories that either dealt with the European election campaign or other EU topics such as EU enlargement.[4] EU stories were weighted by their prominence as recommended in the literature (Brosius 1994; McCombs 1981; McCombs and Gilbert 1986).[5] The tone of coverage of EU actors was computed as the difference between the number of positive and negative evaluations of EU actors as coded in the content analysis (see also chapter 6).[6] Both measures, the amount of coverage (weighted by prominence) and the tone of coverage of EU actors, were centered around their mean in order to reduce multicollinearity when analyzing interaction effects (Aiken and West 1991; Jaccard, Turrisi, and Wan 1990).

Whether elite opinion was consensual or polarized was operationalized in the same way as in chapter 6, using all relevant coded content in both television outlets and the most prestigious newspaper.[7] If all three media in a particular country displayed the same evaluative tendency, the coverage was defined as consonant. If one of the outlets investigated deviated from the remaining outlets in its evaluative tendency, the coverage was defined dissonant (for details see appendix B).

Control variables were included in the analysis to make our test of the effects of media coverage on opinions as unambiguous as possible. The relevant literature on antecedents of attitudes toward European integration, on agenda-setting, and on alternative explanations of media effects suggests to control for the following variables: satisfaction with domestic democracy (Anderson 1998; Sanchez-Cuenca 2000), utilitarian motives (e.g., Gabel 1998b; McLaren 2002), party cues (e.g., Franklin, Marsh, and McLaren 1994), respondents' positions on the left-right spectrum (e.g., Budge, Robertson, and Hearl 1987; McLaren 2002), political interest (e.g., McLeod, Becker, and Byrnes 1974; Wanta 1997), media exposure and media attention (Drew and Weaver 1990), interpersonal communication (e.g., Schmitt-Beck 2000), and need for orientation and demographics (Rössler 1997). In the agenda-setting analysis, the degree of conflict in the coverage was added as a control variable. In the analyses of support for European integration, the number of EU actors covered was used as an additional control variable.

Missing values

In order to prevent nearly half of the cases being lost due to missing data (when using listwise deletion), missing values were replaced by valid scores derived from other, related, responses.[8] This reduced the number of missing cases by 30 percent to 70 percent. Remaining missing values were replaced either by mean substitution (for metric variables) or by the modal value (for dichotomies). These substitutions of missing values were only applied to the control variables. Missing values of the two dependent variables were not imputed to minimize the danger of arbitrary data modification.

Data analysis

The survey data were weighted to equal effective numbers of cases for all countries.[9] Respondents were assigned two exposure scores for each of the two news outlets they claimed to watch regularly, one for amount and one for tone displayed in the EU coverage of the particular news outlets. For example, British respondents who regularly watched BBC *9 o'clock news* were assigned the EU coverage and tone measures of this news outlet. Additionally, contextual information was added to respondent records for consensual (coded 0) or polarized (coded 1) elite opinion and for dissonance (coded as 0) or consonance of the tone of coverage (coded 1).[10] Respondents who never watched any one of the television news outlets were omitted from the analyses, which reduced the EU sample size to 8,863 respondents.[11]

As discussed above, a cross-level interaction is expected between amount (tone) of EU coverage and nature of elite opinion (dissonance-consonance).[12] I analyzed this interaction effect following a procedure suggested by both Jaccard, Turrisi, and Wan (1990) and Aiken and West (1991). In a nutshell, this procedure entails post-hoc probing of the interaction effects by testing the slopes that are conditional on the values of the moderating variable for significant differences from zero. The required computations are not available in standard statistical software packages and have to be conducted separately.[13]

Results

Did the amount of coverage influence citizens' perceptions of how important European integration is? Furthermore, is there evidence that the nature of elite opinion on European integration conditioned this relationship? Table 7.1

Table 7.1 Impact of various cross-level interactions on attitudes toward European integration

	Importance of European integration (n = 8280)	Support for European integration (n = 7853)
Key variables		
Amount EU coverage	−.001 (.002)	
Elite opinion	−.143 (.150)	
Tone of EU coverage		−.032 (.029)
Consonance		−.701 (.395)
Interaction effects		
Amount • Polarized elite opinion	.006 (.002)**	
Tone • Consonance		.115 (.044)*
Constant	2.124	1.606
R^2	0.11	0.10

* $p < 0.05$; ** $p < 0.01$.
Note: Cell entries are unstandardized multiple regression coefficients. Robust standard errors in brackets.
Data sources: EES 1999; content analysis 1999 European election campaign.
The models were controlled for: gender, age, education, work status, subjective social class, interpersonal communication, party cues, left-right position, satisfaction with domestic democracy, political interest, attention to news, TV exposure, newspaper exposure, the number of TV news outlets and newspapers used, need for orientation and conflict in EU coverage (importance perception only), visibility of EU actors (support only).

shows a significant interaction between the nature of elite opinion and the amount of coverage (b = 0.006, p < 0.01). Figure 7.1 visualizes how the nature of elite opinion conditioned the effect of the amount of coverage on respondents' feelings about the importance of European integration. Note that, for computational reasons, the values of the (weighted) amount of coverage are centered. The sample mean of this variable is thus set to 0. Negative values indicate an amount of coverage below the sample mean, positive values indicate an amount of coverage above the sample mean.

Figure 7.1 shows two lines, one for the impact of the amount of coverage when elite opinion is polarized and one for the impact of the amount of coverage when elite opinion is consensual. As the line with the positive slope indicates, higher amounts of EU coverage only have a positive effect on the perceived im-

FIGURE 7.1 Interaction effect of amount of EU coverage and nature of elite opinion on the perceived importance of European integration

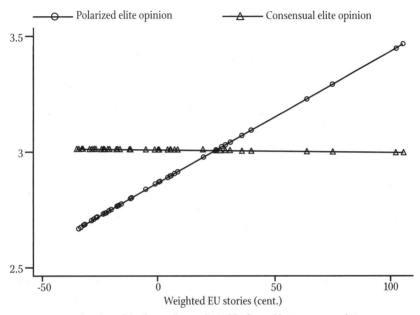

Note: To compute the values of this figure, all control variables from table 7.1 were set to their mean.

portance of European integration when elite opinion on integration is polarized. Conversely, in the case of consensual elite opinion, more EU coverage has hardly any impact on how important respondents felt the issue of European integration to be (see the nearly horizontal line). Post-hoc probing these conditional influences (i.e., the slopes of the lines in figure 7.1) confirmed that only in the case of polarized elite opinion does the amount of coverage have a significant effect (for details of the computation, see Peter 2003). By contrast, the amount of coverage has no (significant) impact when elite opinion is consensual.

The second goal of this chapter was to establish whether the tone of coverage influences citizens' support for European integration more strongly when coverage is consonant than when coverage is dissonant. The tone of television coverage of EU actors was expected to affect people's attitudes toward European integration only if the overall tone of coverage was consonant with the specific tone of coverage an individual was actually exposed to. In such cases, citizens should adjust their attitude toward European integration to the tone of coverage. Table 7.1 demonstrates that the interaction between the tone of coverage of EU actors and consonance or dissonance of the coverage is indeed significant ($b = 0.115$, $p < 0.05$).

FIGURE 7.2 Interaction effect of consonance/dissonance and tone of coverage on support for European integration

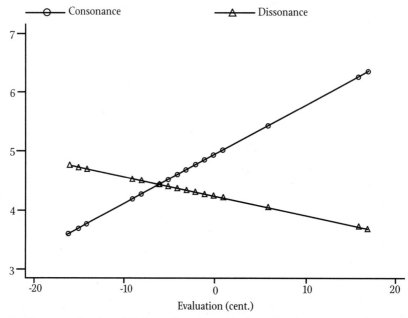

Note: To compute the values of this figure, all control variables from table 7.1 were set to their mean.

Figure 7.2 visualizes the impact of the tone of coverage in the two contexts that I distinguish. The tone of coverage indeed affected attitudes toward European integration positively in a consonant context (see line with positive slope in figure 7.2). The more positive the tone in the coverage of EU actors that people are exposed to, the more favorable their opinions are about European integration. Conversely, the more negative the tone, the less favorable opinions are about European integration. Figure 7.2 also suggests that, in a dissonant context, a more positive tone of coverage is associated with less favorable attitudes toward European integration (see line with negative slope). However, statistical post-hoc probing of these conditional effects (i.e., the slope of the two lines in figure 7.1) showed that this last mentioned effect is not significant. The only significant effect is found in the consonant context.

DISCUSSION

This chapter demonstrated that television coverage matters for citizens' attitudes about European integration. In this respect it supports a commonplace presumption about such effects, which has, however, rarely been investigated empirically. The most important finding, however, is that there is no unified European context in terms of media effects. The cross-national comparative perspective demonstrates that the occurrence of significant effects depends on the (country-specific) context. The effect of the amount of coverage on importance perceptions is conditional on the nature of elite opinion in a country. Similarly, a positive or negative tone does not always and everywhere result in a positive or negative attitude toward European integration—whether it does depends on the consonance of coverage. Three main conclusions can be drawn.

First, consensus or polarization in elite discourse about European integration moderates the impact of the amount of news coverage on citizens. Disagreement among political elites about European integration sensitizes citizens to the importance of the issue. Consensus among political elites seems to have a numbing effect, owing to which larger amounts of coverage have no effect whatsoever on the perceived importance of European integration. Whether European integration is perceived as a soporific and unimportant *fait accompli* or as an exciting and important development depends largely on the interaction of elite discourse and television news coverage.

The second main conclusion is that the tone of coverage of EU actors sometimes affects citizens' attitude toward European integration. This finding dovetails with an emerging, yet small strand of research on media effects on attitudes toward the EU. Norris (2000) and Banducci, Karp, and Lauf (2001) reported evidence of the tone of EU coverage affecting people's opinion on EU matters. However, this chapter points out that the presence of such effects depends on context, more specifically on the consonance of coverage. Meyer (1999) pointed out a 'communication deficit' of the European Union and linked it to the apprehension of EU officials that too much media attention to European affairs may endanger support for European integration. The findings in this chapter suggest that such concerns are exaggerated. Exposure to negative coverage only jeopardizes support for integration in a consonantly negative context, i.e., when the tone of all media coverage is overwhelmingly negative.

Third, contextual characteristics explain how media affect attitudes toward European integration. In much the same way as a particular climate is required for certain plants to grow, particular conditions are required for media to exert effects on the attitudes of those who are exposed to their content. As far as attitudes about European integration are concerned, these conditions were found to exist at the level of the national context.[14] Relevant country characteristics include the degree of consensus of elite opinion and the consonance of the coverage of the media within a given country. It seems worthwhile to extend the kind of analyses presented in this chapter to other contextual variables such as economic ones (e.g., trade dependency on the EU or whether a country is financially a net contributor). Various studies have demonstrated the influence of such economic factors on support for European integration, and further analyses may unravel the interconnections between media coverage, country context, and support for European integration.

In conclusion, this chapter demonstrates that media coverage cannot be ignored with impunity when studying people's attitudes toward European integration. Due to the rudimentary state of research in this respect, this chapter only provides some first evidence of media effects and of the conditions under which they exist. It is up to future research to further develop the basic strategy of linking specific characteristics of coverage to citizens' opinions and to conceptualize that relationship as a conditional one, contingent on particular contexts.

Notes

1. The idea behind this terminology is that media set the agenda of citizens' concerns and possibly also the agenda of politicians' concerns.

2. However, several studies demonstrated how political elites try to influence issue definitions and opinion processes, e.g., Caldeira (1987); Erikson, Wright, and McIver (1989); C. Franklin and Kosaki (1989).

3. The term 'EU actors' refers not only to EU officials (e.g., members of the European Commission), but also to others who are clearly associated with the EU (e.g., national ministers in their capacity as members of the EU's Council of Ministers). Institutions such as the Commission, the Parliament, and the European Central Bank can also be considered EU actors if they, and not individuals representing the institutions, are the subject of a news story.

4. An exclusive focus on the coverage of the election campaign proper would not appropriately mirror the information people actually receive about European integration from television news during the period of investigation.

5. The prominence of the stories was computed with a measure originally developed by Watt and van den Berg (1981) and modified by Watt, Mazza, and Snyder (1993). For further information see Peter (2003). It combines length, placement, or presentation of stories in a news bulletin. Just like amount of coverage, these elements provide cues about the importance of the issues covered.

6. Kepplinger and Maurer (2001) demonstrated that this difference measure is closer to how recipients perceive evaluative tendencies than, for example, the mean evaluation.

7. For each country, the front page of the most prestigious newspaper was analyzed. The front page presents the most important part of each newspaper and gives a good

overview of what a particular newspaper considers important. The most prestigious newspaper of each of the various countries was chosen because it can to some extent be considered as representative of a country's newspaper coverage and, moreover, because it often influences coverage in other newspapers (Dearing and Rogers 1996). Because the analyses in this chapter (and in the previous one) focus on effects of television coverage, the tone of newspaper coverage was only used for the operationalization of the consonance measure.

8. For example, if a respondent had not specified his or her position on the left-right scale, but had indicated the likelihood of voting particular parties, his or her left-right position could be approximated from where he or she had placed the particular party on the left-right scale. Similarly, a substitute measure for missing data on political interest was derived from people's participation in political events, attention to European news was deduced from people's exposure to European election news, news exposure from media use, etc. It was tested with dummy interactions (in which the dummy indicates the substitution of missing data) whether the deduced cases behaved differently than the other cases. There was no evidence of such deviations, indicating that the substitution of missing cases did not affect the validity of the findings.

9. Technically, this weighting resembles the second weight variable described in appendix A, but does not include the weighting for turnout and distribution of party choice.

10. In Austria, no commercial broadcasting exists. In Ireland, the commercial channel attracted, in 1999, an audience too small to warrant attention.

11. No meaningful differences existed between the cases included in the analysis and the original sample in terms of the variables used for the analyses in this chapter.

12. The expected cross-level interaction between the country-level factor nature of elite opinion (dissonance or consonance of coverage as a whole) and the individual exposure to EU coverage creates a problem with the estimation of the standard error. Because the data are located at two different levels and because the respondents are, to some extent, 'nested' in the particular country, the observations (or respondents) within a particular country are no longer independent. If this is not taken into account in the analyses (e.g., by estimating regular OLS regression models), the standard error of especially the cross-level interaction effect is underestimated. This, in turn, leads to an increased chance of a type-I error. Recently, scholars have suggested and employed multi-level modeling as solution to this problem (e.g., Steenbergen and Jones 2002). However, in the context of this study, three important caveats have to be raised against multi-level modeling. First, cross-national comparative research on the EU usually does not meet the requirements of proper multi-level models. Multi-level modeling typically requires the contextual units (here: countries) to be randomly sampled, which is not the case in this study. Second, multi-level models presuppose sufficient power to test cross-level interactions. Scholars agree that at least twenty to twenty-five contextual units (here: systems) are necessary for meaningful multi-level modeling (e.g., Snijders and Bosker 1999). In the context of the EU and its fifteen member states, this is not possible. Third, Steenbergen and Jones (2002) "caution researchers against 'blindly' using these models [i.e., multi-level models; JP] in

data analysis" (p. 235). Instead, they suggest more traditional ways of correcting standard errors in hierarchical data, for example, the 'sandwich' estimation of the standard error used in this study (Huber 1967; White 1980).

13. For details, see chapters 2 and 4 in Aiken and West (1991), and pp. 26–28 and 31–33 in Jaccard, Turrisi, and Wan (1990).

14. It may be that the contextual effects emanate from smaller contextual units than entire countries and that they would be more clearly visible were context to be defined on a smaller scale. Yet, the analyses demonstrate that even when using countries as contextual units, we find these effects.

CHAPTER EIGHT

Non-voting in European Parliament elections and support for European integration

HERMANN SCHMITT
AND CEES VAN DER EIJK

Participation in European Parliament elections is low and has been so since the first of these elections in 1979. While considerable research effort has been invested to explore the causes of the meager turnout in European Parliament elections, the results so far are somewhat inconclusive. On the aggregate level, we know quite well which aspects of the context of the election matter. It does make a difference, of course, whether voting is compulsory or not. It also matters whether European Parliament elections are held concurrently with national first-order (or other 'more important' second-order) elections or whether this is not the case; whether they are conducted close to national first-order elections or not (see chapter 1). We are somewhat less certain about the effects of Sunday (versus weekday) voting; some authors report a positive effect of Sunday voting on turnout (e.g., Oppenhuis 1995; van Egmond, de Graaf, and van der Eijk 1998), but in Franklin's analyses in chapter 1 this factor did not exert any significant effect (see note 5 in that chapter).

On the individual level things seem to be less clear. Traditional predictors of individual turnout—social integration, political mobilization, and party attachment—are found to be as important in European Parliament elections as they are in any other election. But controversy reigns in the literature on a question that is not only of academic interest but that also contains some political dynamite. This question is whether abstentions in European Parliament elections carry a hidden political message like "I don't agree with the whole European business," or "Why do we need a European Parliament. Let's get things right at home," and so on. This chapter sets out to determine the relative importance of 'Euro-skeptic' non-voting in European Parliament elections as compared to what may be called 'Euro-neutral' abstentions. Based on the 1999 European Election Study, two factors that may cause 'Euro-skeptic' non-voting are distinguished: lack of support for the EU ("I don't like Europe"), and lack of EU policy appeal of political parties ("If it comes to Europe there is no reasonable choice"). Four categories of Euro-neutral abstentions are controlled for: lack of support for national politics ("I don't like the way politics is run in this country"); lack of political parties' general appeal ("There is no party I can support"); lack of involvement ("I don't care"); and lack of efficacy ("My vote does not matter"). Social structure is also considered as a more remote social factor which precedes the political ones. Finally, the evolution of Euro-skeptic causes of abstention is determined in a diachronic cross-national perspective by analyzing survey evidence from three European Parliament elections (1989, 1994, and 1999).

MOTIVES FOR NON-VOTING

For European Parliament elections in particular, it might be useful to expand existing notions of the motives and political aims which a voter may pursue by abstaining from the election. These motives are related to different possible outcomes of an election. For present purposes, it suffices to distinguish two kinds of outcome: policies and legitimacy.

Almost every election installs a new, or confirms the old, government. The government's political choices ultimately result in a set of governmental policies. These can be regarded as the policy outcome of elections. Based on past performance and on election programs, voters may develop expectations about likely policy outcomes of an election. To the extent that voters attempt to influence policy outcomes by their choice for one of the parties, non-voting will occur when no relation is perceived between election results and policy outcomes. This is a very likely source of non-voting in European Parliament elections. These elections are different from most other ones because they do *not* contribute to the formation of a government. The policy consequences of different outcomes of a European Parliament election are therefore difficult to determine (which is not to say that they do not exist). This factor goes a long way in explaining why levels of participation are generally much lower in European Parliament elections than in elections for a national parliament (cf. Schmitt and Mannheimer 1991).

However, general elections are not only a way to collectively decide about future policies,[1] they also add to the legitimacy of the political regime. This is the second outcome of elections that is relevant here. Citizens' participation in the electoral process is often taken to indicate system support, while abstentions may signify two things, indifference on the one hand or system opposition (sometimes referred to as alienation) on the other (Pappi 1996).[2] The slate of available choice options seems to matter here a great deal. The smaller the number of anti-system choice options on the ballot, the more likely it is, *ceteris paribus*, that abstention expresses system opposition.[3] If someone abstains because there are no parties that adequately express one's views, particularly views of opposition against the political regime at hand, this would thus express a lack of legitimacy. The possibility that such motives lie behind non-voting in European Parliament elections is not farfetched at all. As chapter 10 will demonstrate, explicitly Euro-skeptic or Euro-hostile parties are absent in many of the member states, and where they do exist they are often unpalatable to many voters because of extremist policy positions that they take in areas other than European integration.

In addition to the motivations mentioned, various other factors are likely to impinge on the likelihood that individual voters abstain rather than go to the polls. At the personal level, political involvement and political efficacy are likely to be of importance. Concerning parties, it is likely that the strength of the appeal that parties generate for voters (general as well as policy appeal) will affect electoral participation, as will voters' satisfaction (or disaffection) with the political situation in their own nation state. Consequently, we will control for these factors in our appraisal of the extent to which the appeal of parties affects individual voters' choices of abstaining or casting their ballot.

In what follows, we will apply these notions about motives of non-voting in European Parliament elections and assess the extent to which electoral abstention is motivated by opposition to the EU or to European integration in general, while taking into account the effects of the auxiliary factors just mentioned.

Euro-skeptic abstentions in European Parliament elections

Politicians and media tend to see the participation rate in European Parliament elections as a crucial indicator of political support for the European Union and, more generally, for the integration process. When the first direct election was called in 1979, the European Parliament launched a broad non-partisan mobilization campaign in all member countries of the Union (Blumler 1983). Those efforts have been repeated on a smaller scale in subsequent elections. In spite of this, turnout was widely considered disappointingly low in 1979. A superficial glance at the development of turnout since then seems to indicate a downward trend. EU-wide participation dropped steadily from a cross-country average of 66 percent in 1979 to 53 percent in 1999 (see table 1.1 in chapter 1). As Franklin argues in chapter 1, this apparent decline is somewhat of an artifact, and thus less alarming than it might seem at first sight. To a large extent, it is the consequence of successive enlargements of the Union with countries without compulsory voting, of the disappearance of a 'first-election boost' and of coincidental variations in the salience of European Parliament elections caused by their timing in the domestic electoral cycle. When these effects of composition and timing are removed, participation in European Parliament elections is relatively stable (see also Wessels and Schmitt 2000). But stable as 'in reality' turnout may be, it is also particularly low. This brings us back to our question of motivations for non-voting in European Parliament elections in general, and to that of Euro-skeptic abstentions in particular.

Past research is somewhat inconclusive with regard to Euro-skeptic abstentions. Schmitt and Mannheimer, in their 1991 analysis of the 1989 European Election Study data, find that participation in European Parliament elections is virtually unrelated to attitudes about European integration. In 1989 at least, electoral participation was mostly a matter of habitual voting: "people went to the polls because they are used to doing so on election day" (1991, 50). Later analyses based on the same 1989 European Election Study included, in addition to individual-level factors, systemic and contextual characteristics and their interaction with individual-level variables (see Franklin, van der Eijk, and Oppenhuis 1996). While this strategy of research meant a big step forward (accompanied by a considerable raise of explained variance), attitudes about European integration and the European Community were again found to be virtually unrelated with electoral participation.

This negative result seems to be quite unpalatable for people who seem emotionally attached to the conventional wisdom of politicians and journalists that non-participation must indicate lack of support for European integration. Smith, for example, is one of those who after correctly noticing that "Franklin, van der Eijk and Oppenhuis have challenged the sort of claims made in this section" dismisses these results and contends without any empirical evidence or argument whatsoever that "[d]espite their skepticism it seems that attitudes do have a part to play in explaining behavior in EP elections" (Smith 1999, 123n10).

Fortunately, other critiques of our previous findings are based on empirical evidence and analysis rather than on beliefs that seem to be impervious to empirical argument. Blondel, Sinnott, and Svensson (1998) conducted an extensive empirical study of electoral participation in the 1994 elections to the European Parliament. They conclude, in contrast to the conclusions about the 1989 elections referred to above, that "voluntary Euro-abstention to be significantly affected by attitudes to European integration, by attitudes to the European Parliament, and by attitudes to the parties and candidates in the election, and that it is not significantly affected by second-order considerations and calculations" (Sinnott 2000, 70 summarizing Blondel, Sinnott, and Svensson 1998, 222–236).

It is quite possible that things have changed since we first explored the issue for the 1989 election. After all, since 1989 the European Union has developed in many important ways. Conceivably, these changes made themselves felt in the 1994 elections, but may have continued in full force thereafter. National sovereignty has been further transferred to Union institutions and authorities (e.g., in the currency domain). The political consequences of the continuously increasing policy scope of the EU are more widely felt (like during the BSE crisis and the foot and mouth disease epidemic). Last but not least, the dynamics of EU membership—i.e., the repeated broadening of the EU citizenry—is a source of concern for many citizens. These and other developments may have changed the relation between mass political orientations toward the European Union and electoral behavior in European Parliament elections. Euro-skeptic abstentions in European Parliament elections may have become more important than in the past. Whether this is the case is the question that is addressed in this chapter, first with an in-depth analysis of the 1999 election and subsequently in a diachronic analysis over the three elections from 1989 on.

While having an open mind for the possibility that the character of non-voting in European Parliament elections may have changed after 1989, we are nevertheless skeptical about the validity of the analyses on which the conclusions of Blondel et al. rest. Their claims have to be questioned on methodological grounds.

Blondel et al. define *voluntary Euro-abstainers* as those respondents who, in the course of the interview, gave one or more of the following reasons when asked (in an open-ended question) why they had abstained: "Lack of interest, distrust of or dissatisfaction with politics and politicians, lack of knowledge and dissatisfaction with the European Parliament electoral process" (1998, 50). Two objections can be made to their procedure. Our first objection concerns the *use of self-reported reasons* or motivations for behavior. Alvarez and Nagler (2000, 61) express in a related context severe doubts about the validity of such information: "researchers using these survey questions do not appear to have seriously considered the quality of the survey responses obtained for questions asking for justifications of reported political behavior." They particularly doubt whether respondents are always able to cognize and verbalize reasons for their behavior. One can equally doubt whether the context of a mass-survey allows them to express *all* the reasons they may have in mind. A related, but somewhat different problem is whether we can assume that what people see as the reasons for their own behavior can be equated with the reasons that a researcher would see. In the words of Abraham Kaplan (1964, 32), "it is of crucial importance that we distinguish between the meaning of the act to the actor . . . and its meaning to us as scientists, taking the action as subject-matter. I call these, respectively, *act meaning* and *action meaning*." He emphasizes that the two will in general be quite different. Open-ended questions about reasons for behavior (in this particular case, for non-voting) may be useful for describing act meaning, although even that claim may be contested (see Alvarez and Nagler, above). By taking these responses as the reasons ('causes') for non-voting that would be satisfactory from a researchers' perspective, Blondel et al. naively assume that act meaning and action meaning coincide. By doing so they shrink away from their own responsibility to formulate falsifiable accounts for the respondents' behavior: their approach leaves no room for falsifying the reasons for non-voting given by respondents. This problem of non-falsifiability leads to our second major objection to the Blondel et al. approach, which is that it suffers from *selection-bias* (King, Keohane, and Verba 1994, 128–136). This often occurs "when we, knowing what we want to see as the outcome of the research (the confirmation of the favorite hypothesis), subtly or not so subtly select observations on the basis of combinations of the independent and dependent variables that support the desired conclusion" (p. 128). In the case of the approach of Blondel et al., it is obvious that the open-ended question about reasons for non-voting can only be asked to non-voters. As a consequence, only non-voters can be found to be uninterested or dissatisfied with the European Parliament electoral process. Therefore, the attribution of non-voting to this lack of interest or dissatisfaction cannot be falsified: we simply do not know how (un)interested or (dis)satisfied those are who did cast a ballot in the European elections. Conceivably, the voters were even less interested and less satisfied than non-voters, which would effectively refute Blondel et al.'s interpretation that lack of interest and dissatisfaction made people stay home. But it is impossible to ask voters questions about their motivations for abstaining, thus the analysis is restricted to only one category of the dependent variable (the non-voters). As a consequence "nothing whatsoever can be learned about the causes of the dependent variable" (King, Keohane, and Verba 1994, 129).

In our approach we explicitly look at voters *and* non-voters, and our independent variables derive from questions that have been asked to *all* respondents, irrespective of their behavior. Therefore our findings are neither tainted by selection bias or by the problems of self-reported motivations. As stated above, it is quite possible that things have changed since we first explored the issue of non-voting for the 1989 election. In the remainder of this chapter we investigate whether or not this is so, first by an analysis of (non-)voting in the 1999 European Parliament election and subsequently by a diachronic analysis over the three European elections since 1989. The analyses reported below are based on the European Election Studies 1989, 1994, and 1999 (see appendix A).

Voting and non-voting in 1999

Our research question does not involve multi-level relationships, so that no tests for interactions of individual factors and systemic or contextual ones are required. In contrast to earlier work we will therefore concentrate here on individual-level relationships. For reasons elaborated above, we do not focus exclusively on non-voters, nor do we separate the sample into groups that are analyzed separately.

The dependent variable in our analysis is dichotomous: participation (or lack thereof) in the 1999 European Parliament election as reported in the post-electoral survey of the EES 1999.[4] Our independent variables can be grouped into a series of clusters. One of these—social-structural characteristics of voters[5]—is not directly political in character, while the other six pertain to genuinely 'political' constructs:

1. support for EU politics,[6]
2. support for national politics,[7]
3. parties' general appeal,[8]
4. parties' policy appeal,[9]
5. political efficacy,[10] and
6. political involvement.[11]

Figure 8.1 displays the components of each of these clusters.

Our central indicator of Euro-skepticism is (the lack of) *support for EU politics* (construct 1). The stronger the (positive) correlation is between support for EU

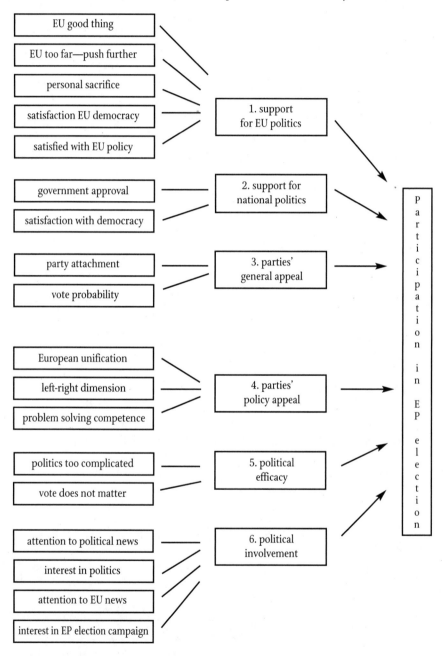

FIGURE 8.1 Indicators, constructs, and the dependent variable: The analytical scheme

politics and participation in European Parliament elections, the more room exists for Euro-skeptic non-voting.[12] Whether such correlations should be interpreted as 'causal' depends of course on the extent to which they can be accounted for by antecedent causal factors.

The policy appeal of political parties (construct 4) indicates the extent to which citizens may feel that they lack an appropriate 'positive' choice option, possibly causing them to abstain. A strong negative correlation of parties' policy appeal with abstention should therefore signal a substantial amount of strategic non-voting. Parties' policy appeal increases as the distance between the (non-)voter and the closest of the relevant national parties regarding European integration and left-right becomes smaller. We also included in this cluster a measure of party competence: parties lack policy appeal if none of the national parties are felt competent to solve the political problem that a citizen regards as the most important.[13] One of the variables in this cluster is related to attitudes regarding European integration, yet cannot be taken as an indicator of Euro-skepticism. The distance between a respondent and the party that is closest to him or her in terms of a European integration dimension indicates the adequacy of the best possible choice in this respect. If this distance is very large, no party whatsoever is very attractive as far as this criterion is concerned, but that does not imply that the respondent is Euro-skeptic or Euro-hostile. The magnitude of this distance does not indicate the respondent's location on a scale about European integration that runs between 'should be pushed further' and 'has already been pushed too far'. The respondents' own location on this scale has been included in cluster 1 (support for EU politics).

Support for national politics (construct 2), *parties' general appeal* (construct 3), *political efficacy* (construct 5), and *political involvement* (construct 6) are all in a way indicators of 'Euro-neutral' participation or abstention. There is no 'hidden' political or substantive message behind the act of non-voting when people abstain due to a lack of mobilization or involvement, party attachment, or political powerlessness and alienation. In particular, there is no hidden Euro-hostility behind these possible causes of non-voting. Among these four, past research has identified political involvement and parties' general appeal as particularly strong predictors of electoral participation.[14]

Strategy of analysis

We are *not* primarily interested in the relative importance of each and every individual variable—let alone in the specification of their interrelationships—

but rather in the importance of the *clusters* of variables described above, each of which represents a general construct (see figure 8.1). Therefore, each of these constructs is represented in the analysis by a single measure that encapsulates the empirical information of its constituent parts to the extent that it contributes to the explanation of the dependent variable: electoral participation. This has been done by the optimal linear transformation and addition of the variables involved: the predicted value of the dependent variable (electoral participation) from a multivariate linear regression using only the variables pertaining to a single construct as independents. In contrast to methods such as factor analysis, this procedure ensures that *all* explanatory power of this set of variables is retained. All constructs have been measured in this way, as well as the entire set of socio-demographic background variables.

We will first investigate for each of the countries[15] in our survey the correlations between electoral participation and each of the clusters of independent variables, which were listed in figure 8.1. These bivariate correlations allow us to gauge to what extent Euro-skeptic factors can conceivably help to explain non-voting, and how important this contribution to explanation can be in comparison to other factors.

As our survey contains different numbers of cases for the different political systems of the EU, we decided to correct for this by weighting the respective country samples to an identical number of effective cases. In this way we avoid the risk that relationships that are found to be significant in one system fail to be so in another only for reasons of a smaller sample size.[16]

In a second step of analyses we will add relevant controls. The aim of this is to correctly assess the explanatory importance of each of the clusters of variables depicted in figure 8.1. We do not want to assume that all the independent variables have equal causal status. Rather, it seems appropriate to look at attitudes as mediating (part of) the effect of background characteristics of respondents, in addition to adding explanatory power to them.[17] Therefore, we use causal analysis methods (structural equation modeling) in this stage of our analysis.

The general structure of the model to be tested is depicted in figure 8.2, which displays the theoretical expectations included in the model that is estimated for each of the political systems of the EU. From these models different kinds of results are important. The first result to inspect is whether or not the causal structure imposed on the models to be estimated is falsified by the structure of the empirical data, which is reflected in so-called 'fit' indices. Second, we have to look at the extent to which all these variables in combination are able to explain individual-level variation in electoral participation, i.e., explained variance. Third, we need

FIGURE 8.2 Determinants of electoral participation in the 1999 European election: 'permissible' arrows

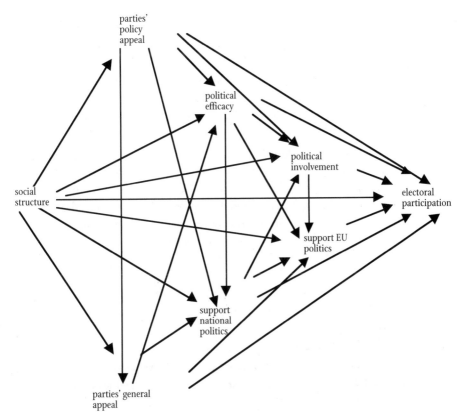

to assess the causal importance of each of the constructs shown in figure 8.1. This is expressed in so-called (standardized) total effects.[18] In view of the research question addressed in this chapter, we are particularly interested in this coefficient for the cluster 'support for EU-politics', as this coefficient tells us how important Euro-skepticism or Euro-hostility is in explaining non-voting, when taking into account relevant controls.

After our causal analysis of electoral participation in the 1999 elections to the European Parliament, we turn to a diachronic analysis in which we compare the 1999 data with similar information from 1994 and 1989. This will allow us to pinpoint systematic changes in the importance of independent variables. Because the survey instrumentation differs somewhat between these three studies, we have at our disposal only a relatively small common denominator of indicators that are available in each of the three consecutive European Election Studies. Only three sets of independent variables were included in each of these studies: the social-structural position of respondents,[19] their general political involvement,[20] and the extent to which they hold Euro-skeptic attitudes.[21] The first of these two represent in our analyses the ubiquitous theoretical wisdom that non-voters are 'peripheral' socially[22] and politically.[23] In line with the logic of figure 8.2, we will use the first two of these as controls to isolate the true effects of the third on turnout.[24] In view of the smaller number of independent variables, we suffice in this diachronic analysis with a block-recursive multivariate regression. This involves a stepwise regression in which social-structural factors are entered first, and their explanatory power is determined. Indicators of political involvement are entered subsequently, and the proportion of *additional* variance explained is determined. Attitudes about Europe and the European Union are entered as a last cluster, and again the proportion of additional variance explained is determined (together with the proportion of variance explained overall).[25]

Findings

Bivariate relationships

In table 8.1 we present for each of the political systems of the EU the bivariate correlation between electoral participation in 1999 on the one hand and each of the clusters of independent variables on the other hand.

In table 8.1 three clusters of independent variables stand out because of the strength of their correlation with electoral participation: political parties' general appeal, political involvement, and political efficacy. The manner in which we constructed the summary indicator for each cluster (see above) necessitates these correlations all to be positive. If however, we investigate the direction of these associations at the level of the separate indicators (not shown here), they are all in the expected direction.

For the other clusters, we find considerable differences between EU member countries. First and foremost, the extent to which voting or abstention can conceivably be explained by support (or lack thereof) for the EU is extremely limited in most of the EU systems. In six systems there is no statistically significant bivariate correlation whatsoever. In no less than eleven out of sixteen systems, the correlation falls below 0.16 (which, squared, would give an upper boundary of 2.5 percent explained variance). This includes such countries as Britain and Den-

Table 8.1 Correlates of participation in European Parliament elections, 1999

	Support for EU politics	Support for national politics	Parties' general appeal	Parties' policy appeal	Political efficacy	Political involvement	Social structural characteristics
Austria	.19	–.00	.27	.09	.14	.31	.32
Belgium: Flanders	.19	.18	.42	.11	.20	.23	.18
Belgium: Wallonia	.24	.08	.09	.24	.35	.27	.17
Britain	.14	.09	.23	.08	.21	.39	.34
Denmark	.14	.06	.15	.06	.21	.43	.20
Finland	.22	.06	.39	.04	.22	.43	.23
France	.10	.02	.30	.22	.19	.33	.30
Germany	.20	.10	.25	.13	.22	.32	.25
Greece	.04	.07	.27	.11	.06	.16	.20
Ireland	.03	.07	.22	.04	.12	.27	.37
Italy	.04	.04	.35	.10	.10	.26	.10
Luxembourg	.18	–.05	.25	.13	.09	.31	.26
Netherlands	.23	.05	.28	.04	.26	.42	.25
Portugal	.02	.05	.37	.17	.21	.30	.25
Spain	.19	.08	.32	.16	.19	.32	.30
Sweden	.33	.21	.37	.05	.30	.47	.34
Country average	.16	.07	.28	.11	.19	.33	.25

Source: European Elections Study 1999.

mark, where Euro-skepticism (possibly even Euro-phobia) is very strong and possibly dominant, as well as traditionally Europhile systems such as Italy and Luxembourg. In all systems but one, the squared correlation (which represents the upper limit of explanatory power of Euro-skepticism, as controls for additional or rivaling explanations have not yet been included) falls below 5 percent. The only real exception to this *pervasive marginality* of the effect of EU support is Sweden. In Sweden more than anywhere else in the EU do bivariate correlations hint at the potential to explain electoral participation by support or lack of support for the EU. When (via analyses using the separate items, see above) we investigate the direction of these correlations, we find that most of them (but not all) reflect that 'supportive' attitudes toward the EU are more prevalent among voters than among non-voters. When disregarding the weakness of these correlations, this seems to be in line with a hypothesis of non-voting motivated by anti-EU attitudes. The exceptions to this general pattern indicate, however, that sometimes Euro-skeptics of one kind or another are more, not less, prevalent among those who turn out to cast their vote. Obviously, contextual differences, such as the way in which political parties are aligned with these attitudes have to be taken into account to understand these differences. The mere fact that (particularly in Britain and Flanders) it is the Europhiles who are more prone to abstain should serve as a warning against hasty conclusions that abstention can only be motivated by a *lack* of support for the EU.

'Support for national politics' is everywhere of limited importance at best, with the exception of—again—Sweden where this correlation is of medium strength.

The cluster 'parties' policy appeal' is also only weakly related to electoral participation, and quite differently so in the various political systems. As the construct is related to contextual phenomena such as the format of the party competition in the different political systems, the differences we find between systems do not come as a surprise. What is surprising, however, is the general weakness of this correlation.

The correlation of socio-demographics with turnout also shows considerable country differences. When descending from the cluster to its constituent variables (analyses not shown here, but see Schmitt and van der Eijk 2003, 296) we find that age is almost everywhere significantly related to electoral participation. Most often this correlation is negative, which indicates that the younger age cohorts are abstaining over proportionally, as could be expected (cf. Franklin 2004). All correlations with education are positive, but in seven of the sixteen systems education is *not* significantly related to participation. Similar remarks can be made about the other background variables. Interesting as these differences may be, they are not central to our research question in this chapter. The main reason for looking at these variables at all is to use them as controls in later analyses.

Causal analysis

On the basis of figure 8.2 a series of causal models (structural equation models) has been estimated with electoral participation as dependent variable, social-structural characteristics as exogenous, and the attitudinal variables as intermediating factors.

A first question to be addressed with this kind of modeling is whether or not the empirical observations contradict the hypothesized ordering of variables, that is, the total set of hypothesized effects. This is indicated by so-called fit coefficients, which are reported in the bottom rows of table 8.2. The value of these coefficients is in each case satisfactory, which implies that empirical observations did not falsify the assumptions of causal ordering implied in the model, and thus that no significant portions of covariance between the variables are left unaccounted.[26]

The next question we can address with the analyses reported in table 8.2 is how well they explain electoral participation. In table 8.2 we ordered the political systems on the basis of explained variance. The explanatory power of this set of independent variables varies considerably between the political systems of the EU. Greece ranks lowest, with a mere 6.7 percent explained variance, Sweden ranks highest with 30.9 percent. Why these differences? The coefficients of the independent variables may help elucidate these contrasts.

In a EU-wide perspective, three constructs or clusters stand out as the most powerful: social structure, political involvement, and parties' general appeal. The first of these, social structure, has by far the weakest (but still significant) effects in those systems where voting is compulsory (Belgium—Flanders and Wallonia—and Luxembourg), or where a quasi-compulsory regime is in place (Italy, Greece).

This underscores the observation by Franklin, van der Eijk, and Oppenhuis (1996) that system characteristics can constrain the playing room for individual-level factors when it comes to electoral participation. It also confirms the expectation of Verba, Nie, and Kim (1978) that compulsory voting diminishes the effect of social inequality on political participation. In line with the reduced impact of social structure under conditions of (semi-) compulsory voting, we also see that in these same systems the effect of political involvement is much weaker than elsewhere. So, the differences between systems in terms of the explanatory power of the model are at least in part a consequence of the limited opportunity for some kinds of variables to exert the effects they would have had when voting is a voluntary act and abstention is legitimate.

Of the other variables, efficacy and parties' policy appeal are the most important, although their effects vary considerably between systems. Support (or lack thereof) of national politics or of EU politics are factors that do generate significant coefficients in only a few of the political systems. Support of national politics is the weakest of these two, which indicates that non-participation in European Parliament elections can hardly be accounted for by citizens' alienation from their domestic political systems. The factor of most central interest in this chapter, support of EU politics, fails to add significantly to explanations of voting or abstention in nine out of sixteen systems. It is significant—but weak—in the other seven. It is strongest in Flanders, Luxembourg, and Sweden, but even in those three

Table 8.2 Determinants of participation in the European Parliament elections of 1999: Standardized total effects, explained variance and model fit indices

	Sw	Fi	Ne	Po	Ir	B-F	De	Brit	Sp	Au	Ge	Fr	It	Lu	B-W	Gr
Support EU politics	.117	.082				.142		.089	.085					.132	.075	
Support ntl politics	.089							.054								
Parties' general appeal	.261	.300	.247	.359	.222	.383	.094	.171	.242	.246	.200	.219	.332	.197	.077	.163
Political involvement	.354	.319	.281	.224	.197	.174	.412	.278	.201	.186	.247	.184	.103	.170	.196	.115
Parties' policy appeal	.167	.089	.248	.131			.086		.083		.142				.203	
Political efficacy	.100											.143		.106		
Social structure	.312	.279	.257	.223	.380	.175	.235	.305	.281	.303	.271	.220	.102	.173	.171	.172
% explained variance of electoral participation	30.9	26.0	24.8	23.8	22.9	22.6	21.7	19.5	18.8	18.3	18.1	14.4	12.9	12.6	10.7	6.7
NFI [1]	.978	.987	.978	.938	.932	.997	.998	.955	.972	.974	.976	.937	.968	.955	.990	.947
NNFI [2]	1.000	.996	.996	1.000	1.000	1.000	1.000	1.000	1.000	1.000	.993	1.000	1.000	1.000	1.000	1.000
CFI [3]	1.000	.999	.998	1.000	1.000	1.000	1.000	1.000	1.000	1.000	.998	1.000	1.000	1.000	1.000	1.000

Source: European Elections Study 1999. The structural equations program used is EQS. Findings are based on weighted data (political weight 2). (1) Bentler and Bonett's Normed Fit Index. (2) Bentler and Bonett's Non-normed Fit Index. (3) Comparative Fit Index. STEs < .05 are not reported.

systems it is by far inferior to the three most powerful factors: social structure, political involvement, and general party support.

Diachronic analysis

Our final question concerns possible changes over time in the importance of Euro-skepticism as a factor leading to electoral abstentions. Did this factor increase in importance, or decrease, or was there not much of a change? Are particular country patterns standing out? These questions can be answered on the basis of the diachronic analysis reported in table 8.3.[27] The first observation is that attitudes about Europe and the European Union do not play much of a role in any of these elections for the decision to go and vote or to abstain after structural determinants of electoral participation have been considered. No countries stand out as exceptions to this overall finding, and we find not much development over time either.

We do see some evolution, however, in the explanatory power of the structural determinants of turnout. Social-structural factors are losing some of their importance for electoral participation. This is most visible in France, but it can be traced elsewhere too. In combination with the generally low level of turnout (see also chapter 1 of this volume) this suggests that an increasing number of people whose social profile traditionally propelled them to turn out and vote increasingly fail to do so nonetheless. Even more pronounced is the decline in importance of political involvement as a facilitator of participation in European Parliament elections. Increasingly, people abstain no matter whether they are interested in politics or not, or whether they feel attached to a political party or not. Both trends accelerate between the 1994 and the 1999 election.

Could it be that controlling for these two factors conceals a stronger direct ('gross') association between turnout and (lack of) support for Europe and the European Union? More detailed analyses, not reported in a separate table, show that, on average, 'gross' and 'net' effects of political support for Europe and the European Union do not differ much—mainly because the 'gross' effects are very modest themselves.[28]

SUMMARY AND PERSPECTIVES

How much of a political—Euro-skeptic or even Euro-hostile—message is hidden behind non-voting in European Parliament elections? Is there any ground

Table 8.3 Participation in European Parliament elections: Effects of social structure, political involvement, and attitudes toward Europe*

Election	1989				1994				1999			
Country	A	B	C	C–B	A	B	C	C–B	A	B	C	C–B
Austria									.09	.13	.14	.01
Belgium	.09	.12	.12	.00	.08	.14	.14	.00	.04	.06	.09	.03
Britain	.12	.20	.21	.01	.08	.16	.17	.01	.12	.15	.16	.00
Denmark	.09	.17	.18	.00	.08	.20	.20	.00	.05	.12	.13	.00
Finland									.07	.19	.20	.01
France	.16	.21	.21	.00	.13	.24	.24	.01	.09	.12	.12	.00
Germany	.07	.15	.16	.01	.07	.18	.21	.03	.08	.12	.12	.00
Greece	.22	.24	.24	.00	.23	.32	.32	.01	.04	.06	.06	.00
Ireland	.18	.20	.20	.00	.11	.19	.19	.00	.13	.14	.14	.00
Italy	.08	.15	.15	.00	.17	.24	.25	.01	.02	.10	.10	.00
Luxembourg	.07	.08	.08	.00	.04	.11	.16	.04	.07	.13	.15	.01
Netherlands	.08	.15	.17	.02	.10	.15	.17	.02	.08	.16	.17	.01
Portugal	.07	.17	.18	.01	.09	.23	.23	.00	.04	.16	.16	.00
Spain	.09	.15	.16	.00	.11	.21	.22	.02	.08	.12	.13	.01
Sweden									.12	.20	.23	.03
Country average	.11	.17	.17	.00	.11	.20	.21	.01	.08	.13	.14	.01

* Figures are R^2 and R^2 changes from block-recursive multiple OLS regressions.
Source: European Election Studies 1989, 1994, and 1999. Missing values have been deleted pairwise. In the above table heading, "A" symbolizes the proportion of variance explained in turnout by social structural factors; "B" stands for a model where in addition to social structural factors those of political involvement are entered; "C" represents a model where in addition to social structural factors and factors measuring political involvement a third block of variables has been entered: attitudes toward European unification and the European Union.

to the common and intuitively almost self-evident interpretation that people stay home because they disagree with the European Union and European integration? The answer, in a nutshell, is negative: nowhere does anti-EU sentiment play a major role in the decision to participate in or abstain from European Parliament elections. Irrespective of their evaluation of the EU and the process of European integration, the decision to vote or to abstain is based on other grounds. Intuitively almost self-evident interpretations can be entirely incorrect, and this is a patent case thereof. The longevity and popularity of this false interpretation is itself surprising. Even without proper controls for antecedent causal factors do we find that the correlation between attitudes toward the EU and electoral participation is exceedingly weak in most countries, and at best of medium strength in a single occasion. The popularity of the notion of Euro-hostile non-voting flows to some extent from the widespread journalistic practice to ask non-voters about their reasons for not voting. As we argued above, this common procedure is tantamount to 'stacking the deck' (in technical jargon: it leads to selection bias). Non-voters have no choice in such situations but to say something that sounds like an intelligible and rational motivation, and stating that one is skeptic about the EU serves this purpose very well.[29] Those who do vote are rarely asked why they do so, but rather for whom they voted. Would they be asked to give a reason for going to the polls, they hardly can profess Euro-skepticism in a context where such an attitude would automatically be considered as a reason for not voting.[30] As we saw, even reputable academics—cf. Blondel et al.—sometimes fall prey to the lure of this fallacious way of using empirical information.

The absence of a 'supportable choice option' also contributes little to the explanation of non-voting, but it is more important than orientations toward the EU, in particular in the Netherlands and Wallonia. This explanation refers to the absence of (at least) one political party that adequately expresses a voter's policy concerns. Given the weight that is attributed to such policy orientations in 'economic' models of party choice, their limited impact on non-voting is actually quite surprising.

Among the individual-level constructs considered in the present analysis, social-structural locations are clearly the single most important predictor of electoral participation. Their causal effect (standardized total effect, see table 8.2) is the most powerful in seven of our sixteen political systems. General party support and political involvement tie for second most important factor, with four first ranks each. Substantive political reasons—be it the Euro-skeptic or the 'choicelessness' variant—matter very little, if at all, just as support for national politics and political efficacy.

In a way this is good news for the prospects of EU democracy. Growing levels of abstention in European Parliament elections are *not* the result of a growing alienation with the EU political system or hostility toward the politics of European integration. They rather seem to result from the fact that those who go and vote on election day—the socially integrated and politically involved—stay home in ever greater numbers when the members of the European Parliament are elected. The lack of excitement that comes with these elections, which itself is largely a function of the shortage of political consequences that can be associated with the election result, may be the main reason for this phenomenon. The second-order logic of European Parliament elections thus seems to diffuse the impact of major factors that cause (non)participation in first-order elections.

But there is another, darker side to all of this. Due to limited turnout, European Parliament elections do not contribute to legitimating the EU political system as much as they possibly could. And in the long run, low turnout figures might contribute to the erosion of political involvement and political support in more general terms. There is a danger of spill-over of apathy to the politics at national and sub-national levels although so far this seems not to have materialized (Franklin 2002b).

Having ruled out Euro-skeptic non-voting as a major factor in explaining abstention in European Parliament elections is one thing, a satisfactory explanation is quite another. Two kinds of extensions of the analyses reported here should result in more satisfactory models, at least as far as explanatory power is concerned. First of all, low R^2s to some extent may be caused by what in statistical jargon is termed 'local independence'.[31] Some factors that impinge on voting versus abstaining are a constant within each of the political systems. They may have 'across-the-board' effects, which cannot be picked up in separate analyses for each of the systems. This suggests a pooled analysis in which systemic and contextual explanatory factors (such as the timing of EP elections in terms of the domestic electoral cycle) are added to individual-level ones. Aspects to be incorporated in such analyses have been reported in chapter 1 of this volume. Integrated with individual-level variables, their addition to R^2 remains limited, however, as analyses on the 1989 European election by Oppenhuis (1995) and by Franklin, van der Eijk, and Oppenhuis (1996) have demonstrated. A second kind of extension of our present analysis involves interactions involving subgroups of citizens. Generational differences and differences in political sophistication come immediately to mind when thinking about the possibility that the specification of an explanatory model may be different for subgroups of respondents. But even then, findings from analyses that elaborate this line of thought also demonstrate limited increases in explained variance. Perhaps, then, we have to consider the possibility that at the individual level not all variance can be explained by structural or substantive factors, but that they also have to be accounted for by forces that are idiosyncratic (or random) in nature.

Notes

1. Obviously, the causal chain from elections to government formation to policies is far from deterministic, and the term 'decide' should not be taken literally.

2. Theoretically one could expect satisfaction also to generate abstentions: "why be active if without doing so things run quite well?" But empirical research on electoral participation in all kinds of contexts has so far failed to present any support for this possibility.

3. An obvious example are elections under communist rule, e.g., in the former GDR. Anti-system parties could not form and participate in general elections, and citizens opposing the regime could therefore not express this opposition other than by abstaining. A good number did, but official turnout figures were sugarcoated in order to mock mass support (Weber 1999).

4. Measurements of electoral participation or abstention regularly suffer from the tendency of over-reporting (i.e., from the fact that people claim to have voted while they actually abstained). One of the reasons for this is the 'social desirability' response set, i.e., that respondents say what they think is socially acceptable or desirable. We have tried to overcome this problem to some degree by lowering the 'social desirability' threshold of having participated by the following wording of the participation question: "A lot of people abstained in the European Parliament election of June 10 while others voted. Did you cast your vote?" In spite of this formulation, the samples still over-represent the voters, and under-represent the non-voters. Evidently, there is a relationship between non-voting and non-participating in a survey (because of refusals or other causes). The number of 'don't know' and other missing data responses is very low, so that there is no need to reconsider (and possibly recode) these as indicative of non-voting.

5. These are age and sex of respondents, their education, church attendance, union membership, and urban-rural residence.

6. This construct is based on the following indicators: EU membership is a good or bad thing (Eurobarometer trend variable); European integration has gone too far vs. should be pushed further (ten-point scale); preparedness for personal sacrifice if member country in crisis; satisfaction with the functioning of EU democracy (four-point scale); satisfaction with national EU policy (four-point scale). Note that this construct is somewhat broader than the conventional indicators of support for European integration as it involves both measures of policy satisfaction and regime support.

7. This construct is based on the following indicators: approval of the government's record to date; satisfaction with the functioning of democracy [in country] (four-point scale).

8. This class includes the following indicators: party attachment (four categories from very close to not close to any party); propensity to vote for the most preferred of the relevant national parties (a value that is usually in the upper regions of a scale ranging from 1 to 10).

9. This construct is based on the following indicators: the smallest of the distances to any of the nationally relevant parties in terms of European integration (see second indicator of note 11; this results in a value that is usually low on a scale ranging from 0 to 9); the smallest of the distances to any of the relevant national parties in terms of left and right (this likewise results in a value that is usually low on a scale ranging from 0 to 9); perceived existence or otherwise (dichotomous coding) of a national political party which is capable of dealing with the most important political problem (party competence).

10. This construct is based on the following indicators: politics is too complicated (four-point agree-disagree scale); vote does not matter (four-point agree-disagree scale).

11. This construct is based on the following indicators: attention to political news (four-point scale from none to a lot); interest in politics (four-point scale from not at all to very); attention to EU news (four-point scale from none to a lot); interest in EP election campaign (four-point scale from not at all to very).

12. Strong negative correlations indicate that Euro-skeptic citizens are more likely to participate than to abstain, and *vice versa*. This can occur when Euro-critical forces are particularly successful in mobilizing the vote.

13. See Schmitt (2001) on the importance of party competence considerations for vote choices.

14. Cf. Schmitt and Mannheimer (1991); Oppenhuis (1995); Franklin, van der Eijk, and Oppenhuis (1996).

15. In these analyses we distinguish between the two parts of Belgium—Flanders and Wallonia—because of the differences in their respective party systems. For the same reason we should differentiate between respondents in Northern Ireland and in Britain. The number of respondents in Northern Ireland is too small, however, to be used as a separate sub-sample, so these cases were dropped from the analysis. Compared to the Belgian and the British–Northern Irish differences in the structure of party competition, the deviation from the national scheme in the two regional party systems of Scotland and Wales are minor and do not require a distinct analysis.

16. The weight used in our analyses weights within each of the countries the data so that (weighted) distribution of electoral behavior in the 1999 European Parliament elections corresponds to the actual election result in that country. The specifics of this method have been reported elsewhere (van der Eijk and Oppenhuis 1991, and appendix B in van der Eijk and Franklin, 1996). After this, the resulting weight was multiplied with a country-specific constant so that the effective number of cases after weighting is equal for each political system.

17. Of course, attitudinal variables can also be seen as *moderators* of the effect of background characteristics on electoral participation. In this chapter, however, we will not pursue this possibility.

18. These express in a way similar to standardized regression coefficients the sum of the direct as well as indirect causal effects of each on the constructs on electoral participation.

19. Sex, age, education, marital status, union membership, and church attendance are used mainly as indicators of social integration and resource attribution.

20. Political involvement is measured somewhat differently than for the 1999 study—we include interest in politics (four-point scale from not at all to very) and party attachment (measured on a four-point scale from not close to any party to very close to a particular party).

21. Support for Europe and the EU is measured by two indicators. One is asking for respondents' support for European unification (in 1989 and 1994 on a four-point scale from very much against to very much in favor; in 1999 on a ten-point scale from has already gone too far to should be pushed further). The other is the familiar membership 'trend'

question from the Eurobarometers, which establishes whether one's country's membership of the EC/EU, according to the respondent, is a good thing, neither good nor bad, or a bad thing.

22. Due to a lack of social integration; see e.g., Lipset 1960; Tingsten 1963; Lancelot 1968; and Wolfinger and Rosenstone 1980.

23. Due to a lack of political involvement; see e.g. Lazarsfeld, Berelson, and Gaudet 1944; Berelson, Lazarfeld, and McPhee 1954; Campbell 1962.

24. The format of the questions to measure electoral participation differs slightly from study to study. This would be a matter of concern if we were estimating *levels* of participation, but not when—as we are here—the object is to identify *causes* of abstention.

25. One could wonder why no method of analysis was used that is specifically designed for dichotomous dependent variables, such as, e.g., logit or probit methods. We refrained to do so for presentational purposes, after having found that such analyses do not lead to substantively different conclusions.

26. This does not exclude the possibility that other models, with different assumptions about the causal ordering, are also not falsified by the data.

27. While we remain faithful to our preference for the OLS algorithm, control runs have been done with multiple logistic regression. We arrived at virtually the same results with Nagelkerke's pseudo R^2 as compared to OLS.

28. When examining forty-two cases (political systems × elections) there are, indeed, a few cases where the control variable (social-structural variables and political involvement) shield some of the 'gross' effect of European attitudes on participation in European Parliament elections, most notably Germany in 1994 and Sweden in 1999. This demonstrates the importance of causal analyses (or semi-causal ones, as in the case of block-recursive regression) as the 'gross' effect is biased owing to the absence of proper controls. Such instances make it explicable, however, that hasty interpretations of uncontrolled associations fuel the (incorrect) interpretation of electoral participation sometimes being motivated by Euro-skeptic attitudes.

29. We now leave aside the additional form of 'stacking the deck' that occurs when journalists select only those responses that fit their own substantive preconceptions and that provide maximum expected news-value (cf. Brants and van Praag 2005).

30. To a certain degree we find similar reactions in the context of national elections: it seems to be socially acceptable to rationalize not voting by referring to lack of trust in 'politics'. For people who do vote such rationalization for their behavior is often seen as 'illogical'. Yet in the context of national elections, too, the difference in distrust and cynicism between voters and non-voters is considerably reduced when one moves from self-verbalized motivations for one's own behavior to measures of distrust and cynicism that are applicable to all respondents.

31. It must be recognized, however, that R^2 is an often misleading measure for explanatory power. It seems almost impossible to eradicate the notion that the magnitude of this coefficient should be gauged in terms of the interval between 0 and 1. This is incorrect, however. Empirical distributions of categorical variables generate an upper limit of R^2 that is usually far below 1.

CHAPTER NINE

EU support and party choice

WOUTER VAN DER BRUG, CEES VAN DER EIJK, AND MARK N. FRANKLIN

Orientations toward European integration and toward the European Union figure prominently in many chapters of this volume. Chapter 4 focused on parties' orientations toward European integration, and on voters' perceptions thereof. Chapter 5 analyzed differences in supportive attitudes toward the EU, looking for explanations at contextual and individual levels. Chapter 7 demonstrated that media news affects citizens' orientations and attitudes toward the EU. In this chapter we investigate the effects of such attitudes toward the EU on party choice.

Attitudes toward the EU can affect party choice both in European elections and in national elections. At the time of European elections, citizens are more likely to be primed to take issues of European integration into account than in national elections when news coverage is predominantly focused on domestic issues. As a consequence, we may expect their attitudes toward European integration to affect their choice of parties. This influence may be limited, however, by the small degree to which issues relating to European integration are politicized in most EU countries. In national elections too, the lack of politicization is likely to restrict the salience of issues concerning European integration. But national elections are potentially more opportune occasions to vote according to one's attitudes about integration, as the future of the integration process is primarily determined by national politicians, not by members or aspiring members of the European Parliament. For different reasons we may thus expect attitudes toward integration to affect party choice in national elections as well as in European elections, making it appropriate to study effects of such attitudes in quite general terms.

In this chapter we do not concern ourselves primarily with differences in party choice between national and European elections. We already know from the analyses in chapters 2 and 3 that such differences are quite common and related to the timing and the second-order character of European elections. In this chapter we address the question whether and how voters' orientations toward European integration affect their choice of parties in general. Our models pertain first of all to national elections, but we provide additional analyses to assess whether effects of EU support on party choice are different among those who vote for the same party in both elections and those who voted for different parties.

Previous studies have shown that orientations toward the European Union and toward European integration contribute little to explaining party choice (e.g., Reif and Schmitt 1980; van der Eijk, Franklin, and Oppenhuis 1996; van der Eijk, Franklin, and van der Brug 1999). There are good reasons, however, for attitudes toward European integration having become more important predictors of the vote in 1999 than they were before. First, in the years before 1999, the member states of the Union increasingly transferred their jurisdiction over a wide set of policy areas to the EU. The actual importance of the European arena for determining policies that directly impinge on citizens' lives increased noticeably during the decade before 1999. To the extent that voters have become aware of this increased importance of EU policies, this may heighten the relevance of elections to the European Parliament as an occasion to express their orientations toward the Union, its policies, and further integration.

Second, citizens in the member states of the Union have witnessed 'Europe' becoming politically more contested in recent years (see also Marks and Steenbergen 2004). Opposition to the deepening and widening of the Union has gradually become an element of mainstream political discourse, often backed by respectable parties, interest groups, and social elites. Failed or nearly failed referenda about the treaties of Maastricht and Amsterdam, or in non-EU states about joining the Union, demonstrated such political contestation not only to the citizens in the countries involved, but in all European countries.[1] Events such as the introduction of the euro generated more discord among politicians and social and economic interests than many earlier steps in the integration process had done, even in the absence of referenda. This political contestation may have helped to 'prime' citizens into making the connection between their attitudes toward European integration and their actual choice of party.[2] Of course, some of these developments were still in the making at the time of the 1999 European elections, but they may well have cast their shadows ahead. Finally, as Marsh showed in chapter 3, attitudes toward European integration are moderately strong determinants of vote *shifts* between European and national elections. All of these considerations suggest the plausibility of voters' EU orientations affecting the choices they make at the ballot box.

Modeling party choice

The analysis of party choice is complicated by the fact that the differences between parties are qualitative in nature. In other words, party choice, the dependent variable, is a nominal-level variable that cannot be handled by common regression methods. Moreover, this variable is different in different countries, as each offers its citizens a different set of political parties from which to choose. Both problems can be 'solved' by redefining the dependent variable as a dummy that distinguishes, for example, between left votes and right and center ones (e.g., Franklin, Mackie, and Valen 1992) or between a vote for a government and an opposition party (e.g., Lewis-Beck 1988). Logistic regression can then be used to analyze such dichotomous dependent variables, which are, moreover, comparable between countries. The drawback of such procedures is that the redefined dependent variable only captures a single aspect of party choice, at the exclusion of all kinds of other aspects that may be of importance to individual voters. An alternative is to analyze party choice in its original nominal form using methods such as multinomial logit. The disadvantage of this approach is that it can only be applied one country at a time, yielding separate results for each country that can only be compared in an impressionistic way.[3]

The solution we prefer is to reconceptualize party choice as a two-stage decision process that follows the logic of individual choice theory (Ben-Akiva and Lerman 1985), which also underlies Downs' (1957) theory of voting. This approach implies that explaining party choice involves two separate analyses. The first of these conceptualizes the dependent variable as the utility that voters would derive from voting for each of the parties in a system—a dependent variable that can be analyzed with straightforward regression models. The second stage of voters' decisions is to translate those utilities into a choice of party, which is usually regarded as a matter of utility maximization, i.e., choosing the party that would yield more utility than any other. The analyses pertaining to this second stage involve assessing the extent to which voters do make their choices in accordance with this maximizing rule. Because utilities are not party-specific (the research question for the first stage is formulated in such terms as "what is it that determines the utility of voting for a party?") there is no problem in analyzing data from multiple countries at the same time.[4]

The measure of electoral utility that we use is based on a direct operationalization of this concept by way of the following survey question: "Some people always vote for the same party. Other people make up their mind each time. Please tell me for each of the following how probable it is that you will ever vote for this party." Downs' concept of 'party utility' (the benefits—subjective or objective—a voter gets from voting for a particular party) is often referred to interchangeably with the notion of party preferences (how much parties are preferred in relation to each other). The concept of party utility has the advantage of connoting a value that can be measured rather than a set of options that can only be ordered. We prefer the phrase 'propensity to support a party' (or simply 'party support') when referring to the Downsian concept of party utility, partly because the word 'utility' has in recent years acquired an overlay of additional meanings from its use in the rational choice approach to theory construction that are too restrictive for our purposes.

Typically, these 'party support' questions are asked for each of the political parties in a country, or at least for each of the parties that can reasonably be expected to win representation in the national parliament. The qualification 'ever' serves to free the respondent from the typical ballot constraint that only preference for a single party can be expressed, or from other restrictions that the ballot may exert over the expression of electorally relevant preferences at a specific moment in time. Respondents were offered a ten-point scale (of which only the polar extremes were labeled as "certainly never" and "certainly at some time") to express the likelihood of ever voting for each of the parties. Note that the question does not specify any particular electoral contest but that it relates to elections in general. These questions are sometimes referred to as the 'probability to vote' questions, but it must be emphasized that they do not measure probabilities in the statistical sense. The responses (or any transformation thereof) do not sum to 1, as they would if they were probabilities. Indeed, the fact that these variables do in fact yield different sums for different respondents is one of the things giving us confidence that the questions do elicit utilities (van der Eijk et al. 2006).

To be interpretable as utilities, responses to these questions need to fulfill two additional criteria. First, the empirical relationship should hold that actual party

Table 9.1 Party choice and propensities to support parties

	Percentage voted for the party with highest support score in European election	Percentage would vote for the party with highest support score in national election
Austria	88.2*	93.6
Belgium: Flanders	89.4	92.9
Belgium: Wallonia	85.1	89.7
Britain	84.5	92.6
Denmark	73.9	92.4
Finland	82.8	92.0
France	82.6	86.8
Germany	90.9	93.9
Greece	89.2	95.4
Ireland	77.5	95.2
Italy	83.4	93.2
Luxembourg	80.3	85.3
The Netherlands	90.7	93.4
Portugal	96.6	96.4
Spain	94.0	94.7
Sweden	75.8	98.2
EU-wide	87.2	93.3

* 88.2% of the respondents who voted in the European election gave the highest support propensity score to the party they had voted for.

choice coincides with the party to which respondents award the highest utility. This implies that actual party choice should only depend on the responses to these questions and that no other factors impinge directly (i.e., without being mediated by electoral utilities) on party choice. Table 9.1 demonstrates that this assumption is empirically well founded. It shows the extent to which party choice can be deduced from the party support propensities.[5]

As can readily be seen, when asked which party they would vote for if a national election would be held on the day of the interview, more than 90 percent of the voters name the party to which they awarded the highest support score. The highest score generally corresponds to actual or intended party choice in national elections. As a consequence, we arrive at valid conclusions about the determinants of choice by analyzing these support propensities.[6]

An additional requirement is that respondents should not routinely give a "certainly never" response to each party they do not vote for, as then the answers for all the parties yield no more information than the ubiquitous party choice question. Without presenting details here, the party support measures are not marred by such problems. The analyses to be presented in chapter 11 demonstrate that there are large numbers of voters in all member states of the EU whose preference for their second most preferred party lags only minimally behind their preference for their most preferred one (for which they actually vote). For some people this is also the case for their third most preferred party.

In the analyses in this chapter the party support propensity is the phenomenon to be explained, the dependent variable. In order to achieve comparability between political systems we require an innovative research strategy, which will be described in detail below. At this point it is mainly important to note that the use of this dependent variable avoids the problems of a nominal-level dependent variable that is different between countries. Therefore, this dependent variable gives a much firmer empirical basis for comparative explanatory propositions about determinants of party choice than one would obtain from the analysis of party choice itself.

DESIGN TO ANALYZE THE DETERMINANTS OF PARTY CHOICE IN COMPARATIVE RESEARCH

The party support propensities yield a large number of variables: one for each party. Yet, they should all be analyzed simultaneously, as if they were a single variable. The logic of the party utility concept suggests a common formulation of the factors that yield party support, rather than party-specific formulations. Obviously, it is an empirical question to what extent the propensities to support various parties can be explained by common factors, and to what extent party-specific factors still play a role.

All the different party support variables can be analyzed as a single dependent variable by employing a variant of the technique suggested by Stimson (1985) for regression in time and space. In practical terms this means performing a regression on a 'stacked' data matrix which, instead of having one case for each respondent, has one case for each party for each respondent (one record for each respondent ×

party combination). Figure 9.1 illustrates graphically how the stacked data matrix is constructed.

In the stacked data matrix each respondent is represented by as many 'cases' as there are parties for which support propensities were measured. Because different parties are represented by different cases rather than by different variables, the dependent variable pertains to parties in general and can be considered as a

FIGURE 9.1 Structure of stacked data matrix

Original Data Matrix

resp-id	Age	left/right position respondent	perceived LR-position pty 1	perceived LR position pty 2	perceived LR position pty 3	L/R Dist. to party 1	L/R Dist. to party 2	L/R Dist. to party 3	Vote-choice	Propensity to support party 1	Propensity to support party 2	Propensity to support party 3
1	59	4	4	6	7	0	2	3	1	9	5	4
2	40	6	3	7	8	3	1	2	2	5	9	7
3	22	9	3	6	8	6	3	1	3	2	4	7

Stacked Data Matrix

resp-id	id-of-party	Age	left/right distance	vote-choice	Propensity to support
1	1	59	0	1	9
1	2	59	2	1	5
1	3	59	3	1	4
2	1	40	3	2	5
2	2	40	1	2	9
2	3	40	2	2	7
3	1	22	6	3	2
3	2	22	3	3	4
3	3	22	1	3	7

measure of generic party support. After having constructed this stacked data matrix for each country separately, all the countries can be pooled into a single country comparative data matrix.[7] The result of these operations in the European Election Study of 1999 is a single matrix, containing 108,364 records, which are weighted down to 13,500, the original number of actual observations. The party support propensities that are the dependent variable relate to a total of 117 different political parties and 16 different electoral contexts (see the appendix of this chapter for details).[8]

In this stacked and pooled data matrix, independent variables that pertain to relations between party and voter have to be specially constructed. A voter's position on the left-right scale, for example, will not capture in this design the effect of ideology on party support, but a *distance* between the left-right positions of a voter and the respective party does capture this effect. Policy distances between the respondent on the one hand, and the respective party in the stacked data matrix were computed for two policy scales: left-right, and the issue of European integration. In both cases respondents had been asked to place themselves as well as the most important parties in their country on a scale ranging from one to ten. In the case of the left-right scale the extremes are labeled 'left' (position 1) and 'right' (position 10). In the case of European integration the extremes are labeled "European integration should be pushed further" (position 1), and "European integration has been pushed too far already" (position 10).

When no appropriate measure of distance or similarity can be straightforwardly computed, for instance because relevant party characteristics are unmeasured, appropriate independent variables have to be constructed by means of specific transformations of the original independent variables (for details, see the appendix of this chapter). This procedure was applied to all voter characteristics other than their orientations toward left or right and toward European integration. As a consequence of this procedure, the regression coefficients associated with these transformed variables will always be positively signed.

In order to assess the importance of domestic and of 'European' considerations in explaining voters' choices in the 1999 elections to the European Parliament, we need to include in our model all relevant determinants of party support.[9] As demographic characteristics we included social class, income, and religion. Ideological and issue considerations are represented by left-right distance and by voters' distance to parties concerning European integration. A measure of EU approval is included, which is based on the classic Eurobarometer question "generally speaking, do you think that [our country's] membership of the European Union is a good thing, a bad thing, neither good nor bad" (appropriately transformed by way of the procedure described in the appendix). Voters' preferences concerning a set of current political issues were combined into an issues variable, and approval (or lack thereof) of the incumbent government was likewise included as an independent variable. In addition, two interactions with voter × party characteristics were added that turned out to affect party choice: interactions of perceptual agreement with, on the one hand, ideological proximity and, on the other hand, issue proximity (van der Eijk and Franklin 1996).[10]

Finally, we included as an independent variable a simple party characteristic, party size, measured by the proportion of seats a party occupies in the national parliament. Party size represents a strategic consideration that voters may take into account.[11] When two parties are about equally attractive otherwise, voters will have a higher propensity to support the largest one because it stands a better chance of achieving its policy goals. Previous research has shown that such strategic considerations are important to voters (e.g., Oppenhuis 1995; van der Eijk, Franklin, and Oppenhuis 1996).

Results

We start by investigating the extent of variance in support propensities that can be explained by the different (groups of) independent variables, taken one at a time. We report this for each of the countries separately, and for the EU-wide dataset as a whole (see table 9.2). We have two measures of attitudes toward the EU (see above), and their bivariate effects on support propensities are reported in the first two columns of table 9.2. Both exert rather limited effects on party support (and thus also on party choice). The highest R^2 for the effect of the European integration variable is 0.11 in Germany, and the lowest is 0 percent in Luxembourg. The EU-wide explained variance is only 4 percent. The explanatory power of EU approval (the classic 'good thing–bad thing' question) is of a similar magnitude (between 1 and 9%, and 3% EU-wide). Even though these effects appear to be limited, they are similar in magnitude to some of the other factors that determine party support: government approval, issue importance, class, and religion.

Ideological distance to parties is a much more important determinant of party support than any other independent variable. The strength of the effects of (distance to party in terms of) left-right, class, religion, and EU approval is quite comparable to what similar analyses yielded for 1989 (van der Eijk, Franklin, and Oppenhuis 1996, 350) and for 1994 (van der Eijk, Franklin, and van der Brug

Table 9.2 Proportion explained variance (R^2-adjusted) of various models to explain party support

	European integration	Approval of EU	Government approval	Importance of issues	Left-right	Class*	Religion
Austria	.03	.04	.02	.02	.13	.02	.03
Belgium: Flanders	.02	.09	.05	.10	.19	.04	.04
Belgium: Wallonia	.03	.03	.01	.07	.15	.04	.02
Britain	.03	.02	.04	.01	.09	.01	.01
Denmark	.06	.06	.02	.02	.17	.02	.01
Finland	.00	.02	.01	.02	.15	.03	.04
France	.04	.02	.03	.02	.24	.01	.04
Germany	.11	.01	.02	.01	.19	.01	.02
Greece	.05	.02	.08	.01	.20	.01	.02
Ireland	.02	.01	.01	.01	.11	.02	.02
Italy	.07	.02	.06	.01	.17	.01	.01
Luxembourg	.05	.03	.01	.03	.17	.04	.05
Netherlands	.07	.01	.01	.01	.19	.01	.06
Portugal	.02	.01	.07	.03	.29	.01	.02
Spain	.05	.01	.09	.00	.21	.01	.03
Sweden	.04	.06	.02	.03	.26	.07	.03
EU	.04	.03	.03	.03	.18	.02	.03

* The effect of social class on party choice is estimated with two predictors (y-hats) of subjective social class and family income.

1999, 174). In comparison to 1994, the variance explained by left-right distance decreased somewhat (from 21% to 18%), as did the effects of issues (from 4% to 3%), social class (from 3% to 2%), and religion (from 6% to 3%).[12] These changes in explained variance from 1989 or 1994 are too small to warrant any conclusions about possible trends. Our findings here can thus be regarded as an independent confirmation of established insights about the importance of factors that impinge on the vote—a fact that greatly increases our confidence in them.

In table 9.3 we present variance explained in a series of block-recursive regression models. The way the models are specified follows the logic of a 'funnel of

Table 9.3 Proportion explained variance (R²-adjusted) of models to explain party support. Each subsequent model contains all independent variables from the previous model and adds some new ones.*

	Model 1	Model 2	Model 3	Model 4	Model 5	Model 6
Austria	.05	.16	.18	.22	.23	.30
Belgium: Flanders	.08	.23	.26	.28	.29	.29
Belgium: Wallonia	.06	.19	.21	.21	.22	.23
Britain	.02	.10	.11	.14	.17	.25
Denmark	.04	.19	.20	.25	.27	.32
Finland	.06	.18	.19	.23	.24	.28
France	.05	.26	.26	.27	.28	.31
Germany	.03	.21	.21	.25	.26	.41
Greece	.03	.22	.22	.23	.26	.32
Ireland	.03	.14	.15	.15	.16	.24
Italy	.02	.18	.18	.19	.22	.24
Luxembourg	.08	.24	.24	.26	.27	.34
Netherlands	.07	.24	.25	.27	.27	.38
Portugal	.03	.30	.31	.32	.35	.40
Spain	.04	.23	.23	.25	.28	.43
Sweden	.09	.30	.30	.34	.35	.36
EU-wide	.05	.21	.22	.24	.26	.31

* The regressions contain the following independent variables:
Model 1: religion and class
Model 2: model 1 + l-r ideology
Model 3: model 2 + issue priorities
Model 4: model 3 + approval of the EU and issue 'EU integration'
Model 5: model 4 + government approval
Model 6: model 5 + party size

causality' (Campbell et al. 1960). The order of the independent variables reflects our assumptions about their causal antecedence with respect to the dependent variable, party support. Short-term effects are located closer to party support (and thus, as we discussed above, also closer to the actual vote), whereas long-term effects are located further away from the actual decision. The first model in table 9.2 represents the long-term effects of socio-structural variables (in this case social class and religion). The second model adds ideological considerations. Ideologies represent long-standing value orientations which are not expected to change over the course of a single election campaign. Issues (added in model 3) and EU-related attitudes (added in model 4) are considered to be less long term than ideologies. This is not to imply that they change within the course of a single election campaign, but they may well do so between elections. Government approval (added in model 5) represents an evaluation of recent performance of the governing parties only and is therefore a short-term factor. Party size (added in model 6) is expected to represent strategic considerations, which are the most immediate ones.[13]

In order to assess the effect of EU attitudes we should compare model 4 to model 3. This comparison makes it clear that the effect of EU attitudes on the vote contributes only marginally to the explanation of party support: additions to explained variance vary from virtually nothing (0%) in Wallonia and Ireland to a maximum of 5 percent in Denmark, and 2 percent for the EU as a whole. The seemingly larger importance of these variables in table 9.1 (particularly for some countries) is thus mainly spurious, generated by more antecedent factors. The entire set of variables that are added in models 2, 3, and 4 relate clearly to voters' substantive policy considerations. If we compare the explained variance of model 1 (with only socio-structural variables) with that of model 4, we see that substantive political orientations have a considerable impact on party-support propensities, raising the explained variance (EU-wide) from 5 percent in model 1 to 24 percent in model 4. By far the largest part of this increase is due to the ideological (left-right) distance between voters and parties, while the more specific issues combined (including EU attitudes) add about 3 percent to variance explained.[14]

The next addition (model 5) concerns government approval. Elections provide citizens with the opportunity to reward incumbents for good performance or to punish them if they did not do well. Such retrospective evaluations of government performance do indeed contribute to voting decisions, but the effects thereof are not large. R^2 goes up by 2 percent for the EU-wide analysis, and nowhere is the increase more than 3 percent.

Finally we added the variable 'party size' (in model 6), which reflects voters' strategic considerations. In the EU-wide analysis, this increases variance explained considerably, from 26 percent to 31 percent. Between political systems, large differences exist in the magnitude of this contribution to the explanatory power of the model, which are mainly due to differences in the fragmentation of their party systems.[15] In Flanders and Wallonia—political systems with many small parties—the effect of party size is almost negligible, whereas in Germany and Spain (both multiparty systems that are dominated by two large parties) R^2 increases by 15 percent when party size is taken into account. This suggests that strategic considerations of voters that are tapped by this variable are much more relevant in systems dominated by a small number of large parties than in systems where grand coalitions are the norm. This explanation for the differences in the effect of party size is not fully satisfactory because it cannot explain why party size has a relatively strong effect in the Netherlands and a relatively weak effect in Britain. An additional factor that could conceivably play a role is whether there are multiple ideologically similar parties. A voter who finds several parties, large and small, close to his own ideological position has indeed to revert to strategic considerations to determine which of these would yield more utility if she or he voted for them. In the Netherlands there are many ideologically similar parties, but in Britain the number is small (primarily Labour and the Liberals).

Of the various models reported in table 9.3, model 6 most closely resembles similar models presented elsewhere for explaining party choice in the 1989 European elections (van der Eijk, Franklin, and Oppenhuis 1996, 357), and in the 1994 European election (van der Eijk, Franklin, and van der Brug 1999, 176). Yet, its explanatory power decreased from 0.43 in 1989, to 0.36 in 1994, to 0.31 in 1999. These differences are partly caused by differences in the measurement of independent variables (see also note 12). Yet, the explanatory power of structural variables such as social class and religion as well as of ideology (left-right) has also somewhat decreased in strength. The implication of this finding is that in 1999 other short-term factors (perhaps including quite idiosyncratic ones) than the ones included in our model were of somewhat more importance for voters' party-support propensities than in earlier elections. This suggests an increased susceptibility to short-term changes in party support (and hence, in voting). In chapters 11 and 12 the ramifications of this will be traced in terms of the propensity for electoral volatility.

After the analyses presented above, three questions still need to be addressed. The first of these concerns the effects of the independent variables. Table 9.3 gave us their explanatory power but not their (causal) effects. The second question is whether or not a Europe-wide analysis (as presented in the EU row of the various tables) is sensible when country-specific analyses (the country rows in the respective tables) seem to indicate considerable differences between the countries. Third, and finally, one may wonder whether a single model is suitable for different groups of respondents, and in particular whether it fits those who indicated

Table 9.4 Regression coefficients (beta's) of the most encompassing models to explain party support (EU-wide)

	Model 6	Model 6 with interaction
Religion	.12	.12
Subjective social class and family income	.10	.10
Left-right perceived distance	−.32	−.32
Issue priorities	.08	.08
EU approval	.09	.09
European integration	−.07	−.07
Government approval	.13	.13
Party size	.24	.24
Interaction left-right distance with structural agreement		−.03
R^2-Adjusted	.31	.31

that they did not vote for the party that they ranked highest in terms of support propensities in the European elections of 1999 (see also table 9.1, above).

Table 9.4 presents the causal effects of the independent variables in the form of the standardized regression coefficients of model 6 (see also table 9.3) on an EU-wide basis, i.e., on the dataset in which the surveys from all the member states of the EU have been pooled. These coefficients show clearly that only two factors have a strong impact on support propensities. First of all the left-right distance between a voter and a party (the larger the distance, the smaller the preference, hence the negative sign of the coefficient). Second, the size of a party, which suggests that voters will, *ceteris paribus,* prefer large parties over small ones, presumably because they offer better prospects for getting ideological or policy stands realized in actual government policies.[16] The causal effects of the more specific issue variables are weak, including those for EU approval and attitudes with respect to European integration. Variables related to class also have a rather weak effect on party support, as has consistently been found in studies conducted after the late 1970s (cf. Franklin, Mackie, and Valen 1992). Religious factors and the (dis)approval of the incumbent government are of intermediate strength.

Yet, how should we look upon these EU-wide effects after having observed in table 9.3 that the explanatory power of the independent variables varies greatly between countries? Is it not necessary, one might wonder, to specify interaction effects that would tap differences between countries in the effects of the independent variables? Earlier research along similar lines on the data from the 1989 European Election Study showed indeed that the regression effect of some variables is so different in the various countries that some interaction terms are warranted (van der Eijk, Franklin, and Oppenhuis 1996, 354). The most important of those was an interaction between left-right distance on the one hand and the perceptual agreement in a country about the position of the various parties on the left-right continuum on the other. The introduction of this interaction is, obviously, only possible in the EU-wide model, since in each country the degree of perceptual agreement is a constant. Including this interaction term in model 6 yields the results that are displayed in the right-hand column of table 9.4. We find for 1999 almost the same value for this coefficient as in 1989 and in 1994, -0.03, which indicates that in countries where voters agree more with one another about parties' left-right positions, left-right distance between a voter and a party has a stronger impact on party support. Adding this interaction term to the model does not, however, increase the R^2.

In addition, a comprehensive scan was performed to assess whether or not any other additional interaction-terms involving the central independent variables of this chapter (EU support) are necessary to capture differences among the different countries in how EU support affects party-support propensities. The results of this scan were also overwhelmingly negative.[17] So, there is no compelling need to complicate the models by including country-specific interaction effects. The differences in the explanatory strengths of the independent variables in tables 9.2 and 9.3 are therefore not to be interpreted as differences between these countries in the process that generates preference for political parties. It merely reflects differences in distributions of the respective variables, not differences in how they impinge on party support. Having discovered this, we may indeed conclude that we are justified in combining the surveys from the different member states of the EU into a single analysis, because the mechanism by which independent variables affect party support (and hence party choice) is fundamentally the same in all these countries.

Our final concern is whether we are justified in applying a single model to all respondents, when we saw in table 9.1 that almost 13 percent of those who voted in the European elections had voted for a different party than the one they rated highest in terms of support propensities. To assess whether this is a problem, we tested whether the parameters of the model are different for two groups of citizens: those who voted in the European election for the party to which they indicated the highest support (at the time of the interviews), and those who voted for a different party. This test showed that model 6 fits the data for both groups of voters equally well.[18]

Discussion and conclusions

While the European Union becomes increasingly more important as an arena in which policies are shaped and implemented that have large consequences for the member countries and their individual citizens, attitudes toward European integration and toward the EU are still of marginal importance for the process leading to voters' party choice. Apparently, voters use neither national nor European elections as occasions to express in their vote their evaluation of the EU or their preferences with respect to the speed of integration.[19] Why not?

A first possible explanation could be that voters do not consider European integration important, or that they all agree with each other as well as with their party elites about the right course of action regarding Europe. Either of these conditions would be sufficient to generate small effects and weak explanatory power. However, as was demonstrated in chapter 5, neither of these conditions is met. Voters clearly disagree among themselves about the desirability of (further) European integration, and about how the existing Union should be evaluated. A different explanation would be that voters do not perceive parties to present a clear set of alternative options. Chapter 10 does show that this is a more plausible explanation.

From the perspective of democratic representation, it is problematic that attitudes toward European integration do not enter the voting decision. The evidence we presented above indicates that, very much in line with the notion of European elections being second-order national elections, these elections are primarily used by voters for expressing domestic political concerns, and not for voicing their concerns about the EU and European integration. As we indicated in this book's introductory chapter, the EU and its decision-making processes are isolated from domestic and popular influence in a number of ways. When voters sense that this is the case, from the actions of elites or from the media, it makes sense for them not to base their vote on substantive orientations regarding the EU, not even in European elections. This is not to imply, however, that their experiences with the consequences of European integration, and their satisfaction or dissatisfaction with those consequences, will never have electoral consequences.

But to the extent that they do, it will be in indirect ways, that will be explored in more detail in chapter 12.

Appendix

In order to analyze the effects of determinants of party support in a stacked data matrix, we need a linear transformation of these independent variables. Appropriate transformations are obtained from a regression of each of the party-support propensities in turn on the original independent variable (in the unstacked data matrix).

The original regression equation for each party is $y_i = a + b \cdot x_i + e_i$, in which y_i is the propensity that respondent i has to support this party (measured with the probability of a future vote question) and x_i is an independent variable. In this equation the predicted values are obtained by $\hat{y}_i = a + b \cdot x_i$. By substituting $a + b \cdot x_i$ with $\hat{y}_i$ in the equation, the new regression equation (using the $\hat{y}_i$ as predictors of party support) becomes: $y_i = \hat{y}_i + e_i$. If we would estimate this latter model, the estimated intercept would be 0 and the estimated slope would be 1, while the residuals e_i (which form the basis for the computation of explained variance) are unaltered. After the predicted values are computed for each party in turn, these predicted values (y-hats) are saved and stacked to become the new independent variable. This is permissible because the y-hats are simply linear transformations of the original independent variable x. To create one independent variable in the stacked data matrix (which contains support measures for 117 parties), we thus did 117 regression analyses, saved the y-hats, and stacked these on top of each other.

When stacking the y-hats on top of each other in the stacked matrix, the actual variable which is added is not the predicted value (y-hat), but the deviation of the y-hats from their mean for each party. This still encapsulates the variance in support propensities caused by the independent variable, but prevents differences among parties in the average level of party support from being incorporated in the newly created independent variable. Such differences among parties in average support are caused by other factors besides x_i, and should hence not contribute to the variance in the newly created predictor. For an elaborate discussion of this procedure, see van der Eijk and Franklin (1996, chapter 20). In the analyses reported in this chapter, this procedure was applied for the variables social class, income, religion, issues, EU-approval, and government approval.

Since multiple observations in the stacked data matrix refer to the same respondent, these observations are not independent of each other. Moreover, the distribution of the dependent variable is rather skewed, so that the data do not conform to standard OLS assumptions. For this reason we also estimated robust standard errors (in STATA), which do not assume a homoskedastic distribution of the error terms. Additionally, multiple observations pertaining to one respondent were defined as mutually dependent (using the option 'cluster' in STATA). All estimates of these robust standard errors turned out to be substantially *smaller* than those obtained when estimating the standard error of a normal OLS regression on a stacked data matrix in which the number of respondents is weighted down to the original sample size. In this chapter we therefore present the results of the latter procedure, which provides the most conservative estimates of statistical significance.

NOTES

1. Often, failed or near-failed referenda are interpreted as evidence of popular apprehension about (further) European integration. In many of such instances, however, support for or opposition to the national government that was responsible for the topic of the referendum was of greater importance in explaining referendum votes than support for or opposition to further European integration (see, e.g., Franklin, Marsh, and McLaren 1994; Franklin, Marsh, and Wlezien 1994; Franklin, van der Eijk, and Marsh 1995; for a contrary view see Garry, Marsh, and Sinnott 2005). For further discussion about this domestic background see also de Vreese and Semetko (2001, 2002) and Franklin (2002a).

2. Concerning priming processes, see, e.g., Krosnick and Kinder 1990; Iyengar and Simon 1993; Krosnick and Brannon 1993.

3. This problem can be solved by using conditional logit (CL) models for comparative analyses on data that are pooled across countries (cf. Kroh 2003). This is only possible, however, to the extent that the independent variables can be construed as relationships between individuals and voters. For many of the variables of interest here this cannot easily be done in a way that is appropriate to CL. As a consequence, one has to use mixed models which comprise elements of conditional logit and multinomial logit side-by-side, with the latter component defying pooled analyses across countries. An additional problem with these various kinds of logit models (also known as discrete choice models) is that simulation studies have demonstrated the results of such analyses to be extremely vulnerable to specification bias (van der Eijk and Kroh 2002; van der Eijk et al. forthcoming).

4. Earlier applications of this approach have demonstrated its value particularly for comparative analyses; see, e.g., Tillie 1995; Oppenhuis 1995; van der Eijk and Franklin 1996; van der Brug, Fennema, and Tillie 2000; van der Brug and Fennema 2003: van der Brug, van der Eijk, and Franklin 2006). For a more detailed elaboration of the rationale, see also van der Eijk, 2002 and van der Eijk et al. 2006.

5. In the European Elections Studies of 1989 and 1994 the relationship between party choice and highest utility was equally strong (e.g., van der Eijk, Franklin, and Oppenhuis 1996; van der Eijk, Franklin, and van der Brug 1999). A great number of additional validating analyses have been reported elsewhere (cf. Tillie 1995; van der Eijk et al. 2006).

6. Many other analyses can be performed to demonstrate that the replacement of actual party choice with this specific set of utility scores is justified. The most important of these is an unfolding analysis that demonstrates that the scores on the probability to vote questions can be understood to emanate from the same latent factors for all parties, implying that the origins of these scores are identical for all parties, including the one actually voted for. Such validating analyses have been reported in detail by Tillie (1995).

7. Obviously, all these manipulations require that identifying variables for party and for country are added to the data matrix. These enable party and country characteristics to be used as independent variables (or as terms in interaction with voter characteristics), and they are necessary to conduct empirical checks on the implied assumption of unit homogeneity of all individual × party combinations across parties and across countries. Such checks have been run extensively and this assumption could not be rejected. These tests will not be reported here in detail. What they entail and how they are conducted is discussed more extensively in van der Eijk, Franklin, and Oppenhuis 1996, 356–362.

8. We distinguish within Belgium between Flanders and Wallonia because of the differences in their party systems. This yields a total of sixteen different electoral contexts.

9. The selection of these variables has been inspired by previous studies of party choice in European elections (van der Eijk, Franklin, and Oppenhuis 1996; van der Eijk, Franklin, and van der Brug 1999), as well as by the multitude of analyses of party choice based on national election studies (for good reviews, see e.g., LeDuc, Niemi, and Norris 2002). The obvious limitation is the availability of variables in the European Election Study 1999.

10. Perceptual agreement of party positions is a measure of the extent to which respondents in each country agree as to the location of their political parties in left-right terms (van der Eijk 2001).

11. This variable will only be used in multivariate analyses. It is somewhat less appropriate in bivariate analyses, as people's preferences for parties are particularly affected by 'size' in conjunction with substantive considerations (e.g., issues, left-right, religion, etc.).

12. The decrease in the effect of religion is, however, largely due to the fact that the 1999 study had no separate sample of Northern Ireland as was the case in 1994. The 1999 study contained only thirty-one respondents from Northern Ireland, too small a number to be analyzed. These respondents were omitted from our analyses. The comparison with 1989 and 1994 is slightly marred, moreover, by differences in the number of available indicators or in the wording of items concerning issues and EU approval.

13. Although party size is a consequence of the number of people who support a party, and thus in the long term may be seen in part as the consequence of issue preferences, at any one election the sizes of parties can be regarded as exogenous to the individual voter. For a more detailed discussion on the interpretation of party size as reflecting voters'

strategic considerations, see van der Eijk, Franklin, and Oppenhuis 1996, 352–353, and Tillie 1995.

14. One could argue that adding left-right to the equation after (rather than before) the position and valence issue variables would increase the contribution of issues to the explanation. Still, the causal ordering implied by such an analysis does not appear compatible with the notion that left-right orientations function as political schema (Conover and Feldman 1984; Kerlinger 1984), super issues (Inglehart 1984), or ideological identification (van der Eijk and Niemöller 1983).

15. It might be wondered whether party size would suffer from circularity as a predictor of party support: parties are large because they are supported by large numbers of people who consequently also vote for them. But this concern arises from a level of analysis confusion. No one vote affects the size of a party appreciably, so at the individual level of analysis there is no circularity. To be large, parties need to be attractive to large numbers of people. Once they have grown large, additional people may vote for them because of their size, but size in itself is not an explanation for their size.

16. Tillie (1995) demonstrated that the effect of size is an average effect that differs in strength for different groups of voters. He distinguishes, on the basis of a special series of survey questions, between pragmatists and idealists, the first group supposedly being more sensitive to the strategic considerations that we ascribe to voters in our interpretation of the effect of party size. When introducing that distinction in the analysis, he finds that most of the effect of party size has been absorbed by it, which validates the interpretation used here.

17. The scan was performed as follows. Model 6 plus the interaction term concerning perceptual agreement and left-right distance was run on the EU-wide dataset, and the residuals were saved. Subsequently, these saved residuals were used as the dependent variable in a country-by-country analysis with the same independent variables (except the interaction because it would be perfectly collinear with left-right distance) as in the EU-wide model. Any significant coefficients point then to the potential need for adding more interactions to the model so as to account for differences in the strength of independent variables between countries. This procedure thus allows us to diagnose the need for interaction effects between political systems on the one hand and the independent variables on the other. When looking at the issue of European integration we checked for each of the systems, sixteen in total. None of these sixteen interaction terms was significant. When using the same procedure for the other independent variables, we find five significant interaction effects (at $p < 0.01$), all of which involve party size. The EU-wide analysis overstates the effect of party size somewhat for two systems (Flanders and Sweden), while it somewhat understates it for three systems (Germany, Spain, and the Netherlands). We were unable to interpret these interactions in substantive terms (i.e., by which characteristics of countries they might have been generated). Moreover, in similar analyses for 1989 and 1994 we did not find these significant interactions. This combination of uninterpretability and instability over time made us refrain from including these interaction effects in the models displayed in table 9.4.

18. The scan was performed in the following way. We constructed a dummy variable that distinguishes between the group of citizens who did and who did not vote for the party to which they gave highest utility at the time of the interview. This dummy was added to that model displayed in table 9.4 (right-most model). Then this model was run on the EU-wide dataset, and the residuals were saved. The effect of this dummy variable was not significant (b = −0.061; se = 0.106; beta = −0.007), which shows that overall levels of party preferences were not different among the two groups of citizens. Subsequently, the saved residuals of the overall regression were used as dependent variables in an analysis with the same independents but run only for those respondents who voted for a different party in the European elections than the one they gave the highest utility rating at the time of the interview. Any significant coefficients point then to the potential need for adding more interactions to the model so as to account for differences in the strength of independent variables between the two groups of citizens. Of the nine parameters estimated in this way, none was significant. We have no reason therefore to assume that our model misrepresents the behaviors of the specific group of voters who voted for a different party in the European election than the one they preferred the most.

19. The reader may recall that our questions about party preferences were not formulated in regard to any specific type of election.

CHAPTER TEN

The sleeping giant: Potential for political mobilization of disaffection with European integration

CEES VAN DER EIJK
AND MARK N. FRANKLIN

Progress toward European Unity has been characterized as occurring in the context of a high degree of 'permissive consensus' (Lindberg and Scheingold 1970). Institutions have been created, policies have been enacted, and sovereignty has effectively been transferred to European institutions with little interference from the general public. Until the late 1990s no great manifestations of enthusiasm have been evident, but neither has there been much in the way of consistent opposition. This was often regarded as 'natural' on the grounds that moves toward European unity were a matter of foreign policy—something that traditionally falls within the purview of the executive in European countries. More recently, it has been ventured that this permissive consensus is eroding, were it only because of the fact that foreign and domestic policies have become increasingly intertwined and that the effects of European regulation have started be noticed in the daily lives of European citizens (van der Eijk and Franklin 1996). Indeed, occasional outbursts of anger and even protest have been seen on the part of specific groups like truckers, farmers, or lovers of traditional foodstuffs.

Yet most of these eruptions have appeared to be isolated and unconnected events, uncoordinated and apparently without long-term political

189

consequences in the member countries or within the institutions of the European Union. Above all, political entrepreneurs (such as party leaders, interest organizations, and social movements) appeared reluctant to exploit these eruptions as a basis for political mobilization. Even the Danish political movements that contest their country's membership and oppose further deepening of European integration have not systematically aligned themselves with protests on matters like BSE, milk prices, farm subsidies, and so forth.

Nevertheless, opinion polls do seem to show that there are sizeable groups in the populations of EU member countries who are not happy with the existing degree of unification, let alone with further deepening or widening of European integration. This suggests that the eruptions referred to above might not be as isolated and unconnected as they appear. So, in spite of the absence of visible connections between these various protests, we cannot discard the possibility that they are all manifestations of a deeper anxiety among sections of the European public about the course and consequences of European integration—an anxiety that constitutes a potential basis for political mobilization.

How can we tell whether these opinion polls demonstrate the presence of an opportunity for political entrepreneurs? In national politics discontented publics can express their discontent politically by 'throwing the rascals out'. But in European matters voters are unable to throw out whatever rascals might be seen as responsible for unpopular developments. Neither in national elections nor in elections to the European Parliament can voters unseat members of the European Commission or Council.

In this chapter we will argue that this disaffection does provide an opportunity for political entrepreneurs, and that the likelihood that it will be capitalized upon increases with the passage of time.

A commonplace of political commentary is that citizens of European Union countries differ in their attitudes regarding Europe. Some favor their country's membership in the EU, others oppose it. Some, while thinking that membership is generally a good thing, feel that steps toward unification have gone far enough—or even too far. Others believe that further steps should be taken.

Citizens of EU countries also differ in terms of more traditional political orientations—attitudes on the proper role of government in society, welfare provision, and other matters which have increasingly over the past half century come to be subsumed within a single orientation toward government action, generally referred to as the left-right orientation (Lipset 1960; Lijphart 1980; Franklin, Mackie, and Valen 1992).

These two orientations are often assumed to be unrelated, which implies that the newer pro- or anti-EU orientation cuts across the more traditional left-right orientation (see, e.g., Hix and Lord 1997; Hooghe and Marks 1999). Our own research (see chapter 9, and also van der Eijk and Franklin 1996; van der Eijk, Franklin, and van der Brug 1999; van der Brug, van der Eijk, and Franklin 2007) demonstrates that EU orientation does not currently have much impact on party choice at EU elections. Elections to the European Parliament have been described as 'second-order national' elections at which the arena supposedly at issue (the European arena) takes second place to the national arena as a focus for issue and representational concerns (Reif and Schmitt 1980; Reif 1984, 1985a; Marsh and Franklin 1996). In the national arenas of the EU it is almost invariably the left-right dimension that dominates voters' preferences and choice. Nevertheless, in this chapter we will argue that the pro- or anti-EU orientation, despite its apparent irrelevance for political behavior, constitutes something of a 'sleeping giant' that has the potential, if awakened, to change the political landscape drastically in many EU member states. We find that attitudes toward the EU and left-right orientations are largely independent (see below). Thus, if EU attitudes would gain in importance as determinants of party choice, they would undermine the current dominant basis for contemporary party mobilization that is rooted in the left-right dimension in most European polities.[1] We will also show that the prerequisites are present for these consequences to show themselves under certain specifiable conditions.

Initially we employ two measures of EU orientation (which will be described in some detail in the next section), both of which are found to be largely unrelated to the standard measure of left-right position (see table 10.1). Responses to the question "do you think that the European Union is a good or bad thing?" show least correlation with left-right position in any country, with only three significant relationships (see middle panel of table 10.1). The variable derived from the question whether European unification has gone too far or should be pushed further shows slightly higher correlations (see left-most panel of table 10.1). Nevertheless, even those correlations are generally very low with none even as strong as 0.3.[2] The good-bad variable is one that has been used ever since the earliest days of research into public attitudes toward Europe. The other variable is of more recent vintage. In this chapter we make greater use of the newer variable because it is a more sensitive measure (using a ten-point scale rather than a threefold distinction) and because we have corresponding data on where voters perceive the parties to be, which we do not have for the other variable. Table 10.1 demonstrates that the pattern of relationships for this newer variable across countries is very similar to the pattern found for the more established measure. The final two columns show the intercorrelation between the two EU measures in each country. When the data from all countries are pooled, the correlation is 0.42.[3]

Table 10.1 Correlations between left-right and pro- and anti-EU measures

	Left-right and more-less EU integration		Left-right and EU is good-bad thing		More-less EU integration and EU good-bad thing	
	correlation	p-value	correlation	p-value	correlation	p-value
Austria	−0.136	0.000	0.056	0.886	−0.489	0.000
Belgium: Flanders	−0.286	0.000	0.196	0.751	−0.586	0.000
Belgium: Wallonia	−0.079	0.313	0.034	0.244	−0.303	0.000
Britain	−0.099	0.005	0.099	0.063	−0.474	0.000
Denmark	0.145	0.000	−0.176	0.000	−0.485	0.000
Finland	0.023	0.663	−0.029	0.536	−0.391	0.000
France	−0.102	0.005	0.058	0.481	−0.358	0.000
Germany	0.019	0.573	0.03	0.549	−0.445	0.000
Greece	0.012	0.805	−0.074	0.833	−0.300	0.000
Ireland	0.045	0.348	0.077	0.090	−0.290	0.000
Italy	0.122	0.000	−0.011	0.463	−0.269	0.000
Luxembourg	−0.033	0.599	0.060	0.462	−0.340	0.000
Netherlands	−0.100	0.003	0.049	0.669	−0.338	0.000
Portugal	0.067	0.213	−0.051	0.926	−0.297	0.000
Spain	0.020	0.565	−0.104	0.023	−0.323	0.000
Sweden	0.253	0.000	−0.274	0.000	−0.543	0.000
EU-15	−0.01	ns	−0.01	ns	−0.423	0.000

Of course, the low correlations shown in the left two panels of table 10.1 could result from the two EU measures reflecting non-attitudes, without meaningful content. We need to consider this possibility but, assuming for the moment that the correlations are not just manifestations of random data, they indicate whether and how, in various systems, EU attitudes are related to left-right orientations.[4] In most systems these correlations are negligible, as already pointed out. Exceptions are Flanders, and to a lesser extent Austria (and possibly France, Netherlands, and Britain), where negative feelings toward the EU are mainly harbored by right-wing people. In Denmark and Sweden (and to a much lesser extent in Spain and Italy), however, negative feelings toward the EU are mainly harbored by left-wing people.

The differences between these two groups of countries indicate that, to the extent that differences in opinion about EU integration are being politicized, there is no 'natural' connection of 'what goes with what'. The interactions in the domestic political arena—domestic politics, in other words—may generate a connection of Euro-skeptic attitudes with either the right or the left (there is also the possibility of a connection with both right and left—a curvilinear relationship—which we will return to in a later section of this chapter). This means that any such 'colonization' of contestation over EU integration threatens the perspective that we sketched in *Choosing Europe?* (1996) of a common European electorate that responds in common ways to political problems and political stimuli.[5] We will have reason in later sections to refer back to the occasionally non-zero correlations between left-right and EU orientations, and to the fact that these correlations are not all in the same direction.

THE DATA

Our data are taken from the voters' component of the European Election Study 1999 (see appendix A for details). These data contain two measures of EU orientation. As already mentioned above, one is a ten-point scale on which respondents were asked to indicate whether European unification had gone too far or had to be pushed further. The other is a three-point scale on which respondents were asked whether their country's membership of the EU was a good thing, a bad thing, or neither good nor bad. The second of these questions, suitably recoded to place 'neither good nor bad' in the middle of the scale, is the same question as has been asked in Eurobarometer studies since 1970 and which, in other research, has been found to be a valid measure of preferred position on European integration (Franklin and Wlezien 1997; Scheuer 2005). That is, people who say European unification is a good thing favor a high level of unification, those who say it is neither good nor bad favor a medium level, and those who say it is a bad thing want a low level or no unification at all. In this respect, the variable is closely equivalent to our measure of left-right position, though measured only on a three-point scale in contrast to the ten-point scale that we have for left-right. Note that those who want a low level of unification might or might not want actions to be taken that would change the extent of unification currently in place, as is true of those who say they want a high level of unification.

The other variable (responses to the 'gone too far' question) though measured on a ten-point scale is a measure of policy preference. Those who pick a low value want actions to be taken to reduce the current level of unification while those who pick a high value want actions to be taken to increase the extent of unification. Because this variable contains a policy implication, we would rather expect it to be somewhat related to the left-right measure, at least to the extent that EU integration has been politicized in party-political terms. After all, left-right position is the dominant cleavage in the domestic politics of the member states of the EU, and political scientists have argued since at least the time of Schattschneider (1960) that for a concern to have policy implications it needs to have been incorporated at least to some extent into the dominant dimension of current political contestation. Thus significant correlations were to be expected in table 10.1, where left-right orientation was correlated with this variable. Indeed, it is surprising that these correlations were so weak and that so few of them were significant.

In addition to these two measures we have a set of variables very similar to the 'gone too far' measure but which relate not to respondents' own positions but to their perceptions of the positions of parties measured on the same ten-point scale. We also have a set of measures of the perceived left-right position of each party, which correspond to the left-right position of respondents in much the same way. These are the variables we will employ in the present chapter.

THE CONFLICT POTENTIAL OF VOTERS' EU ORIENTATIONS

Table 10.2 shows a number of univariate statistics relating to the left-right and 'gone too far' measures using the former as a point of reference since it is a ubiquitous scale that is understood to tap a phenomenon that is generally understood as being of real importance in structuring domestic politics. For each variable the table shows three such statistics: the percentage of respondents who failed to answer the question and, for those who did answer, the extent to which they are in agreement about this answer (the peakedness of the distribution)[6] and the extremity of their answers (the difference between the median answer and the midpoint of the scale). Several things stand out from this table. Most notably, the percentage of missing data for the EU integration scale is little more than half what it is for the left-right scale. This implies that what is tapped by the scale is not so moot that people have difficulty placing themselves—quite the contrary. The second thing to note is that agreement in terms of where people place themselves on the left-right scale is much greater than for the 'gone too far' scale. Third, on average respondents place themselves further away from the midpoint of the ten-point response scale (i.e., from 5.5) on the 'gone too far' scale than on

Table 10.2 Characteristics of voters self-placement on EU integration and left-right scales

		EU Integration scale			Left-right scale		
	N	Percent missing	Agreement	Extremity	Percent missing	Agreement	Extremity
Austria	501	3.39	0.15	0.54	12.57	0.52	0.38
Belgium: Flanders	274	7.66	0.19	0.39	25.55	0.45	0.03
Belgium: Wallonia	226	10.18	−0.07	0.04	23.45	0.33	0.50
Britain	978	7.57	0.15	0.74	11.96	0.44	0.46
Denmark	1001	6.69	0.13	0.43	8.79	0.36	0.09
Finland	501	16.97	0.19	0.76	16.77	0.34	0.01
France	1023	12.41	0.22	1.12	18.77	0.31	0.56
Germany	1001	1.40	0.25	0.85	6.49	0.45	0.54
Greece	500	7.60	0.29	2.50	8.80	0.07	0.25
Ireland	502	2.99	0.20	0.08	10.76	0.45	0.24
Italy	3707	22.85	0.27	1.10	25.65	0.22	0.33
Luxembourg	301	9.30	0.23	1.62	11.63	0.43	0.40
Netherlands	1001	4.40	0.35	1.14	11.29	0.34	0.12
Portugal	499	13.83	0.07	0.86	22.04	0.48	0.33
Spain	998	6.91	0.09	1.20	13.83	0.22	0.63
Sweden	505	6.93	0.13	0.46	6.53	0.17	0.32
Across-system average		8.82	0.18	0.86	14.68	0.35	0.33

the left-right one. In other words, their positions with respect to EU integration are (on average) more 'extreme' than for left-right.[7]

These coefficients make two things clear. First, the measures we have of EU orientation are unlikely to have emanated from the kind of random response process that would be triggered by non-attitudes, that is, when people have no 'real' orientations. If people were pulling their preferences regarding the EU out of thin air then we would see much more missing data for the EU variable than for the left-right variable. In fact we see less. Moreover, random response would result in a combination of low agreement and low extremity. In fact, we find that this combination is more characteristic of the left-right scale, the validity of which is rarely questioned. The combination of lower agreement together with higher extremity is particularly indicative of real attitudes rather than random response. Second, the low degree of agreement regarding their self-placements signifies that people do differ considerably among themselves as to whether EU integration has gone too far or not. The smaller this coefficient, the higher the potential for political contestation. After all, if agreement is high in terms of where people put themselves then there is not much to fight about politically. On top of this, the higher extremity scores for the EU measure (more than twice as high as for left-right) indicates on average a greater intensity of feeling regarding this issue. Evidently, the ingredients for contestation over EU integration are even more powerful than over the more traditional issues that are subsumed under the left-right divide.

The greater dispersion of attitudes regarding Europe as compared to left-right attitudes can be seen particularly clearly if we graph the joint distribution, which is done in figure 10.1. In this graph, voters are located according to their support

FIGURE 10.1 Party positions on left-right (horizontal) and less-more EU integration (vertical) dimensions, measured from positions of party supporters; all EU countries combined. Local linear regression fit line added.

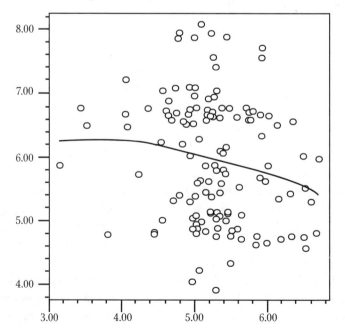

for different political parties, which provides us with a 'quasi-party space'.[8] The greater dispersion of opinions regarding Europe is clear in this graph from the fact that points are much more spread out in the vertical than in the horizontal dimension; actually the picture shows a bimodality in the vertical dimension as opposed to a more unimodal clustering in the middle on the horizontal one. It is also evident that there is no clear curvilinear relationship between the two dimensions. Extreme attitudes toward Europe are not more evident at any particular point on the left-right scale.[9]

The potential for contestation over issues regarding Europe is clear from these findings. The important question is why such potential for contestation has not so far been realized in elections to the European Parliament, or, for that matter, in the domestic political arenas of the EU member states.

The supply-side of electoral politics

One possible reason for lack of contestation would be that political parties do not provide the vehicles for contestation. If voters are not offered a choice between different visions of Europe then, whatever the differences between voters, these cannot be expressed on their ballots. One of the questions we may therefore ask is how much choice voters have in terms of the parties' positions on European integration. Is there a large variety of choice, or is there only a choice between Tweedledum and Tweedledee?

This question is of relevance in the context of political contestation, as parties are important vehicles for expressing political disagreements and for mobilizing citizens in this respect. Of course, parties are not the exclusive actors in this regard, as social movements, interest groups, and media also play a role in mobilizing and expressing contestation. However, for the 'authoritative allocation of values' and public policy, these other actors depend on political parties (and the governments that they populate). So, when there is little difference between parties, there is also little room for expressing differences in opinion in a politically potent manner. Perhaps existing parties should in such circumstances fear the potential lure of new parties catering to these different preferences, but how easy it is for newcomers to gain access and representation depends on institutional arrangements.

The easiest way to assess whether parties are offering a relevant choice between different policies regarding European integration is by considering the range of party positions in terms of this issue. We can measure these positions on the basis of voters' perceptions of where the parties stand.[10] Following the same logic as before, we will consider these measures both for EU position and also for left-right party location. The dispersion of party locations on each of these dimensions in the member states of the European Union tells us how much choice is on offer on that dimension in that country. The degree of dispersion (which we measure in terms of variance) is not, however immediately comparable between political systems, owing to differences in numbers of parties whose locations we know, but within each system the dispersion of the parties can easily be compared as between the two dimensions.

Moreover, these variances can be computed in two different ways. One way is to have each party contribute equally to them, which is sensible from the perspective of choices on offer (irrespective of whether a party is small or large, it offers a choice to the voters). The other way is to weight parties according to their size (measured as percent of votes in the last national election), which makes sense from the perspective of political culture, political communication, and 'mobilization of bias' (Schattschneider 1960). The reasoning that leads us to employ the second measure in addition to the first is that larger parties contribute (on average, and other things being equal) more than smaller ones to the dominant climate of opinion and to what is considered 'mainstream.'

Table 10.3 reports these variances, computed in both ways, for each system of the EU separately as well as for the EU as a whole (meaning for all parties for which these perceptions have been obtained in all EU countries). The table shows that, in general (and irrespective of whether they are weighted by size) parties offer voters more choice on the left-right dimension than on the EU dimension (see the columns labeled 'difference' where positive values signify a larger dispersion of parties on the left-right dimension, while negative values show a larger dispersion on the EU dimension). In each sub-table there is only one country (Denmark) in which parties differ more on the EU dimension than on the left-right dimension.[11] This finding helps us to understand why, in most countries, there is so little contestation on European issues at European Parliament elections, but it makes it even more remarkable that the preferences of individuals were found in the previous section to be so much more diverse on the EU dimension than on the left-right dimension.

Comparing the weighted and unweighted variances by country shows to what extent the palette of choice on each of these dimensions is dependent on small parties. On the EU dimension, much of the variance is generated by small parties in Wallonia, Denmark, Germany, Portugal, and Spain. On the left-right dimension, small parties contribute much to the variance in party positions in Portugal, Germany, France, and Denmark. In all other countries, the smaller parties usu-

Table 10.3 Variance in party positions on left-right and EU orientation

	Parties weighted on size			Parties weighted equally		
	Integration	Left-right	Difference	Integration	Left-right	Difference
Austria	1.57	1.89	0.32	1.17	2.15	0.98
Belgium: Flanders	0.16	4.07	3.91	0.15	4.65	4.50
Belgium: Wallonia	2.31	5.46	3.15	5.08	7.18	2.10
Britain	0.55	1.14	0.59	1.46	1.44	−0.02
Denmark	4.03	3.66	−0.37	6.36	5.80	−0.56
Finland	0.08	4.18	4.10	0.68	3.43	2.75
France	1.02	5.82	4.80	1.46	8.90	7.44
Germany	1.52	2.80	1.28	4.50	7.33	2.83
Greece	2.52	6.69	4.17	3.51	6.73	3.22
Ireland	0.60	1.28	0.68	0.99	2.02	1.03
Italy	0.48	4.88	4.40	0.43	3.53	3.10
Luxembourg	0.91	1.87	0.96	1.67	3.36	1.69
Netherlands	0.53	2.36	1.83	2.16	3.92	1.76
Portugal	3.27	3.28	0.01	7.33	9.40	2.07
Spain	1.16	5.88	4.72	3.22	6.27	3.05
Sweden	4.17	4.60	0.43	5.05	5.77	0.72
Entire EU	2.13	3.50	1.37	2.53	4.54	2.01

ally offer some, but not very much more choice (in terms of variance of party positions) than the larger parties do.

A second way to look at the contribution of parties to contestation over European matters is to consider the extent to which the party space corresponds to the attitude space in the two dimensions that we investigate. Although we saw in our introductory section that individual voters' attitudes on European matters are largely orthogonal to their left-right orientations, such near-independence might not be true for the positions that parties occupy on both dimensions. Figure 10.2 displays a number of thumbnail graphs, one for each country, in which each party's position is plotted on the left-right and EU dimensions.

As can readily be seen, for most countries the dispersion of parties in terms of left-right (across the graph) is considerably greater than the dispersion of parties

FIGURE 10.2 Parties' positions on left/right (horizontal) and anti/pro integration (vertical) dimensions

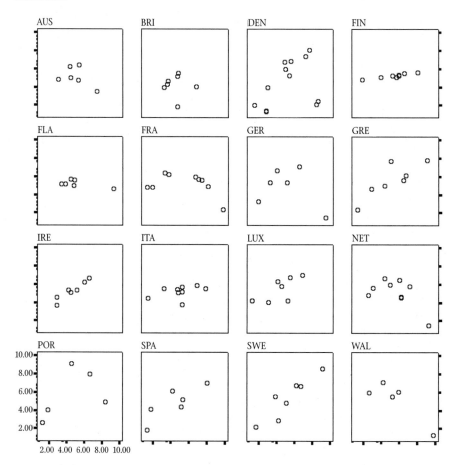

in terms of European integration (up and down the graph). In Finland, Flanders, France, and Italy, indeed, the parties are spread out in virtually a straight horizontal line across the center of the graph. In several other countries (Austria, Britain, Netherlands, and Wallonia) there is a virtually amorphous scattering along the center of the graph. In some cases (Denmark, Greece, Ireland, Luxembourg, Spain, and Sweden) the willing eye can discern a positive relationship between the two dimensions, such that left parties are more likely to be Euro-skeptical while right parties are more likely to be in favor of European integration. In Portugal, by contrast, the pattern seems to resemble an inverted U, with extreme parties of both left and right being more likely to oppose European unification. If we look hard for this pattern we seem to see it also in some of the other countries: France, Germany, Netherlands, and even Denmark. Indeed, traces of an upside down U can be seen in most of the countries where the party spread encompasses both extremes of the left-right scale. This suggests that the apparently different patterns in the different countries are in reality due to the fact that the left-right continuum is differently populated by parties in each of them. Some countries have no party of the extreme right; other countries have no party of the extreme left. Consequently, what we could be seeing in these thumbnails are country-specific projections of a common pattern filtered in each country by the party system that exists there.

To assess this conjecture we superimpose in figure 10.3 the thumbnails from figure 10.2 on top of each other, producing a single graph for all countries of the EU in 1999. This single graph plots the location of all parties on the left-right and pro- or anti-European integration dimensions. Two patterns seem to be present in figure 10.3. One pattern is of a positive relationship between the two dimensions,

FIGURE 10.3   Party positions on left-right (horizontal) and less-more EU integration (vertical) dimensions, all parties in the EU

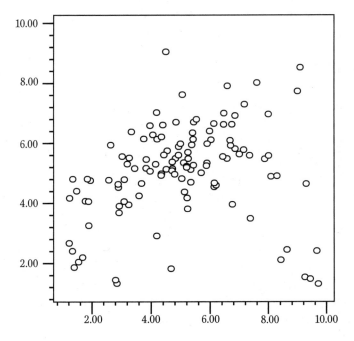

as seen more clearly in some of the thumbnails of figure 10.2, where parties of the right are most inclined to favor European integration. The other pattern is the inverted U, where extreme parties at both ends of the left-right spectrum are most in opposition to European integration. Of these two patterns, the latter is more pronounced. Except for a single party in each of Greece and Sweden (the two top right outliers in figure 10.3) the inverted U is quite clear.

Earlier we saw no evidence of a tendency among voters for pro- or anti-European attitudes to be related in any particular way to left-right attitudes. The positive relationship and inverted U that we see among parties was not similarly evident among voters. More specifically, we found that over the full range of the left-right scale voters vary considerably in terms of their European attitudes. This is not true for parties—and especially not within any particular political system, as was apparent in the thumbnail graphs presented in figure 10.2. For whatever reasons, voters at all positions of the left-right scale are offered little choice with respect to EU integration by the parties in their systems. As a consequence, many voters are forced to choose between either expressing in their party choice their left-right ideological concerns, which forces them to ignore their preferences regarding European integration, or the other way around: choosing parties on the basis of their positions regarding Europe, at the cost of not being able to select the party they would have preferred in left-right terms.

Indeed, the situation is even worse than initially appears since not all parties are equally viable options for choice. Most European countries have very few large parties together with a larger number of small ones, and voters often have reservations about supporting parties that have little chance of influencing government policy (cf. Tillie 1995; van der Eijk, Franklin, and Oppenhuis 1996). Parties that are anti-Europe are particularly likely to be small parties. Thus figures 10.2 and 10.3 mislead to some extent by portraying all parties as though they were equally viable as choices for all voters. In figure 10.4 we provide an alternative perspective by representing the parties in terms not only of their locations but also in terms of their size (measured as share of the vote in the most recent national election). Larger parties are indicated by larger symbols and the smallest parties by mere specks.

In figure 10.4 the inverted U is much less prominent than in figure 10.3. The figure shows more clearly, however, a positive relationship between political parties' left-right and integration positions. Evidently political parties of the left are less likely to favor (further) integration. The extremities of the U (where most anti-European parties are found) are mainly populated by small parties. In view of the internal differences of opinion of their actual and potential voters, we can under-

FIGURE 10.4 Party positions on left-right (horizontal) and less-more EU integration (vertical) dimensions; all parties in the EU, parties weighted by size

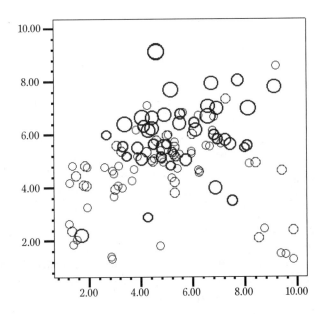

stand why large, moderate (in left-right terms) parties are apprehensive to compete on the basis of the EU dimension (which would mean to politicize it). But to the extent that they fail to do so, each of them is supported by a constituency of voters that is deeply divided on European matters as pointed out in previous research (Franklin, van der Eijk, and Marsh 1996). Up to and including 1999, those constituencies appear to be rather docile in the face of their lack of choice but, given the strongly held nature of these opinions, the question is how long this state of affairs can endure.[12] This question relates to the image of the 'sleeping giant' that we introduced early in this chapter.

THE SLEEPING GIANT

Since we view European parties through the lens provided to us by European voters (our measures of party position are those provided by respondents to our survey), it is clear that many European voters are aware of the fact that they cannot choose a party on the basis of its position on European integration while also maintaining their ability to choose a party on the basis of its position in left-right terms. At present in most countries voters are willing to put their preferences regarding integration on ice and make their choices between parties on other grounds, but how long this state of affairs can continue is a question that does not have an unequivocal answer. Certainly it would be a brave commentator who would assert that the present state of affairs could continue indefinitely. Already the pro- or anti-integration policy dimension appears to hold promise for mobilizing voters in a way that the left-right dimension lacks (see the proportions of voters who hold positions and the extremity of these positions). This being the case, it seems only a matter of time before policy entrepreneurs in some countries seize the opportunity presented by these quite polarized opinions to differentiate themselves from other parties in EU terms. Indeed, this has already happened in some countries where small parties of the far left or far right have taken up distinctly pro- or (more often) anti-EU stances. In some countries these stances even appear to have paid electoral dividends.

As EU integration becomes more politicized, this could result in still more voters being pulled toward party choices they would not have made on the basis of left-right concerns. This could have unfortunate consequences for the development of a European party system. We saw in table 10.1 that the more policy-relevant measure of preference for unification was somewhat more orientated in left-right terms than was the less policy-relevant measure. We also saw that there was considerable incoherence (between different countries) of the left-right and pro- or anti-EU linkage: some of the non-zero correlations in table 10.1 were positive, some negative. So the increasing politicization of EU issues in the domestic political arenas of the member states might ironically interfere with the development a European party system that consistently offers comparable choices on both dimensions to the citizens of the various member states (e.g., van der Eijk and Franklin 1996, chapter 21). It will also make it increasingly more difficult for party groups in the European Parliament to maintain the cohesion that they have so far been able to maintain on the basis of their internal (left-right) ideological agreement (cf. Katz and Wessels 1999).

What are the prerequisites for greater politicization of EU matters? We can think of four different sets of facilitating conditions: the activities of elites, external events, chance, and shifts in voter orientations. The last of these has already happened. As documented earlier in this chapter, the erstwhile permissive consensus has disappeared as voters are more strongly divided over matters of European integration than they are over matters related to left and right. Thus, the preconditions for voter mobilization on the basis of pro- or anti-EU arguments are already present. But voter readiness is not enough. Some policy entrepreneur or entrepreneurs have to come along who are willing to capitalize on these preconditions in order to win votes that otherwise would have gone elsewhere. The only reason this has been slow to happen is because established elites have so far been largely able to prevent it from happening. Existing parties are very resilient. Existing party elites know which side their bread is buttered on. As argued extensively in *Choosing Europe?* (van der Eijk and Franklin 1996, 370–371), all party leaders understand from long experience the danger to them of an issue that is not integrated into the left-right spectrum of concerns. European issues have as a matter of fact proved easier to manage than other new issues in most European countries (the exception is probably Denmark). Environmental, feminist, gay rights, and energy issues have provided far greater headaches to party elites in most countries than European issues, no doubt mainly because the EU has in most countries successfully been presented as a matter of foreign policy, which is in all European countries a branch of policy making traditionally left in the hands of governments. But one only has to read the newspapers to see how issues that were once viewed as purely foreign have become domesticized in recent decades. Moreover, as the EU increasingly moves into areas that directly impinge on the lives of individuals, it becomes more difficult for governments to argue successfully that these are areas in which they should be allowed free rein.

Government ministers do not make matters easier for themselves in this regard when they return from Brussels blaming the EU for domestic policy repercussions that were in fact the consequences of their own policies. By using the EU as a shield to hide behind in order to avoid voters' wrath, governments increase the likelihood that voters will respond to any proposals that may be made to address that shield directly.

From where might such proposals come? We have to remember that political elites are not monolithic. Though the leaders of large parties have an interest in keeping European matters off the political agenda, the same is increasingly not true of the leaders of small parties (accounting for the anti-European positions of so many small parties in figure 10.4), or of challengers from within large parties, as we saw in the British Conservative Party in 1997 when the pro-European leadership of John Major was successfully challenged by an anti-European upstart, William Hague, after the party was decimated in the 1997 British general election. Such challengers, where successful, can capture a major party and use it as a vehicle for gathering anti-European support. But it is only a matter of time before a chance occurrence or an external event will favor entrepreneurs that mobilize support by emphasizing an anti-integration position. And there is plenty of time for this to happen. The problems generated by the evolution of the European Union are not going to go away, much as the established leaders of large parties might wish that they would. To the contrary, the evolution of the EU in terms of its internal market and in terms of its external enlargement is guaranteed to generate contentious political issues within the member countries for years (probably generations) to come. Think only of the domestic political impact of large numbers of legal migrants into Holland, Germany, or Britain from Poland or Slovenia. And it is only a matter of time before an economic downturn provides new and potent possibilities for politicization by blaming the EU.

When the British prime minister of the late 1950s, Harold Macmillan, was asked by a young (male) reporter what had been the greatest challenges to his leadership, his answer was "Events, dear boy, events." Events are going to be the greatest challenge to existing major party leaders and to their success in keeping European issues off the domestic political agenda in their countries. Some of these might be chance events that we cannot possibly anticipate. Others are only too easy to anticipate: labor market stresses, as already mentioned; taxation problems; energy crises; knock-on effects from the single currency in most EU countries. The potential sources of issues to politicize the pro- or anti-EU dimension are limitless. In some country at some time they will result in a new alignment of domestic political forces, either by giving support to what is now a minor party (or to a party that arises in response to the new issue) or by giving support to opposition forces within an existing large party. And if this happens in one country, the contagion effect on other countries can be expected to be virtually immediate. One development that has already changed the balance of forces in Europe is precisely the fact that developments in any EU country that might be of interest to parties and politicians in other member countries are immediately reported there.

Of course, even when the European dimension becomes politicized in this way, the effect will not be permanent. The left-right dimension, because it subsumes so many issues of continuing importance and because of its absorptive capacity to integrate new issues, will certainly retain its dominance (cf. Silverman 1985). The role we expect to see for the pro- or anti-integration dimension in Europe is one similar to the role played in the United States by the conflict over the proper scope of federal versus states' rights. By shifting attention to this issue-dimension, American politicians can often change a minority position to a majority position (cf. Schattschneider 1960). Thus the battle for supremacy in that nation is often a battle about the arena that has to 'solve' it. We expect the same thing to happen in

Europe—perhaps not immediately and perhaps not everywhere, but sometime soon and somewhere not a thousand miles from Brussels. In the final chapter of this volume we explore what would be the consequences for European as well as national elections of a politicization of the issue of European integration.

Notes

1. The analyses reported in this chapter pertain to the European Parliament elections of 1999 and are based on surveys from the electorates of all member states (see below for details).

2. The—by and large—opposite signs of relationships with these two variables reflect the fact that their codings run in opposite directions.

3. Correlations are somewhat depressed by the fact that about 70 percent of respondents answer "good" on the second of these variables, whereas these responses are distributed across the higher values of a ten-point scale on the first variable.

4. The rather strong correlations between the responses to the two EU measures (see the most right-hand panel of table 10.1) challenge the suggestion that we deal with random responses.

5. Although we have in EES 1999 no other issue variables of relevance, there are no indications from other comparative research that the contents of the left-right dimension is different between the countries of the EU (everywhere, left is associated with equality, state intervention in the economy, support for the welfare state, feminism, ecology, whereas right is everywhere associated with freedom, support for restricted government, free markets, etc.).

6. This coefficient attains a value of 1 when all respondents place themselves at the same point on the scale; it takes on a value of 0 if they are uniformly distributed over the entire scale; and it takes on a value of -1 when half the respondents place themselves at each extreme of the scale (see van der Eijk 2001).

7. One reason for this is precisely the fact that party choices are not based on this variable (see also chapter 9). The fact that these positions are not related to choice removes the need to temper their extremity.

8. Each symbol in the graph signifies the median positions on the two dimensions of the potential electoral supporters of a particular party. Who is counted as a supporter and who is not depends on the response to the question of how likely it is that one would ever vote for the party in question. Answers to these questions range from 1 ('never') to 10 ('will certainly vote for this party'). Respondents were weighted according to these responses: answering 1 ('never') resulted in a weight of 0, as these respondents cannot in any way be considered as electoral supporters of the party in question. An answer of 10 (will certainly vote for this party) yields a weight of 1. Intermediate answers were associated with weights that were linearly interpolated between these extremes.

9. The same pattern is obtained by graphing the prevalence of each conjunction of positions regarding Europe without reference to parties, but that graph consists of equally spaced points that differ in their weight. It is therefore more difficult to interpret than the picture we have chosen to present in figure 10.1.

10. One may wonder how well these perceptions reflect actual positions of parties regarding policy. In terms of the motivations of voters to choose a particular party, this question is of little relevance, but it is of vital importance for assessing the quality of the communication between parties and voters and for the actual degree of political representation of voters' policy preferences in the parliamentary arena. Analysis of the 1994 election study indicates that voter perceptions may differ considerably from other indicators of party positions (in that instance the positions of parties as reported by their candidates), particularly in the case of issues that are hardly politicized (cf. van der Brug and van der Eijk 1999) or that get little coverage in the mass media. When comparing voters' perceptions of party positions in 1999 with the positions of parties' that can be derived from their manifestos (see chapter 4) we likewise find considerable differences. Yet, to the extent that we focus on voters, it is their perceptions that count irrespective of whether these perceptions are consistent with other indicators of party positions. In all analyses to follow in this chapter, when parties are characterized by perceptions, it is the (interpolated) median of individual respondents' perceptions that is used.

11. This is caused by the existence of the two Euro-skeptic movements (Junibevaegelsen and Folkebevaegelsen) that compete only in European Parliament elections. When weighting parties by size, Portugal shows no real differences in variance between the two dimensions. Unweighted, there is more of a difference in Portugal, but less of a difference in Britain (owing to the effect of the tiny UKIP, positioned extremely against EU integration in 1999).

12. Occasionally parties and politicians may be more distinct from one another than they are perceived to be by voters (see note 10). This is because effective communication about party positions is often missing. Policy entrepreneurs, especially at the European level, often fail to connect with voters who are still oriented primarily to their national party systems.

CHAPTER ELEVEN

Prospects for electoral change

MARTIN KROH, WOUTER VAN DER BRUG,
AND CEES VAN DER EIJK

European elections provide potentially important prospects for electoral change, and thus for affecting the subsequent development of domestic politics. This may seem like a somewhat surprising perspective on elections that are mainly characterized by a low intensity of campaigning, by scant media attention, and by shallow voter involvement. Yet from previous European elections we know that the outcomes of European elections can indeed affect the domestic political landscape, the more so the larger their divergence is with previous national elections. European elections have been referred to as the 'midwife assisting in the birth of new parties', on occasion they effectuated the replacement of party leaders or changes in parties' stances on important issues, and they have at times altered the internal relations of governing coalitions. In short, the results of European elections and changes in party support that become visible in European elections have important consequences for domestic politics.[1]

In this chapter we investigate the potential for electoral change at the time of three European elections: 1989, 1994, and 1999. Two factors conspire to provide European elections with the potential to generate electoral change. As we will argue in more detail below, the first is a country's party system and the pattern of electoral competition it shaped. This factor is not at all specific to European elections, and it is equally responsible for the potential of electoral change in first-order national elections. The second factor is that in second-order national elections less seems to be at stake in terms of political power, which encourages voters not to 'vote with their head' but rather 'with their heart' or 'with their boot'.[2] In combination, these two factors generate a large potential of voters who may change their vote between elections.

Until the 1960s election results were highly stable from one election to the next in most European countries, the reason for Lipset and Rokkan (1967) to refer to the party systems as 'frozen'. The cause of this stability was that electoral decisions were largely determined by voters' positions in the structure of social cleavages of their societies. As these social positions are hardly amenable to change, party choice and election results were comparatively stable. However, the impact of social characteristics on party choice has generally decreased in Western democracies (e.g., Franklin, Mackie, and Valen 1992), and voters started to choose between parties rather than just registering a vote for the party that appeared to be the 'natural' representative of a particular segment of society.[3] As a consequence of this process, voters had to compare political parties and decide which was—for whatever reasons—the most attractive to support. This provides room for electoral change of a nature that did not exist before, or at least not to the same extent. Indeed, since the 1970s electoral change has increased in most European countries, sometimes dramatically so (Dalton, McAllister, and Wattenberg 2000). In this chapter we assess for each the member states of the EU how large this potential of vote-switchers is. We subsequently look into factors that cause this potential to vary between countries and between different kinds of individuals. We conclude this chapter by discussing the conditions under which these potential vote-switchers may indeed change their party choice in national or in European elections, thereby setting the stage for the next chapter, in which we evaluate the consequences of some of these conditions. But before we can turn to these matters, we first explicate how we analyze (potential) vote switching.

Measuring the Potential for Vote Switching

Vote switching refers to voters who vote in one election for a different party than in another election. It is thus defined in terms of choice, yet we contend that in order to understand it, one has to focus on party preferences—or the propensities to vote for parties, as explained in chapter 9[4]—rather than on choice itself. We illustrate this by a hypothetical example in which only two parties vie for people's votes: party A and party B. We assume that voters vote for the party they prefer the most and that we can observe these preferences. Table 11.1 (left panel)

Table 11.1 Hypothetical effects of an electoral shock on preferences and choice

	Preferences and choices before the shock that affected Party A			Preferences and choices after the shock that affected Party A		
	Preference for Party A	Preference for Party B	Vote choice	Preference for Party A	Preference for Party B	Vote choice
Voter 1	9	4	A	7	4	A
Voter 2	8	5	A	6	5	A
Voter 3	7	6	A	5	6	B
Voter 4	6	7	B	4	7	B
Voter 5	5	8	B	3	8	B

presents for five different voters their preferences for each of these parties, expressed in terms of a ten-point scale. It also presents their choice between the parties, which corresponds for each voter with the party that registers the highest preference. The right panel of this table presents the same information—preferences and choice—at a later election. In the interval between the two elections something has happened that has uniformly lowered the preferences of all voters for party A by two units on the ten-point scale. This could have been caused by all sorts of things, such as a scandal involving politicians of party A or an economic recession for which voters hold party A responsible. Comparing the left- and right-hand panels of table 11.1 shows the consequences of this shift in preferences for voters' choices.

In the hypothetical example in table 11.1, the events between the two elections have the same effect on all voters' preferences for party A. Yet the consequences thereof in terms of their choices are not the same for all. For four out of the five voters displayed, the changes in preferences did not affect their vote choice. Voters 1 and 2 had preferences for party A that were so much stronger than those for party B that the drop of preference for party A does not change the fact that party A is preferred over B, so that these voters' choices are unchanged. Voters 4 and 5 already preferred party B to party A so that any drop in preference for party A cannot alter this; their votes are also unchanged. Only for voter 3 does the drop in preference for party A lead to a change in which party is *most* preferred, and hence in a change of choice. This is not because voter 3 was affected more than other voters by the events between the two elections. It is only because this voter's preferences for the two parties were rather close in strength. Changes in choice between parties (i.e., actual vote switching) are thus not necessarily indicative of a greater change in the evaluation of a party than is stability in vote choice. Whether or not changes in evaluation (i.e., in preference) lead to changes in choice depends on how far apart the options involved were in terms of preference, and on the magnitude of changes in preferences. When the most preferred parties differ only little in the electoral utility they would yield, small changes in preferences can lead to vote switching. If, on the other hand, there is a wide gap between the preferences for the highest and second highest ranked parties, it requires very large changes in preference to make a voter alter his or her choice.[5]

We may look upon the relationship between preference and choice in terms of electoral competition between political parties. A party can, for all practical purposes, only realistically hope to acquire the votes of those people who have high preferences for it. When, however, people have high preferences for more than one party, the parties involved have to compete for these voters. The closer a voter's preferences are for their first and second most preferred parties, the stronger the competition between these parties for this voter's support.[6] When looked upon from this perspective, the analyses to be reported in this chapter highlight what one might call the 'electoral opportunity structure' for political parties: the prospects and the risks that an election offers them. It defines the realistic possibilities for parties' electoral strategies and tactics.

We use these perspectives on the relationship between preferences and choice to assess the potential for vote switching in the countries of the European Union. We consider the most likely switchers to be those who see their two most preferred parties as almost equally attractive. Electoral preferences (or electoral utilities) are measured with the same variables as used in chapter 9. They derive from a question "how likely is it that you will ever vote for this party?" that was asked for each party in a country.[7] The responses vary from 1 ("I will certainly never vote for this party") to 10 ("I will certainly vote for this party at some time in the future"), and we define 'almost equally attractive' as a difference of at most 1 on this ten-point scale. Thus, likely switchers are those who have a tied first preference, or whose second preference is only one point less than their first.[8] In the example presented in table 11.1 only voters 3 and 4 are potential switchers: their choice is very sensitive to small changes in preferences. The information about electoral preferences or utilities not only allows the identification of voters who may easily switch between parties (who are subject to intense electoral competition), but also of those voters who are quite unlikely to switch (who are for all practical purposes beyond competition). We defined these as the voters for whom the difference between their highest and second highest preference is more than three points on the ten-point preference scale.[9] The extent to which a country is likely to experience electoral change depends largely on the sizes of these groups of voters who are very likely or very unlikely to switch between parties.

DIFFERENCES IN POTENTIAL VOTE SWITCHING BETWEEN COUNTRIES AND PERIODS

Table 11.2 presents for each of the EU countries the proportions of voters who are likely switchers (who are subject to intense competition) and of voters who are unlikely to switch (who are by and large beyond electoral competition).[10] This information is presented for three European election years: 1989, 1994, and 1999. When looking at the averages of these proportions for the EU, we see that the group of likely switchers has increased from 36 percent on average in 1989 to 42 percent in 1999, while the group that is unlikely to switch has decreased in size, on average from 41 percent in 1989 to 31 percent in 1999. Particularly the latter change is quite substantial and reflects a decreasing basis for electoral stability in most member states of the Union.

Table 11.2 shows considerable variation between the EU countries. Most countries mirror the development in the EU averages. Spain shows very little change in either direction, and only two systems show a strong decline in this potential for electoral change since 1989. In Flanders the group of likely switchers has noticeably dropped, while in Portugal the group beyond electoral competition has increased substantially. In most countries these changes took shape during the entire period since 1989, except for Britain where they were concentrated in the period between 1994 and 1999.

Apart from their occasionally different patterns of change since 1989, countries also differ in the extent of their vulnerability to electoral change. Looking at 1999, France, Ireland, Finland, Italy, and the Netherlands clearly show the greatest potential for electoral change, more than half of the voters in these countries regard their two most preferred parties as almost equally attractive. The consequences thereof in terms of actual choices can be drastic: relatively small incidents, which cause small changes in party preferences, can generate an avalanche of party switching. But even in the countries that apparently have the largest potential for electoral stability, about one-third of the electorate is subject to intense competition. In other words, the electoral environment in each of the member states is characterized by a potential for vote switching that is much

Table 11.2 Proportions of voters subject to intense competition and beyond competition (1989, 1994, and 1999)

	Subject to intense competition			Beyond competition		
	1989	1994	1999	1989	1994	1999
Austria	—	—	0.37	—	—	0.36
Belgium: Flanders	0.41	0.39	0.33	0.39	0.36	0.34
Belgium: Wallonia	0.26	0.30	0.38	0.52	0.45	0.30
Britain	0.29	0.28	0.42	0.45	0.45	0.28
Denmark	0.37	0.39	0.40	0.34	0.28	0.28
Finland	—	—	0.56	—	—	0.22
France	0.58	0.53	0.62	0.19	0.20	0.14
Germany	0.29	0.33	0.34	0.39	0.34	0.36
Greece	0.23	0.30	0.42	0.63	0.49	0.36
Ireland	0.50	0.47	0.52	0.26	0.28	0.17
Italy	0.36	0.45	0.53	0.42	0.27	0.23
Luxembourg	0.38	0.37	0.36	0.41	0.32	0.32
Netherlands	0.35	0.44	0.51	0.40	0.25	0.18
Portugal	0.32	0.29	0.31	0.45	0.47	0.57
Spain	0.33	0.29	0.29	0.48	0.50	0.48
Sweden	—	—	0.42	—	—	0.26
Mean EU-12	0.36	0.37	0.42	0.41	0.35	0.31
Mean EU-15	—	—	0.43	—	—	0.30

Notes: Subject to intense competition: difference between the two highest ranked parties is 0 or 1.
Beyond competition: difference between the two highest ranked parties is more than 3.

larger than is often assumed, and that is staggeringly higher than portrayed by studies before the 1970s. Therefore, none of these countries can nowadays expect that voters' choices will be stable and easily predictable.

Table 11.2 strongly suggests that many of the differences between systems and between moments in time are explicable by characteristics of parties and party systems. The changes in Britain fit perfectly qua timing with the transformation of the Labour party under Tony Blair, which was designed to increase Labour's electoral competitiveness. Similarly, the increase in the number of potential and likely vote-switchers in the Netherlands since 1989 coincides with a period of sustained ideological and policy convergence of the major parties which has undermined the demarcation of electoral niches (cf. Van Wijnen 2001; Thomassen, Aarts, and van der Kolk 2000; Pennings and Keman 2003). But not all changes have to be attributed to the behavior and positioning of parties. Changes in the generational composition of electorates are also likely to contribute to an increase in the potential for electoral change (cf. Franklin 2004). Generations that have been socialized in periods of stable cleavage politics are replaced by new generations that have reached adulthood in times where such electorally stabilizing conditions had weakened or even disappeared. And, finally, changes in the distribution of individual characteristics such as education, party attachment, and political attentiveness may contribute to the likelihood of electoral change—at least to the extent that these characteristics are related to the potential for vote switching at the individual level.

Explaining the potential for vote switching

What accounts for potential vote switching? As suggested above, we can think of at least two different levels of explanation, one relating to voters, the other to parties and party-systems. At the individual level, theory and previous research suggest some factors to be relevant, albeit that different strands of research lead to different and sometimes contradictory expectations. At least two traditions exist that differ starkly in the differences they ascribe to stable and switching voters. One tradition—represented by, e.g., Lazarsfeld, Berelson, and Gaudet (1944), Campbell et al. (1960), Trenaman and McQuail (1961)—portrays switchers as comparatively little involved and informed about politics. In contrast, analysts such as Daudt (1961), Kaase (1967), Benewick et al. (1969), van der Eijk and Niemöller (1983), and Zelle (1995) contest the existence of such differences in involvement and sophistication between switchers and stable voters. They report that consistent differences between switchers and stable voters exist only in terms of age and party attachment. This not entirely consistent literature suggests that we should take all variables into account that somewhere have been suggested as relevant in determining party switching: various aspects of political involvement and sophistication,[11] party attachment and age. In addition we are also interested in the social[12] and political correlates[13] of switching, even in the absence of any specific hypotheses about their effects.

With respect to parties, we expect that small differences between policy positions of the parties on offer will increase the extent to which voters are likely to switch between them. From chapter 9 we know that left-right ideology and issues are the most important substantive determinants of party preferences in most EU countries, so we can expect that large perceived differences between parties' positions will impede the likelihood of vote switching. We can elaborate this hypothesis in general terms by looking at the left-right dimension, and in more specific terms by focusing on the European integration dimension.[14] For both, we express the variety of party positions in the system by way of a measure of polarization.[15] In addition we expect the number of parties in a party system to be of relevance, the larger the number of viable parties,[16] the larger the likelihood that a voter will find more than just one of them electorally attractive and will thus be a potential switcher. The number of parties in each system and the polarization of parties are variables at the systemic rather than individual level.

The dependent variable, potential vote switching, was so far defined as a dichotomous variable. A respondent was defined as a potential switcher if the difference between the two most preferred parties is no more than one point on the ten-point scale for electoral preference (or utility). This dichotomy was particularly useful for the descriptive analyses presented in table 11.2, but for explanatory analyses it has the disadvantage of disregarding the sometimes large differences in preference patterns of all those people who were not classified as potential switchers. Therefore, we use a slightly different measure as our dependent variable in the following analyses: the inverse of the difference in preference between the two most preferred parties.[17] A high score on this measure thus indicates a high likelihood to switch between parties. Since this measure has ten possible values, we treat it as an interval level variable that allows us to make use of regression methods for analyzing the impact of the independent variables on the potential for switching. Although the independent variables pertain to two different levels of analysis—individuals and party systems—multi-level analysis was not opportune in our situation.[18] Because of the different levels of analysis represented in the model, we computed robust standard errors, and we report significance on the basis of these. For all variables in the model, missing data were replaced by imputed values.[19] In order to avoid misspecification of the model, we included country dummies to absorb differences in the level of the dependent variable. The results of our analyses are displayed in table 11.3.

The table presents two models with the same individual-level predictors, but each with different contextual variables. In model 2 each country is represented by a dummy variable (with the exception of Sweden which functions as the base category) in order to adequately account for the differences in the averages of the dependent variable. In model 1 these country dummies are replaced by three substantive contextual variables relating to the nature of the party systems. Neither

Table 11.3 Models to explain potentials for electoral change

	Model 1 B (SE)	Model 2 B (SE)
Individual characteristics		
Social background		
Age	−.016 (.003)***	−.015 (.002)***
Gender	.024 (.051)	.031 (.046)
Education	.009 (.003)**	.004 (.003)
Class	.048 (.027)	.068 (.029)
Union membership	.136 (.060)	.124 (.059)*
Church attendance	.008 (.025)	.029 (.024)
Political involvement		
Political interest	.071 (.043)	.092 (.042)*
Strength of party ID	−.570 (.032)***	−.520 (.027)***
Frequency of watching TV news	−.057 (.014)***	−.038 (.014)**
Frequency of reading daily newspaper	.019 (.012)	.007 (.012)
Political attentiveness	.107 (.041)**	.074 (.038)
Political attitudes and opinions		
Positions on a left-right scale	−.024 (.016)	−.027 (.015)
Left-right extremism	−.101 (.028)***	−.133 (.023)***
Positions on European integration	.032 (.014)*	.027 (.011)*
Extremism on European integration	−.054 (.024)*	−.021 (.020)
Politics too complicated	−.061 (.035)	−.034 (.031)
Parties quarrel too much	.013 (.040)	.042 (.038)
Voting does not matter	.072 (.039)	.078 (.035)*
No difference between parties	.192 (.037)***	.150 (.037)***
Contextual variables		
Polarization of left-right positions	−.498 (.090)***	
Polarization of EU positions	−.421 (.081)***	
Effective number of parties in parliament	.144 (.017)***	
Country dummies (Sweden is base category)		
Austria		−.440 (.167)*
Flanders		−.905 (.223)***
Wallonia		−.213 (.244)
Britain		−.390 (.165)*
Denmark		−.345 (.162)*
Finland		.340 (.185)

Table 11.3 Continued.

	Model 1 B (SE)	Model 2 B (SE)
France		.433 (.184)*
Germany		−.723 (.170)***
Greece		−.401 (.196)*
Ireland		.218 (.169)
Italy		.326 (.167)
Luxembourg		.010 (.234)
Netherlands		.516 (.171)**
Portugal		−1.518 (.239)***
Spain		−1.286 (.197)***
Intercept	−.662 (.357)	−1.940 (.269)***
n	13,518	13,518
R^2-Adjusted	0.110	0.134

*** $p < 0.001$, ** $p < 0.01$, * $p < 0.05$. Data Source: EES 1999

of these models is very successful in accounting for the potential for switching (R^2 equals 11.0% and 13.4% respectively). Two quite different conditions may be at the basis of this low explained variance. The first is that we may have omitted major factors that, if they were included in the analysis, would have boosted explained variance considerably. It is irrelevant whether such omissions are due to the unavailability of the necessary data or to oversight and lack of imagination on our part. To the extent that this is the cause of low explained variance, our failure is reached in commission, as the relevant literature provides no suggestions for additional factors that should be taken into account. A second, quite different interpretation of the low explanatory power of the analysis is that the potential of switching is to a considerable extent determined by random and idiosyncratic factors.[20] In either case, the implication of our analyses is that the potential for switching is spread quite equally among different groups in society.

Of the variance in the dependent variable, 8.5 percent can be accounted for by the individual-level determinants only (not presented in table 11.3). This implies that almost 5 percent of the total variance can be attributed to contextual differences. This is the difference between the explained variances of model 2 and the individual-level variables only. The fifteen country dummies do of course not elucidate the substantive nature of this contextual variation. To provide a substantive explanation for these contextual differences, the fifteen country dummies are replaced by three contextual variables in model 1. The explained variance of this model is 11.0 percent. The three contextual variables thus pick up about half of the variance that can be attributed to country differences.

All three contextual variables have a clearly significant effect. Polarization between parties has a negative effect. This is the case for both dimensions. The more strongly that parties are differentiated from each other, the smaller the potential for vote switching.[21] The effective number of parties in a political system also has a strong and plausible effect on voters' potential to switch between parties. Its positive sign implies that when there are more parties to choose from, the potential for switching increases.

To assess individual-level effects, model 2 is more appropriate than model 1 because it is fully specified at the contextual level. Of the variables representing people's social background, only age stands out as significant. Its negative effect tells us that young voters are on average more likely to switch between parties than older voters. This is not unexpected. As the number of elections in which people can take part increases, so do the possibilities for reinforcement, which promotes people getting set in their choice (see also Converse 1969; Franklin 2004).[22]

Three of the measures of political involvement reach significance: party attachment, political interest, and watching television news.[23] The negative effect of party attachment is as expected: feelings of attachment or identification with a party will, *ceteris paribus,* decrease the potential for vote switching. The positive effect of interest is less obvious. From the tradition exemplified by Lazarsfeld, Berelson, and Gaudet (1944) one would expect the likelihood of switching to be most pronounced among the least interested voters, which would yield a negative coefficient. The critics of this view would not have expected any kind of significant effect. But in our data we do find a positive (albeit not very strong) effect of attentiveness. This somewhat unexpected finding requires corroboration in subsequent studies. Moreover, further analysis has to address concerns with respect to the direction of causality: does political interest increase people's likelihood to switch between parties, or does the latter promote a greater level of interest in order to arrive at a choice between almost equally attractive parties?[24] Furthermore, we find that watching television news has a negative effect on the potential for changing one's vote, whereas reading newspapers does not have a significant effect. As in the case of the effect of attentiveness, these coefficients require replication and probing for endogeneity. It is therefore too early to use them for grounding new theoretical propositions, but they are sufficiently provocative to merit replicatory analysis in a wide variety of contexts.

When looking at political attitudes and opinions we find that people's positions on the left-right and the EU integration dimensions are hardly related to their potential to switch votes. More easily interpretable is the finding that the more extreme one's own position is on either of these continua (irrespective of the side one is on) the less likely one is to switch parties. A combination of a less party supply at the extremes of ideological and policy dimensions and of greater psychological involvement of people who place themselves close to one of the poles of such dimensions accounts for the (negative) signs of these two extremity variables.

Respondents' opinions on a series of statements about parties and politics (for details, see note 13) are not significantly related to their likelihood of switching, except for the statement that there is no difference between parties, which in this context is a quite intelligible finding. This attitudinal statement corresponds to some extent with lack of polarization of party systems.

Discussion

Large segments of the electorates of the member states of the European Union are very likely to switch their vote from one election to the next—more than 40 percent on average. The electoral preferences for the two parties that each of these voters prefers the most are very close. Therefore, it takes very little to change the rank order of the first and second most preferred party, which thus changes the party that stands to get their vote. As we discussed earlier, this is neither new nor specific for European elections. At earlier European elections the incidence of potential switchers was high too—even if it seems to have increased since the late 1980s, witness table 11.2—and in the context of national first-order elections it is so as well.[25] Therefore one could conclude that European elections provide just an extra moment on the calendar at which this potential for electoral change can manifest itself. But there is an added element that is particular for European elections, and that gives a different flavor to the opportunities that these elections provide for electoral change. The second-order character of European elections provides voters with different strategic incentives than first-order national elections do. The latter decide—directly or after coalition formation—who will govern the country, whereas the political implications of European elections are of a more indirect nature. Reif and Schmitt (1980) already observed that citizens are more prone in European elections to vote 'with their heart' than with their 'head', which called attention to the diminished relevance of voter considerations concerning who they would like to see entrusted with government power. Their line of reasoning has been extended by Oppenhuis, van der Eijk, and Franklin (1996) who argued that sometimes protest considerations will be stimulated in the context of a European election: voting 'with the boot'.[26] In short, European elections differ from national ones in terms of the weights of different kinds of strategic considerations that make a party more or less attractive to vote for. All of this implies that electoral change generated by a European election is somewhat different from what a national election at the same time would have brought forth. European elections are not just another moment for the manifestation of electoral change; they add an extra 'twist' to it.[27]

Not all vote switching leads to changes in parties' electoral strength, as some of the movements at the level of individual voters cancel out. From chapter 2 in this volume we know, however, that it occasionally does affect parties' strengths.[28] Moreover, when European elections effectuate sizeable net electoral change this often has its impact on the domestic political landscape. Poor electoral performance erodes parties' clout in parliament and, if applicable, in government. In much the same way does a very good showing elevate parties' standing in parliament, in the media, and in the eye of the general public. In spite of the often dismissive attitude of parties, media, and citizens toward the importance of European elections, and in spite of the fact that the strategic incentives for voters are somewhat different from first-order elections, European elections do alter the domestic political arena in which parties compete for control over policy direction and where they prepare themselves for the 'next round'.[29] How wisely they subsequently operate in this redefined structure of prospects and risks is, of course, a matter that lies outside the realm of electoral politics proper.

What possibilities, if any, exist for parties to try and better themselves by tapping into the large potential of vote-switchers? The gains to be expected from successfully targeting specific groups in electorates seem limited in view of the low explanatory power of the model reported in table 11.3. This implies that to a very large extent all kinds of voter segments are almost equally prone to harbor potential switchers. But parties may conceivably try to change the salience of the issues on which they take different stands or to change their positions on issues. In view of the comparatively small differences between parties (see chapter 10), the issue of European integration seems to lend itself as potential option in this respect. Whether there would be particular parties that would gain from that cannot be assessed with the analyses presented so far in this volume. Gaining additional votes requires that changes in issue emphasis and party positioning result in a *comparative* advantage in electoral preferences. Whether any parties could hope to obtain this, and which parties that would be, will be addressed in the next chapter.

Notes

1. The political consequences of European elections include, of course, also the opposite of what is mentioned in the main text: depending on their outcomes and the existing context they may also help to strengthen the position of party leaders, to solidify parties' positions on issues, and to bolster coalitions. For examples, see van der Eijk and Franklin (1996) as well as the various country reports on European elections and their political consequences in *Electoral Studies* and *West European Politics*.

2. See the discussion on the implications of the second-order character of European elections elsewhere in this volume, in particular in chapters 1, 2, 3, and 12.

3. See also Dalton, Flanagan, and Beck (1984), Crewe and Denver (1985), Rose and McAllister (1985).

4. To avoid too contrived a text, we use the terms 'preference', 'propensity to support a party', and '(electoral) utility' as interchangeable. This concept is discussed in more detail in chapters 9 and 12 and elsewhere, see in particular van der Eijk and Franklin (1996, chapter 20), Tillie (1995), and van der Eijk et al. (2006).

5. All of this implies that when assessing and analyzing electoral change the ubiquitous focus on actual choice has to be supplemented with a focus on the preferences underlying those choices.

6. One may, correctly, notice that this conception of party competition is process-oriented and not necessarily action-oriented, as it does not require parties to be aware of their competitive relationships. On the other hand, astute political entrepreneurs are usually quite aware of who their competitors are, and particularly so in the current day and age where polling informs them about this.

7. We refrain here from repeating the background, validity, and characteristics of this set of questions, and refer for that to the discussion and references in chapter 9, and the discussion on additional uses of this information that is presented in chapter 12 and its appendix.

8. This kind of dichotomy is very helpful for comparing political systems. It is, obviously, also somewhat arbitrary. The distinction between likely and not-likely switchers can be relaxed—resulting in larger numbers of potential switchers—or sharpened so that only those who have a tie at their highest preference are considered as likely switchers. Such variations in the cut-off point do affect the magnitudes of the group defined as likely switchers, but not the pattern of differences between countries and periods that we analyze below. A ten-point scale forces respondents to 'round' their preferences to an integer.

This implies that our operationalization of 'nearly equal preferences' includes preference differences between 0 and 1.5 on the underlying continuous preference scale.

9. These definitions are slightly different from those used by van der Eijk and Oppenhuis (1991), who used data from the 1989 European elections for similar analyses as are reported here. It will be clear that criteria for classifying voters as subject to intense competition or as beyond competition can vary in threshold while employing the same logic. The definitions used here are somewhat more suited for the over-time comparison presented in this chapter, and that were not part of the research question addressed by van der Eijk and Oppenhuis in 1991.

10. The two groups we distinguish do not exhaust the electorates. The complement of their sum to 1 reflects the group that is somewhat less likely to switch votes, yet not classified as beyond competition.

11. More specifically: political interest, political attentiveness, exposure to mass media (television and newspaper), and education as an often used proxy for sophistication.

12. In particular: gender, class membership, union membership, and church attendance.

13. Including: position and extremity of voters' positions on the left-right and European integration dimensions (see also chapter 10), and whether or not the respondent subscribes to the following four statements: "Sometimes politics is so complicated that someone like me just cannot understand what is going on" ('Politics too complicated'), "Parties and politicians are more concerned with fighting each other than with furthering the common interest" ('Parties quarrel too much'), "So many people vote in elections that my vote does not matter" ('voting does not matter'), and "Most of the parties in [country] are so much alike that it does not make much of a difference which one is in government" ('no difference between parties').

14. We use here the survey questions that asked respondents to indicate parties' positions on a scale, the poles of which are "European unification has gone too far" and "European unification should be pushed further." We refer to this dimension as an *integration*-dimension, as we see this as a more encompassing term that reflects its meaning better than the term *unification*. The nature of this dimension was discussed in chapter 10, and will be reviewed in more detail in chapter 12, in the context of how matters relating to 'Europe' are framed and politicized.

15. To measure the extent of polarization in each system, we first computed the means of the perceived party positions on a dimension. Then we computed the weighted sum of the distances between (mean perceived) positions of all these parties. The weight is assigned on the basis of the size of the parties (proportions of seats in parliament). This measure has been proposed by Klingemann (2002).

16. As a measure we use the effective number of parties parties suggested by Laasko and Taagepera (1979).

17. More specifically: potential for switching $= -1 \times$ ((preference for most preferred party) $-$ (preference for second most preferred party)). As the electoral preferences for parties are measured on a ten-point scale, this measure ranges from -9 to 0, with the

latter value indicating the strongest potential for vote switching. Obviously, this more continuous measure is strongly correlated with the dummy variable which was used earlier in this chapter for descriptive analyses (at the individual level the correlation is 0.721 and at the system level 0.715).

18. First, multi-level methods require at least twenty units sampled at the highest level (Kreft and de Leeuw 1998, 126), whereas we have only sixteen systems. Second, these sixteen systems cannot sensibly be regarded to constitute a (random) sample from a wider universe.

19. To impute missing data we used King et al.'s (2001) EMis algorithm and the associated AMELIA program. This generated five datasets with missing data imputed. In each of these five generated datasets, the observed data are identical, as is the algorithm that leads to random draws. However, each random draw generates (possibly) different parameters. The results reported for the b-coefficients in table 11.3 are the means of the b-coefficients emanating from the analyses of these five datasets. The standard errors associated with the b-coefficients consist of the mean variance of standard errors over all five imputations (i.e., the within-imputation variance), and the variance of parameters between imputations (i.e., the between-imputation variance) (cf. Rubin 1987; Little and Rubin 1987).

20. To some extent this is indeed the case by statistical necessity. The dependent variable is the difference between two observations and its variance therefore contains more random error than either of the component parts from which it was derived. In the absence of covariance between the errors in the original measures the error variance of the difference is the sum of their separate error variances. This causes by necessity a drop in attainable levels of explained variance; nevertheless, the value of 0.13 for R^2 is not very impressive.

21. This finding is consistent with related research into the correlates of party system polarization as reported by, e.g., Bartolini and Mair (1990), Bowler (1996), Schmitt and Holmberg (1995), Roberts and Wibbels (1999), and Klingemann and Wessels (2000). This effects of extremity and of (perceived) polarization can also be understood as implications of spatial theory (cf. Downs 1957).

22. One should be cautious not to over-emphasize this argument. First, irrespective of age, voters are confronted with changing party landscapes that sometimes compel them to discard set ways: parties disappear, merge, or split. Moreover, even though older voters may be less sensitive to this, they are not entirely impervious to drastic changes in parties' positions on issues important to them. Finally, reinforcement of choice requires an uninterrupted series of identical choices. Any interruption sets the process back, and in some periods such interruptions are likely to occur because of charismatic leaders, deep-cutting political scandals, etc.

23. Attentiveness was measured by asking respondents how much they pay attention to news about politics. The response categories are 'none', 'a little', 'some', and 'a lot'.

24. This latter possibility is implied in Popkin's 'reasoning voter' argument (1991).

25. This has been documented for a number of countries, most extensively so for the Netherlands, where electoral utility items have been included in all national election

studies since 1982. In other countries these items have more recently also been included in studies of national elections (Britain, Ireland, Germany, Spain).

26. Oppenhuis, van der Eijk, and Franklin argued that the strategic incentives generated by European elections are not always the same, but dependent on the domestic political context in which they take place (1996, 301–304). When national governments are stable and secure, the outcome of a European election is not likely to change this. Tacitly this is communicated to voters by the behavior of parties and media, and this promotes 'sincere' voting (i.e., 'with the heart'). This kind of situation usually exists shortly after first-order national elections. When governments are less stable and secure, parties look at a European election as updates of popular support for rivaling parties and policies and implicitly communicate to voters that they pay attention to this election. As there is still no direct implication for the allocation of government power, those kinds of strategic considerations will not be triggered, but protest considerations will become more attractive: voting 'with the boot'.

27. See also chapter 2 of this volume.

28. From Oppenhuis, van der Eijk, and Franklin 1996 we know this, too, for the 1989 European elections.

29. It is evident that not all (net) changes in party strengths are equally important alterations of the political landscape of a country. Yet, for the parties involved the relevance of their (net) losses or gains is much clearer. A more elaborate analysis of systemic consequences of electoral change requires an assessment for each of the parties of the magnitudes and likelihood of their (net) gains and losses in a specific election. Such an analysis is beyond the scope of this chapter, but it will be taken up in chapter 12.

CHAPTER TWELVE

European elections, domestic politics, and European integration

WOUTER VAN DER BRUG
AND CEES VAN DER EIJK
WITH HERMANN SCHMITT, MICHAEL MARSH, MARK FRANKLIN,
JACQUES THOMASSEN, HOLLI SEMETKO, AND STEFANO BARTOLINI

European elections provide unique opportunities for studying the complex interactions between elites and citizens in the interrelated spheres of domestic and European politics, partially because these elections link domestic and European politics. While their nature as second-order national elections makes European elections an integral part of the domestic political sphere, the temptation to interpret them as popular verdicts on the state and course of European integration has repeatedly proved irresistible. Irrespective of the veracity of such an interpretation—extremely limited until now, see the findings from chapters 8 and 9—it affects the way in which politicians and political parties position themselves with respect to European integration. Some of these—governing parties and politicians—directly affect policy making in the European political arena by virtue of their membership of the Council. This is particularly important because, as we will argue in detail in this chapter, we expect that the consequences of European integration will become politically more important and more contested in the years to come. Such changes will first and foremost take place in the domestic political arenas of the member states and thus impact

European elections as well as first-order elections, i.e., the elections for the national parliaments of the member states. For these reasons, the results of the analyses presented in the previous chapters of this book not only document what went on during the European elections of 1999 but, possibly more importantly, they also serve as a stepping stone for making informed inferences about the way in which these complex interactions may evolve in the future. This is the agenda of the present chapter. We will first elaborate the linkage between European elections and domestic politics, focusing on the most important actors involved: common citizens, political elites, and media. Subsequently, we discuss why European integration can be expected to increase in electoral importance in the decade to come. Finally, we use the results from our analyses in previous chapters and the data of the European Election Study 1999 to estimate the electoral consequences of a number of scenarios each of which reflects a plausible change in the salience and politicization of 'Europe'.

One of the leading themes in the previous chapters of this volume was that European elections have to be regarded primarily as national political events. They are second-order national elections, the outcomes of which are to be understood as deriving primarily from domestic factors rather than from European ones. In spite of the fact that they are not commonly seen that way, European elections are thus an integral part of national politics. For expository convenience and lack of better terminology we will ourselves also distinguish between European elections and (other aspects of) domestic politics, while keeping in mind that they both belong to one and the same system. One may wonder whether this characterization of European elections as second-order national elections is still as justified as it was in 1980 when Reif and Schmitt coined the concept. Since then, the importance of the European Union has increased tremendously in all kinds of policy areas that directly impinge on individual voters' lives and well-being. New accessions, the introduction of the euro in most of the member states, and the drafting of an EU constitution (subjected to referenda in several countries) have undoubtedly heightened popular awareness of the EU.[1] This raises the question whether these events have altered the importance and the nature of European elections in the eyes of the voters, transforming them into something more than the seemingly inconsequential kind of 'beauty contest' that is implied in the concept of a second-order national election. Without in any way underestimating the breadth, depth, and consequences of all such changes at the level of European governance, we argue in this chapter that European elections are, and will be for the foreseeable future, second-order national elections. Precisely because of this, we can utilize the insights from previous chapters to explore how in years yet to come the elections to the European Parliament can be expected to interact with other aspects of domestic politics. This is the first theme to be elaborated in this chapter.

When looking at the way in which European elections are affected by (other aspects of) domestic politics we will build upon some of the previous chapters. These illustrated how European elections are affected by the domestic political context—in particular the location of these elections in the first-order electoral cycle of the member states. We will review the implications thereof for what we can expect to happen in future European Parliament elections.

In the second part of this chapter, we explore how the consequences of advancing European integration may affect first-order national elections. Our point of departure is the expectation that—for reasons briefly alluded to above—it is more likely than not that 'Europe' will become more visible and probably also more politicized in years to come. As already stated, and as will be argued in more detail below, we do not think that increased salience and politicization of the EU, of the process of European integration, and of the consequences of European policies will alter the second-order character of European elections. But that does not imply that these changes are of no relevance. On the contrary, heightened salience and politicization have their effects on voter behavior, and hence on election outcomes. And, as we will argue, such consequences are not limited to European elections, but will make themselves equally felt in first-order elections, i.e., elections to the national parliaments of the EU member states. Obviously, changes in voter behavior will also affect the behavior of politicians, political parties, and media and, therefore the entire domestic political landscape in the member states of the Union.[2] From the results of the analyses of voter behavior that were reported in chapter 9 we can derive inferences about voter preferences in a range of 'scenarios' defined in terms of (changing) salience and politicization of issues related to the EU and European integration. We will assess the electoral consequences of some such scenarios for national (and European) elections and we will demonstrate that under specifiable and realistic conditions EU-related issues can generate considerable electoral changes.

European elections and domestic politics

Since their first occurrence in 1979, and in large measure up to this very moment, it was obvious that the direct elections to the European Parliament are of a different nature than national parliamentary elections, which were most often studied until then. The campaigns and the outcomes illustrate this most clearly. The campaigns are generally lackluster, as issues connected to the European Union (earlier the European Community) and European integration are scarcely politicized and, in fact, hardly discussed by parties, politicians, and the media. Therefore, and because of the lack of a direct linkage between executive power in the EU and the composition of the European Parliament, these elections provide voters little possibility to influence EU policy making.[3] As a consequence, domestic political issues generally dominate the campaigns, but usually also without much fervor because the composition of the European Parliament has no direct bearing either on the course of domestic politics or on the allocation of domestic government power. Low turnout demonstrates that all of this provides little motivation for voters. Moreover, the understanding that these elections have no direct political consequences frees voters from some of the considerations that help determine their choice in national parliamentary elections: they can vote with their 'heart' rather than with their 'mind'. In general, this has the effect that large parties (among which many government parties) do worse and small parties (predominantly opposition parties) do better than in the case of more important (first-order) elections. Of course, this stylized picture does not apply equally to all European elections in each of the member states and important exceptions exist, but that is exactly what they are: exceptions.[4]

Reif and Schmitt (1980) were among the first to try to conceptualize the peculiar character of these kinds of elections. They referred to them as second-order national elections. Such elections are characterized by the national political arena being dominant over the specific political arena for which the election is ostensibly meant. Yet, in contrast to other—first-order—elections in which the national political arena is dominant, they do not have direct consequences for the allocation of government power: there is less 'at stake'. Other phenomena, such as lackluster campaigns, limited attention in the media, low turnout, losses for large parties, and 'voting with the heart' are not defining characteristics of second-order elections, but consequences thereof, which are sometimes more and at other times less pronounced. Subsequent research has contributed much to further refining our understanding of these phenomena and particularly of the circumstances that cause European elections to differ between themselves in these aspects.[5] Such variations seem to be attributable predominantly to the extent to which second-order elections can be expected to have *indirect* consequences for (government) power, and this, in turn is largely related to their timing in the domestic electoral cycle.[6]

From this conceptual discussion follows that—irrespective of the importance and politicization that 'European' issues may attain—elections to the

European Parliament cannot be but second-order national elections for the foreseeable future. They remain to be of no direct consequence for the allocation of power in the executive and policy-initiating bodies in the European Union, which are the Commission and the Council. The composition of the Commission is decided upon by the Council and the governments of the member states. Although a new Commission has to be confirmed by the European Parliament, it is virtually impossible that European elections could be a forum of popular influence on its composition and its ideological complexion (see also note 3). The composition of the Council is equally little at stake in European elections as it is determined by national (first-order) elections and—in most countries—by the vagaries of coalition formation. So, indeed, as discussed in the introduction of this volume, the design of the EU shields these institutions well against direct popular influence via European elections. Moreover, neither the proposals contained in the constitution drafted by the Convention nor ongoing debates about the constitutional order of the EU suggest that this is going to change.[7] At the same time, the dominance of the national political arena in European elections is also built in by design. The fragmentation of European elections along the boundaries of the member states guarantees that the relevant actors in European Parliament elections are virtually indistinguishable from those in national (first-order) elections: the electorate,[8] the political parties,[9] and the media.[10] Yet, in spite of their semblance to national elections, no national government power is directly at stake. Stated differently: European elections are second-order national elections as an unavoidable consequence of the institutional design of the EU.

Because of their second-order character, what happens in European elections will be determined in the future—in much the same way as it has been in the past—by the domestic political context and by the *indirect* political importance that this context bestows upon European elections. This, in turn, depends to a considerable extent on the timing of European elections within the national (first-order) election cycle—or to specific circumstances, such as, e.g., disarray within or between government parties that may give rise to early elections (see also note 6). As far as timing in the domestic electoral cycle is concerned, we can summarize several of its effects from previous chapters.

If European elections occur briefly before a national election, parties are likely to pay more attention than otherwise because they consider them as early indicators of what may happen in the upcoming 'real' election. With the passage of time, a previous national election gradually loses its validity as an indicator of the electoral strength of the various parties. Therefore, the longer the period since a previous national election, the more politicians and voters will turn to second-order national elections to 'update' their perception of popular support for the various parties. Since nothing succeeds like success, the outcomes of European elections impinge upon the dynamics of subsequent national election campaigns. Parties are therefore particularly eager to do well in a European election if it takes place briefly before a national one.[11] Therefore, a European election close before a domestic election confronts voters with national political elites who are active in the campaign and highly attentive to whatever 'messages' voters are inclined to convey with their choice.

Their increased campaign activities serve to heighten voters' motivations to participate by signaling that something is at stake. After all, why would politicians spend their time on non-important matters? These cycle-related variations in cognitive and motivational requirements for participation result (on average) in higher turnout for European elections that fall late in the electoral cycle. Franklin modeled this relationship in detail in chapter 1 of this volume.

Not only voter turnout is affected by the timing of European elections; voters' choices are too, at least in the aggregate. Marsh demonstrated in chapter 3 that the relationship between support for governing parties and the time since the last national elections is curvilinear in nature.[12] In comparison to their vote share at the previous national election, government parties lose the most when the electoral cycle is roughly at its midpoint. These losses are considerably smaller at earlier or later moments when government parties may even win in vote share. Several factors loom behind these findings, some of which could be explored in more detail by comparing—party-by-party rather than by a government-opposition dichotomy—parties' vote shares in European elections with the vote share they would have acquired had it been national elections (chapter 2). One factor causing government loss is that strategic considerations are weaker in European elections than in national ones ('voting with the heart'), which works predominantly at the disadvantage of larger parties, and government parties are on average larger than those in opposition. But strategic considerations are not entirely absent, and they, too, vary over the course of the cycle (cf. Oppenhuis, van de Eijk, and Franklin 1996), contributing to this curvilinear pattern of government losses. A second factor behind the findings of chapters 2 and 3 is that Euro-skeptic parties did comparatively well in 1999, with government parties almost by necessity being more positively associated with 'Europe' than opposition parties are. Whatever the specific mix of factors that generate the curvilinear relationship modeled by Marsh here, too, it is obvious that it arises from the second-order character of European elections.

Table 12.1 Effects of timing of European elections in first-order electoral cycle

	Four years before first-order national election	Two years before first-order national election	One month before first-order national election
Turnout, compared to EE being consecutive with a first-order national election	−17.8%	−8.9%	−0.4%
Electoral performance of government parties compared to previous first-order national election	+4.9%	−4.4%	+0.6%

In table 12.1 we indicate the magnitude of these two relationships between the domestic electoral cycle and what happens in European elections. We do so by evaluating the respective models that were presented in chapters 1 and 3 for different moments in the electoral cycle: four years before the next election (usually this means, shortly following the previous national election), two years before the next election (roughly the midpoint of the electoral cycle), and one month before the next national election.[13] It is obvious that these timing effects are far from trivial in their magnitude. The electoral instability that they generate will be overlaid on top of the electoral effects of other political developments, some of which relate to the process of European integration, which we will discuss in the next section. Consequently, in some situations, these timing effects will be muted by countervailing developments that have been abstracted away by the *ceteris paribus* clause that underlies the models that were used in the analyses presented in table 12.1. In other situations, however, timing effects will reinforce what was already in the making due to other factors. In all situations, however, the source of this timing variability is the second-order character of European elections, and that is, as we argued above, an inescapable consequence of the constitutional arrangements of the EU. These arrangements therefore may be successful in shielding important institutions and policy processes in the EU from popular influence (see the introduction of this volume), but they do so only by burdening the political systems of the member states with electoral instability that—in contrast to what one would hope to find in democratic polities—cannot be simply interpreted in terms of approval or disapproval with policies, either at the national or at the European level.

European integration, electoral preferences, and election outcomes

Our argument that European elections will remain second-order national elections for years to come does not imply that they may not change in other aspects. On the contrary, we do expect their appearance to change in important ways, most notably because they will, on average, become more focused on 'European' issues than they have been until now. This will also increase their political relevance for the process of European integration, but only indirectly so. Below, we argue that 'Europe' will increasingly become a topic of domestic political contestation, and that this will augment its electoral salience. The domestic nature of this increase in salience and politicization will, obviously, not only affect European elections, but also the (first-order) elections for the national parliaments. We will analyze the potential electoral consequences of these changes, making use of the insights gained in the previous chapters of this volume.

European integration has become increasingly more important and more visible to ordinary citizens since the first direct elections to the European Parliament in 1979. All indications are that this development has not yet run its full course and that it will continue in years to come. EU policy covers more areas than ever before and affects not only matters that are distant in citizens' experiences, but also progressively more affairs that are close by and of daily importance. The fact that most European legislation has to be 'translated' into national regulation and that it has to be implemented at the national level may help to obscure exactly how and by whom it was shaped, but it cannot completely obscure that it finds its roots in 'Europe'. Politicians, journalists, and sundry other opinion leaders have become accustomed to pointing to the EU or 'Brussels' as the origin of policies, particularly those they disagree with.[14] For these reasons it is likely that not only the 'objective' weight of the EU in terms of regulatory impact will continue to increase for quite some time to come, but even more so the perceived importance of the EU in the eyes of ordinary citizens, and this will, if given the opportunity to do so, make itself felt in their electoral behavior.

The perception of 'Europe' being important is by itself not sufficient for a greater impact of opinions about Europe on party preferences and voting. In fact, the perception that Europe matters is already present in large segments of the populations of the member states of the EU, and yet, as documented by many studies in the past decade and by the results in chapters 8 and 9, voters' opinions on Europe, the EU, and European integration are in most instances of marginal importance at best for explaining their electoral behavior. Perceived importance is thus only a necessary condition for opinions and preferences to have an impact on political behavior. It needs to be complemented by other conditions, most notably the politicization of 'Europe' as an issue on which parties take conflicting positions. 'Europe', 'European integration', and the 'EU' are, however, multifaceted phenomena.[15] Economic integration is not the same as political integration, and parties or voters who are in favor of one are not necessarily in favor of the other. Whether or not to join the common currency (the euro) is a different issue than is the CAP. The debate about the constitutional make-up of the EU may divide people and parties in different ways than policy making within the framework of ratified treaties. There is no logical reason why positions on all these different matters should be related. But there is a behavioral one: the need for parties, politicians, journalists, and citizens to reduce complexity in order to limit their information costs and to allow rational choice.[16] The successful construction of an overarching framework for political contestation about Europe is a precondition for European opinions and preferences to become more important in determining voters' choices. The main actors to bring this about are political parties and mass media, as they are the primary aggregators of specific concerns into more generic ones as well as professional manipulators of cognitive and emotive symbols. But political parties—particularly mainstream ones—have until now not been very instrumental in this respect.[17] Neither have most media risen above the level of isolated coverage of events and incidents—with the exception of those catering to small, professional niches. There are no reasons to expect mainstream parties and media to change in this respect, except in the face of powerful incentives. These may derive from a combination of challenging political entrepreneurs, social movements, and unintended consequences of short-term rational behavior of mainstream politicians.

Challenges to existing political parties originate in particular from the political entrepreneurs that start new parties. They need to differentiate themselves from established competitors, and European integration offers a cluster of issues that lends itself easily to this. It does so mainly because the (sizeable) segments of the electorates that are opposed to or ambivalent about further integration are poorly represented by the major political parties as was demonstrated in chapter 10[18] and, more recently, in the outcomes of referenda on the EU constitutional treaty that were held in 2005. Because most of the existing parties have in the past promoted or accepted the deepening of integration and the broadening of the Union, a contrasting Euro-skeptic position may be quite attractive to newcomers. Such new parties need not be of one particular kind, and not all of them will be successful at the polls. But as soon as any such upstart does perform well in an election, the existing parties are challenged to take issue with it and they will have to clarify their positions on the issue(s) that are believed to be responsible for the newcomer's success.[19] Particularly in the case of an electoral breakthrough in a European election, chances are that the new party's position on European integration will be regarded as the cause of success, irrespective of the veracity of such an interpretation.[20] One contribution of new parties to the politicization of European integration is thus that they prod older parties to explicate their positions. In addition, they may assist in reducing the multifarious nature of European affairs into a simple frame, which lends itself better to an overarching form of politicization and mobilization. In recent years, new parties have done so mainly by emphasizing that integration has *gone too far* (or is on the verge of doing so) and that the country in question should reassert its autonomy and independence.[21]

A second contribution to framing and politicizing European integration may come from the anti-globalist movement. Over the past decade, anti-globalists have vociferously portrayed the EU as 'fortress Europe' that disallows the Third World access to the European market and that helps to perpetuate or even to bolster unfair advantages for its own agricultural sector. In the process, the EU's emphasis on economic performance over humane values would also have aggravated damage to the environment. While not restricting themselves to the EU as a target, anti-globalists have launched spirited and at times violent demonstrations at a series of EU summits and have strongly denounced the treaties of Amsterdam and Nice. Although the anti-globalist movement is small, and even though it enjoys only limited support in public opinion, it has strong communicative and rhetorical skills, which give it media exposure beyond its numbers. Its generally negative portrayal of the EU thus contributes to the familiarity of an overarching anti- or pro-integration frame that can be applied to all kinds of matters European.

A third factor that may help to attain an overarching framing of a great variety of loosely connected EU-related matters derives from the unintended consequences of routine behavior of government politicians. Normal behavior of governments includes claiming credit for situations that are expected to enhance popular support and trying to shift the blame for everything that may endanger this. It has been documented repeatedly that the tendency to externalize blame to 'Brussels' is often irresistible for national governments, even when they themselves have been involved in making the policy in question by way of their position in the Council of Ministers and the European Council.[22] This kind of routine behavior contributes to reducing complexity by framing Europe in terms of a struggle between one's own national interest on the one hand, and the interests of other countries or of the EU in general on the other. This unintended framing is easily augmented and reproduced by the mass media, particularly because they cater almost exclusively to country-specific audiences and as their primary focus is toward the domestic political arena.

These various schemata of structuring all kinds of diverse issues relating to the EU are not identical, but they seem mutually compatible and can therefore easily be used in conjunction. The *'has gone too far'* frame is often motivated by a claim that specific *national interests* are endangered by European policy,[23] which is a short step away from *opposing* European integration. It stands to reason that Europhobia or Euro-skepticism in one form or another is not the only possible position for parties, media, and voters as it represents only one of the poles of a continuum, the other pole of which could be termed Europhilia. Yet any politicization of issues relating to European integration is likely to be propelled particularly by expressions of Euro-skepticism, were it only because the position that integration should be furthered (both in 'deeper' and in 'broader' ways) has until now been dominant in the political arenas of most of the member states, which is reflected in the public perception that most major political parties favor rather than oppose European integration.

Successful politicization will be a self-sustaining and irreversible process at least for some time. The attainment of an overarching frame will reduce information cost for media and voters; its conflictuous aspect will represent news value for media and thus generate media coverage. Increased attention for an issue by media and parties heightens its salience to voters, and vice versa, as was demonstrated in chapters 6 and 7: media attention to the EU not only increases when a viable anti-EU party arrives on the scene (see chapter 6), it has a stronger effect on attitudes when there is more contestation among elites (chapter 7).

However, not everyone stands to gain from the politicization of European integration—on the contrary. Established parties are not homogeneous in this respect and run the risk of internal strife and schisms when other matters than those that unite them increase in political importance. Moreover, issues compete with each other for agenda priority, so that the ascendance of some concerns implies that other ones will suffer neglect or oblivion. For reasons exposed above, however, it seems unlikely that the de-politicization of 'Europe' that has been successfully maintained for decades can be sustained indefinitely. Moreover, the process of European integration itself has also promoted convergence of issues and frames between the countries of the EU. Because of this, successful politicization of European integration in one country will be noticed in other countries and function as a source of inspiration and as an example to be emulated.[24]

The conclusion of our discussion in this section is that it is exceedingly likely that the politicization and salience of European integration will increase, although it is impossible to predict where or when this will occur first, or what the specific catalyst for it will be. The likelihood of these developments, however, raises questions about their electoral consequences.

ELECTORAL CONSEQUENCES OF INCREASING SALIENCE AND POLITICIZATION OF 'EUROPE'

We can explore the electoral consequences of increasing politicization and salience of European integration by using results from the analyses of earlier chapters in this volume. Chapter 6, for example, documented that prior to the European elections of 1999 the media dedicated on average about 10 percent of their attention to these elections or to other European topics (see table 6.1). In countries with elite dissent (Austria, Denmark, France, Greece, and Sweden) this percentage was substantially higher (14%) than in countries with elite consensus on the integration issue (7%). For the reasons elaborated earlier, we can expect that the number of countries will increase where at least one viable anti-integration party exists. From the analyses presented in table 6.3 we can estimate what changes in media attention the emergence of such a party will generate in those countries where no such party existed in 1999 (Belgium, Germany, England, Ireland, Italy, Luxembourg, the Netherlands, Portugal, Spain, and Finland): the volume of media coverage would increase by 4.8 percent of all news. This, in turn, would directly affect citizens. From chapter 7 we know that citizens are much more inclined to feel that integration is an important issue when elite consensus is replaced by elite dissent on that issue (the difference being almost a full point on a four-point scale).[25] This, in turn, would create an environment in which further attempts at politicization could flourish.

When estimating the effects on voter behavior of increasing politicization and salience of European integration it has to be kept in mind that these processes have different effects. In the process of politicization, political parties change their position (or at least some of them will do so). This affects the policy distances between voters and parties, and thus the attractiveness of each of the parties to different kinds of voters: smaller policy distances make parties more attractive (*ceteris paribus*), larger distances make them less attractive to vote for. Because voters differ in their positions on the pro or contra integration dimension, changes in the positions of parties will have different consequences for different voters. The second process, increasing saliency, implies that voters will give more weight to the integration issue (in comparison to other considerations) when deciding which party to vote for. Even without any changes in policy distances between voters and parties, changes in salience may affect party choice, particularly when different considerations do not point to the same party as the 'best' choice.

We can assess the consequences of increasing polarization and salience of the European integration issue for election results by using the models presented in chapter 9. In that chapter, the aim was to explain propensities to vote for parties from a series of independent variables, among which was policy distance on European integration. The effects (weights) of these explanatory variables were estimated on the data from the European Election Study 1999. The estimated model can subsequently be used to predict what the vote propensities would be for each of the parties under circumstances different than those that existed when the data were collected. This yields for each voter an estimate of the attractiveness of each of the parties for particular—counterfactual—conditions. From these vote propensities we can derive voters' choices of parties, using the assumption that people vote for the party which is most attractive to them (an assumption that is strongly supported by empirical information, as documented in chapter 9). Finally, by aggregating these individual choices, we arrive at estimated election outcomes for the conditions that were specified. In this manner, it is possible to evaluate how election results would be in a counterfactual world, i.e., a world that differs from the one that yielded the estimated model that was reported in chapter 9.

When evaluating the electoral consequences of counterfactual conditions, we have to bear in mind that the actions of all actors in the electoral process are interrelated. If one party changes its position, other parties are likely to react, journalists may become more interested in the issue, and this in turn has consequences for the choices of voters, and these affect party behavior again, etc. It is therefore not realistic to 'predict' the long-term consequences of counterfactual conditions. We can, however, fruitfully assess how election results would be affected in the short term, and particularly if only a few of the aspects of the estimated model would change. We will therefore limit ourselves to two aspects, salience and politicization. We do so by looking at three different counterfactuals, or scenarios.

The first scenario involves increased saliency, which is represented by the effect (weight) of voter-party distances on the integration dimension. The question to be answered is simply how election outcomes would change if the issue of European integration were to become more important to voters than it was in 1999, while all other factors would be the same. We defined this 'increased saliency' counterfactual by setting this weight equal to that of voter-party distances on the left-right dimension, which we found to be the strongest substantive factor affecting propensities to vote for parties (see chapter 9, table 9.4).[26]

The second scenario involves increased salience, in the same way as in first scenario, but adds changes in party positions that could arise from increased politicization of the integration issue. Given the predominance in 1999 of pro-integration positions among political parties, particularly mainstream parties, politicization would in all likelihood result in all parties shifting in a Euro-skeptic direction. This scenario is inspired by the development of the immigration issue in countries such as the Netherlands and Denmark since the mid-1990s. When anti-immigrant parties became electorally successful, virtually all other political parties adapted their positions and began to advocate more restrictive immigration policies. Our second scenario defines a counterfactual world in which all parties have become somewhat more Euro-skeptic (a change of one position on the ten-point scale), while voters' positions on this dimension remain as they were.[27]

In the third scenario, we add to increased salience and changes in party positions yet a different factor: voters' positions on European integration. What would happen if the distribution of both party and voter positions on this dimension would resemble that on the left-right dimension? The left-right dimension was chosen as the point of comparison because it is in all countries of the EU the dominant structuring dimension that relates parties and voters' substantive political opinions. This counterfactual was defined by a transformation at the level of individual voters of the independent variable 'distances on the integration dimension' in such a way that their distribution is set to be identical to that of distances on the left-right scale, while preserving the ordering of parties' positions on the integration dimension. Technical details of this, and of the other two scenarios are provided in an appendix to this chapter.

We estimate the electoral consequences of these three scenarios. The results pertain to first-order elections in the EU member states, and, with some more slippage, also to elections to the European Parliament. As discussed in chapter 9 (see table 9.1) the vote propensities data that are at the heart of our analysis are very closely linked to individual party choice in both kinds of elections. Our findings can be expressed in different ways. In its most detailed form, we can look at all individual respondents in our samples and determine what party they would choose in the modeled conditions and compare that with their behavior in the 1999 baseline. Table 12.2 illustrates this, for the first scenario and for Austria. The table shows how many voters would make a different choice if the world would have been according to the stipulated scenario, what their original choice was (as predicted by the model), and to which party they switched. By summing rows and columns, we also see how these individual changes affect the vote shares of the various parties. This kind of table is very helpful in demonstrating that the

Table 12.2 Exemplary case. Changes in party choice in Austria as a consequence of scenario 1.*

Party choice predicted by scenario 1	Predicted party choice by baseline						
	SPÖ	ÖVP	FPÖ	GRUENEN	LIB F.	CSA	Total
SPÖ	116	4	8	1	0	0	129
ÖVP	5	102	14	2	0	0	123
FPÖ	7	10	59	3	0	0	79
GRUENEN	3	2	1	21	0	0	27
LIB FORUM	1	0	0	0	2	0	3
CSA	0	0	0	0	0	1	1
Total	132	118	82	27	2	1	362

* Gross change is the total number in the off diagonal cells (those who changed) divided by N (= 60/362 x 100% = 16.6%). The net change is the sum of the absolute differences in the margins divided by N and divided by 2 (and multiplied by 100%). The net change is thus: ((|129 – 132| + |123 – 118| + |79 – 82| + |27 – 27| + |3 – 2| + |1 – 1|) / 2) x 100% = (12 / 362 / 2) × 100% = 1.66%.

consequences of the various scenarios are not evenly spread across all political parties. As a case in point, the Austrian FPÖ would lose 28 percent (23/82) of its original voters as a consequence of increased salience of European integration, but it would at the same time also acquire new votes (20), resulting in a net loss of almost 4 percent (net loss 3, on the original base of 82). The much larger SPÖ and ÖVP would experience much less turbulence in their electoral support, which is interesting from a party-specific or system-specific analysis. Reporting forty-eight analyses (three scenarios for each of sixteen systems) in this way provides, however, little possibility of arriving at a Europe-wide perspective.

In the remainder of this chapter, we summarize these detailed individual-level tables for the countries of the EU. Table 12.3 presents for each country, and for each scenario, two different perspectives on electoral change. It gives, first, the proportions of individual voters who would change their vote (gross change), which is indicative of the extent to which conditions other than those in 1999 can 'move' people to make different choices. Second, it expresses the consequences of these—sometimes countervailing—individual changes for the distribution of parties' shares of the vote (net changes), which is indicative for the political consequences that greater salience and politicization of European integration would have in the respective member states.[28]

Table 12.3 Predicted electoral change (in percent) in election results in different scenarios

Change in party choice	Scenario 1 Gross Change	Scenario 1 Net Change	Scenario 2 Gross Change	Scenario 2 Net Change	Scenario 3 Gross Change	Scenario 3 Net Change
Austria	16.6	1.7	17.8	4.2	15.3	1.9
Belgium: Flanders	10.7	3.9	10.6	3.2	17.8	3.5
Belgium: Wallonia	20.9	11.3	17.5	8.0	21.0	6.7
Britain	6.5	1.6	6.4	1.5	6.9	1.4
Denmark	15.0	7.4	14.4	4.8	13.6	5.4
Finland	16.5	4.7	13.4	3.0	13.5	5.0
France	10.8	3.4	12.2	3.8	24.9	11.8
Germany	5.1	0.9	5.1	0.9	8.5	2.1
Greece	8.9	1.2	8.9	2.3	13.2	2.6
Ireland	12.3	3.5	12.7	2.8	13.8	5.0
Italy	5.3	2.6	6.5	2.7	7.2	2.7
Luxembourg	8.8	3.6	7.9	4.9	15.2	6.0
Netherlands	10.2	2.6	11.6	4.2	14.6	4.0
Portugal	6.1	3.4	5.8	3.1	11.1	3.1
Spain	3.8	1.5	4.2	1.2	7.1	2.7
Sweden	21.8	12.6	20.9	7.8	25.8	14.0
Average	11.2	4.1	11.0	3.7	14.3	4.9

When inspecting the consequences of the three scenarios for the members of the EU, table 12.3 gives rise to a number of general conclusions. First, we find that the conditions that we modeled result in considerable numbers of voters who switch to a different party. Gross change (the proportion of voters switching) averages across the countries between 11 percent and 14 percent for the three scenarios. In eleven out of these forty-eight contexts (three scenarios for sixteen political systems), the percentage of switchers surpasses 16 percent, which is one out of every six voters. In six instances, at least one out of every five voters would switch between parties as a consequence of the political changes modeled in the three scenarios, leaving all other factors unchanged. This magnitude of electoral volatility is far from negligible. It must be kept in mind, however, that there also are contexts where increasing salience and politicization of European integration would make very few voters switch their vote. The size of the group of switchers is obviously related to the number of voters whose first and second best choices differ relatively little in terms of vote propensities, and who can therefore easily switch. This number is determined by all kinds of other factors that impinge on the propensities to vote for parties and that were kept unchanged in the scenarios: left-right orientations, other issues, the political translation of factors such as religious and class, government approval, etc.[29]

A second general conclusion from table 12.3 is that net electoral change is quite limited. Net change averages 4.2 percent and exceeds a level of 5 percent in only twelve out of forty-eight situations. Comparing these figures with those for gross change highlights that more than half of all individual vote switching is cancelled out by aggregation. Compared to the net change commonly found in national first-order elections in European countries, the counterfactuals that we evaluate seem to be quite limited in the electoral volatility they generate. Mair (2002a, b) reports an average net change of 13 percent for parliamentary elections in Western European countries in the 1990s. So, on average, the scenarios will not generate large-scale electoral upheavals of the kind that resulted from sundry domestic political developments at different occasions.[30] The political significance of whatever amount of net change would result from one of our scenarios cannot, however, be determined by its numerical size only. Some 4 percent to 5 percent net change may, depending on how it is distributed over political parties, make or break a majority, and hence affect the composition of the government. Moreover, the fall-out in public discourse of even a limited amount of net electoral change can be quite different depending on whether it is concentrated around few parties or fragmented among many political parties. It would be incorrect, therefore, to restrict our view to only the *average* degree of net change that would be generated by the scenarios. In a small number of cases (Sweden, France, and Wallonia) net electoral change would be quite considerable, and considerably above 'normal' levels for first-order elections. As we discussed above, such cases would function as catalysts for political change in other countries, by stimulating media attention and public debate, by encouraging new political entrepreneurs to emulate successes elsewhere, and by motivating established party elites to preempt this by anticipatory changes in their own positions on European integration.

A third general observation from table 12.3 is that large differences exist between countries in the extent to which the circumstances modeled in our scenarios affect election outcomes. In Sweden the gross and net changes are generally the highest, whereas in Spain the smallest effects are generally observed. This is to some extent the consequence of differences in numbers of volatile voters (see chapter 11). In table 11.2 we showed that Spain and Portugal have the smallest groups of volatile voters and the largest proportions of voters who are beyond electoral competition. The sheer number of volatile voters does not explain all the differences between these countries though. For example, Italy has many volatile voters, but the counterfactual scenarios result in only moderate (net) changes in party strengths. The most likely explanation is that Italian volatile voters waver between parties that have similar positions toward European integration, so that changes in salience and politicization of this issue have for most Italian voters little differential effects between their first and second most preferred parties.

As repeatedly indicated above, electoral change is not necessarily distributed evenly across all political parties. So, when investigating the electoral consequences of the three scenarios, we should not only address the question how much change would be generated by plausible counterfactual conditions, but also which kinds of parties would be most affected. In order to do so, we analyzed the net gains or losses that individual parties would experience in the three scenarios (see the detailed information in the appendix of this chapter). We compared parties according to three criteria: whether they are a government or an opposition party, whether they are large or small, and where they are located on the left-right dimension.[31] A simple regression analysis—reported in table 12.4—is sufficient to demonstrate that indeed not all kinds of parties are equally affected by changes in salience and politicization of European integration.

Table 12.4 shows that, largely irrespective of their ideological background, large parties are most vulnerable. This is consistent with the findings from chapter 10 that Euro-skeptic voters are in general not well represented by large

Table 12.4 Predicting gain or loss of parties in three scenarios by party characteristics

	Scenario 1	Scenario 2	Scenario 3
Right party (dummy)	.047	.158	.059
Government party (dummy)	−.033	−.018	−.038
Party size (scale)	−.216*	−.241*	−.340**
R^2-adjusted (n = 115)	.030	.057	.106

Entries are standardized regression coefficients (* significant at $p < 0.05$; ** significant at $p < 0.01$)

Table 12.5 Predicting gain or loss of parties in three scenarios by party characteristics

	Scenario 1	Scenario 2	Scenario 3
Right party (dummy)	.032	.142	.036
Government party (dummy)	−.022	−.007	−.021
Party size (scale)	−.056	.072	−.098
Government party * party size	−.209	−.220	−.317*
R^2-adjusted (n = 115)	.038	.068	.138

Entries are standardized regression coefficients (* significant at $p < 0.05$; ** significant at $p < 0.01$)

political parties, that orientations concerning European integration are orthogonal to left-right orientations among voters, and that there is little variation in large parties' positions on European integration. An increase in salience and politicization will therefore, at least in the short run, hurt large parties in particular. Table 12.4 suggests that the government or opposition status of a party is irrelevant for its electoral performance in the three scenarios. To some extent this is misleading, and the consequence of multicollinearity and of small numbers of cases. A slightly more elaborate regression analysis is reported in table 12.5, which includes in addition to the explanatory variables reported in table 12.4 an interaction between party size and government status. From the magnitude of the coefficients it is immediately clear that large government parties in particular are vulnerable to electoral loss when European integration becomes electorally more important and when parties become more differentiated in their positions.[32]

In conclusion

European elections are inescapably, we argued, second-order *national* elections. As a consequence, the outcomes of European elections are first and foremost affected by domestic politics. Although it seems quite plausible to interpret the outcomes of European elections as indicative of popular support for European integration, or the lack thereof, such interpretations are largely incorrect, as was demonstrated in chapters 8 and 9. Indeed, most of the chapters in this volume presented overwhelming empirical support for the relevance of the second-order conceptualization of European elections which implies that the

EU-arena is indeed secondary at best (sometimes even hardly relevant at all) in explaining the behavior of voters, parties, and media and in interpreting the outcomes of the electoral process.

But European elections do not yield identical outcomes to those that national first-order elections would produce at that moment in time (cf. chapter 2). How preferences and orientations of citizens are expressed in their propensities to support parties—and thus in their party choices—is moderated by strategic considerations that themselves are subject to the vagaries of timing. The analyses reported in chapters 1, 2, and 3 demonstrate that the timing of a European election in the domestic electoral cycle determines the indirect domestic political consequences of a second-order contest, which affects the behavior of voters and parties. As these effects of timing are not related to voters' substantive political preferences, they reduce the capacity of elections to perform one of their key roles in representative democracies, that of a channel of communication between citizens and elites that helps legitimize policies and power. This is particularly problematic because European elections are so prone to be erroneously interpreted as gauging voters' orientations regarding 'Europe'.

The dominance of the domestic political arena does not imply that issues related to European integration are never of any importance in European elections. But the extent to which this issue (or cluster of issues) is of relevance is determined by its role in the domestic political arena. If voters' opinions about European integration affect their choices in European elections, they will only do so by virtue of the fact that they will have the same kind of impact in national first-order elections. And, we argued, it seems difficult to imagine that the successful de-politicization of these matters can endure indefinitely. On the contrary, all indications are that political contestation over European integration will increase in the years to come, which will also raise the salience of integration issues. We investigated the electoral consequences thereof by using the explanatory models from earlier chapters as the basis for estimating election results for counterfactual scenarios that were defined in terms of increased salience and politicization of 'Europe'. These findings teach us that increasing politicization and salience will—on average— generate a considerable amount of electoral volatility at the level of individual voters, but much less so at the level of parties' electoral strengths. But behind these averages there is considerable variation, and in a small number of systems (particularly Sweden, France, and Wallonia) the potential exists for large net electoral changes. Moreover, at the same time the process of European integration has augmented the likelihood of 'contagion' between countries. What happens in one country has in other countries the function of an example—to be emulated or to be avoided—and thus affects parties and political entrepreneurs, media, and voters.

The electoral consequences of increased salience and politicization of European integration will be overlaid on whatever electoral developments arise from other factors. These other factors were not varied in our simulations, they were held constant as part of a necessary *ceteris paribus* clause. But evidently they will not be constant in the years to come. This implies that the potential for electoral change owing to the changing political importance of European issues will sometimes be dampened by other factors, but at times it will also exacerbate them. In most countries larger parties, which are usually seen as part of the establishment, are at risk when the issue becomes more politicized. This prospective could be interpreted as an invocation for governments (and particularly for large government parties) to keep investing in the de-politicization of the issue of European integration. We feel, however, that the chances of such a strategy being successful in the long run are exceedingly small—particularly after the French and Dutch electorates rejected by referendum the draft EU Constitution in 2005. It would make more sense to reinvent the basic principles of electoral representation in the EU and particularly how these connect with citizens' electoral representation in the domestic political arenas of the member states. Necessary elements of such an attempt have been discussed in political and in academic circles for at least a decade and a half. Much of that discussion was theoretical, or based upon unsubstantiated hunches and assumptions. Only systematic empirical research provides fundamental insights in the existing defects of the electoral connection at the European level, and its undermining effects on the electoral connection at the domestic level.

Such insights have been elaborated at length in the previous flagship books of the European Election Studies Group—*Choosing Europe?* and *Political representation and legitimacy in the European Union* (see also the preface of this volume)—and these are still much of relevance today. In this book—and particularly in this chapter—these insights were updated and elaborated. They imply that the results of European Parliament elections can generally not be interpreted as indicative for voters' support of the existing forms and directions of European integration. Moreover, they imply that the second-order character of European Parliament elections is the consequence of existing constitutional arrangements in the EU which insulate the most important institutions and policy processes in the EU from popular influence. This democratic deficit can be diminished by making the composition of these institutions or the substance of European policies directly and predictably dependent on Europe-wide electoral verdicts. The empirical research embodied in the two previous books and the current one demonstrate how the second-order character of European Parliament elections burdens the political systems of the member states with electoral instability that cannot be interpreted in political terms, either at the national or at the European level, and that therefore undermines some of the basic functions of elections in representative democracy. The analyses in this book clearly demonstrate that in 1999—as much as in 1989 and 1994 (see in particular the arguments by Franklin, van der Eijk, and Marsh [1996]) and by Thomassen and Schmitt [1999a])—we can sensibly speak of a single European electorate, and that the preconditions do exist for effective electoral representation in the EU. They also demonstrate that neither of these can be taken for granted, particularly not when issues of European integration will increase in saliency and politicization.

Appendix: Scenario simulations

In this appendix we present the method and results of estimating electoral outcomes for each of the sixteen political systems, specifying three different scenarios. First, we calculated a baseline election outcome on the basis of model 6 presented in table 9.3. This baseline was based on models estimated for each system separately. From the estimated parameters individual vote propensities were calculated for each of the parties. From these, party choice is determined, using the assumption that voters choose the party for which the vote propensity is highest. Aggregation over all respondents yields a baseline election result.

In a second step, we changed one of the parameters of the model or the distribution of one of the independent variables or both and recomputed predicted vote propensities, individual party choice, and the aggregate result. The difference between the two calculated election outcomes indicates the effect of the counterfactual elements of the scenarios. The three scenarios that we evaluate below are the following:

Scenario 1: Attitudes toward EU become more important determinants of electoral utilities. Modeling this scenario requires a change in the regression coefficient of the independent variable 'distance between respondent and party on the issue of EU integration'. As counterfactual value of this regression coefficient we chose the same value as the unstandardized coefficient of left-right distances between respondent and party in the respective country. Because both distances are measured on the same scale, this change implies substantively that policy distances for the unification issue are modeled to be of equal importance as ideological distances.

Scenario 2: Attitudes toward EU become more important predictors of electoral utility (as in scenario 1), and at the same time all parties become more Euro-skeptic in their own position. This scenario requires the same changes to the model as in scenario 1 and in addition a change in the perceived position of each of the parties: all parties were made one unit more Euro-skeptic.

Scenario 3: Attitudes toward EU become more important predictors of the electoral utility (as in scenario 1). In addition the distribution of distances between voters and parties on the integration dimension is altered so that it equals the distribution of the distances between voters and parties on the left-right dimension. As in the two other scenarios, the regression coefficient of the independent variable 'distance to party on the issue of EU integration' was changed. The adaptation of the distances on the integration dimension was achieved as follows. For each voter we determined the rank order of parties in terms of distances on left-right and distances on European unification. Then we replaced the smallest distance on the issue of European unification by the (observed) smallest distance on left-right. The same was done for the second distance, and for the third, and so on. Table 12.A.1 illustrates the procedure for a hypothetical case of three voters in a country with only three parties.

Voter 1 in table 12.A.1 is closest to party B on the integration issue. In order to mirror the distribution of left-right distances, the value of this distance should thus be the same as the smallest distance to a party on the left-right dimension. The smallest distance on left-right is 0, so that the transformed value for distance to party B on European unification is now 0 as well. The second closest party on integration is party C. The distance to the second closest party on left-right is 4, to which value the distance on the integration issue is changed.[33]

Table 12.A.1 Illustration of changes made to the distribution of the variable distances on EU unification, so that it mirrors the distribution of LR distances.

	Observed distance to party on L-r			Observed distance to party on integration			Transformed distance to party on integration		
	Party A	Party B	Party C	Party A	Party B	Party C	Party A	Party B	Party C
Voter 1	0	4	5	8	3	5	5	0	4
Voter 2	6	2	4	3	5	7	2	4	6
Voter 3	8	5	1	3	6	1	5	8	1

Table 12.A.2 Simulations for Austria

	Scenario 1	Scenario 2	Scenario 3
SPÖ	−0.8	−1.4	−1.9
ÖVP	+1.4	+4.2	+0.9
FPÖ	−0.8	−1.7	+0.7
Grüne	0.0	+1.0	+0.3
Lib. Forum	+0.3	0.0	0.0
CSA	0.0	0.0	0.0
Total net change	1.7	4.2	1.9
Total gross change	16.6	17.8	15.3
Total n		360	

When focusing only on party choice, the consequences of these three scenarios can be expressed in different forms. Table 12.2 illustrates the perspective of individual party switching. Aggregating these data to the level of individual parties, their net gains or losses (compared with the 1999 baseline) are reported below for each of the political systems under analysis (tables 12.A.2 to 12.A.17). These values constitute the dependent variable in the regression analyses reported in tables 12.4 and 12.5. Finally, for entire systems, aggregation across parties yields the gross and net changes reported in table 12.3.

Table 12.A.3 Simulations for Flanders (Belgium)

	Scenario 1	Scenario 2	Scenario 3
VLD	−0.9	+1.7	−0.5
CVP	−1.1	−1.1	−1.2
SP	+1.2	+1.5	+0.8
AGALEV	−1.9	−0.5	−1.8
Vlaams Blok	+0.3	−1.1	+0.8
Volksunie	+2.4	−0.4	+1.8
Total net change	3.9	3.2	3.5
Total gross change	10.7	10.6	17.8
Total n		184	

Table 12.A.4 Simulations for Wallonia (Belgium)

	Scenario 1	Scenario 2	Scenario 3
PS	+4.8	+2.5	+1.9
PRL	−1.5	−0.7	+1.1
ECOLO	−9.7	−7.2	−6.6
PSC	+3.2	+3.2	+0.7
FN	+3.3	+2.3	+3.0
Total net change	11.3	8.0	6.7
Total gross change	20.9	17.5	21.0
Total n		135	

Table 12.A.5 Simulations for Britain

	Scenario 1	Scenario 2	Scenario 3
Conservatives	−0.4	−0.7	−0.3
Labour	−1.1	−0.7	−1.0
Liberal Democrats	+0.9	+1.2	+1.3
SNP	0.0	0.0	0.0
Plaid C	0.0	0.0	0.0
Green party	+0.2	−0.1	+0.1
UKIP	+0.5	+0.2	−0.1
Total net change	1.6	1.5	1.4
Total gross change	6.5	6.4	6.9
Total n		705	

Table 12.A.6 Simulations for Denmark

	Scenario 1	Scenario 2	Scenario 3
Soc dem	−4.3	−3.5	−3.0
Venstre	−3.1	−0.9	−2.5
Konserv	+0.6	+0.7	+0.5
Soc. Folk P.	+2.0	−0.3	+1.6
Dansk fp	+2.1	+1.7	+0.7
CD	0.0	0.0	+0.1
Rad Venstre	+0.1	+0.4	+0.2
Rod-gronne	+1.8	+1.3	+1.8
Christel FP	0.0	+0.3	+0.0
Fremskridtspartiet	+0.8	+0.5	+0.4
Total net change	7.4	4.8	5.4
Total gross change	15.0	14.4	13.6
Total n		728	

Table 12.A.7 Simulations for Finland

	Scenario 1	Scenario 2	Scenario 3
SDP	+2.6	+0.9	−0.1
Keskusta	+0.4	−0.2	−0.5
Kokoomus	−3.7	−1.9	−4.1
SFP/RKP	−0.3	−0.3	−0.3
Vihreat	−0.7	−0.6	+1.2
Vasemm.	+0.2	+0.5	+1.7
SKL/Kristilllisit	+1.4	+1.6	+2.0
PS Perussuomalaiset	0.0	0.0	0.0
Total net change	4.7	3.0	5.0
Total gross change	16.5	13.4	13.5
Total n		214	

Table 12.A.8 Simulations for France

	Scenario 1	Scenario 2	Scenario 3
PS-PRG	−2.3	−1.7	−7.9
RPR	−0.1	−0.9	−3.0
UDF	+1.4	+1.9	+3.9
PC	+0.5	+0.6	+1.4
Verts	+0.9	+0.4	+4.5
LO-LCR	+0.2	+0.3	+0.2
DL	−0.1	+0.3	+1.5
FN/MN	+0.4	−0.2	+0.4
RPF	−0.8	−1.1	−0.9
Total net change	3.4	3.8	11.8
Total gross change	10.8	12.2	24.9
Total n		529	

Table 12.A.9 Simulations for Germany

	Scenario 1	Scenario 2	Scenario 3
CDU/CSU	−0.2	+0.3	−0.9
SPD	−0.6	−0.8	−1.2
B90-Grünen	+0.2	+0.2	+1.1
FDP	0.0	0.0	0.0
Republikaner	+0.3	+0.3	+0.5
PDS	+0.4	+0.1	+0.5
Total net change	0.9	0.9	2.1
Total gross change	5.1	5.1	8.5
Total n		876	

Table 12.A.10 Simulations for Greece

	Scenario 1	Scenario 2	Scenario 3
Pasok	−0.1	+0.5	−1.4
ND	+0.6	+1.2	+0.1
KKE	−0.8	−1.4	−1.2
Synasp	+0.1	+0.1	+0.4
DIKKI	−0.3	−0.8	+1.6
Polit Annix	+0.2	+0.2	+0.2
Fileleyther	+0.3	+0.3	+0.3
Total net change	1.2	2.3	2.6
Total gross change	8.9	8.9	13.2
Total n		368	

Table 12.A.11 Simulations for Ireland

	Scenario 1	Scenario 2	Scenario 3
FF	−3.5	−2.7	−4.2
FG	+0.4	+0.6	+2.2
Labour	+0.4	0.0	−0.8
Prog. Dem.	+0.4	+0.4	+0.6
SF	+0.3	+0.5	+0.6
Green Party	+1.9	+1.3	+1.6
Democratic Left	0.0	0.0	0.0
Total net change	3.5	2.8	5.0
Total gross change	12.3	12.7	13.8
Total n		328	

Table 12.A.12 Simulations for Italy

	Scenario 1	Scenario 2	Scenario 3
Forza Italia	−1.4	−1.0	−1.7
Dem. di Sinistra	−1.2	−1.7	−1.0
AN	+1.2	+1.2	+1.5
Lista Panella/Bonini	+0.6	+0.6	+0.6
I Democratic	+0.7	+0.7	+0.4
Lega Nord	0.0	0.0	0.0
Rifond. Comm.	+0.1	+0.1	+0.1
PPI	0.0	0.0	+0.1
CCD/CDU	0.0	0.0	0.0
Total net change	2.6	2.7	2.7
Total gross change	5.3	6.5	7.2
Total n		1880	

Table 12.A.13 Simulations for Luxembourg

	Scenario 1	Scenario 2	Scenario 3
CSV/PSC	+2.6	+3.3	+3.2
DP/PD	+0.9	+1.5	−0.3
LSAP/POSL	−3.2	−4.1	−4.6
ADR	+0.1	+0.1	+0.9
Dei Greng	−0.4	−0.7	−1.4
Gei Lenk	0.0	0.0	+1.6
GAL	0.0	0.0	0.0
Total net change	3.6	4.9	6.0
Total gross change	8.8	7.9	15.2
Total n		209	

Table 12.A.14 Simulations for the Netherlands

	Scenario 1	Scenario 2	Scenario 3
PvdA	−1.9	−2.6	−1.9
CDA	+0.2	+1.3	−0.8
VVD	−0.6	−1.3	−1.0
D66	+0.7	+1.2	+1.2
Groen Links	+1.3	+1.4	+1.9
SGP	0.0	0.0	0.0
SP	+0.2	+0.2	+0.6
CD	0.0	0.0	0.0
RPF	0.0	−0.2	−0.2
GPV	+0.2	+0.2	+0.3
Total net change	2.6	4.2	4.0
Total gross change	10.2	11.6	14.6
Total n		632	

Table 12.A.15 Simulations for Portugal

	Scenario 1	Scenario 2	Scenario 3
PS	−2.8	−2.8	−2.8
PSD	−0.6	−0.3	−0.2
CDS/PP	+2.5	+2.5	+3.1
CDU	+0.9	+0.6	0.0
Bloco de Esquerda	+0.0	+0.0	0.0
Total net change	3.4	3.1	3.1
Total gross change	6.1	5.8	11.1
Total n		294	

Table 12.A.16 Simulations for Spain

	Scenario 1	Scenario 2	Scenario 3
PP	+0.1	−0.5	−2.2
PSOE	−1.5	−0.7	−0.5
IU	+1.3	+1.1	+2.3
CIU	0.0	0.0	0.0
PNV	0.0	0.0	0.0
EH	+0.1	+0.1	+0.4
Total net change	1.5	1.2	2.7
Total gross change	3.8	4.2	7.1
Total n		632	

Table 12.A.17 Simulations for Sweden

	Scenario 1	Scenario 2	Scenario 3
Vansterp	+2.8	−0.4	+1.3
Soc. Dem.	−5.8	−6.0	−3.9
Miljop.	+3.4	+3.5	+2.0
Center Party	0.0	0.0	0.3
Folkp.	+4.6	+2.3	+6.0
Krist. Dem.	+1.8	+1.9	+4.4
Moderaterna	−6.7	−1.4	−10.1
Total net change	12.6	7.8	14.0
Total gross change	21.8	20.9	25.8
Total n		325	

Notes

1. In 1999, some of these events were still lying in the future. Their occurrence was, however, anticipated by politicians, journalists, and aware citizens owing to the fact that many of the critical decisions resulting in these events had already been taken or were under discussion at the time. Many of the considerations that we discuss in this chapter were of equal relevance in 1999 as they are at the time of writing.

2. Our argument may not be read as implying that voter behavior is totally exogenous to that of parties, politicians, media, and other elites. Changes in voter behavior may very

well be the result of actions of, e.g., politicians, and such actions may even be motivated by entrepreneurial considerations. It is, however, of crucial importance whether or not strategic calculations and entrepreneurial activities of elites are 'vindicated' by voter responses. It is only in that sense that our argument in the text can be read.

3. In spite of its formidable and gradually increasing powers in the legislative process of the EU, the European Parliament does not initiate the course of European policy and of the integration process. Steps toward further integration have been largely the responsibility of the European Council, which consists of leaders of national governments. In as far as EU politicians have influenced this process, this has been predominantly the domain of the European Commission. The ideological and personal composition of neither of these bodies is under the control of the European Parliament, and therefore not at stake in European elections. The powers of the European Parliament with respect to the composition of the European Commission are limited to granting or withholding confirmation to nominations that are either made by the Council (as far as the president of the Commission is concerned) or by the national governments (for the other members of the Commission).

4. Portrayals of the various European elections since 1979 in the member states of the EU can be found in a number of sources, most notably Blumler and Fox (1982), Reif (1984, 1997), van der Eijk and Franklin (1996) and in short election reports in journals such as *Electoral Studies* and *West European Politics*.

5. Reif (1997) clarified aspects of the intended conceptualization (and their implications for operationalization), while Oppenhuis, van der Eijk, and Franklin (1996) and Marsh (1998) contributed to further elaborations of second-order election theory.

6. The location of European elections in the domestic electoral cycle is, of course, only a proxy for the likelihood of domestic political actors to adapt their behavior and mutual relations in reaction to (their interpretation of) the outcome of European elections. It is therefore obvious that numerous occasions exist in which this receptivity is high in spite of a location in the first-order electoral cycle that would not suggest so (cf. Franklin, van der Eijk, and Oppenhuis 1996, 312–313). As long as such occasions can only be indicated by their 'proper names', they may contribute to our understanding of specific situations, yet not to generalizable propositions.

7. The fact that the prospects of the draft constitution are dim after the 'no' votes in the French and Dutch referenda of 2005 does not conclude further debate about the constitutional order of the EU, nor does it for future purposes reduce in importance the separate components of this draft.

8. For European elections, EU citizens have voting rights in other member states if they live there. Yet, as a proportion of those eligible to vote, this group is close to negligible in almost all countries.

9. The political parties on the ballot in European elections are usually the same as those which traditionally contest national elections, even using the same names. There are some noteworthy exceptions to this rule. In France, the national parties (or segments or combinations thereof) that vie for votes in European elections do so often under different names than those by which they are known domestically. As a case in point, in 1994 the

Front National was listed on the ballot as Liste contre l'Europe de Maastricht, Allez la France! but all indications are that ordinary French voters knew very well to which of the traditional national parties these names on the ballot referred. Another exception to the rule that the same parties compete for votes in national and European elections is Denmark, where two lists exist that only compete in European elections and not in national ones: the Folkebevaegelsen and the Junibevaegelsen (see also Worre 1996). Finally, it is very common to find new parties on the ballots of European elections, and occasionally these are quite successful. The very fact that almost without exception the successful ones of these newcomers subsequently attempt to establish themselves as national political parties underscores our contention that it is a single set of parties that competes in national and European elections. It also underscores our argument made in the outset of this chapter, namely that European elections should be regarded as an integral part of domestic politics.

10. Media systems are even more country specific than party systems are, and in each country it is the same set of media that covers national and in European elections using similar formats.

11. Unfortunately, we have no explicit and systematic analyses of variations in party behavior (campaign activity, campaign spending, deployment of 'big guns', etc.) as a function of the timing of European elections in the electoral cycle. Our basis of evidence consists of somewhat fragmented and ad hoc observations by a number of the authors of this volume, reinforced by inferences from the kind of analyses of media and voter behavior as reported in previous chapters. No significant timing effects on media attention were found in the aggregate analyses (N = 12) in chapter 6. Future research should verify whether this effect does indeed not exist, or whether the failure to find such effects is due to the small number of cases in combination with country-specific crises that dominated their respective media agendas.

12. In a recent contribution Schmitt and Reif (2003) come to compatible results on the basis of analysis of different kinds of data. Van der Brug, van der Eijk, and Franklin (2007) also find a similar curvilinear relationship at the level of individual respondents.

13. The specific models used are: model C in table 1.2 and the model in table 3.1 with the largest number of cases (n = 52). Of course, these analyses are based on *ceteris paribus* conditions.

14. Actually, the lack of clarity of who is involved in European policy making (particularly as far as the role of cabinet ministers of national governments is concerned) makes the EU an easy target to blame, even for matters that are quite unrelated to its policies. Moreover, the EU is more easily blamed for policy consequences that are disliked than it is credited for those that are applauded. For a more detailed discussion of these phenomena and their causes, see, e.g., Franklin, van der Eijk, and Marsh (1996).

15. See, e.g., Marks and Steenbergen (2004).

16. With regard to the general argument about reducing complexity as a condition for rational behavior, see, e.g., Downs (1957). For empirical studies of how citizens reduce informational complexity, see, e.g., Conover and Feldman (1984), Granberg and Holmberg (1988), and van der Brug (1997).

17. Clear and well-known exceptions exist, particularly Euro-skeptic ones, such as the anti-integration lists in Denmark and Sweden, the Conservative Party and more recently the UKIP in Britain. Yet the majority of political parties in the member states have been conspicuous in their lack of contribution to public debate over European integration.

18. The analyses by Schmitt and Wüst demonstrated that this perceived lack of variation may be questioned when inspecting party manifestos. Although they report that party positions as derived from their content analysis of manifestos are significantly correlated with voters' perceptions of these positions, a noticeable difference between the two is that the manifestos exhibit more variation between parties than perceptions do. This discrepancy calls for further analysis, but a likely factor in its explanation is lack of salience of and media attention to European integration. Low prominence generates uncertainty, which manifests itself by a centripetal tendency in the distribution of perceptions. Across the 115 parties for which the relevant data are available, perceptual agreement about party positions on the left-right dimension is 0.43 on average, whereas for positions on European integration it is substantially lower: 0.30. This clearly indicates that voters are somewhat uncertain about parties' positions on the integration dimension. (For perceptual agreement measured by van der Eijk's coefficient of agreement, see van der Eijk 2001.)

19. It is, of course, not necessary that a newcomer's success is attributed to its position on European integration, and in that case it does not generate an incentive for established parties to be more outspoken on 'Europe'. The astounding success of the Dutch LPF (the party of the murdered politician Pim Fortuyn) in 2002 was generally attributed to its anti-immigration platform, while such a position was widely believed to be off-limits by the established political parties, leaving it wide open to challengers. As a consequence, all parties were forced to reassess their position on matters relating to immigration, and although all parties shifted toward a more restrictive position, the result was greater politicization and initially a greater diversity of party positions on this issue. In this context it should be noted that the LPF was also considerably more Euro-skeptic than other parties, but because this position was not attributed to be the cause of its electoral success, it did not force other parties to explicate their positions on European integration.

20. Recent examples are the successes in the European elections of 2004 of the UKIP in Great Britain and of the two successful lists of Van Buitenen in the Netherlands and Martin in Austria, both of whom gained renown by exposing financial improprieties at the European level.

21. This way of framing the issue may be fruitfully employed by parties irrespective of its more specific roots. Some parties may dispute further integration because they fear its effects on existing welfare arrangements (a sentiment often encountered among left voters in the low countries and Scandinavia), others may oppose integration because of its alleged secularizing influence, or because it would swell immigration, or for other reasons yet. Whether or not such attributions of consequences to 'Europe' are correct is irrelevant.

22. For examples, see, e.g., the country chapters in van der Eijk and Franklin (1996).

23. The 'too far' frame could, of course, also be invoked on totally different grounds, such as considerations of efficiency and effectiveness. Although this is not uncommon in

discussions among scholars and officials, it is rarely invoked by mass media or by politicians when addressing ordinary citizens.

24. In spite of all the country-specific aspects of the various party systems in the EU, such processes of (selective) imitation are historically quite prevalent. Lipset and Rokkan documented this for the more distant past, and for more recent times this phenomenon is illustrated by the evolution of green parties, and later of anti-immigrant parties across Europe. Political developments in each of the countries of the EU provide, of course, examples that some will try to emulate, while others will attempt to prevent them. The opportunity structure for specific developments differs, however, between countries, which implies that attempts to emulate will not necessarily lead to success. For an illustration of such processes in the context of the (anti)immigration issue during the 1990s, see, e.g., Pellikaan, van der Meer, and de Lange (2003).

25. This is the outcome of evaluating the model presented in table 7.1 under the counterfactual condition of the emergence of a viable anti-integration party and its consequences on media attention to integration.

26. Technically, it is the weight of the *distances* between voters and parties on both dimensions that has been set to an equal value, which is the estimated effect of left-right distance in model 6 from chapter 9.

27. Changes of this magnitude are not uncommon, particularly when they concern issues in which parties have no strongly vested interests (see, e.g., van der Brug 1997; van Wijnen 2001). The issue of nuclear energy, for example, was not strongly politicized among the mainstream parties in the Netherlands until the Three Mile Island–Harrisburg nuclear incident in 1979. Between 1977 and 1981, the three largest Dutch parties changed on average about one full position on a seven-point scale in the eyes of the voters (e.g., van der Brug 2001, 61). In comparison to this the change of one point on a ten-point scale, as used in this second scenario, is of a realistic magnitude.

28. As a summary measure of net change for an entire political system we use the so-called Pedersen index (Pedersen 1979), which is defined as the summation of all (absolute) changes in parties' vote shares, divided by 2. This measure is directly comparable to gross change: in the absence of any countervailing effects of individual switching, this index is identical to the amount of gross change. For a numerical example see the note with table 12.2. The Pedersen index does not reflect party-specific consequences of switching. We report such net changes at the level of political parties separately in the appendix of this chapter.

29. See chapter 11 for analyses of the proportions of voters in each of the countries that can switch easily because their first and second choices are of roughly equal attractiveness. The correlation between gross electoral change on the one hand and the size of the groups that have no more than one point difference in the utility of their first and second preferences on the other hand is, for the three scenarios, 0.19, 0.25, and 0.27 respectively (the last two coefficients are significant at $p = < 0.10$, with $n = 16$). The weakness of these correlations indicates that the consequences of our scenarios are stronger than only affecting 'tie breakers' that tip the balance in the case of near equally

attractive electoral options. Also the conditions implied in the scenarios would give rise to vote propensities that affect more parties than just the two most preferred ones.

30. Compare, e.g., the Dutch Parliamentary elections of 1994 and 2002 (Pedersen values 21% and 31% respectively), the Italian election of 1994 (37% net change).

31. These three characteristics of parties are defined in terms of the 1999 baseline context. Size was measured by the proportion of seats each party occupied in their national parliaments at the time of the elections of 1999. Parties with a median position larger than 5.5 on the ten-point left-right scale were classified as 'right leaning', whereas the other parties were classified as 'left leaning'.

32. The differences in terms of significance between tables 12.4 and 12.5 are caused by smaller degrees of freedom in table 12.5 and by some multicollinearity between government status and party size.

33. Performing these transformations for respondents who provided valid responses for the same parties on both scales (N = 4,484) results in a transformed distance on integration variable that has exactly the same distribution as the left-right distances (mean = 2.92 and sd = 2.36). In order not to lose cases owing to missing data, a special procedure was designed for individual-level missing value substitution for those respondents who did not place the same parties on both dimensions. Details can be obtained from the authors upon request.

Postscript

The research agenda beyond the 2004 European elections

CEES VAN DER EIJK
AND WOUTER VAN DER BRUG

While this volume, which analyzes European elections through 1999, was being finished, new elections to the European Parliament were held in June 2004. As always since 1989, the 2004 elections were accompanied by large-scale collecting of empirical information on voters, media, and parties.[1] Preparing, linking, and analyzing these data will take a considerable amount of time—years rather than months—which makes it not opportune to try to include in-depth analyses of the 2004 European elections. Yet, we cannot conclude this volume without witnessing the very fact of these new elections having taken place and without calling attention to some observations about them. This postscript therefore addresses two questions. First, how do the 2004 elections—based upon impressionistic accounts—compare to the insights generated in this volume? Second, what are the implications of the 2004 elections for the agenda of future research? In addressing these questions we focus on four different topics that were of central concern in this volume: 1) media attention to European integration and European elections, 2) the positioning of political parties on the issue of European integration, 3) electoral turnout, and 4) party choice and election outcomes.

Media attention to European integration and European elections

In chapter 6 of this volume, de Vreese, Lauf, and Peter concluded that the European Parliament election of 1999 was regarded by the mass media as a non-event. Mass media paid very little attention to the campaign (a single exception notwithstanding), and to the extent that they did cover the campaign, it was usually framed in a domestic context. Therefore, the authors conclude that the character of EP elections as second-order national elections is clearly reflected in media coverage.

As we argued in chapter 12, there is no reason to expect that European elections will be anything but second-order national elections in the foreseeable future. This does not imply that media attention will necessarily be minimal. Indeed, the analyses of chapter 6 demonstrated that media pay considerably more attention to European elections in countries with a viable anti-EU party. It can be expected therefore that European elections will draw more media attention when integration becomes a more salient and contested issue in the domestic political arena, which will provide incentives for some parties at least to position themselves toward an anti-integration position. We consider this a very plausible development, which may already have started in the period since 1999 (see our discussion in chapter 12).

The generally small extent of media coverage of the European elections in 1999 may to some extent be attributable to more dramatic concurrent events, most notably the war in Kosovo. The results of an analysis of the media content during the run-up to the European elections of 2004 indicate that the visibility of the elections on television news had increased compared to 1999 in most of the fifteen 'old' member states of the EU and that the coverage of the elections was higher in most of the 'new' member states than in the 'old' member states (de Vreese et al. 2005). Indeed, this increase may be caused by the absence of war at the borders of the Union in 2004. It may, conceivably, also be caused by changes in salience of and political contestation over European integration since 1999. Naturally, at this moment in time and without more pertinent empirical information, it cannot be determined which of these interpretations is most apposite. Yet, even without the necessary factual information, we can indicate what kind of findings would support the one or the other of these rivaling interpretations. To the extent that increases in coverage are the result of increased political salience and contestation, we would also expect—following the argument elaborated in chapter 12—an increase in the use of pro versus contra integration frames and in attention to diverging positions of political parties. To the extent that the war of Kosovo deflected attention to the 1999 European elections, we would not expect any major changes in use of frames between 1999 and 2004.

Irrespective of which of these interpretations will eventually turn out to be more to the point, any increases in coverage are of relevance by themselves. Jochen Peter demonstrated in chapter 7 of this volume that, in the presence of a viable anti-EU party, more coverage leads citizens to perceive European integration as more important than they otherwise would. Under these circumstances, increases in coverage are thus one of the conditions that lead to more salience of the issue of European integration, the effects of which were analyzed in the simulated scenarios presented in chapter 12.

The second-order character of European elections is thus not incompatible with increases in media attention to European elections beyond the extremely low levels of 1999. The observation that media attention is predominantly framed in terms of the domestic political context is less likely to change, however.[2] This finding from chapter 6 is inherently linked to the second-order nature of these elections. It implies that we can expect national politicians to get more media exposure than European ones, and that media will focus more on consequences of European elections for the domestic political arena than for that of the EU.

Parties and their positions on the issue of European integration

With some exceptions, major political parties in the member states of the EU in 1999 were little distinct in terms of their position with respect to European integration, at least in the perceptions of voters (see chapter 10). When looking at positions that can be derived from election manifestos (chapter 3), there seems to be somewhat more variety between parties than voters perceive, but this remains electorally ineffective as long as it is not reflected in how voters perceive what is offered to them.[3] Until analyses similar to those from chapters 3 and 10 can be reported for 2004 we cannot state definitively where parties positioned themselves in 2004 on the issue of European integration and how this was perceived by voters. Yet a variety of impressionistic observations suggest that political parties have become more clearly differentiated on integration.

In the 2004 elections Euro-skeptic and even outright anti-EU parties have won their best results ever. This group includes new anti-EU parties from old member states (such as the British UK Independence Party, the French Movement for France, and the Swedish June Movement, which is inspired by the Danish Euro-skeptic party under the same name) as well as from the new member states (particularly the second-largest Polish party, the Catholic League of Polish Families). In addition many small parties of the far right and far left have voiced opposition against the EU for a period far antedating 1999. Electoral support for these Euro-skeptic parties is considerably smaller than for pro-integration parties, but it is no longer negligible. The proportion of the European electorates that in 2004 supported parties opposed to further integration has grown sufficiently large to make other parties (which were traditionally pro-integration) and governments pay attention, and occasionally reconsider their established positions on this issue.[4]

In addition to growing support for anti-EU parties, the proposals for the European constitutional treaty were voted down in referenda in the Netherlands and France. Even though one has to be careful not to interpret the no-vote too easily as a sign of Euro-skepticism, the outcomes of these referenda demonstrated that even in founding member states of the EU citizens will not support each and every step toward further integration.[5] These referenda prompted a considerable amount of soul-searching among the established parties about the future course of European integration, particularly among those parties who fear that they stand to lose votes if they do not adapt their own positioning (generally in a more Euro-skeptic direction).

The evidence referred to above is obviously anecdotal and possibly incomplete. It thus requires—once the relevant data become available—systematic assessments of party positions in 2004 in terms of voter perceptions as well as in terms of policies and manifestos. Such assessments would involve tracking party positions over time and establishing which kinds of parties have shifted most and in which directions. It would also involve an investigation of the relation between perceived changes and 'objective' changes in party positions. Our expectation would be, first, that parties holding government responsibility are less likely to shift positions than opposition parties, and that the reflection of such changes in public perceptions is contingent on salience and politicization of the integration issue.

When new issues become politicized, they often represent challenges to the cohesion of existing parties. New issues carry the risk of dividing parties that derive their character from their stances on other matters. Moreover, forging coalitions becomes infinitely more complex if new issues give rise to multi-dimensional party constellations. Such problems can be resolved if existing parties manage to successfully integrate a new issue in the existing dominant left-right conflict dimension. Historically this has happened in the 1980s with issues such as environmental protection, opposition to nuclear energy, and emancipation of women. More recently, positions on the new issue of immigration have become increasingly absorbed in left-right. In the process, the left-right dimension also evolves in its content and meaning.[6] Such absorption could very well happen with the issue of European integration. An important question for future research is thus whether such aligning processes can be observed at the time of the 2004 election, or at later moments in time. If so, the obvious subsequent question is which of the poles of the integration issue has become aligned with 'left' and which with 'right', and whether the answer to this latter question is or is not country specific.

These questions are of greater importance than merely satisfying academic curiosity. If the integration issue were to become aligned in the same manner in different member states of the Union, this would greatly enhance the viability of shared pan-European political discourse. If, on the other hand, left-right would become positively correlated with European integration in some countries and negatively in others, it becomes unlikely that a Union-wide shared political discourse will emerge. Such a development will have momentous consequences for the kind of democratic representation and electoral control that can evolve in the near future. Alternatively, parties' positions on left-right and on European integration may remain rather unconnected as they were through 1999. In the long run, such a situation tends to erode party cohesion, particularly when, as we expect (see the discussion in chapters 10 and 12), integration becomes a more important and politically more contentious issue.

Turnout

In chapter 1 of this volume, Mark Franklin analyzed the development of turnout in European elections over time. He showed that levels of turnout in European elections had decreased in the EU on average, and that this can be explained by three conditions: a decline in the number of countries benefiting from a so-called 'first-time boost', a decline in the number of compulsory voting countries, and happenstansical variations in the timing of European election in the respective national electoral cycles. How does turnout in 2004 compare with this analysis? This postscript is not the appropriate place for a full replication of his analysis, but a brief inspection of registered turnout at the 2004 European elections is informative nonetheless. Table PS.1 presents the relevant information for all member states of the Union since 1979 and through 2004.

Table PS.1 shows that, on average, the trend of gradually decreasing levels of turnout has continued. At 48.3 percent, the average level of turnout in 2004 was slightly lower than the 53.2 percent registered in 1999. However, when only considering the fifteen countries that were members of the Union in both years, there is no decrease, but a slight increase in the average level of turnout in 2004. The overall decrease is thus due to below-average levels in the new member states.

The first explanatory factor in Franklin's model is the 'first-time boost': turnout is, *ceteris paribus*, about 10 percent higher at the first European elections in a country. When considering the turnout levels of the ten member states that acceded the Union in 2004 one may doubt whether they indeed experienced such a boost in 2004. If they did, then the 2004 levels of turnout in Slovakia (17%), Poland (21%), Slovenia, and the Czech Republic (both 28%) would project a rather grim outlook for turnout in future European elections. The 2004 turnout levels in other new member states are, at first sight, less at odds with the notion of a first-time boost. However, the decision to join the EU was subjected in most of the new member states to popular approval by referendum, and it is not inconceivable that a first-time boost would in some countries have exerted its effect not in 2004, but earlier, in the preceding accession referenda. Whether or not this is the case and whether such reasoning would apply to all countries that conducted referenda is obviously high on the agenda for future research.[7]

The second factor in Franklin's model is the presence or absence of compulsory voting in the member states. At the time of the first European elections in 1979, voting was compulsory in three out of nine countries. In 1999, this had declined to three out of fifteen, and in 2004 even further to four out of twenty-five, the only new country with compulsory voting being Cyprus. Part of the difference between 1999 and 2004 may thus be explained by the 2004 enlargement, which caused a further decline in the proportion of compulsory voting countries.

The third factor in Franklin's explanation of turnout levels is the timing of a European election within the national election cycle. European elections conducted shortly before a national election yield higher turnout than when they are held soon after a first-order national election. Without entering in a full-scale re-estimation of this effect, a cursory glance seems to indicate that this timing factor in 2004 has remained to be of relevance. The 2004 European elections in Finland and the Netherlands were considerably later in the domestic cycle than in 1999 when in both countries they followed just a few months after national parliamentary elections. The increase in turnout in these countries supports the Franklin

Table PS.1 Turnout at elections for the European Parliament, 1979–2004

Country	1979	1981	1984	1987	1989	1994	1995	1999	2004	Average
Austria							67.7	49.4	42.4	53.2
Belgium+	90.4		92.2		90.7	90.7		91.0	90.8	91.0
Britain	32.2		32.6		36.2	36.1		24.0	38.8	33.3
Cyprus+									71.2	71.2
Czech Republic									28.3	28.3
Denmark	47.8		52.4		46.2	52.9		50.5	47.9	49.6
Estonia									26.8	26.8
Finland							60.3	31.4	39.4	43.7
France	60.7		56.7		48.7	52.7		46.8	42.8	51.4
Germany	65.7		56.8		62.3	60.0		45.2	43.0	55.5
Greece+		78.6	77.2		79.9	71.2		75.3	63.2	74.2
Hungary									38.5	38.5
Ireland	63.6		47.6		68.3	44.0		50.2	58.8	55.4
Italy+	84.9		83.4		81.5	74.8		70.8	73.1	78.1
Latvia									41.3	41.3
Lithuania									48.4	48.4
Luxembourg+	88.9		88.8		87.4	88.5		87.3	89.0	88.3
Malta									82.4	82.4
Netherlands	57.8		50.6		47.2	35.6		30.0	39.3	43.4
Poland									20.9	20.9
Portugal				72.4	51.2	35.5		40.0	38.6	47.5
Slovakia									17.0	17.0
Slovenia									28.3	28.3
Spain				68.9	54.6	59.1		63.0	45.1	58.1
Sweden							41.6	38.8	37.8	39.4
Country Average*	65.8	78.6	63.8	72.4	63.6	58.4	64.0	53.2	48.3 (54.4**)	56.9
N	9	1	10	2	12	12	3	15	25 (15)	89

* Average of cell-entries per column.
** Only counting the 15 'old' member states.
+ Compulsory voting country (in Italy only until 1993).
Source: Compiled from official sources.

model and second-order election theory. Greece and Spain also support this model. In these countries the difference in timing was just the other way around. National parliamentary elections in both countries took place in March 2004, just three months before the EP elections, whereas in 1999 they were located considerably later in the domestic election cycle. The sharp drop in turnout in these countries in 2004 is thus well in accordance with the model.

A preliminary inventory of turnout levels in 2004 thus suggests that much of our earlier insights into the dynamics of turnout are still very relevant. The additional twenty-five observations provided by the 2004 elections are invaluable for further analyses to help disentangle the effects of first-time boosts and accession referenda, but also because they add statistical power that allows further detail in other analyses of turnout.

PARTY CHOICE AND ELECTION OUTCOMES

In chapter 2 Marcel van Egmond analyzed the differences in electoral success of parties in national and European Parliament elections. Some of his findings confirmed earlier findings (cf. Oppenhuis, van der Eijk, and Franklin 1996), such as small parties doing better in EP elections than in national parliamentary elections, particularly when European elections are held shortly after national elections. Other results, however, set the 1999 election to the European Parliament apart from previous ones. This is particularly so for his conclusion that parties with an outspoken critical position toward European integration fared better in the 1999 EP elections than they would have in national elections, would these have been held on the same day. It is tempting to eyeball the outcomes of the 2004 European elections and conclude that Euro-skeptic parties did well again. Obviously, it would not be difficult to single out particular cases as illustrations. One could, for example, think of the rather spectacular successes of a number of extremely Euro-skeptic parties, such as the UKIP in Britain, the Junilistan in Sweden, and the Catholic League of Polish Families. Yet, it makes little sense to yield to this temptation. After all, it is virtually impossible to survey the results of some 150 different parties in the EU informally, let alone to detect any pattern. Moreover, any judgment as to how well or how poorly parties fared in the 2004 elections has to be based on comparing their results with either a counterfactual that has to be constructed—as van Egmond did— or with another election result, such as that from the most recent national elections—as Marsh did in chapter 3. Therefore, we have to leave the verdict about possible electoral advantages or disadvantages of Euro-skeptic party positions to the agenda for further research.

Van Egmond's finding of an electoral advantage of Euro-skeptic parties may seem somewhat puzzling in view of the analyses in chapter 9, which demonstrated that attitudes toward European integration had only a marginal effect on electoral utilities, and hence on party choice. We can think of different rivaling explanations for this apparent contradiction, each with different implications for what we can expect to happen at future European elections.[8] One possibility is that the apparent electoral advantage of Euro-skeptic parties is no more than a one-off aggregation artifact, in which case it is unlikely to be found again in 2004. A second possibility is one of 'aliasing': some omitted variable showing its effects via another one that is included and correlated with it. In 1999, we find, for instance, that at the individual level government satisfaction is significantly (and negatively) correlated with Euro-skepticism in most of the member states. It is near to impossible to include the individual-level government satisfaction variable in van Egmond's type of analysis, but this would not prevent this variable from exerting its impact, particularly after aggregating from the individual level to the party level. To assess the merit of this explanation of the ostensible electoral advantage of Euro-skeptical parties in 1999, more detailed modeling of electoral utilities and resulting choice is required, mainly by way of structural modeling.[9] Finally, it is also possible that the very weak individual-level effect of Euro-skepticism on electoral utilities does generate significant electoral advantages of Euro-skeptic parties. After all, our explanation of party choice is based on a two-stage model, where the first stage involves the explanation of utilities, and the second stage consists of choice driven by maximization of utility. Depending on the competitive structure between political parties, small changes in utilities may lead to different choices, or, as we expressed this elsewhere, "small effects may have large consequences" (van der Brug, van der Eijk and Franklin 2007). If this last explanation were to be upheld in further analyses, it implies that in future European elections too, party positions with respect to European integration will be related to success in European elections, at least when compared to how they would have fared had national elections been held at the same moment in time. This will be even more so if, as we argued in chapter 12, the integration issue will gain in salience and politicization in the domestic political arenas of the member states.

It is obvious that this volume and the analyses presented in its various chapters have not exhausted the agenda of research into European elections; on the contrary, they have added to it. Juxtaposition of the findings of different chapters generates new questions, as discussed in these chapters and in this postscript. A first and informal inspection of some of the outcomes of the 2004 European election leads to new questions, which can only be addressed by analyzing the new data that will derive from the studies about voters, parties, and media that were conducted at the occasion of these elections. Those forthcoming data will serve future studies in a number of ways. They are indispensable for 'normal' replicatory analysis, which tests the generality of our insights by flagging changes and anomalies. They will allow for better modeling of evolutionary and developmental processes by adding an extra time-point to data covering previous European elections. They will be used to assess the differences and commonalities of electoral processes across member states, which is particularly important in view of the 2004 enlargement of the Union. The new data will increase the number of political and economic contexts that can be studied by twenty-five, providing more power to unravel the effects of interrelated contextual factors that influence the electoral process. It is a full agenda indeed, which deserves to be addressed in the years to come because of the real-world importance of what European integration is all about.

Notes

1. See the websites of the European Election Studies Workgroup at www.ees-homepage.net.
2. Our expectation that European elections will remain being framed in a domestic context is not at odds with the question that we raised about the degree to which media coverage will be framed in terms of a conflict between pro- and anti-integration forces. These are just two different perspectives on media content that can be assessed independently of each other.
3. It is likely, however, that voter perceptions are not only driven by manifestos (to the extent that the contents thereof is conveyed to voters via media, directly or indirectly), but also by other manifestations of party positioning, such as speeches, media appearances and campaign pledges by leading politicians, or by opposition (or the absence thereof) to government policy regarding 'Europe'.
4. How long such effects last is, again, mainly determined by the dynamics in the domestic political arena. As a case in point, the electoral success of the British UKIP in 2004 strengthened the anti-integration position of the Conservative party, which feared losing its anti-EU supporters to it. This effect lasted only until the next general elections of May 2005, however, when the UKIP incapacitated itself because of internal strife over leadership. This new party lost its electoral appeal in a very short period, thus removing the

threat to the Conservative Party, which therefore could afford once again not to resolve its internal divisions over European integration.

5. The dominant interpretation of these referenda in the press and among political parties seems to be that voters rebelled against further integration, and, possibly, against the prospect of future EU membership of Turkey. Such sentiments undoubtedly did play a role among large segments of the electorates in the Netherlands, but other considerations were important too. Aarts and Van der Kolk (2005) showed that the main motives to vote 'no' in this referendum were the fear of loss of wealth, of national identity, and of existing social welfare arrangements, as well as discontent with the introduction of the euro. According to them, rejection of the unpopular domestic government did not play a major role in the Dutch referendum. What exactly the mix was of ant-integrationist versus other political motivations in France is a matter for future studies.

6. Obviously, such developing alignments are not the result of careful planning by politicians, let alone the result of a single party's actions. They are rather to be seen as the unanticipated result of numerous interactions between a series of political actors. One of the best general accounts of the logic behind such processes is Schattschneider's classic discussion of "The Displacement of Conflicts" (1960, chapter 4).

7. Teasing out whether the effect of a first-time boosts manifests itself in a country's first European election or in a preceding accession referendum is helped by the fact that some of the fifteen older member states also subjected their entry into the EU to popular approval by way of a referendum.

8. Forthcoming data from the 2004 European election may allow these rivaling explanations to be tested.

9. This line of reasoning also compels us to consider endogeneity problems: does dissatisfaction with the government fuel Euro-skeptic responses (in conditions where the government is seen as pro-integration), or does Euro-skepticism lead to lack of satisfaction with a pro-integration government? Obviously, questions such as these can only be posed, but not answered in this postscript. Yet, they evidently deserve a place on the agenda for future research.

Appendix A

The voter study

CEES VAN DER EIJK
AND **WOUTER VAN DER BRUG**

The European Election Study (EES) 1999 comprises a voter study consisting of surveys of representative samples of the electorates of the then fifteen member states of the European Union: Austria, Belgium, Denmark, Finland, France, Germany, Greece, Ireland, Italy, Luxembourg, the Netherlands, Portugal, Spain, Sweden, and the United Kingdom. The fieldwork for this study began immediately after the European Parliament elections of 9 and 13 June 1999. The first interviews were conducted on 14 June, the last ones on 8 July. The main part of the interviews was conducted in the two weeks between 14 and 27 June.

The EES 1999 was organized by the European Elections Studies Group, an international group of researchers that, on the occasion of previous European elections in 1989 and 1994, organized similar surveys of the voting age populations of the member states of the European Union (see, e.g., Schmitt et al., 1997; van der Eijk et al., 1993).[1] In spite of each study's unique emphasis on particular aspects of European elections and the contexts within which they take place, each of these three studies is designed along similar principles. Therefore, the three European Election Studies of 1989, 1994, and 1999 offer not only ample opportunities for comparisons across political systems, but also for longitudinal comparisons (see e.g., chapter 11 of this volume). All three studies are archived by and can be obtained from Steinmetz Archives (http://www.dans.knaw.nl/nl/data/steinmetz_archief/), as well as from most other social science data archives (such as the Zentral Archiv in Cologne, or the ICPSR in Ann Arbor). The European Elections Study Group maintains a website that contains additional information about the EES data and about the work and publications of the EES group: http://www.europeanelectionstudies.net.

The data from the EES 1999 were released to the general scholarly community in March 2002. This appendix provides some general information about the EES 1999, such as the sample sizes for each country and weighting of cases.

The questionnaires of the EES 1999 were identical in the various member states, apart from minor but unavoidable differences generated by differences in party names and country-specific institutions. As a consequence the study offers wide opportunities for comparative analyses. Owing to a different form of data collection, the Italian data differ from those of the other member states in minor ways. A full documentation of these differences, and of all other characteristics of the study—including sampling procedures, response rates, wording of questions, response categories, and the exact wording of questions and response categories in the original languages—is provided in the codebook (van der Eijk et al. 2002).

General Profile of the Study

The EES 1999 is a stratified sample of the European population, in which each of the fifteen member states represents a stratum. In each of the fifteen member-states of the EU random samples were drawn of citizens eligible to vote in the European Parliament elections. The interviews were conducted by means of *Computer Assisted Telephonic Interviewing* (CATI), with the exception of Italy, where a tele-panel was used. The number of interviews conducted in the different member states of the European Union is presented in table A.1.

Weighting

Two kinds of weight variables are provided with the data and are used in this book. The first one is a political weight variable, which is described in more detail in the codebook. When applied, it generates a distribution of turnout and

Table A.1 Number of interviews conducted in different countries

Austria	501
Belgium	500
Flanders	274
Wallonia	226
Denmark	1001
Finland	501
France	1020
Germany	1000
Greece	500
Ireland	503
Italy	3708
Luxembourg	301
Netherlands	1001
Portugal	500
Spain	1000
Sweden	505
United Kingdom	1008
Britain	977
N. Ireland	31
Total	13549

party choice that is identical to the actual results of the June 1999 European election in the respective countries (see appendix D). This variable was constructed in the same way as its counterparts in the 1989 and 1994 European election study datasets. Applying this weight leaves the effective number of cases unchanged from the raw data for each country, with the exception of Northern Ireland, where the number of interviews conducted was so small that it did not seem appropriate to weight them. The Northern Irish records have been assigned a value of zero (0) on this variable, so that using this weight excludes Northern Irish cases from the analysis. This variable was used in the country-specific analyses reported in this book.

The second weight variable is a transformation of the first. This transformation consists of a multiplication with a country-specific constant, so that the effective number of cases is equal for each of the systems. When applying this weight to analyses that are conducted for each of the political systems separately, it produces results identical to those obtained when using the first weight variable, except for the (effective) number of cases (and consequently for standard errors and tests of significance). When applied in pooled analyses, however, it yields unbiased estimates of the effects of systemic (or contextual) factors. It was used in all pooled analyses reported in this book.

NOTE

1. In its preparation of the 1999 study, the Group convened several times, in particular in Enschede (the Netherlands, July 1997) and Mannheim (March 1999). The core group that organized the 1999 Voter Study consisted of Wouter van der Brug (University of Amsterdam, the Netherlands), Cees van der Eijk (University of Amsterdam, the Netherlands), Mark Franklin (Trinity College, Hartford, Connecticut), Sören Holmberg (University of Gothenburg, Sweden), Renato Mannheimer (University of Genova, Italy), Michael Marsh (Trinity College, Dublin), Hermann Schmitt (University of Mannheim, Germany), Klaus Schönbach (University of Amsterdam, the Netherlands), Holli Semetko (University of Amsterdam, the Netherlands), Jacques Thomassen (Twente University, Enschede, the Netherlands) and Berhard Wessels (Wissenschaftszentrum, Berlin).

The study would not have been possible without generous support from a variety of sources. Data collection was made possible first of all by a major grant from the Dutch Science Foundation (NWO, the Netherlands) with matching funds and additional support from the University of Amsterdam, as well as from the German Bundespresseamt. Additional important grants came from the CIS (Madrid), the University of Genoa (Italy), the University of Mannheim (Germany), and Trinity College (Hartford, Connecticut). Nonfieldwork costs for cleaning, data file production, and documentation were covered by the University of Amsterdam. Costs of meetings of the scholars who designed and carried out the study were covered by the Dutch National Science Foundation (NWO, the Netherlands) and the University of Mannheim.

Appendix B

The media study

EDMUND LAUF
AND JOCHEN PETER

Research on television news has shown that the election coverage tends to cluster shortly before Election Day, and European election content is mainly broadcast in the main evening news (see Blumler 1983; Reiser 1994). Rather than short bulletins or current affairs programs, television news during the 1999 European election campaign was therefore analyzed for the two weeks prior to Election Day. When the first European Parliamentary elections were held in 1979, public service television was the norm in each country. By 1999, however, most countries had strong private television channels, and research indicates that there may be consequences for regular viewers' perceptions of, knowledge about, and willingness to participate in, democracy (Aarts and Semetko 2003).

We selected the main evening public and commercial news programs with the highest viewership at the time of the post-election survey in 1999. For Belgium we analyzed Dutch-speaking Flanders and French-speaking Wallonia separately. Given that no private channels existed in Austria or were of no importance in Ireland in 1999, only the public broadcasting channel with the largest reach was included in these two countries. Because only a minority watched the Greek public broadcasting channel, ET1 (Seri 2002), a second private channel was analyzed in Greece. Due to its limited reach in comparison to networks in other countries, the channel in Luxembourg was not part of the analysis.

The content analysis was organized centrally at the University of Amsterdam, supported by grants from the Dutch National Science Foundation. The research team in Amsterdam (Semetko, Schönbach, de Vreese, Peter, and Lauf) developed the codebook, drawing upon topic and actor coding used in numerous national election campaign studies (Semetko et al. 1991; Semetko and Schönbach 1994; Diez-Nicolas and Semetko 1999; Semetko 2000; de Vreese, Peter, and Semetko 2001), as well as variables used by Schulz (1983) in his analysis of information in the first European Election campaign in 1979. Research on news frames (Semetko and Valkenburg 2000) and on the effects of news on public opinion about European integration (Semetko, van der Brug, and Valkenburg 2003) contributed to the measures developed to assess the visibility of frames in the news. We focused on election and economic frames. Some broad categories about the program were coded on the outlet level, but the focus was on the news story level. The single news story (defined as semantic entity with at least one topic delimited from another story by a change of topic) was the coding unit, a paper sheet had to be filled per story. Main parts of the codebook (including e.g. framing categories, election categories, and actors) had to be coded only if the story was political. Political stories were defined as follows: in the story, politicians or political groups, institutions, or organizations were verbally mentioned at least twice, or were verbally mentioned once and quoted, or were verbally mentioned at least once and depicted at least once. Because the period of investigation was heavily dominated by stories about the Kosovo war and because the focus of the study lay on the coverage of the European election campaign, Kosovo stories were only coded if they clearly referred to the EU. Up to six actors were coded in each story. In addition, the evaluation of the actor in the story was coded for tone, if any, as well as the function of the actor. The codebook also captured whether actors were cited in the news or quoted.

The project was organized bilingually. Codebooks and sheets were solely in English language, coder training, pre- and reliability testing was done using English language material while coding was done by native speakers. They were trained over six weeks before coding, then there were tests for inter-coder reliability, and they were supervised throughout the entire coding process. For each country, the stories were randomly assigned to the coders. Because in cross-national comparative content analyses, differences between the countries can be the unintended result of lacking coordination of the various country groups, the coder trainers of the country groups were in daily contact to coordinate the coding in the country groups and to resolve problems. Moreover, the majority of the coding was centrally done at the University of Amsterdam to keep the coding process as comparable as possible.[1]

For the reliability test, coders of all country groups had to code at least eighteen randomly selected television stories per channel.[2] The reliabilities are reported when discussing the relevant measures. For the calculation a reliability dataset with a pairwise coded unit was created.

General profile of the study

Taken together, thirty-seven native speakers coded overall 5,477 stories in 369 news programs. Of these, there were 1,808 'political' stories, which met our definition of political.

Data transformation and inter-coder reliability

For the analysis presented in this book we used only a selection of the variables. Here we present briefly the transformations and the reliabilities.

Topic. This is the major subject of the story, the subject taking the most space or time—often mentioned in the headline. The original topic list contained seventy-two topics, under eleven general categories. Because weather forecasts in some channels are placed in a distinct, subsequent newscast (e.g., Dutch RTL News) and are therefore not present in some countries, we excluded all stories with the topic weather from this comparative analysis. Intercoder-agreement for the recoded topics is 0.93 (Cohens kappa 0.86).

Visibility/Length of a story. The length of the news stories was coded in seconds. The intercoder-agreement is 0.96 (Pearson correlation).

Importance/Story number. Each story was numbered in chronological order.

Location and affected location. We asked coders to code the main location, the location where the story, or the actions it depicts, (mainly) take place (in terms of prominence in the story or length). We also coded the affected location: where primarily (in terms of prominence in the story or space/ time devoted to it) are people directly affected, influenced, harmed by, or profit from what the story is about. The list of locations consists of each EU country, the EU, and other countries collapsed to regions. We recoded the variable in two categories: 1) own country (country of the newscast) and 2) other country. Intercoder-agreement for location is 0.96 (kappa 0.92), affected location 0.94 (kappa 0.87).

Actors: nationality. For our analysis here, we selected only actors coded in all stories with the topic EU election if a political actor was mentioned (in 17 of the 312 EU stories no actor was coded). For each actor, his or her country membership

Table B.1 Summary information about content analysis of news

	Sum of news stories	Sum of political stories	Mean number actors/story	Channels analyzed	Missing days* analyzed	Newspaper polarized	Elite opinion coverage	Consonant
Austria	142	69	4.3	ORF "ZiB" (pb)	None	Die Presse	Yes	No
Belgium: Flanders	480	251	4.3	VTR "Het Journaal" (pb) VTM "Nieuws" (co)	3/6 None	De Standard	No	Yes (−)
Belgium: Wallonia	488	159	2.8	La Une "JT Meteo" (pb) RTL "Le Journal" (co)	None 10/6	La Libre Belgique	No	No
Denmark	272	107	4.7	TV1 "TV-Avisen" (pb) TV2 "Nyhederne" (co)	29/5 27/5	Morgenavisen Jyllandsp.	Yes	Yes (−)
Finland	273	62	2.9	Yle "Finish News" (pb) MTV3 "News" (co)	None None	Helsingin Sanomat	No	No
France	647	193	3.6	TF1 "Le Journal" (co) F2 "Le Journal" (pb)	None None	Le Monde	Yes	Yes (−)
Germany	361	134	3.4	ARD "Tagesschau" (pb) RTL "RTL Aktuell" (co)	None None	Frankurter Allgemeine Zeitung	No	No

Country				Programme	Dates missed*	Newspaper		
Greece	610	213	4.2	Antenna "Ta Nea Tou" (co) Mega "Kentriko deltio" (co) ET1 "News" (pb)	8/6–13/6 1/6, 6+7/6, 9–13/6 1/6, 6+7/6, 9–13/6	Kathimerini	Yes	No
Ireland	125	60	4.5	RTE1 "News (21.00)" (pb)	3/6, 7/6	Irish Independent	No	Yes (–)
Italy	370	88	4.4	Rai Uno "TG1" (pb) Canale5 "TG5" (co)	30/5 30/5	Corriere della Sera	No	No
Netherlands	219	105	4.0	NOS "Het Journaal" (pb) RTL "Nieuws" (co)	31/5, 1/6 1/6	NRC Handelsblad	No	No
Portugal	371	72	2.9	RTP1 "News" (pb) SIC "News" (co)	None None	Publico	No	No
Spain	597	126	1.8	TVE1 "Telediario" (pb) Tele5 "Telecino" (co)	None None	El Pais	No	Yes (+)
Sweden	272	77	3.6	TV2 "Rapport" (pb) TV4 "Nyheterna" (co)	None None	Dagens Nyheter	Yes	No
UK	254	82	4.4	BBC "Nine o'clock news" (pb) ITV "News at 6.30" (co)	28+29/5 30+31/5-99, 6/6-99	Guardian	No	No

* These days were missed because of altered schedules, country-specific holidays, or bulletins not broadcast on particular days of the week.

had to be coded with a list similar to the location list. We computed a new variable to record whether an actor is from the country of the outlet, from another EU country, from the EU/Euroland, or from somewhere else. Because only the main actor was defined by the codebook, we estimated the reliability coefficients only for the main actor. Intercoder-agreement for this category was 0.92 (kappa 0.85).

Actors: quotes. The total number of direct, literal quotes (also if translated simultaneously or dubbed) of each actor was measured. Because this variable is metric we calculated Pearson's r = 0.88.

Actors: evaluation. For each actor, we coded whether they were evaluated favorably, unfavorably or neutral/not evaluated. Intercoder-agreement is 0.86 (kappa 0.57, n = 359 pairs). We subtracted negative from positive evaluations of EU actors in stories and divided the result by the numbers of EU actors in a story.

Actors: evaluation by whom: If an actor was evaluated the coder had to decide if the evaluation came mainly from the actor him or herself, from journalists/media, or from other sources. Intercoder-agreement is 0.81 (kappa 0.57).

Notes

1. Only the Italian, Greek, Portuguese, and Spanish coders worked at their home institutions in Genoa, Athens, Lisbon, and Madrid. However, coder trainers had visited all country groups and intensively trained the coders at the various locations. Moreover, the coder trainers closely monitored the coders' work throughout the whole coding phase.

2. For Germany, only twelve stories were coded. In Spain and Demark, coding was carefully monitored throughout the coding process with regular testing of reliabilities between the coders and the coder-supervisor. Danish news was coded by one coder, and this was closely checked by the coder trainer.

Appendix C

Euromanifesto content

ANDREAS M. WÜST

The party manifestos issued on the occasions of elections to the European Parliament have been collected and analyzed for all parties ever represented in the EP. Although Euromanifestos have been collected for the complete period from 1979 to 2004, analyses presented in this book exclusively rely on the 1999 Euromanifestos (total N = 117).[1] In general, national parties issue their own Euromanifesto, but in some cases the national parties adopted their European party federation's Euromanifesto completely (4) or in part (1), so these documents have also been collected and coded. In sixteen cases, national parties have neither issued an Euromanifesto nor adopted the Euro-parties' manifesto, but six of them at least issued an official document pertaining to the EP election (such as, for instance, press releases), while in the remaining ten cases, an acceptable substitute (excerpt of the national manifesto; party leader manifesto etc.) could be identified and analyzed. Altogether, only seven parties lack documents for the 1999 EP election of which four are Italian (of a twenty-two record total), two Spanish (regionalists), and one Belgian (CSP).

PROJECT INFORMATION

The Euromanifestos Project was funded by two grants of the German Research Foundation (DFG, Germany) starting in January 2002 and ending in December 2005. Research director was Hermann Schmitt of the MZES at the University of Mannheim. Supported by expert coders of all EU countries, the Euromanifesto team has collected, coded, processed, and is currently analyzing the documents. The analysis is done both by computer-assisted content analysis (Tanja Binder and Daniel Lederle) and by expert coder content analysis (Andreas M. Wüst). First results of the latter analysis are presented by Wüst and Schmitt in chapter 4 of this book. The Euromanifestos have been archived at the MZES (QUIA archive), and the data will later on be made publicly available. An internet page on the Euromanifestos project provides background and up-to-date information on the project: www.euromanifestos.de.

Coding

For the expert coding of the Euromanifestos, a Euromanifesto Coding Scheme (EMCS) has been developed (Wüst and Volkens 2003).[2] The EMCS is a modified and 'mirrored' coding scheme compatible to and based on the classical coding frame used for the Comparative Manifesto Project (CMP) (Volkens 2002; Budge, Klingemann, Volkens, et al. 2001). The EMCS provides the fifty-six original content categories in seven policy domains, but to include EU-specific issues, one domain ('political system') has been split into the classical political system domain and a new European Union political system domain, which includes thirteen new EU-specific categories. In total, the EMCS thus provides sixty-nine content categories and various new sub-categories. Further, the mirroring technique enables us to simultaneously identify the governmental frame a party refers to when it is talking about each of the sixty-nine issues covered by the EMCS: national, European, worldwide, and unspecific. Consequently, the Euromanifesto expert coding results in empirical information on the content of the Euromanifestos (like the CMP does for the national party manifestos) combined with data on the political arena in which each of these issues is discussed.

Weighting

Euromanifesto data are not weighted except for cumulated results for the European party federations, for the parliamentary groups, or for countries. In these cases, each party's Euromanifesto was weighted on the basis of the number of seats they received in the European elections for which the manifesto was written.

Notes

1. There were 118 documents collected and coded, but due to an extremely short document with only twelve arguments, the Belgian Front National has been excluded from the analyses presented in this book.

2. Also available online: http://www.mzes.uni-mannheim.de/publications/wp/wp64.pdf.

Appendix D

Election results, quasi-switching and turnout effects

MARCEL VAN EGMOND

This appendix contains country tables reporting the outcomes of the 1994 and 1999 European Parliament elections as well as the results of counterfactual national elections, which form the bases for the analyses of chapter 2. For each party in the different countries, the following figures are reported: vote share in the 1994 and 1999 European Parliament elections; the counterfactual vote share, had national parliamentary elections been held instead; followed by the signed difference in percentage points between these two figures. This difference is subsequently assigned to quasi-switching and turnout effects (as explained in chapter 2), both reported in percentage points (positive effects indicate gain in European election compared to hypothetical national elections). The country tables can be seen as a contraction of the more detailed tables that were presented for Germany in tables 2.2 and 2.6 in the main text of chapter 2.

Asterisks indicate government parties at the time of the EP elections. For Luxembourg and Belgium, actual national parliament vote was registered. For France and the Netherlands, ballot list agreements required that for several parties only combined figures can be presented. The party names for these parties are reported in italics.

AUSTRIA

	EP Vote (%) 1996	EP Vote (%) 1999	Counterfactual NP Vote (%)	Difference (EP – NP)	Quasi-switching	Turnout Effect
SPÖ*	29.2	31.7	35.9	–4.2	–7.0	2.8
ÖVP*	29.6	30.7	24.1	6.6	5.5	1.1
FPÖ	27.5	23.6	29.2	–5.6	–0.6	–5.0
Grüne	6.8	9.1	6.5	2.6	1.5	1.1
Liberales Forum	4.3	2.6	2.0	0.6	0.4	0.2
Other	2.6	2.3	2.3	0.0	0.2	–0.2
Pedersen index				9.8	7.6	5.2

BELGIUM: FLANDERS

	EP Vote (%) 1994	EP Vote (%) 1999	Counterfactual NP Vote (%)	Difference (EP – NP)	Quasi-switching	Turnout Effect
SP*	16.6	14.1	15.2	–1.1	–1.2	0.1
VLD	18.4	21.7	16.4	5.3	5.2	0.1
Agalev	10.7	12.0	12.6	–0.6	–0.7	0.1
CVP*	27.4	21.6	21.0	0.6	1.1	–0.5
Vlaams Blok	12.6	15.1	20.8	–5.7	–5.8	0.1
VU-ID21	7.1	12.1	8.4	3.7	3.6	0.1
Other	6.2	1.8	1.0	0.8	0.8	0.0
Pedersen index				8.9	9.2	0.5

BELGIUM: WALLONIA

	EP Vote (%) 1994	EP Vote (%) 1999	Counterfactual NP Vote (%)	Difference (EP – NP)	Quasi-switching	Turnout Effect
PS*	30.4	25.6	25.4	0.2	0.9	–0.7
PRL-FDF-MCC	24.3	26.8	31.4	–4.6	–4.8	0.2
Ecolo	13.0	22.5	24.7	–2.2	–2.3	0.1
PSC*	18.8	5.7	3.4	2.3	2.1	0.2
FN	7.9	1.6	3.3	–1.7	–1.9	0.2
Other	5.6	8.1	5.0	3.1	3.3	–0.2
Pedersen index				7.1	7.7	0.8

BRITAIN

	EP Vote (%) 1994	EP Vote (%) 1999	Counterfactual NP Vote (%)	Difference (EP – NP)	Quasi-switching	Turnout Effect
Conservative	27.9	35.7	31.9	3.8	−0.1	3.9
Labour*	44.2	28.1	45.3	−17.2	−6.2	−11.0
Liberal Democrat	16.7	12.6	15.2	−2.6	−5.5	2.9
SNP	3.2	3.3	1.9	1.4	0.9	0.5
Plaid Cymru	1.1	2.8	1.0	1.8	0.0	1.8
Green Party	3.2	6.2	2.5	3.7	2.9	0.8
UKIP UK Independent Party	—	7.0	0.0	7.0	7.0	0.0
Uk Unionist Party	0.8	0.0	0.5	−0.5	−0.7	0.2
SDLP	1.0	0.0	0.3	−0.3	−0.3	0.0
Other	1.9	4.2	1.5	2.7	1.8	0.9
Pedersen index						

DENMARK

	EP Vote (%) 1994	EP Vote (%) 1999	Counterfactual NP Vote (%)	Difference (EP – NP)	Quasi-switching	Turnout Effect
Socialdemokratiet*	15.8	16.5	24.1	−7.6	−7.8	0.2
Venstre	19.0	23.3	34.7	−11.4	−11.4	0.0
Det Konservative Folkeparti	17.7	8.6	6.2	2.4	2.5	−0.1
Socialisk Folkeparti	8.6	7.1	14.9	−7.8	−7.7	−0.1
JuniBevaegelsen	15.2	16.2	0.0	16.2	16.2	0.0
FolkeBevaegelsen mod EU	10.3	7.3	0.0	7.3	7.3	0.0
Dansk Folkeparti	—	5.8	6.1	−0.3	1.3	−1.6
Centrum-Demokraterne	0.9	3.5	2.2	1.3	1.4	−0.1
Det Radikale Venstre*	8.5	9.0	5.0	4.0	2.7	1.3
Enhedslisten— Dei RodGronne	—	0.0	2.2	−2.2	−2.8	0.6
Kristeligt Folkeparti	1.1	2.0	1.6	0.4	−0.1	0.5
Fremskridtpartiet	2.9	0.4	1.8	−1.4	−0.5	−0.9
Other	0.0	0.3	1.2	−0.9	−1.0	0.1
Pedersen index				31.6	31.4	2.8

FINLAND

	EP Vote (%) 1996	EP Vote (%) 1999	Counterfactual NP Vote (%)	Difference (EP – NP)	Quasi-switching	Turnout Effect
SDP*	21.5	17.8	21.4	−3.6	−4.4	0.8
Keskustas	24.4	21.2	20.5	0.7	1.3	−0.6
Kokoomus*	20.2	25.4	28.4	−3.0	−8.5	5.5
RKP*	—	5.4	4.0	1.4	0.2	1.2
Vihreät*	7.6	13.4	12.5	0.9	5.2	−4.3
Vasemmistoliito*	10.5	9.1	7.6	1.5	3.0	−1.5
Krisrilliset /SKL	2.8	1.8	2.4	−0.6	0.4	−1.0
SFP	6.8	—				
Other	6.2	6.0	3.2	2.8	3.0	0.2
Pedersen index				7.3	13.0	7.6

FRANCE

	EP Vote (%) 1994	EP Vote (%) 1999	Counterfactual NP Vote (%)	Difference (EP – NP)	Quasi-switching	Turnout Effect
UDF/RPR	25.6	—				
UDF	—	9.3	8.6	0.7	0.8	−0.1
PC*	6.7	6.8	6.2	0.6	−0.4	1.0
Les verts*	2.9	9.7	8.5	1.2	1.5	−0.3
Lutte Ouvrier-LCR (Laguiller/Krivine)	2.3	4.7	3.8	0.9	1.1	−0.2
Rassemblement pour la France		13.0	0.0	13.0	13.0	0.0
PS-PRG-MDC (Holland/Chevenement)	14.5	22.1	33.8	−11.7	−11.5	−0.2
RPR-DL (Sarkozy/Madelin)*	—	12.8	22.5	−9.7	−10.0	0.3
FN (Le Pen)	10.5	2.9	1.9	1.0	0.8	0.2
MN Megret	—	1.2	0.0	1.2	1.2	0.0
CNPT Saint Josse	4.0	4.1	1.3	2.8	3.3	−0.5
PR Leotard			0.2	−0.2	−0.2	0.0
UDC			1.0	−1.0	−0.4	−0.6
List of the Majority for another Europe (de Villiers)	12.3	—				
Radical energy (Tapie)	12.0	—				
Other	9.2	13.5	12.2	1.3	1.0	0.3
Pedersen index				22.7	22.6	1.9

GERMANY

	EP Vote (%) 1994	EP Vote (%) 1999	Counterfactual NP Vote (%)	Difference (EP – NP)	Quasi-switching	Turnout Effect
CDU/CSU	38.8	48.7	52.8	−4.1	−5.9	1.8
SPD*	32.2	30.6	33.2	−2.6	0.9	−3.5
Bundis90/Grünen*	10.1	6.4	5.9	0.5	0.0	0.5
FDP	4.1	3.0	2.0	1.0	0.8	0.2
PDS	4.7	5.8	1.0	4.8	4.7	0.1
Other	10.1	5.4	5.1	0.3	−0.6	0.9
Pedersen index				6.7	6.5	3.5

GREECE

	EP Vote (%) 1994	EP Vote (%) 1999	Counterfactual NP Vote (%)	Difference (EP – NP)	Quasi-switching	Turnout Effect
PASOK*	37.7	32.9	34.7	−1.8	−1.8	0.0
New Democracy	32.7	36.0	42.1	−6.1	−6.3	0.2
KKE (communists)	6.3	8.7	7.3	1.4	0.8	0.6
Synaspismos	6.3	5.2	3.9	1.3	1.1	0.2
DIKKI	—	6.9	5.5	1.4	1.5	−0.1
Politiki Anixi	8.6	2.3				
Other		8.0	6.4	3.9	4.7	−0.8
Pedersen index				8.0	8.1	1.0

IRELAND

	EP Vote (%) 1994	EP Vote (%) 1999	Counterfactual NP Vote (%)	Difference (EP – NP)	Quasi-switching	Turnout Effect
Fianna Fail*	35.0	38.5	42.7	−4.2	−5.9	1.7
Fine Gael	24.3	24.6	24.4	0.2	−1.4	1.6
Labour	11.0	8.7	11.9	−3.2	−2.8	−0.4
Progressive Democrats*	6.5	0.0	2.0	−2.0	−2.7	0.7
Sinn Fein	3.0	6.3	8.2	−1.9	0.3	−2.2
Green Party	7.9	6.7	7.0	−0.3	1.0	−1.3
Democratic Left	3.5	0.0	0.2	−0.2	−0.3	0.1
Independent	6.9	13.1	0.0	13.1	13.1	0.0
Other	1.9	2.0	3.5	−1.5	−1.4	−0.1
Pedersen index				13.3	14.5	4.1

ITALY

	EP Vote (%) 1994	EP Vote (%) 1999	Counterfactual NP Vote (%)	Difference (EP – NP)	Quasi-switching	Turnout Effect
Forza Italia	30.6	25.2	26.4	–1.2	–2.1	0.9
Democratici di sinistra*	19.1	17.4	21.3	–3.9	–3.9	0.0
Alleanza nazionale	12.5	10.3	13.8	–3.5	–3.8	0.3
Lista Panella\Bonino	2.1	8.4	6.4	2.0	2.2	–0.2
I Democratici*		7.7	7.1	0.6	0.8	–0.2
Lega Nord	6.6	4.5	4.1	0.4	0.7	–0.3
Rifondazione communista	6.1	4.3	5.3	–1.0	–1.1	0.1
PPI Partido Populare Italiane*	10.0	4.3	3.1	1.2	1.0	0.2
CCD Centro Dristiano Democratico	—	2.6	2.1	0.5	0.6	–0.1
SDI Socialistici Democratici Italiani	0.7	2.1	2.2	–0.1	–0.1	0.0
CDU Cristiani Democratici Uniiti	—	2.1	0.9	1.2	1.1	0.1
Communisti Italiani	—	2.2	1.5	0.7	0.7	0.0
Federazione dei Verdi	3.2	1.8	1.5	0.3	0.4	–0.1
UDR Unione Democratici per europa	—	1.6	0.9	0.7	0.8	–0.1
Movimento Sociale Fiamma Tricolore	—	1.0	0.8	0.2	0.1	0.1
Liberali\Repubblicani	—	0.1	0.0	0.1	0.1	0.0
Rinnovamento Italiani	—	1.1	0.5	0.6	0.7	–0.1
Pensionati	—	0.8	0.4	0.4	0.4	0.0
Other	9.1	2.5	1.6	0.9	1.4	–0.5
Pedersen index				9.8	11.0	1.7

LUXEMBOURG

	EP Vote (%) 1994	EP Vote (%) 1999	Counterfactual NP Vote (%)	Difference (EP – NP)	Quasi-switching	Turnout Effect
CSV/PCS*	31.5	31.9	30.3	1.6	1.1	0.5
DP/PD	18.9	20.8	23.8	–3.0	–3.0	0.0
LSAP/POSL*	24.8	23.1	22.2	0.9	0.9	0.0
ADR	7.0	8.6	9.8	–1.2	–1.6	0.4
GLEI/GAP (1994) Déi Greng (1999)	10.9	10.7	11.1	–0.4	0.7	–1.1
Other	6.9	4.8	2.8	2.0	1.8	0.2
Pedersen index				4.6	4.6	1.1

THE NETHERLANDS

	EP Vote (%) 1994	EP Vote (%) 1999	Counterfactual NP Vote (%)	Difference (EP – NP)	Quasi-switching	Turnout Effect
PvdA*	22.9	20.0	24.7	−4.7	0.9	−5.6
CDA	30.8	26.9	20.9	6.0	1.2	4.8
VVD*	17.9	19.8	23.3	−3.5	−0.5	−3.0
D66*	11.7	5.8	7.7	−1.9	0.0	−1.9
Groen Links	3.7	11.9	12.6	−0.7	−1.0	0.3
SP	1.3	5.0	4.8	0.2	−0.9	1.1
RPF, GPV, SGP	7.8	8.7	4.8	3.9	−0.3	4.2
Other	3.9	1.9	1.3	0.6	0.5	0.1
Pedersen index				10.8	2.7	10.5

PORTUGAL

	EP Vote (%) 1994	EP Vote (%) 1999	Counterfactual NP Vote (%)	Difference (EP – NP)	Quasi-switching	Turnout Effect
PS*	36.0	43.1	50.2	−7.1	−4.8	−2.3
PSD	35.5	31.1	30.0	1.1	0.9	0.2
CDS/PP	12.8	10.3	7.6	2.7	2.2	0.5
CDU	11.6	13.8	8.8	5.0	3.1	1.9
Other	4.1	1.7	3.4	−1.7	−1.4	−0.3
Pedersen index				8.8	6.2	2.6

SPAIN

	EP Vote (%) 1994	EP Vote (%) 1999	Counterfactual NP Vote (%)	Difference (EP – NP)	Quasi-switching	Turnout Effect
PP Partido Popular*	40.7	39.8	43.6	−3.8	−3.8	0.0
PSOE	31.0	35.3	33.2	2.1	1.0	1.1
Izquirda Unida	13.6	5.8	6.0	−0.2	−0.2	0.0
CiU Convergencia i Unio*	4.7	4.4	3.4	1.0	0.6	0.4
BNG Bloq nacionalista Galego	0.8	1.9	1.6	0.3	0.3	0.0
P Coalicion Nacionalista & Europa de los Pueblos	1.3	0.4	0.0	0.4	0.4	0.0
CE Coalicion Europea	—	0.4	0.0	0.4	0.4	0.0
Other	7.9	12.0	12.2	−0.2	1.2	−1.4
Pedersen index				4.2	4.0	1.5

SWEDEN

	EP Vote (%) 1995	EP Vote (%) 1999	Counterfactual NP Vote (%)	Difference (EP – NP)	Quasi-switching	Turnout Effect
Vänsterpartiet	12.9	15.9	21.7	–5.8	0.6	–6.4
Socialdemokraterna*	28.1	26.1	27.1	–1.0	–3.0	2.0
Miljöpartiet	17.2	9.4	5.5	3.9	3.5	0.4
Centerpartiet	7.2	6.0	4.7	1.3	2.3	–1.0
Folkpartiet	4.8	13.7	5.8	7.9	5.3	2.6
Kristdemokraterna	3.9	7.7	8.4	–0.7	–0.5	–0.2
Moderaterna	23.2	20.6	26.4	–5.8	–8.4	2.6
Other	2.7	0.6	0.4	0.2	0.3	–0.1
Pedersen index				13.3	12.0	7.7

References

Aarts, Kees, and Holli A. Semetko. 2003. The divided electorate: Effects of media use on political involvement. *The Journal of Politics* 65:759–84.

Aarts, Kees, and Henk van der Kolk, eds. 2005. *Nederlanders en Europa; het referendum over de Europese grondwet.* Amsterdam: Prometheus-Vassallucci.

Aiken, Leona S., and Stephen G. West. 1991. *Multiple regression: Testing and interpreting interactions.* Newbury Park, CA: Sage.

Aldrich, John H. 1993. Rational choice and turnout. *American Journal of Political Science* 37:246–78.

Alvarez, R. Michael, and Jonathan Nagler. 2000. A new approach for modelling strategic voting in multiparty elections. *British Journal for Political Science* 30:57–75.

Anderson, Christopher J. 1998. When in doubt, use proxies. Attitudes toward domestic politics and support for European integration. *Comparative Political Studies* 31:569–601.

Anderson, Christopher J., and Daniel S. Ward. 1996. Barometer elections in comparative perspective. *Electoral Studies* 15:447–60.

Anderson, Peter J., and Antony Weymouth. 1999. *Insulting the public. The British press and the European Union.* London: Longman.

Angé, Hans, Cees van der Eijk, Brigid Laffan, Britta Lejon, Pippa Norris, Hermann Schmitt, and Richard Sinnott. 2000. *Citizen participation in European politics.* Stockholm: Statens Offentliga Utredningar.

Banducci, Susan A., Jeffrey A. Karp, and Edmund Lauf. 2001. Elite leadership, media coverage and support for European integration. Paper presented at the regional meeting of the World Association for Public Opinion Research, June 2001, in Hamburg, Germany.

Bartolini, Stefano, and Peter Mair. 1990. *Identity, competition and electoral availability: The stabilisation of European electorates 1885–1985.* Cambridge: Cambridge University Press.

Beck, Nathaniel, and Jonathan N. Katz. 1995. What to do (and what not to do) with time-series—Cross-section data in comparative perspective. *American Political Science Review* 89:634–47.

Beck, Nathaniel, and Jonathan N. Katz. 1996. Nuisance vs. substance: specifying and estimating time-series—cross-section models. *Political Analysis* 6:1–36.

Ben-Akiva, Moshe, and Steven R. Lerman. 1985. *Discrete choice analysis. Theory and application to travel demand.* Cambridge, MA: MIT Press.

Benewick, Robert J., A. H. Birch, Jay G. Blumler, and Alison Ewbank. 1969. The floating voter and the liberal view of representation. *Political Studies* 17:177–95.

Bennett, W. Lance, and Bob R. Entman. 2001. *Mediated politics. Communication and the future of democracy.* Cambridge: Cambridge University Press.

Berelson, Bernard R., Paul F. Lazarsfeld, and William N. McPhee. 1954. *Voting.* Chicago: University of Chicago Press.

Blais, Andre, and Agnieszka Dobrzynska. 1998. Turnout in electoral democracies. *European Journal of Political Research* 33:239–61.

Blondel, Jean, Richard Sinnott, and Palle Svensson. 1997. Representation and voter participation. *European Journal of Political Research* 32:243–72.

———. 1998. *People and parliament in the European Union: Participation, democracy, and legitimacy.* Oxford: Oxford University Press.

Blumler, Jay G. 1983. *Communicating to voters: Television in the first European Parliament elections.* London: Sage.

Blumler, Jay G., and Anthony D. Fox. 1982. *The European voter: Popular responses to the first European Community elections.* London: Policy Studies Institute.

Blumler, Jay G., and Michael Gurevitch. 2001. Americanization reconsidered: UK-US campaign communication comparisons across time. In *Mediated politics. Communication and the future of democracy,* edited by W. Lance Bennett and Robert M. Entman. Cambridge: Cambridge University Press.

Blumler, Jay G., and Gabriel Thoveron. 1983. Analysing a unique election: Themes and concepts. In *Communicating to voters. Television in the first European Parliamentary Elections,* edited by Jay G. Blumler. London: Sage.

Bosch, Agusti, and Kenneth Newton. 1995. Economic calculus of familiarity breeds content? In *Public opinion and internationalized governance,* edited by Oskar Niedermayer and Richard Sinnott. Oxford: Oxford University Press.

Bowler, Shaun. 1996. Reasoning voters, voter behaviour, and institutions: The decision dependence of voting behaviour. In *British elections and parties yearbook 1996,* edited by David Farrell, David Broughton, David Denver, and Justin Fisher. London: Frank Cass.

Brants, Kees, and Philip van Praag. 2005. *Politiek en Media in Verwarring—De Verkiezingscampagnes in het Lange Jaar 2002.* Amsterdam: Het Spinhuis.

Brosius, Hans-Bernd. 1994. Agenda-setting nach einem Vierteljahrhundert Forschung: Methodischer und theoretischer Stillstand? *Publizistik* 39:269–88.

Budge, Ian, Hans-Dieter Klingemann, Andrea Volkens, Judith Bara, and Eric Tanenbaum. 2001. *Mapping policy preferences. Estimates for parties, electors, and governments 1945–1998.* Oxford: Oxford University Press.

Budge, Ian, David Robertson, and Derek Hearl, eds. 1987. *Ideology, strategy, and party change.* Cambridge: Cambridge University Press.

Caldeira, Gregory A. 1987. Public opinion and the U.S. Supreme Court: FDR's court-packing plan. *American Political Science Review* 81:1139–53.

Campbell, Angus. 1960. Surge and decline: A study of electoral change. *Public Opinion Quarterly* 24:397–18.
———. 1962. The passive citizen. *Acta Sociologica* 6:9–21.
———. 1966. Surge and decline: A study of electoral change. In *Elections and the political order*, edited by Angus Campbell, Philip Converse, Warren Miller, and Donald Stokes. New York: Wiley.
Campbell, Angus, Philip Converse, Warren Miller, and Donald Stokes. 1960. *The American voter.* New York: Wiley.
Campbell, James E. 1997. *The presidential pulse of Congressional elections.* Lexington: University Press of Kentucky.
Cappella, Joseph N., and Kathleen Jamieson. 1997. *Spiral of cynicism. The press and the public good.* New York: Oxford University Press.
Cayrol, Roland. 1983. Media use and campaign evaluations: Social and political stratification of the European electorate. In *Communicating to voters. Television in the first European Parliamentary Elections*, edited by Jay G. Blumler. London: Sage.
———. 1991. European elections and the pre-electoral period: Media use and campaign evaluations. *European Journal of Political Research* 19:17–29.
Chaffee, Steve, and Stacey F. Kanihan. 1997. Learning about politics from mass media. *Political Communication* 17:421–30.
Conover, Pamela J., and Stanley Feldman. 1984. How people organize the political world: A schematic model. *American Journal of Political Science* 28:95–26.
Converse, Philip E. 1969. Of time and partisan stability. *Comparative Political Studies* 2: 139–71.
Crewe, Ivor, and David Denver. 1985. *Electoral change in Western democracies.* London: Croom Helm.
Dalton, Russell J. 1996. Comparative politics: Micro-behavioral perspectives. In *A new handbook of political science*, edited by Robert E. Goodin and Hans-Dieter Klingemann. Oxford: Oxford University Press.
Dalton, Russell J., Scott Flanagan, and Paul A. Beck, eds. 1984. *Electoral change in advanced industrial democracies: Realignment or dealignment?* Princeton: Princeton University Press.
Dalton, Russell J., Ian McAllister, and Martin P. Wattenberg. 2000. The consequences of partisan dealignment. In *Parties without partisans: Political change in advanced industrial democracies*, edited by Russell J. Dalton and Martin P. Wattenberg. Oxford: Oxford University Press.
Daudt, Hans. 1961. *Floating voters and the floating vote.* Leiden: Stenfert Kroese.
Dearing, James W., and Everett M. Rogers. 1996. *Agenda-setting.* Thousand Oaks, CA: Sage.
Del Castillo, Pilar. 1996. Spain: A dress rehearsal for the national elections. In *Choosing Europe? The European electorate and national politics in the face of union*, edited by Cees van der Eijk and Mark Franklin. Ann Arbor: University of Michigan Press.
De Vreese, Claes H. 2001. Election coverage—new directions for public broadcasting: The Netherlands and beyond. *European Journal of Communication* 16:155–79.

———. 2003a. *Framing Europe: Television news and European integration.* Amsterdam: Aksant Academic Publishers.

———. 2003b. Television reporting of second order elections. *Journalism Studies* 4:183–98.

De Vreese, Claes H., Susan Banducci, Holli A. Semetko, and Hajo G. Boomgarden. 2005. The news coverage of the 2004 European parliamentary election campaign in 25 countries. Manuscript under review.

De Vreese, Claes H., Jochen Peter, and Holli A. Semetko. 2001. Framing politics at the launch of the euro: A cross-national comparative study of frames in the news. *Political Communication* 18:107–22.

De Vreese, Claes H., and Holli A. Semetko. 2001. The effects of a referendum campaign on public evaluation of political leaders, the campaign, and vote choice. Paper presented at the annual meeting of the World Association for Public Opinion Research (WAPOR), September 2001, in Rome, Italy.

———. 2002. Cynical and engaged: Strategic campaign coverage, public opinion and mobilization in a referendum. *Communication Research* 29:615–41.

De Winter, Lieven, and Marc Swyngedouw. 1999. The scope of EU government. In *Political representation and legitimacy in the European Union,* edited by Hermann Schmitt and Jacques Thomassen. Oxford: Oxford University Press.

Diez-Nicolas, Juan, and Holli A. Semetko. 1999. Los programmas de noticias de television y los campagnes electorales de 1993 y 1996: propiedad, contenido e influencia. In *Democracia mediatica y campanas electorales,* edited by Alejandro Munoz-Alonso and Juan Ignacio Rospir. Barcelona: Ariel Communicacion.

Dinan, Desmond. 1999. *Ever closer union: An introduction to the European Union.* 2nd edition. London: Macmillan.

Downs, Anthony. 1957. *An economic theory of democracy.* New York: Harper and Row.

Drew, Dan, and David Weaver. 1990. Media attention, media exposure, and media effects. *Journalism Quarterly* 67:740–48.

Duch, Raymond, and Michael Taylor. 1997. Economics and the vulnerability of pan European institutions. *Political Behavior* 19:65–78.

Easton, David A. 1975. A re-assessment of the concept of political support. *British Journal of Political Science* 5:435–57.

Eichenberg, Richard C., and Russell J. Dalton. 1993. Europeans and the European Community: The dynamics of public support for European integration. *International Organization* 47:507–34.

Erikson, Robert S., Gerald C. Wright, Jr., and John P. McIver. 1989. Political parties, public opinion, and state policy in the United States. *American Political Science Review* 83: 729–49.

Eurobarometer 51. 1999. *Public opinion in the European Union.* Brussels: European Commission.

Eurobarometer 54. 2001. *Public opinion in the European Union.* Brussels: European Commission

European Election Study. 1999. http://www2.trincoll.edu/~mfrankli/EES99.html.

Fisher, Stephen. 2000. Tactical voting in England—1987 to 1997. Ph.D. diss., University of Oxford.
Franklin, Charles H., and Liane C. Kosaki. 1989. Republic schoolmaster: The U.S. Supreme Court, public opinion, and abortion. *American Political Science Review* 83:751–71.
Franklin, Mark. 1985. *The decline of class voting in Britain: Changes in the basis of political choice, 1964–1983.* Oxford: Oxford University Press.
———. 1992. The decline of cleavage politics. In *Electoral change. Responses to evolving social and attitudinal structures in western countries*, edited by Mark Franklin, Tom Mackie, and Henry Valen. Cambridge: Cambridge University Press.
———. 1999. Electoral engineering and cross-national turnout differences: What role for compulsory voting? *British Journal of Political Science* 29:205–16.
———. 2000. More means less: How successive enlargements of the European Union caused turnout decline in European Parliament elections. Paper presented at the annual meeting of the American Political Science Association, September 2000, in Washington, D.C.
———. 2001. How structural factors cause turnout variations at European Parliament elections. *European Union Politics* 2:309–28.
———. 2002a. Learning from the Danish case: A comment on Palle Svensson's critique of the Franklin thesis. *European Journal of Political Research* 41:751–57.
———. 2002b. The dynamics of electoral participation. In *Comparing democracies: Elections and voting in global perspectives*, edited by Laurence LeDuc, Richard Niemi, and Pippa Norris. Thousand Oaks, CA: Sage.
———. 2004. *Voter turnout and the dynamics of electoral competition in established democracies since 1945.* New York: Cambridge University Press.
———. 2005. European elections and the European voter. In *European Union: Power and policy-making.* 3rd ed. Edited by Jeremy Richardson. London: Routledge.
Franklin, Mark, and John Curtice. 1996. Britain: Opening Pandora's box. In *Choosing Europe? The European electorate and national politics in the face of union*, edited by Cees van der Eijk and Mark Franklin. Ann Arbor: University of Michigan Press.
Franklin, Mark, and Wolfgang Hirczy. 1998. Separated powers, divided government and turnout in U.S. presidential elections. *American Journal of Political Science* 42:316–26.
Franklin, Mark, Patrick Lyons, and Michael Marsh. 2000. The tally of turnout: Understanding cross-national turnout decline since 1945. Paper presented at the annual meeting of the American Political Science Association, September 2000, in Washington, DC.
Franklin, Mark, Tom Mackie, and Henry Valen. 1992. *Electoral change. Responses to evolving social and attitudinal structures in western countries.* Cambridge: Cambridge University Press.
Franklin, Mark, Michael Marsh, and Lauren McLaren. 1994. Uncorking the bottle: Popular opposition to European unification in the wake of Maastricht. *Journal of Common Market Studies* 32:455–72.

Franklin, Mark, Michael Marsh, and Christopher Wlezien. 1994. Attitudes towards Europe and referendum votes: A response to Siune and Svensson. *Electoral Studies* 13:117–21.

Franklin, Mark, Cees van der Eijk, and Michael Marsh. 1995. Referendum outcomes and trust in government: Popular support for Europe in the wake of Maastricht. *West European Politics* 18:101–17.

———. 1996. Conclusions: The electoral connection and the democratic deficit. In *Choosing Europe? The European electorate and national politics in the face of union*, edited by Cees van der Eijk and Mark Franklin. Ann Arbor: University of Michigan Press.

Franklin, Mark, Cees van der Eijk, and Erik Oppenhuis. 1995. Turnout decline and the motivational basis of British participation in the European elections of 1994. In *British elections and parties yearbook 1995*, edited by Colin Rallings, David Farrell, David Broughton, and David Denver. Ann Arbor: University of Michigan Press.

———. 1996. The institutional context: Turnout. In *Choosing Europe? The European electorate and national politics in the face of union*, edited by Cees van der Eijk and Mark Franklin. Ann Arbor: University of Michigan Press.

Franklin, Mark, and Christopher Wlezien. 1997. The responsive public: Issue salience, policy change, and preferences for European unification. *Journal of Theoretical Politics* 9:347–63.

Gabel, Matthew J. 1998a. *Interests and integration. Market liberalization, public opinion, and European Union*. Ann Arbor: University of Michigan Press.

———. 1998b. Public support for European integration: An empirical test of five theories. *The Journal of Politics* 60:333–54.

Garry, John, Michael Marsh, and Richard Sinnott. 2005. 'Second-order' versus 'issue-voting' effects in EU referendums—evidence from the Irish Nice Treaty referendums. *European Union Politics* 6:201–21.

Granberg, Donald, and Sören Holmberg. 1988. *The political system matters. Social psychology and voting behavior in Sweden and the United States*. Cambridge: Cambridge University Press.

Gray, Mark, and Miki Caul. 2000. Declining voter turnout in advanced industrialized democracies, 1950 to 1997. *Comparative Political Studies* 33:1091–1122.

Grunberg, Gérard, Pascal Perrineau, and Colette Ysmal. 2000. *Le Vote des Quinze*. Paris: Presses de Science Po.

Herr, J. Paul. 2002. The impact of campaign appearances in the 1996 election. *Journal of Politics* 64:904–13.

Hewstone, Miles. 1986. *Understanding attitudes to the European Community*. Cambridge: Cambridge University Press.

Hix, Simon, and Christopher Lord. 1997. *Political parties in the European Union*. London: Macmillan.

Hooghe, Liesbet, and Gary Marks. 1999. The making of a polity: The struggle over European integration. In *The politics and political economy of advanced industrial societies*, edited by Herbert Kitschelt, Peter Lange, Gary Marks, and John Stephens. Cambridge: Cambridge University Press.

Huber, P. Joel. 1967. The behavior of maximum likelihood estimates under non-standard conditions. *Proceedings of the fifth Berkeley Symposium on mathematical statistics and probability* 1:221–33.

Inglehart, Ronald. 1970. Cognitive mobilization and European identity. *Comparative Politics* 3:45–70.

———. 1984. The changing structure of political cleavages in western society. In *Electoral change in advanced industrial democracies: Realignment or dealignment?* edited by Russell J. Dalton, Scott C. Flanagan, and Paul A. Beck. Princeton, NJ: Princeton University Press.

———. 1997. *Modernization and postmodernization. Cultural, economic, and political change in 43 societies.* Princeton, NJ: Princeton University Press.

Inglehart, Ronald, and Karlheinz Reif. 1991. Analyzing trends in west European opinion: The role of the Eurobarometer surveys. In *Eurobarometer. The dynamics of European public opinion. Essays in honour of Jacques-René Rabier,* edited by Karlheinz Reif and Ronald Inglehart. Houndmills: Macmillan.

Iyengar, Shanto, and Adam F. Simon. 1993. News coverage of the Gulf crisis and public opinion: A study of agenda setting, priming, and framing. *Communication Research* 20:365–83.

Jaccard, James, Robert Turrisi, and Choi K. Wan. 1990. Interaction effects in multiple regression. *Sage university papers series on quantitative applications in the social sciences.* Series No. 07–072. Thousand Oaks, CA: Sage.

Jackman, Robert. 1987. Political institutions and voter turnout in industrial democracies. *American Political Science Review* 81:405–23.

Jackman, Robert, and Ross Miller. 1995. Voter turnout in the industrial democracies during the 1980s. *Comparative Political Studies* 27:467–92.

Jacoby, William G. 1991. Data theory and dimensional analysis. *Sage University Paper Series on Quantitative Applications in the Social Sciences.* Series No. 07–078. Newbury Park, CA: Sage.

Kaase, Max. 1967. *Wechsel von Parteipräferenzen. Eine Analyse am Beispiel der Bundestagswahl 1961.* Meisenheim am Glan: Anton Hain.

Kaplan, Abraham. 1964. *The conduct of inquiry. Methodology for behavioral science.* Scranton: Chandler.

Katosh, John P., and Michael W. Traugott. 1981. The consequences of validated and self-reported voting measures. *Public Opinion Quarterly* 45:519–35.

Katz, Richard S., and Bernhard Wessels, eds. 1999. *The European Parliament, the national parliaments, and European integration.* Oxford: Oxford University Press.

Kepplinger, Hans Mathias. 1998. *Die demontage der politik in der informationsgesellschaft.* Freiburg: Alber.

———. 2002. Mediazation of politcs: Theory and data. *Journal of Communication* 52: 973–86.

Kepplinger, Hans Mathias, and Marcus Maurer. 2001. Saldo oder Mittelwert? Eine vorläufige Antwort auf eine ungestellte Frage. In *Die Politik der Massenmedien. Heribert Schatz zum 65. Geburtstag,* edited by Frank Marcinkowski. Köln: Halem Verlag.

Kerlinger, Fred N. 1984. *Liberalism and conservatism*. Hillsdale, NJ: Lawrence Erlbaum.

Kernell, Samuel. 1977. Presidential popularity and negative voting: An alternative explanation of the midterm congressional decline of the president's party. *American Political Science Review* 71:44–66.

King, Gary, James Honacker, Anne Joseph, and Kenneth Scheve. 2001. Analyzing incomplete political science data: An alternative algorithm for multiple imputation. *American Political Science Review* 95:49–69.

King, Gary, Robert O. Keohane, and Sidney Verba. 1994. *Designing social inquiry: Scientific inference in qualitative research*. Princeton, NJ: Princeton University Press.

King, Gary, Michael Tomz, and Jason Wittenberg. 2000. Making the most of statistical analyses: Improving interpretation and presentation. *American Journal of Political Science* 44:347–61.

Kleinnijenhuis, Jan, Dirk Oegema, Jan A. de Ridder, and P.C. Ruigrok. 1998. *Paarse polarisatie: de slag om de kiezer in de media*. Aalphen aan de Rijn: Samsom.

Klingemann, Hans-Dieter. 2002. Policy supply and policy demand: Does party system polarization matter? Presentation at the TMR Conference on Political Representation in Europe, April 2002, in Cadenabbia, Italy.

Klingemann, Hans-Dieter, Richard I. Hofferbert, and Ian Budge. 1994. *Parties, policies, and democracy*. Boulder: Westview.

Klingemann, Hans-Dieter, and Bernhard Wessels. 2000. Political consequences of Germany's mixed-member system: Personalization at the grass-roots? In *Mixed-member electoral systems: Best of both worlds?* edited by Matthew Shugart and Marty P. Wattenberg. Oxford: Oxford University Press.

Kreft, Ita G.G., and Jan de Leeuw. 1998. *Introducing multilevel modeling*. London: Sage.

Kroh, Martin. 2003. *Parties, politicians, and policies—orientations of vote choice across voters and contexts*. Ph.D. diss., University of Amsterdam.

Krosnick, Jon A., and Laura A. Brannon. 1993. The impact of the Gulf War on the ingredients of presidential evaluations: Multidimensional effects of political involvement. *American Political Science Review* 87:963–75.

Krosnick, Jon A., and Donald R. Kinder. 1990. Altering the foundations of support for the president through priming. *American Political Science Review* 84:497–512.

Laasko, Markku, and Rein Taagepera. 1979. Effective number of parties: A measure with application to West Europe. *Comparative Political Studies* 1979:3–27.

Lancelot, Alain. 1968. *L'Abstentionisme électoral en France*. Paris: Colin.

Lazarsfeld, Paul F., Bernard Berelson, and Hazel Gaudet. 1944. *The people's choice*. New York: Duell Sloan and Pierce.

LeDuc, Laurence, Richard Niemi, and Pippa Norris, eds. 2002. *Comparing democracies: Elections and voting in global perspectives*. 2nd ed. Thousand Oaks, CA: Sage.

Leroy, Pascal, and Karen Siune. 1994. The role of television in European elections: The cases of Belgium and Denmark. *European Journal of Communication* 9:47–69.

Lewis-Beck, Michael S. 1988. *Economics and elections*. Ann Arbor: University of Michigan Press.

Lijphart, Arend. 1980. *Democracies*. New Haven, CT: Yale University Press.
Lindberg, Leon, and Stuart Scheingold. 1970. *Europe's would-be polity: Pattern of change in the European Community*. Englewood Cliffs, NJ: Prentice Hall.
Lipset, Seymour M. 1959. Some social requisites of democracy: Economic development and political legitimacy. *American Political Science Review* 53:69–105.
——. 1960. *Political man*. Garden City, NJ: Doubleday.
Lipset, Seymour M., and Stein Rokkan. 1967. Cleavage structures, party systems, and voter alignments: An introduction. In *Party systems and voter alignments*, edited by Seymour M. Lipset and Stuart Rokkan. Glencoe, IL: The Free Press.
Little, Roderick J., and Donald B. Rubin. 1987. *Statistical analysis with missing data*. New York: John Wiley.
Mackie, Thomas. 1991. *Europe votes 3*. Aldershot: Gower.
——. 1996. Appendix D. The results of the 1989, and 1994 European Parliament elections. In *Choosing Europe? The European electorate and national politics in the face of union*, edited by Cees van der Eijk and Mark N. Franklin. Ann Arbor: University of Michigan Press.
Mackie, Thomas, and Frederick Craig. 1980. *Europe votes 1*. Aldershot: Gower.
——. 1985. *Europe votes 2*. Aldershot: Gower.
Mackie, Thomas, Mark Franklin, and Cees van der Eijk. 1996. The dog that did not bark: The 1994 elections in the light of 1989. In *Choosing Europe? The European electorate and national politics in the face of union*, edited by Cees van der Eijk and Mark N. Franklin. Ann Arbor: University of Michigan Press.
Mair, Peter. 2000. The limited impact of Europe on national party systems. *West European Politics* 16:231–46.
——. 2002a. De eigenaardigheden van de Nederlanders. De verkiezingen van 2002 in een vergelijkend perspectief. *B en M Tijdschrift voor Beleid, Politiek en Maatschappij* 29:160–63.
——. 2002b. In the aggregate: Mass electoral behaviour in Western Europe, 1950–2000. In *Comparative democratic politics. A guide to contemporary theory and research*, edited by Hans Keman. London: Sage.
Mannheimer, Renato. 1996. Italy: Consulting the oracle. In *Choosing Europe? The European electorate and national politics in the face of union*, edited by Cees van der Eijk and Mark N. Franklin. Ann Arbor: University of Michigan Press.
Marks, Gary, and Marco Steenbergen, eds. 2004. *European integration and political conflict*. Cambridge: Cambridge University Press.
Marsh, Michael. 1995. Policy performance. In *Political representation and legitimacy in the European Union*, edited by Hermann Schmitt and Jacques Thomassen. Oxford: Oxford University Press.
——. 1998. Testing the second-order election model after four European elections. *British Journal of Political Science* 28:591–607.
Marsh, Michael, and Mark N. Franklin. 1996. The foundations: Unanswered questions from the study of European elections, 1979–1994. In *Choosing Europe? The European*

electorate and national politics in the face of union edited by Cees van der Eijk and Mark N. Franklin. Ann Arbor: University of Michigan Press.

McCombs, Maxwell E. 1981. The agenda-setting approach. In *Handbook of political communication*, edited by Dan D. Nimmo and Keith R. Sanders. Beverly Hills, CA: Sage.

McCombs, Maxwell E., and S. Gilbert. 1986. News influence on our pictures of the world. In *Perspectives on media effects*, edited by Jennings Bryant and Dolf Zillmann. Hillsdale, NJ: Erlbaum.

McCombs, Maxwell E., Esteban Lopez-Escobar, and Juan Pablo Llama. 2000. Setting the agenda of attributes in the 1996 Spanish general election. *Journal of Communication* 50:77–92.

McCombs, Maxwell E., and Donald L. Shaw. 1972. The agenda-setting function of the mass media. *Public Opinion Quarterly* 36:176–87.

McKelvey, Richard D., and Peter C. Ordeshook. 1972. A general theory of the calculus of voting. In *Mathematical applications in political science VI*, edited by J. F. Herdon and J. L. Bernd. Charlottesville: University of Virginia Press.

McLaren, Lauren M. 2001. Immigration and the new politics of inclusion and exclusion in the European Union: The effects of elites and the EU on individual-level opinions regarding European and non-European immigrants. *European Journal of Political Research* 39:81–108.

———. 2002. Public support for the European Union: Cost/benefit analysis or perceived cultural threat? *The Journal of Politics* 64:551–66.

McLeod, Jack M., Lee B. Becker, and James E. Byrnes. 1974. Another look at the agenda-setting function of the press. *Communication Research* 1:131–66.

McQuail, Denis, and Frans Bergsma. 1983. The European dimensions of the campaign. In *Communicating to voters. Television in the first European elections*, edited by Jay G. Blumler. London: Sage.

Meyer, Christoph. 1999. Political legitimacy and the invisibility of politics: Exploring the European Union's communication deficit. *Journal of Common Market Studies* 37:617–39.

Miller, Joanne M., and Jon A. Krosnick. 2000. News media impact on the ingredients of presidential evaluations: Politically knowledgeable citizens are guided by a trusted source. *American Journal of Political Science* 44:301–15.

Mokken, Robert J. 1971. *A theory and procedure of scale analysis. With applications in political research*. Den Haag: Mouton.

Morgan, David. 1985. British news and European Union news: The Brussels news beat and its problem. *European Journal of Communication* 10:321–43.

Niedermayer, Oskar. 1995. Trends and contrasts. In *Public opinion and internationalized governance*, edited by Oskar Niedermayer and Richard Sinnott. Oxford: Oxford University Press.

Niedermayer, Oskar, and Richard Sinnott, eds. 1995. *Public opinion and internationalized governance*. Oxford: Oxford University Press.

Niemi, Richard, and Herbert Weisberg, eds. 1993. *Controversies in voting behaviour*. Washington, DC: CQ Press.

Noelle-Neumann, Elisabeth. 1973. Return to the concept of powerful mass media. *Studies of Broadcasting* 9:67–112.
Norris, Pippa. 2000. *A virtuous circle. Political communications in postindustrial societies.* Cambridge: Cambridge University Press.
Norris, Pippa, John Curtice, David Sanders, Margaret Scammell, and Holli A. Semetko. 1999. *On message. Communicating the campaign.* London: Sage.
Oppenhuis, Erik V. 1995. *Voting behavior in Europe. A comparative analysis of electoral participation and party choice.* Amsterdam: Het Spinhuis.
Oppenhuis, Erik V., Cees van der Eijk, and Mark Franklin. 1996. The party context: Outcomes. In *Choosing Europe? The European electorate and national politics in the face of union,* edited by Cees van der Eijk and Mark Franklin. Ann Arbor: University of Michigan Press.
Pacek, Alexander, and Benjamin Radcliff. 2003. Voter participation and party-group fortunes in European Parliament elections, 1979–1999: A cross-national analysis. *Political Research Quarterly* 56:91–95.
Papke, Leslie E., and Jeffrey M. Wooldridge. 1996. Econometric models for fractional response variables with an application to 401 (K) plan participation rates. *Journal of Applied Econometrics* 11:619–32.
Pappi, Franz Urban. 1996. Political behaviour: Reasoning voters and multi-party systems. In *A new handbook of political science,* edited by Robert E. Goodin and Hans-Dieter Klingemann. Oxford: Oxford University Press.
Pedersen, Mogens N. 1979. The dynamics of the European party systems: Changing patterns of electoral volatility. *European Journal of Political Research* 7:1–26.
Pellikaan, Huib, Tom van der Meer, and Sarah de Lange. 2003. The road from a depoliticized to a centrifugal democracy. *Acta Politica* 38:23–50.
Pennings, Paul, and Hans Keman. 2003. The Dutch parliamentary elections of 2002 and 2003: The rise and decline of the Fortuyn Movement. *Acta Politica* 38:51–68.
Peter, Jochen. 2003. *Why European television news matters.* Ph.D. diss., University of Amsterdam.
Peter, Jochen, and Edmund Lauf. 2002. Reliability in cross-national content analysis. *Journalism and Mass Communication Quarterly* 79:815–32.
Popkin, Samuel. 1991. *The reasoning voter.* Chicago: University of Chicago Press.
Powell, G. Bingham. 1980. Voting turnout in thirty democracies: Partisan, legal, and socio-economic influences. In *Electoral participation: A comparative analysis,* edited by Richard Rose. Beverly Hills, CA: Sage.
Powell, G. Bingham. 1986. American voter turnout in comparative perspective. *American Political Science Review* 80:17–43.
Przeworski, Adam, and Henry Teune. 1970. *The logic of comparative social inquiry.* New York: Wiley.
Ray, Leonard. 1999. Measuring party orientations towards European integration: Results from an expert survey. *European Journal of Political Research* 36:283–306.
Reif, Karlheinz, ed. 1984. *European elections 1979/81 and 1984. Conclusion and perspectives from empirical research.* Berlin: Quorum.

———, ed. 1985a. *Ten European elections*. Aldershot: Gower.

———. 1985b. Ten second order national elections. In *Ten European elections*, edited by Karlheinz Reif. Aldershot: Gower.

———. 1985c. National electoral cycles and European elections 1979 and 1984. *Electoral Studies* 3:244–55.

———. 1997. European elections As member state second-order elections revisited. *European Journal of Political Research* 31:115–24.

Reif, Karlheinz, and Hermann Schmitt. 1980. Nine second-order national elections. A conceptual framework for the analysis of European election results. *European Journal for Political Research* 8:3–44.

Reiser, Stefan. 1994. *Parteienkampagne und Medienberichterstattung im Europawahlkampf 1989: Eine Untersuchung zu Dependenz und Autonomieverlust im Verhältnis von Massenmedien und Politik*. Konstanz, Germany: Ölschläger.

Riker, William H., and Peter C. Ordeshook. 1968. The theory of the calculus of voting. *American Political Science Review* 62:25–42.

Roberts, Kenneth, and Erik Wibbels. 1999. Party systems and electoral volatility in Latin America. *American Political Science Review* 93:575–90.

Robertson, David. 1976. *A theory of party competition*. London: Wiley.

Rogers, Everett M., and James W. Dearing. 1988. Agenda-setting research: Where has it been, where is it going? In *Communication Yearbook*, Vol. 11, edited by J. Anderson. Beverly Hills, CA: Sage.

Rosch Inglehart, Marita. 1995. Gender differences in sex-role attitudes: A topic without a future? In *Eurobarometer. The dynamics of European public opinion. Essays in honor of Jacques-René Rabier*, edited by Karlheinz Reif and Ronald Inglehart. Houndsmills, Basingstoke: Macmillan.

Rose, Richard, and Ian McAllister. 1985. *Voters begin to choose*. Beverly Hills and London: Sage.

Rössler, Patrick. 1997. *Agenda-setting. Theoretische Annahmen und empirische Evidenzen einer Medienwirkungshypothese*. Opladen: Westdeutscher Verlag.

Rubin, Donald B. 1987. *Multiple imputation for nonresponse in surveys*. New York: John Wiley.

Sanchez-Cuenca, Ignacio. 2000. The political basis of support for European integration. *European Union Politics* 1:147–72.

Sartori, Giovanni. 1976. *Parties and party systems. A framework for analysis*. Cambridge: Cambridge University Press.

Sayrs, Lois. 1989. *Pooled time series analysis*. Thousand Oaks, CA: Sage.

Schattschneider, E.E. 1960. *The semi-sovereign people*. New York: Holt Rinehart and Winston.

Scheuer, Angelika. 2005. *How Europeans see Europe. Structure and synamics of European legitimacy beliefs*. Amsterdam: Amsterdam University Press.

Schmitt, Hermann. 2001. *Politische Repräsentation in Europa*. Frankfurt: Campus.

Schmitt, Hermann, and Tanja Binder. 2004. Political representation in the European Union. Agendas of voters and parties in the EP election 1999. Research paper of Mannheoimer Zentrum für Europaische Sozialforschung (MZES)

Schmitt, Hermann, and Cees van der Eijk. 2003. Die politische Bedeutung niedriger Beteiligungsraten bei Europawahlen. Eine empirische Studie über die Motive der Nichtwahl. In *Europäische Integration in der öffentlichen Meinung*, edited by Frank Brettschneider, Jan van Deth, and Edeltroud Roller. Opladen: Leske and Budrich.

Schmitt, Hermann, Cees van der Eijk, Farnz Urban Pappi, Evi Scholz, et al. 1997. *European elections study 1994: Design, implementation, and results* (computer file and codebook). Köln: Zentralarchiv für Empirische Sozialforschung.

Schmitt, Hermann, and Sören Holmberg. 1995. Political parties in decline? In *Citizens and the state*, edited by Hans-Dieter Klingemann and Dieter Fuchs. Oxford: Oxford University Press.

Schmitt, Hermann, and Renato Mannheimer. 1991. About voting and non-voting in the European Parliament elections of June 1989. *European Journal of Political Research* 19:31–54.

Schmitt, Hermann, and Karlheinz Reif. 2003. Der Hauptwahlzyklus und die Ergebnisse von Nebenwahlen. In *Politbarometer*, edited by Andreas Wüst. Opladen: Leske und Budrich.

Schmitt, Hermann, and Angelika Scheuer. 1996. Region—nation—Europa. Drei Ebenen politischer Steuerung und Gestaltung in der Wahrnehmung der Bürger. In Das Europische Mehrebenensystem (Mannheimer Jahrbuch fr Europische Sozialforschung Bd. 1), edited by Thomas König, Elmar Rieger, and Hermann Schmitt. Frankfurt: Campus.

Schmitt, Hermann, and Jacques Thomassen, eds. 1999. *Political representation and legitimacy in the European Union*. Oxford: Oxford University Press.

Schmitt-Beck, Rüdiger. 2000. *Politische Kommunikation und Wählerverhalten: ein internationaler Vergleich*. Wiesbaden: Westdeutscher Verlag.

Schoenbach, Klaus. 1981. Agenda-setting im Europawahlkampf 1979: Die Funktionen von Presse und Fernsehen. . *Media Perspektiven* 7:537–47.

Schoenbach, Klaus. 1983. What and how voters learned. In *Communicating to voters. Television in the first European Parliamentary Elections*, edited by Jay G. Blumler. London: Sage.

Schoenbach, Klaus, Jan de Ridder, and Edmund Lauf. 2001. Politicians on TV: Getting attention in Dutch and German election campaigns. *European Journal of Political Research* 39:519–31.

Schram, Arthur J.C. 1989. *Voter behavior in economic perspective*. Alblasserdam: Kanters

Schulz, Winfried. 1983. One campaign or nine. In *Communicating to voters. Television in the first European parliamentary elections*, edited by J.G. Blumler. London: Sage.

Semetko, Holli A. 2000. Great Britain: The end of the News at Ten and the changing news environment. In *Democracy and the media: A comparative perspective*, edited by Richard Gunther and Anthony Mughan. Cambridge: Cambridge University Press.

Semetko, Holli A., Jay G. Blumler, Michael Gurevitch, and Denis H. Weaver. 1991. *The formation of campaign agendas: A comparative analysis of party and media roles in recent American and British elections*. Hillsdale, NJ: Lawrence Erlbaum.

Semetko, Holli A., and Maria Jose Canel. 1997. Agenda-senders versus agenda-setters. Television in Spain's 1996 election campaign. *Political Communication* 14:459–79.

Semetko Holli A., and Klaus Schönbach. 1994. *Germany's unity election: Voters and the media*. Cresskill, NJ: Hampton Press.

Semetko, Holli A., and Patty M. Valkenburg. 2000. Framing European politics: A content analysis of press and television news. *Journal of Communication* 50:93–109.

Semetko, Holli A., Wouter van der Brug, and Patty M. Valkenburg. 2003. The influence of political events on attitudes towards the European Union. *British Journal of Political Science* 33 621–34.

Seri, P. 2002. Das Mediensystem Griechenlands. In *Internationales Handbuch Medien, 2002/2003*, edited by Hans-Bredow-Institut. Baden-Baden: Nomos.

Silverman, L. 1985. The ideological mediation of party political responses to social change. *European Journal of Political Research* 19:393–417.

Sinnott, Richard. 1995a. Bringing public opinion back. In *Public opinion and internationalized governance*, edited by Oskar Niermayer and Richard Sinnott. Oxford: Oxford University Press.

———. 1995b. Policy, subsidiarity, and legitimacy. In *Public opinion and internationalized governance*, edited by Oskar Niermayer and Richard Sinnott. Oxford: Oxford University Press.

———. 2000. European Parliament elections: Institutions, attitudes, and participation. In *Citizen participation in European politics*, edited by Hans Angé, Cees van der Eijk, Brigit Laffan, Britta Lejon, Pippa Norris, Hermann Schmitt, and Richard Sinnott. Stockholm: Statens Offentliga Utredningar.

Siune, Karen. 1983. The campaign on television: What was said and who said it? In *Communicating to voters*, edited by Jay G. Blumler. London: Sage.

Smeets, Ingrid. 1995. Facing another gap: An exploration of the discrepancies between voting turnout in survey research and official statistics. *Acta Politica* 20:307–34.

Smith, Julie. 1999. *Europe's elected parliament*. Sheffield: Sheffield Academic Press.

Snijders, Tom A. B., and Bosker, Roel J. 1999. *Multilevel analysis. An introduction to basic and advanced multilevel modeling*. London: Sage.

Stata. 1999. *Stata reference manual release 6*. College Station, TX: Stata Press.

Steenbergen, Marco R., and Bradford S. Jones. 2002. Modeling multilevel data structures. *American Journal of Political Science* 46:218–37.

Stimson, James A. 1985. Regression in space and time: A statistical essay. *American Journal of Political Science* 29:914–47.

Swanson, David, and Paolo Mancini, eds. 1996. *Politics, media, and modern democracy. An international study of innovation in electoral campaigning and their consequences*. Westport: Praeger.

Thomassen, Jacques. 2000. From comparable to comparative electoral research. In *Die Republik auf dem Weg zur Normalität?*, edited by Jan van Deth, Hans Rattinger, and Edeltraud Roller. Opladen: Leske and Budrich.

Thomassen, Jacques, Kees Aarts, and Henk van der Kolk, eds. 2000. *Politieke Verandering in Nederland 1971–1998*. The Hague: SDU.

Thomassen, Jacques, and Hermann Schmitt. 1999a. In conclusion: Political representation and legitimacy in the European Union. In *Political representation and legitimacy in the European Union*, edited by Hermann Schmitt and Jacques Thomassen. Oxford: Oxford University Press.

———. 1999b. Issue Congruence. In *Political representation and legitimacy in the European Union*, edited by Hermann Schmitt and Jacques Thomassen. Oxford: Oxford University Press.

———. 2004. Democracy and legitimacy in the European Union. In *Elections, parties, and political representation. Festschrift for Henry Valen's 80th anniversary*, edited by Hanne M. Narud and Anne Krogstad. Oslo: Universitetsforlaget.

Tillie, Jean. 1995. *Party utility and voting behavior*. Amsterdam: Het Spinhuis.

Tingsten, Herbert. 1963. *Political behavior: Studies in election statistics*. New York: Bedminster Press.

Tomz, Michael, Jason Wittenberg, and Gary King. 2000. CLARIFY: Software for interpreting and presenting statistical results. Version 1.2.2. Cambridge, MA: Harvard University, March 3. [http://gking.harvard.edu/]

Trenaman, Joseph, and Denis McQuail. 1961. *Television and the political image*. London: Methuen.

Tufte, Edward R. 1975. Determinants of the outcomes of midterm congressional elections. *American Political Science Review* 67:540–54.

Valentino, Nicholas A., Matthew N. Beckmann, and Thomas A. Buhr. 2001. A spiral of cynicism for some: The contingent effects of campaign news frames on participation and confidence in government. *Political Communication* 18:347–67.

Valentino, Nicholas, Thomas A. Buhr, and Matthew N. Beckmann. 2001. When the frame is the game: Revisiting the impact of strategic campaign coverage on citizens' information retention. *Journalism and Mass Communication Quarterly* 78:93–112.

Van der Brug, Wouter. 1997. Where's the party? Voters' perceptions of party positions. Ph.D. diss., University of Amsterdam.

———. 2001. Perceptions, opinions, and party preferences in the face of a real world event: Chernobyl as a natural experiment in political psychology. *Journal of Theoretical Politics* 13:53–80.

Van der Brug, Wouter, Meindert Fennema, and Jean Tillie. 2000. Anti-immigrant parties in Europe: Ideological or protest vote? *European Journal of Political Research* 37:77–102.

Van der Brug, Wouter, and Meindert Fennema. 2003. Protest or mainstream? How the European anti-immigrant parties have developed into two separate groups by 1999. *European Journal of Political Research* 42:55–76.

Van der Brug, Wouter, Mark N. Franklin, and Cees van der Eijk. 2000. The economy and the vote: Electoral responses to economic conditions in 15 countries. Paper presented at the annual meeting of the American Political Science Association, September 2000, in Washington, DC.

Van der Brug, Wouter, and Cees van der Eijk. 1999. The cognitive basis of voting. In *Political representation and legitimacy in the European Union*, edited by Hermann Schmitt and Jacques Thomassen. Oxford: Oxford University Press.

Van der Brug, Wouter, Cees van der Eijk, and Mark N. Franklin. 2007. *The economy and the vote*. Cambridge: Cambridge University Press.

Van der Eijk, Cees. 2001. Measuring agreement in ordered rating scales. *Quality and Quantity* 35:325–341.

———. 2002. Design issues in electoral research: Taking care of (core) business. *Electoral Studies* 21:189–206.

Van der Eijk, Cees, and Mark N. Franklin. 1991. European Community politics and electoral representation: Evidence from the 1989 European Elections study. *European Journal of Political Research* 19:105–27.

———, eds. 1996. *Choosing Europe? The European electorate and national politics in the face of union.* Ann Arbor: University of Michigan Press.

———. 2004. Potential for contestation on European matters at national elections in Europe. In *European integration and political conflict*, edited by Gary Marks and Marco Steenbergen. Cambridge: Cambridge University Press.

Van der Eijk, Cees, Mark N. Franklin, and Wouter van der Brug. 1999. Policy preferences and party choice. In *Political representation and legitimacy in the European Union*, edited by Hermann Schmitt and Jacques Thomassen. Oxford: Oxford University Press.

Van der Eijk, Cees, Mark N. Franklin, and Tom Mackie. 1996. The dog that did not bark: The 1994 elections in the light of 1989. In *Choosing Europe? The European electorate and national politics in the face of union*, edited by Cees van der Eijk and Mark N. Franklin. Ann Arbor: University of Michigan Press.

Van der Eijk, Cees, Mark N. Franklin, and Michael Marsh. 1996 What voters teach us about Europe-wide elections; what Europe-wide elections teach us about voters. *Electoral Studies* 15:149–66.

Van der Eijk, Cees, Mark N. Franklin, and Erik V. Oppenhuis. 1996. The strategic context: Party choice. In *Choosing Europe? The European electorate and national politics in the face of union*, edited by Cees van der Eijk and Mark N. Franklin. Ann Arbor: University of Michigan Press.

Van der Eijk, Cees, Mark N. Franklin, Klaus Schönbach, Hermann Schmitt, Holli Semetko, et al. 2002. *European election study 1999: Design, data description, and documentation.* Amsterdam: Steinmetz Archives.

Van der Eijk, Cees, and Martin Kroh. 2002. Alchemy or science? Discrete choice models for analyzing voter choice in multi-party contests. Paper presented at the annual meeting of the American Political Science Association, August 2002, in Boston.

Van der Eijk, Cees, and Kees Niemöller. 1983. *Electoral change in the Netherlands. Empirical research and methods of measurement.* Amsterdam: CT Press.

Van der Eijk, Cees, and Erik V. Oppenhuis. 1990. Turnout and second-order effects in the European elections of June 1989: Evidence from the Netherlands. *Acta Politica* 25: 67–94.

———. 1991. European parties' performance in electoral competition. *European Journal of Political Research* 19 55–80.

———. 1996. Variables employed and methods of analysis. In *Choosing Europe? The European electorate and national politics in the face of union*, edited by Cees van der Eijk and Mark N. Franklin. Ann Arbor: University of Michigan Press.

Van der Eijk, Cees, and Ger Schild, with Marian Visser. 1992. Het Landelijk Kompas van de Provinciale Kiezer. In *Verkiezingen Zonder Mandaat Politieke Communicatie en Provinciale Verkiezingen*, edited by Cees van der Eijk, Irene van Geest, Peter Kramer, and Lisette Tiddens. The Hague: SDU.

Van der Eijk, Cees, Erik V. Oppenhuis, Hermann Schmitt, et al. 1993. *European elections study 1989: Design, implementation and results* (computer file and codebook). Amsterdam: Steinmetz Archives.

Van der Eijk, Cees, and Hermann Schmitt. 1991. The role of the Eurobarometer in the study of European elections and the development of comparative electoral research. In *Eurobarometer: The dynamics of European opinion*, edited by Karlheinz Reif and Ronald Inglehart. London: Macmillan.

Van der Eijk, Cees, Wouter van der Brug, Martin Kroh, and Mark N. Franklin. 2006. Rethinking the dependent variable in electoral behavior—on the measurement and analysis of utilities. *Electoral Studies*, forthcoming.

Van der Eijk, Cees, and Marcel van Egmond. Forthcoming. Political effects of low turnout in national and European elections. *Electoral Studies* 25:424–47.

Van Deth, Jan, ed. 1998. *Comparative politics. The problem of equivalence*. New York: Routledge.

Van Egmond, Marcel, Nan Dirk de Graaf, and Cees van der Eijk. 1998. Electoral participation in the Netherlands: Individual and contextual influences. *European Journal of Political Research* 34:281–300.

Van Wijnen, Pieter 2001. *Policy voting in advanced industrial democracies. The case of the Netherlands 1971–1998*. Enschede: University of Twente.

Verba, Sidney, Norman H. Nie, and Jae-on Kim. 1978. *Participation and political equality*. Cambridge: Cambridge University Press.

Visscher, Gerard. 1995. *Kiezersonderzoek op een dwaalspoor: De in politiek geïnteresseerde kiezer als selffulfilling prophecy*. The Hague: SDU

Volkens, Andrea. 2002. Manifesto coding instructions (WZB Discussion Paper FS III 02–201), Berlin: WZB. [http://skylla.wz-berlin.de/pdf/2002/iii02-203.pdf].

Wanta, Wayne. 1997. *The public and the national agenda. How people learn about important issues*. Mahwah, NJ: Erlbaum.

Watt, James H., and Sjef van den Berg. 1981. How time dependency influences media effects in a community controversy. *Journalism Quarterly* 58:43–50.

Watt, James H., Mary Mazza, and Leslie Snyder. 1993. Agenda-setting effects of television news coverage and the effects decay curve. *Communication Research* 20:408–35.

Weber, Hermann. 1999. *Die DDR 1945—1990*. München: Oldenbourg.

Wessels, Bernhard. 1995. Support for integration: Elite or mass driven? In *Public opinion and institutionalized government*, edited by Oskar Niedermayer and Richard Sinnott. Oxford: Oxford University Press.

Wessels, Bernhard, and Hermann Schmitt. 2000. Europawahlen, Europäisches Parlament, und nationalstaatliche Demokratie. In *Die Zukunft der Demokratie*, edited by Hans-Dieter Klingemann and Friedhelm Neidhardt. Berlin: Sigma.

White, Halbert. 1980. A heteroskedasticity-consistent covariance matrix estimator and a direct test for heteroskedasticity. *Econometrica* 48:817–38.

Wolfinger, Raymond, and Steven Rosenstone. 1980. *Who votes?* New Haven and London: Yale University Press.

Worre, Torben. 1996. Denmark: Second-order containment. In *Choosing Europe? The European electorate and national politics in the face of union*, edited by Cees van der Eijk and Mark N. Franklin. Ann Arbor: University of Michigan Press.

Wüst, Andreas M., and Andrea Volkens. 2003. Euromanifesto coding instructions. MZES Working Paper 64, Mannheim: MZES [http://www.mzes.uni-mannheim.de/publications/wp/wp-64.pdf].

Zelle, Carsten. 1995. *Der Wechselwähler.* Opladen: Westdeutscher Verlag.

Author Index

Aarts, Kees, 215, 272, 277
Aiken, Leona S., 136, 137, 144
Alvarez, R. Michael, 150
Anderson, Christopher J., 17, 136

Banducci, Susan A., 133, 134, 141
Bartolini, Stefano, 224
Beck, Nathaniel, 19, 30
Beck, Paul A., 222
Becker, Lee B., 136
Beckmann, Matthew N., 134
Ben-Akiva, Moshe, 170
Benewick, Robert J., 215
Bennett, W. Lance, 116
Berelson, Bernard R., 167, 215, 219
Bergsma, Frans, 124
Binder, Tanja, 83, 87, 284
Blais, Andre, 15
Blondel, Jean, 17, 29, 149, 150, 163
Blumler, Jay G., 16, 17, 116, 117, 120, 131, 148, 257, 277
Bosch, Agusti, 79
Bosker, Roel J., 143
Bowler, Shaun, 224
Brannon, Laura A., 185
Brants, Kees, 167
Brosius, Hans-Bernd, 136
Budge, Ian, 74, 136, 284
Buhr, Thomas A., 134
Byrnes, James E., 136

Caldeira, Gregory A., 142
Campbell, Angus, 52, 54, 55, 60, 63, 68, 69, 71, 167, 178, 215
Campbell, James E., 55, 60, 63, 71
Canel, Maria Jose, 130
Cappella, Joseph N., 134
Caul, Miki, 15
Cayrol, Roland, 131
Chaffee, Steve, 119
Conover, Pamela J., 187, 258
Converse, Philip E., 219
Craig, Frederick, 20
Crewe, Ivor, 222
Curtice, John, 48

Dalton, Russell J., 95, 97, 133, 210, 222
Daudt, Hans, 215
De Graaf, Nan Dirk, 145
De Lange, Sarah, 260
De Leeuw, Jan, 224
De Ridder, Jan A., 130
De Vreese, Claes H., 10, 120, 128, 129, 130, 185, 263, 278
De Winter, Lieven, 85
Dearing, James W., 132, 133, 143
Del Castillo, Pilar, 48
Denver, David, 222
Diez-Nicolas, Juan, 278
Dobrzynska, Agnieszka, 15
Downs, Anthony, 170, 171, 224, 258

313

Drew, Dan, 136
Duch, Raymond, 134

Easton, David A., 87
Eichenberg, Richard C., 95, 97, 133
Entman, Bob R., 116
Erikson, Robert S., 142

Feldman, Stanley, 187, 258
Fennema, Meindert, 186
Flanagan, Scott, 222
Fox, Anthony D., 16, 257
Franklin, Mark, 4, 5, 6, 8, 10, 11, 13, 15, 16, 17, 18, 25, 26, 29, 30, 31, 33, 38, 43, 44, 46, 48, 49, 53, 54, 61, 71, 87, 88, 91, 98, 101, 111, 115, 116, 117, 118, 133, 134, 136, 145, 148, 158, 159, 164, 166, 169, 170, 176, 180, 181, 182, 184, 185, 186, 187, 189, 190, 191, 193, 202, 203, 204, 205, 210, 215, 219, 221, 222, 225, 226, 231, 247, 257, 258, 259, 266, 267, 269, 270, 276
Franklin, Charles H., 142

Gabel, Matthew J., 95, 136
Garry, John, 185
Gaudet, Hazel, 167, 215, 219
Gilbert, S., 133, 136
Granberg, Donald, 258
Gray, Mark, 15
Gurevitch, Michael, 120

Herr, J. Paul, 118
Hewstone, Miles, 95
Hirczy, Wolfgang, 17
Hix, Simon, 191
Hofferbert, Richard I., 74
Holmberg, Sören, 224, 258, 276
Hooghe, Liesbet, 191
Huber, P. Joel, 45, 144

Inglehart, Ronald, 95, 98, 103, 133, 187
Iyengar, Shanto, 185

Jaccard, James, 136, 137, 144
Jackman, Robert, 15
Jacoby, William G., 114
Jamieson, Kathleen, 134
Jones, Bradford S., 143

Kaase, Max, 215
Kanihan, Stacey F., 119
Kaplan, Abraham, 150
Karp, Jeffrey A., 133, 134, 141
Katosh, John P., 49
Katz, Jonathan N., 19, 30, 204
Katz, Richard S., 204
Keman, Hans, 215
Keohane, Robert O., 150, 151
Kepplinger, Hans Mathias, 119, 127, 134, 142
Kerlinger, Fred N., 187
Kernell, Samuel, 56
Kim, Jae-on, 159
Kinder, Donald R., 185
King, Gary, 71, 150, 151, 224
Kleinnijenhuis, Jan, 130
Klingemann, Hans-Dieter, 74, 223, 224, 284
Kosaki, Liane C., 142
Kreft, Ita G.G., 224
Kroh, Martin, 11, 185
Krosnick, Jon A., 132, 185

Laasko, Markku, 223
Lancelot, Alain, 167
Lauf, Edmund, 10, 130, 133, 134, 141, 263, 278
Lazarsfeld, Paul F., 167, 215, 219
LeDuc, Laurence, 186
Lerman, Steven R., 170
Leroy, Pascal, 117, 118, 119
Lewis-Beck, Michael S., 170
Lijphart, Arend, 190
Lindberg, Leon, 189
Lipset, Seymour M., 167, 190, 210, 260
Little, Roderick J., 224

Llama, Juan Pablo, 118
Lopez-Escobar, Esteban, 118
Lord, Christopher, 191

Mackie, Thomas, 20, 38, 43, 170, 181, 190, 210
Mair, Peter, 124, 224, 242
Mancini, Paolo, 116
Mannheimer, Renato, 29, 48, 147, 148, 166, 276
Marks, Gary, 5, 169, 191, 258
Marsh, Michael, 6, 10, 16, 17, 29, 31, 54, 58, 71, 91, 97, 115, 116, 117, 136, 170, 185, 191, 203, 231, 247, 257, 258, 269, 276
Maurer, Marcus, 142
Mazza, Mary, 142
McAllister, Ian, 210, 222
McCombs, Maxwell E., 118, 132, 133, 136
McIver, John P., 142
McLaren, Lauren M., 6, 115, 133, 136, 185
McLeod, Jack M., 136
McPhee, William N., 167
McQuail, Denis, 124, 215
Meyer, Christoph, 141
Miller, Joanne M., 132
Miller, Ross, 15
Mokken, Robert J., 112, 113, 114

Nagler, Jonathan, 150
Newton, Kenneth, 79
Nie, Norman H., 159
Niedermayer, Oskar, 95, 97
Niemi, Richard, 72, 186
Niemöller, Kees, 187, 215
Noelle-Neumann, Elisabeth, 134
Norris, Pippa, 118, 130, 134, 141, 186

Oppenhuis, Erik V., 6, 13, 15, 16, 17, 25, 29, 44, 46, 53, 71, 101, 111, 116, 117, 118, 145, 148, 159, 164, 166, 169, 176, 180, 182, 185, 186, 187, 202, 221, 223, 225, 231, 257, 269

Pacek, Alexander, 46
Papke, Leslie E., 50
Pappi, Franz Urban, 147
Pedersen, Mogens N., 35, 36, 37, 41, 42, 49, 260, 261, 287, 288, 289, 290, 291, 292, 293
Pellikaan, Huib, 260
Pennings, Paul, 215
Peter, Jochen, 10, 11, 117, 139, 142, 263, 264, 278
Popkin, Samuel, 224
Powell, G. Bingham, 15
Przeworski, Adam, 109

Radcliff, Benjamin, 46
Ray, Leonard, 119
Reif, Karlheinz, 5, 9, 16, 33, 43, 52, 53, 68, 95, 116, 169, 191, 220, 227, 229, 257, 258
Reiser, Stefan, 277
Roberts, Kenneth, 224
Robertson, David, 74, 136
Rogers, Everett M., 132, 133, 143
Rokkan, Stein, 2, 210, 260
Rosch Inglehart, Marita, 98
Rose, Richard, 222
Rosenstone, Steven, 167
Rössler, Patrick, 132, 136
Rubin, Donald B., 224

Schattschneider, E.E., 194, 198, 206, 272
Scheingold, Stuart, 189
Scheuer, Angelika, 10, 85, 95, 97, 98, 99, 101, 133, 193
Schild, Ger, 130
Schmitt, Hermann, 4, 5, 6, 8, 9, 10, 11, 29, 33, 43, 52, 53, 68, 83, 85, 87, 88, 89, 93, 95, 116, 136, 147, 148, 158, 166, 169, 191, 220, 224, 227, 229, 247, 258, 259, 273, 276, 284

Schmitt-Beck, Rüdiger, 136
Schoenbach, Klaus, 130, 131
Schulz, Winfried, 131, 278
Semetko, Holli A., 95, 130, 185, 226, 276, 277, 278
Seri, P., 277
Shaw, Donald L., 132
Silverman, L., 206
Simon, Adam F., 185
Sinnott, Richard, 17, 29, 95, 149, 185
Siune, Karen, 117, 118, 119, 127
Smeets, Ingrid, 49
Smith, Julie, 148, 149
Snijders, Tom A.B., 143
Snyder, Leslie, 142
Steenbergen, Marco R., 5, 143, 169, 258
Stimson, James A., 173
Svensson, Palle, 29, 149
Swanson, David, 116
Swyngedouw, Marc, 85

Taagepera, Rein, 223
Taylor, Michael, 134
Teune, Henry, 109
Thomassen, Jacques, 4, 6, 8, 74, 89, 93, 95, 215, 226, 247, 276
Thoveron, Gabriel, 131
Tillie, Jean, 61, 185, 186, 187, 202, 222
Tingsten, Herbert, 167
Tomz, Michael, 71
Traugott, Michael W., 49
Trenaman, Joseph, 215
Tufte, Edward R, 55, 56, 60, 67, 72
Turrisi, Robert, 136, 137, 144

Valen, Henry, 170, 181, 190, 210
Valentino, Nicholas A., 134
Valkenburg, Patty M., 95, 278
Van den Berg, Sjef, 142
Van der Brug, Wouter, 10, 11, 30, 88, 89, 95, 101, 169, 176, 180, 186, 191, 208, 258, 260, 270, 276, 278

Van der Eijk, Cees, 4, 5, 6, 8, 11, 13, 15, 16, 17, 18, 25, 29, 31, 33, 38, 43, 44, 46, 49, 50, 53, 54, 61, 71, 88, 89, 91, 101, 111, 115, 116, 117, 118, 130, 133, 134, 145, 148, 158, 159, 164, 166, 169, 171, 176, 180, 182, 184, 185, 186, 187, 189, 191, 202, 203, 204, 205, 207, 208, 215, 221, 222, 223, 225, 231, 247, 257, 258, 259, 269, 270, 273, 274, 276
Van der Kolk, Henk, 215, 272
Van der Meer, Tom, 260
Van Deth, Jan, 93
Van Egmond, Marcel, 10, 50, 71, 145, 269, 270
Van Praag, Philip, 167
Van Wijnen, Pieter, 215, 260
Verba, Sidney, 150, 151, 159
Visscher, Gerard, 49
Volkens, Andrea, 77, 92, 284

Wan, Choi K., 136, 137, 144
Wanta, Wayne, 136
Ward, Daniel S., 17
Watt, James H., 142
Wattenberg, Martin P., 210
Weaver, David, 136
Weisberg, Herbert, 72
Wessels, Bernhard, 133, 148, 204, 224, 276
West, Stephen G., 136, 137, 144, 222, 257
White, Halbert, 45, 144
Wibbels, Erik, 224
Wittenberg, Jason, 71
Wlezien, Christopher, 87, 115, 185, 193
Wolfinger, Raymond, 167
Wooldridge, Jeffrey M., 50
Worre, Torben, 31, 258
Wright, Jr, Gerald C., 142
Wüst, Andreas M., 10, 77, 92, 259, 284

Zelle, Carsten, 215

Subject Index

abstention. *See* electoral participation
accountability, 4–5, 91
act meaning vs action meaning, 150
agenda setting, 136
agenda-setting effects, 132, 133
Austria, 19, 21, 24, 46, 79, 86, 90, 103, 110, 122, 143

Belgium, 20, 33, 34, 36, 39, 46, 57, 82, 97, 110, 120, 122
blame. *See* credit and blame
Britain, 16, 18, 24, 25, 73, 97, 100, 110, 122, 125

campaign coverage. *See* TV news
coding procedures for media content, 119, 277–82
commercial TV channels, 143
compulsory voting, 14, 15, 20–21, 145, 267
concurrent national and European elections, 145
conflict potential of EU-orientations, 196–97
consonance of media supply, 134, 135, 136
constitutional treaty, 6, 257
contagion between countries, 245, 260
context effects on media behavior, 126–29

context effects on voter behavior, 131, 141
counterfactual, 32–33. *See also* scenario
credit and blame, 258
—attribution of, 235
Cyprus, 1, 115
Czech Republic, 1

democracy. *See* accountability; legitimacy; representation
democratic deficit, 246
Denmark, 16, 18, 19, 24, 37, 39, 43, 73, 79, 90, 97, 105, 122

effects of electoral context: of timing. *See* electoral cycle
effects of media context, 131, 135, 140, 141
effects of party context
—of party polarization, 133
—on potential for electoral change, 216, 219
—presence of anti-EU party, 237
election outcomes, 286
—and EU-support, 244, 245
—parties' vote shares, 269–70
—potential for change, 210
—turnout, 13–31
—turnout, first-time boost, 267
—turnout effects, 39–48

317

election outcomes (*cont.*)
— turnout in European Parliament elections 2004, 266–69
elections: second-order national elections, 220, 221
electoral change, 209–10
— measuring potential for, 210
— over-all change (Pedersen index), 37, 242, 260
— potential for, 209–10
— quasi-switching, 32–48
— vote switching, 60–68
electoral cohort. *See* voter characteristics, cohort
electoral competition: extent of, 223
electoral cycle
— consequences for campaign coverage, 118, 128, 230–32
— consequences for government support, 51–71, 230–32
— consequences for strategic voter considerations, 45, 225, 245
— consequences for turnout, 15, 17–18, 21, 25, 27, 230–32, 267
electoral participation, 66, 67
— competing interpretations, 148–51, 161–64
— correlates of, 151, 154
— Euro-skeptic non-voting, 146, 161–62
— motives for, 146, 148
electoral utilities, 159, 171, 210, 222, 270
electoral volatility. *See* electoral change; potential for electoral change
Estonia, 1
EU enlargement, 1–3. *See also* new member states
EU institutions, 257
— constitutional treaty, 230
European Commission, 230
European Council, 230
Eurobarometer, 98, 119

Euromanifesto data, 8, 75–77
Euromanifestos. *See* party manifestos
European attitudes. *See* voter attitudes, EU-support
European Commission, 6, 28, 124
European Council, 6, 7, 28, 128
European Election Studies, 7, 35, 61, 74, 77, 100, 135, 193, 271, 273–75
European elections and domestic politics, 4–6, 17–18, 32–33, 52–54, 168–70, 183, 191, 209, 221, 222, 225, 230, 245
Euro-skeptic parties, 48, 119, 259, 264–65, 269–71
Euro-skepticism among voters. *See* voter attitudes, EU-support

Finland, 19, 21, 24, 46, 49, 79, 86, 97, 114, 122
first-time election boost, 15, 16–17, 25
Flanders, 97, 100, 105
food safety scandal, 120
framing. *See* news frames
France, 39, 79, 97, 103, 112, 122

generation. *See* voter characteristics, cohort
Germany, 36, 79, 82, 97, 100, 103, 122, 125
Great Britain. *See* Britain
Greece, 1, 2, 13, 16, 19, 20, 39, 79, 95, 100, 103, 114, 122

Hungary, 1

ideological voting, 176–77
information cost and rational choice, 258
Ireland, 2, 39, 46, 79, 97, 103, 122, 143
issues. *See* political issues
Italy, 20, 39, 57, 97, 100, 105, 122, 125

Kosovo war, 120, 122, 129, 263

Latvia, 1
legitimacy, 4–5, 95, 129, 147, 245
length of EU-membership, 79, 97, 100, 109
Lithuania, 1
Luxembourg, 8, 18, 20, 33, 34, 36, 39, 46, 52, 57, 61, 95, 97, 110

Malta, 1, 115
measuring potential for electoral change, 222
media data, 8, 119, 277–82
midterm elections. *See* electoral cycle

Netherlands, 26, 28, 42, 43, 57, 79, 97, 103, 112, 122
new member states, 1, 26, 111, 115
new political parties, 209, 234, 235, 259
news frames, 118, 125, 263–64
non-voting. *See* electoral participation
Northern Ireland, 49

party choice
—determinants of, 175–80, 203–4
—EU-support, 169, 176
—ideological voting, 181
—modeling party choice, 170–73, 177–78
party size, 181, 187
party manifestos, 73–91, 283–84
party positions
—on European integration, 44, 73–91, 133, 197–202, 216, 264
—on left/right, 197–202, 216
permissive consensus, 189
Poland, 1
polarization: of elites on European integration, 133, 136, 141
political contestation over European integration, 234, 245, 263
political issues
—new issues, 265
—salience, 134

—salience of European integration, 137
politicization of European integration, 204–7, 233–37
—and anti-globalist movement, 235
—and increasing importance of EU policy, 3, 5, 6, 233
—and new political parties, 3, 6
Portugal, 1, 2, 19, 21, 39, 46, 49, 79, 95, 100, 103, 114, 122, 126
potential for electoral change: variation across countries and periods, 213–15

referenda on EU treaties, 265, 272
representation, 73–91, 246, 247, 266

scenario, 7, 9
—effects for government parties, 243–44
—effects for large parties, 243–44
—effects for right parties, 243–44
—estimating election outcomes for scenarios, 237–38, 247–49
—gross electoral change, 240–42
—increased saliency, changed party positions and changed voter positions, 239, 248
—increased saliency and changed party positions, 239, 248
—increased saliency of integration, 238, 247
—net electoral change, 242
second-order election theory, 17–18, 28, 33, 35, 44, 52–54, 68, 70, 116, 118, 128, 228–30, 257, 264
second-order national elections, 227
simulations. *See* scenario
sleeping giant, 191
Slovakia, 1
Slovenia, 1
Spain, 1, 2, 19, 21, 37, 39, 48, 79, 92, 100, 103, 114, 122

Sweden, 19, 21, 24, 73, 79, 95, 97, 103, 105, 122

television. *See* TV news
tone of news, 126–27, 134, 136, 139, 141
—effects on voter attitudes, 141
Turkey, 272
turnout. *See* electoral participation; election outcomes
TV news, 119–29, 131, 135
two-stage model of electoral choice, 170, 210–11

United Kingdom. *See* Britain

visibility of campaign in news, 117, 120–25
visibility of news, 136, 263–64
—effects on voter attitudes, 139
volatility. *See* electoral change; potential for electoral change
vote switching, 210, 215
—in different scenarios, 240–42
voter attitudes
—correlation left/right orientation and EU-support, 193–94
—EU-support, 61, 67, 70, 88, 91, 94–112, 131, 132, 136, 183, 190, 220, 270
—left/right orientation, 99, 136, 190, 220
—party attachment, 219
—party identification, 99
—political attentiveness, 99, 108, 131, 219
—political involvement, 159, 215, 219
voter characteristics
—age, 98, 219
—cohort, 215
—demographics, 159, 210
—education, 98
—gender, 98
—religion, 98, 108
—social class, 98
voters and electoral competition, 210–11, 243

Wallonia, 100